Potatoes rock!
Peggy Keener

Potato in a Rice Bowl

D1007632

Peggy Keener

iUniverse, Inc.
New York   Bloomington

Potato in a Rice Bowl

The views expressed in this work are solely those of the author and do not necessarily reflect the views of the publisher, and the publisher hereby disclaims any responsibility for them.

iUniverse books may be ordered through booksellers or by contacting:

iUniverse
1663 Liberty Drive
Bloomington, IN 47403
www.iuniverse.com
1-800-Authors (1-800-288-4677)

Because of the dynamic nature of the Internet, any Web addresses or links contained in this book may have changed since publication and may no longer be valid.

ISBN: 978-1-4502-2043-9 (sc)
ISBN: 978-1-4502-2041-5 (dj)
ISBN: 978-1-4502-2042-2 (ebk)

Printed in the United States of America

iUniverse rev. date: 4/28/2010

To

Glen, Jeff, Matt and Erin,
the memory makers.

With thanks to Carol
who really knows stuff.

And to Glen who
knows stuff that even
Carol doesn't know.

Life is like the links of a melded chain:
a casserole of encounters that
bind, configure and coalesce us
into who we are according to the
way in which we respond to them.

I see the act of living through the
quirky eye—the eye that refuses to
take living so darned seriously that
I cannot find lurking somewhere
within each event a germ of humor.

Irreverently, I now recall our wacky
life in the Japan of the sixties. This is
not a travelogue. Good grief no!
God created special cicerones
like the Fodor boy for that!

Rather, it is a look back at our bewildering
and unexotic life in Asia as I, a housewife
from Austin, Minnesota, observed it
through my convoluted, though honest,
small-town-America perception.

In all of life's pleasures, there is
nothing quite so delicious as the
precise moment when your—
or anyone else's finger—
comes into contact with
the exact center of your itch.

Why, oh, why is it that no
matter when or where I
sweep a pile of anything into
a nice, neat mound,
my dog comes over and stands
smack dab in the middle of it—
then stares at me?

Someday I'll be moseying along
reflecting back on all this, and
thwack right into a parking meter.

"Nothing stinks like a pile
of unpublished writing."
Sylvia Plath

ONE

NEVER IN THE farthest reaches of my mind did I ever imagine I would one day die on the other side of the world. That I would die in water on the other side of world.

And yet, that is exactly what I was doing.

Mind you, it wasn't by choice. And to make matters worse, I wasn't even a water person! None of it made any sense. There I was the mother of two wee boys, six-thousand, seven-hundred-and-eighteen miles from home, only twenty-four years old, and sinking into the unfathomable depths of an ocean.

The turbulent waves curled around my body like the gripping fingers of a sea serpent, sinuously grasping at me and repeatedly pulling me under. Over and over I rose only to sink again as the winds and water and wreckage thrashed about me. How utterly insignificant was I in that illimitable expanse of ocean swells; no more obvious to another human being than is a single 'i' dot on an enormous billboard crammed with writing.

For Pete's sake! Drowning was not part of the plan. And yet, what was a girl to do? Concentrate! Yes, that is what I had to do. So, while the serpent momentarily rested, allowing me a breath, I conjured up my little ones waiting for their mommy and daddy's return. Would the Japanese woman who was caring for them wait for however many days it would take

1

for my parents to come from the other side of the world? Or would that woman simply go home at suppertime because that was when I told her she could expect to leave? Leave because Glen and I would be returning. Returning, as I had promised.

Now my promise looked empty. Surely the woman would never simply walk out, abandoning our babies. No woman would do that, would she? Our boys were so young: Jeff only two-years-old and Matt, barely weaned, less than a year of age.

"Please," I chanted to her soul in drenched, hopeful gasps, "stay until Gramma and Grampa can get here. Stay! Stay!" But, I knew all too well that Japan was as far away as a place could be from Minnesota, half the circumference of the earth.

TWO

IT HAD ALL begun so simply, so predictably. Not in the least bit quirky or scary—or wet!

In the autumn of 1962, we were living in Boulder, Colorado with our two baby sons. As a veteran, Glen was studying there on the G.I. Bill, having already served a tour of duty in Japan. He was now about to graduate with a degree in Asian Studies from the University of Colorado. But, before that even transpired, he was hired again by the military. Not as a soldier, mind you, but rather as a civilian in the Intelligence Branch of the United States Army. The tassel on his mortarboard had barely flipped when his first assignment arrived. He was to report immediately to Baltimore for four months of training, after which would follow another assignment in Japan.

Japan! Yikes! Okay, so it wouldn't be strange to Glen, but wrapping my head around such an alien destination was barely conceivable; way too exotically peculiar for my simple small-town limitations. So, I didn't. Besides, folks there were different. Like weren't they a sort of barbarian tribe who all wore either a kimono or an army uniform? How on earth could I picture us living there?

But, I wouldn't think about it now because I had way more pressing, more immediate needs. The Baltimore invitation had not included the boys and me. We were left out to dry.

Getting the cold shoulder like that prompted some serious reflection. Would I rather the three of us stay behind utterly alone and isolated ten miles up in the Rocky Mountains in Crisman, Colorado, the 1874 gold mining town where we lived during the last year of college, or should we spend the next four months with my parents in Minnesota?

Hmmm, let's see now ... work my head off day and night all by myself in that lonely, secluded, crusty town (a settlement of only three other families of which I knew one because the other two were creepy—really creepy!), or spend the time in the lap of luxury with my mom and dad?

It was one of those arduous decisions that sometimes confront us in life, demanding a thorny analysis of all the options. Taking a few more minutes, I again reviewed my choices. Boiled down they came to this: hang by my earlobes from a telephone wire, or get a massage and a facial? Stay in a deserted exiled monastic godforsaken mountain hamlet alone with two babies, or return to the absolute security of home? Hellooo!

Why, the very thought of my folks and my hometown made me itch all over, to say nothing of the chance for my boys to get to know their grandparents up-close and personal, and they in turn discovering the remarkableness of my children. Exhilarated was an understatement for the sudden hunger I felt at the thought of returning to the familiar sanctuary of my family.

THREE

AT THIS POINT Glen and I had been married just over three years. During that time I had made some intense observations. Before marriage I read somewhere that women were born with an innately elevated moral code, mountains more refined than their husbands'. Right off the bat it was the responsibility of wives everywhere to mold their hubbies into the righteous clones of their more highly refined feminine selves. Having always been one to take my obligations seriously, I immediately formed a private pre-nuptial pact with myself. I would, in earnest, file down any gritty edges I might find in Glen.

> "A wife is a gift bestowed
> upon man to reconcile him
> to the loss of paradise."
> Johann Goethe

I had heard it said that the only time a woman can really succeed in changing a man is when he's a baby, but I didn't believe it. Besides, I was a little late for that. The truth was, whether he realized it or not, Glen needed me. After all, without me at his ungodly side, he was surely doomed; destined to a life of sin, sloth and savagery. Saving him was ultimately up to me, don't you see?

But, alas, in this all-encompassing female task there was much to do, with few of us women to do it. Our duties seemed endless. We were, nonetheless, determined to refine our men. Somebody sure had it right when they figured out if it weren't for people getting married, men and women the world over would be reduced to fighting with total strangers!

> "Woman would be more charming
> if one could fall into her arms
> without falling into her hands."
> Ambrose Bierce

Only a few weeks into our newly spliced life and with my irrefutable assignment already staring me in the face, I buckled down to the job. Yes, it was as clear as that spot of soup on Glen's shirt that I had been put on this earth to be his exalted cynosure: the guide he needed to contour his dents and spikes. What a package he got when he married me—a wife *and* a make over!

No doubt about it, love was indeed blind. On the other hand, marriage was turning into a real eye-opener. It was, therefore, with much delight that after a thorough analysis, I found I had surprisingly little saving to do. Other than Glen's inability to dance (due, no doubt, to his being overly Caucasian), he was pretty much sinless, slothless and savageless, except for … well, that one thing … that one mere pesky peccadillo.

It was like this. Callously, Glen had unflinchingly waltzed right into our marriage with a Safeway grocery bag full of ishy, really stupefying, unglamorous socks. Oddly, the nylon beasties had no adverse effect whatsoever on his sense of social acceptance, to say nothing of his grasp of their negative impact on world order, but they turned me—me of a more advanced punctilious nature—into a silent, raving mad, sock zealot!

Lamentably, there was no mention anywhere in the higher female code of just how to right this kind of wardrobe wrong. Therefore, left completely on my own with only my innately extolled sense of suavity, I was forced to flounder through this small, but bilious blemish in my new husband in order to create my—*er, our*—complete happiness. The honeymoon was over. This would be the first confrontation in our very short marriage, but like a hamster on a wheel, I couldn't be stopped.

In hot pursuit, I went about formulating a plan to refashion the snarly sock flaw. What to do? Actually, there was only one thing. It was so simple; so all embracing. I would replace Glen's entire stock of footwear for him! Yes, that was it! Keep in mind here, we had only been married a few weeks, so I was treading on really risky, really uncertain marital ground.

> "The music at a wedding procession
> always reminds me of the music
> of soldiers going into battle."
> Heinrich Heine

During the next days I worked tirelessly on my sock proposal, spending hours in dedicated rehearsal, but in the end it took only one well memorized, but nonetheless ardent appeal, to point out to my groom the lack of glory

I found in his limp, uncomely Ban-Lon hosiery. Naturally, thanks to many repeated dry runs, I portrayed them in less harsh terms, not yet having the wifely confidence to be brutally honest. Furthermore, I let him know that I would ask nothing whatsoever of him—not one blooming iota of action, for I'd save him any trouble this discussion might create by replacing the entire offensive lot by myself.

There, I'd said it!

To my everlasting wonder, by the end of my supplication, the enormous stocking mountain had diminished to nothing. Just a little anklet knoll. Our—*my*—first conjugal hurdle had been leaped. Peace o' cake! Shazam! Glen's sacrificial socks went from Frankenstein to Frankenfine! Life, in a heartbeat, was simple again. Along with it I learned the power of that well-known and wise adage: never, ever belittle the joy of good sox.

> "In olden times,
> sacrifices were made
> at the altar,
> a custom which
> is still continued."
> Helen Rowland

Freed from the inelegant smudge of this pedi impediment, I was liberated to move on to other matters of quite possibly even more import. Yes, matters like having babies and moving! Little did I know when Glen proposed that we'd be doing both, and doing them so soon and so often. Golly, I was a girl who had lived in only one house for all her growing-up years, and suddenly with the slip of a ring on my finger, I had become an overnight itinerant.

So far, in only three years of marriage, we had lived in four homes all the way from Colorado to New York, and back again to Colorado. Moving, I soon came to realize, was a rebirthing, reenergizing, titillating adventure, and much to my wonder, I was getting used to it. I liked the developing pattern of not knowing where I might be in six months as I knew by now each change was accompanied by remarkable newness. Without a single mote of army know-how, as well as a complete unawareness of what I was getting myself into, I had already developed the appropriate mindset of the military wife.

Glen's training in Baltimore would be our first separation. One hundred and twenty days seemed an inordinate amount of time. I would soon learn it was not. Sheesh, it was peanuts compared to what our future held. Even so, as green and inexperienced as I was, contemplating these months without Glen did not frighten me. In fact, it was quite the opposite. I found I had an instilled belief in my own ability to cope, and besides, it all felt like an adventure. Shucks, this—our fledgling flight apart—was nothing, because the boys and I would be with my parents, for goodness sake.

Just the same, I genuinely regretted that Glen would miss out on seventeen weeks of his young sons' lives when they not only seemed to change on a daily basis, but actually did. Duty, nonetheless, called. Duty was everything. Duty was more than the boys and me. Always more. In *all ways* more.

FOUR

IN THE WINTER of 1962, Glen dropped Jeff, Matt and me off at my parents' home in Austin, Minnesota. Gene and Margaret McLaughlin's big house allowed the three of us, with all of our stuff, to slip in nearly unnoticed. Well, almost, if you didn't have ears and eyes and weren't prone to ulcers. Just imagine. Like a seismic shift, this sedately retired couple had their previous existence jolted when their returning daughter and her two youngsters barged into their calm, sequestered midst. A flexible Mom and Daddy rose to the challenge, notwithstanding, and seemed believably overjoyed at our arrival, making us feel like beloved guests who did not smell at all fishy after the third day—if, that is, you discounted those diapers! You know the ones I mean.

"A soiled baby,
along with a neglected nose,
cannot be conscientiously regarded
as a thing of beauty."
Mark Twain

Within moments we had taken over the entire unoccupied second floor, spreading out luxuriantly. To say it felt emotional and sheltering didn't begin to cover it. Especially so was settling into the room I had shared for years with my beloved sister, Mary. Contained in that space was every sensation I'd ever heard people say about "going home." All over again, I felt encapsulated in utter security as if I were nesting in a birdcage ribbed with plush, velvet-covered wires. There my past intimacies were reawakened, enveloping my babies and me like a warm blanket just out of the dryer. In that special place—just a room to anyone else—I was taken aback by the strength of those cherished memories that now rushed into my innermost places, imbuing me with a nurturing peacefulness.

As the luscious feelings of home soaked in, I learned just how deeply the objects in Mary's and my bedroom recalled my past, all the way from my earliest days as a toddler up to the day I married Glen and left them all behind. Close as we were, though, Mary and I had never been the kind of sisters who were glued together, confiding every last one of our thoughts and secrets while tittering under the bedcovers at night. Well, I guess we did do that tittering part, but we kept private about the intimate stuff. Like she didn't know my bra size and I didn't know hers. And how was I supposed to know that during tenth grade I was dating the boy she loved if she didn't tell me?

We were also the kind of sisters who did not squabble and fuss with each other. We had the good sense to know not to squander our reserves on that kind of nonsense, for we needed our combined strength to face our two brothers. In that combatant area alone, we *were* glued together.

Returning home was sublimely sumptuous, and if I were being truthful, not a little unsettling. Mercy me! What was I, Peggy, Peggy, *Married* Lady, doing back in my parents' house; their home which I had now turned into the boys' and my own personal B & B?

But, hold on here. We three Keeners were neither vagrants nor were we a Steinbeck family on the skids, forced to return for shelter and sustenance to our Joad kith and kin. Gimme a break! That wasn't us by a long shot. On the contrary, we were on the bright, promising side of life fully taking on our responsibilities, and ready to launch into a world waiting just for us. This reappearance at home was never meant to be an extended stay with unstipulated limits; only a lengthy, drawn out, protracted vacation in which we dominated my parents' every scrap of order and tranquility. That's all!

As I said, the Army extended its Baltimore invitation/order to Glen only, not to his family. Boy, would we get used to that in a hurry. It was amazing how many Glen-only invites we would receive in the next thirty years. Good thing I didn't take it personally, like it was my breath or something.

On the contrary, here was Austin, a swoon of lusciousness. After all, it was my sanctuary, and life within its borders was permanently bountiful. My parents, thank you Lord, erupted with love and adoration, their unbridled ardor showered upon the boys who soaked it up like cotton balls in Kool-Aid. Of course it came as no surprise to me that Mom and Daddy were enraptured by the cherubic qualities of my sons, to say nothing of the easily recognized promise within each boy. Some things in life were just so obvious.

There was, however, more to it than only this child adoration thing. You must understand that my folks were a significantly social couple. At least three times a week, they and their friends got together in the early evening hours for their own bouncy version of happy hour. This now included Jeff, Matt and me. Overnight we became the main attraction, the happy hour epicenter. Well, maybe not me, but certainly the boys. It seemed the members, all grandchildless, couldn't get enough of my babies. As for me, I couldn't get enough of their adulation of my babies; further affirmation of their perspicacity.

> Bless the souls of such children
> with their over-loving, but well-intentioned mothers.
> Someday in the far-off future some mad scientist
> may discover the center of the universe,
> and these glorified children will probably
> be very shocked to learn
> they are not it.
> Unknown

YOU SEE, LIFE before this had been very different. Living, as we did, in the married veterans' half-Quonsets at the University of Colorado, followed by the secluded Crisman buried deep in its mountain valley, had not been exactly dull, but it was nothing like the convivial, chummy brotherhood my folks had with their long time friends. From house to house, happy hour moved like a tray of hors d'oeuvres on a well olive-oiled conveyor belt—with us now on it. All the members lived in wonderful homes (they couldn't even spell Quonset!), and all were gourmet cooks. What was not to love? I ate it up like a famished grasshopper on a congenial corn stalk.

> "In America,
> you can always find a party.
> In Russia,
> the party finds you."
> Yakov Smirnoff

There was also money, frivolous fun funds. Glen and I hadn't had much of that, I can tell you. We'd had to count our G.I. Bill nickels and dimes very carefully, indeed regarding each coin with the utmost of respect. This was not a bad thing as it molded us from the very start into particularly savvy, small-scale business partners. First and foremost was the monthly rental payment of twenty-seven dollars paid to the university for our sumptuous half-Quonset. (Jeff would later tell people we lived in a pipe!) Once that was out of the way, we could breathe easy for another thirty days, thus freeing us up to start a saving plan.

"A penny saved is
a Congressional oversight."
Hal Lee Luyah

First it was quarters, putting them all in a jar. In only a week's time, however, we realized a quarter was ridiculously over-the-top precious. Then going to the extreme, we decided to save all our nickels. But even in 1958, nickels turned out to be too paltry. In the end, we saved dimes. By the time Glen graduated three years later, our personal March of Dimes amounted to four-hundred dollars. The grandeur of it was staggering.

"When they asked
George Washington
for his I.D., he just
took out a quarter."
Steven Wright

Such frugality, it turned out, served us well. Now more than fifty years later, Glen and I have never, in all that time, had an argument over money. But, hold on! Way more important than money, what was it I just said? *Fifty plus years?* Oh, m'gosh, that means I've washed Glen's undies at least 18,250 times, minus a few for those days when we went camping!

Before we amassed our first $400 fortune, we would occasionally relax and sometimes even feel flush enough to splurge on an evening out. Without a doubt, we were where we ate, and "an evening out" was another way of saying "McDonalds." Not to knock it. This brand new fast food concept with hamburgers at fifteen-cents apiece was a big, for crying out loud, splashy deal for folks like us who thought ritzy dining was where you left the trays on the table.

But, the jovial Austin fling that we three were now enjoying was something else altogether. I, as the adult member of the trio, became the newest official member of The Happy Hour Gang. Its roster included a judge and his Minnesota state representative wife, a shopping center developer and his wannabe golf-pro wife, a scientist and his women's activist wife, a nurse and her goofy husband, and some executives and their wives from the hometown Hormel meat packing company. Every last one of them was civically elevated, and I relished the stimulating talk and subtle humor of their spirited gatherings, sponging it up as if I'd never get enough.

"The best thing
about a cocktail party
is being asked to it."
Gerald Nachman

Like, for example, the story the nurse told one evening as the gang was mellowing out on cheese rolls and highballs. It seemed that only that morning she had been in a parking lot where she spotted a woman some distance away, slumped over the hood of a car. The woman's body was heaving up and down across the slick metal surface. Being a medical caregiver, our friend immediately scurried across the asphalt to administer first aid.

As she drew nearer, she realized the woman was pregnant. Very pregnant! She was, however, neither in distress nor in labor, but rather laughing uncontrollably. "Are you alright?" our perplexed friend inquired.

"Oh, yes, I am … but … well … I'm sooooo glad you're here!" gasped the woman. "I've got to tell someone—anyone—what just happened!"

"As you can see," she blurted out between spurts of laughter, "I am nine months pregnant. I was on my way to the doctor for my weekly exam. Naturally, I had to take a urine specimen. At the last minute I could find no appropriate jar or bottle of any kind to put it in, so running out of time, I grabbed an empty Johnnie Walker bottle, filled it and tossed it in the car. On my way to the clinic, I decided to dash in that store for some milk. When I came back, I discovered the bottle had been stolen!"

I leave the rest to your imagination.

> "Never accept a drink
> from a urologist."
> Erma Bombeck's father

Often Happy Hour moved on to a restaurant, a succulent extension of the evening that came with a hired baby sitter, a concept new to me, but one I found remarkably easy to oblige. Just the same, I will admit to trepidation as I believed in my heart-of-hearts that no one could do this mothering job as well as I. Still, upon returning home, I did notice the babysitters had somehow muddled through, for there I would find both dumplings safe, sound and somniferous. And, oh, my dad paid for everything! Life with him *was* a March of Dimes, repeatedly marching in my direction!

The Wagon Wheel was one of my folks' favorite eating spots, a place on the far side of town specializing in not just dinner-plate-sized steaks, but platter-sized. The beef, aged to perfection, literally hung over the rims of the china. Clearly Minnesota cows were beamier. The Wagon Wheel's steaks, along with their preeminent butter-fried hash browns, were enough to levitate an extolling diner right off his seat, rising to epicurean heights along with his cholesterol count.

FIVE

WHEN MOM AND Daddy first dated, my father claimed that from the very get-go the thing that really turned him on to Mom was the gorgeous awareness of, little as she was, her capacity to consume a steak of commendable proportions all in one eating. Could anything be better than that, he marveled? It was like divine bovine providence: Gene and Margaret, beef magnets. As she, while chewing, gave him a look you could have poured over ice cream, they rhythmically ruminated their way into white hot romance.

> "You know 'that look'
> that women get
> when they want sex?
> Me, neither."
> Steve Martin

It may sound as though I'm painting a picture of gluttony here. Trust me, it was no such thing. As it happened, Daddy was raised in the food business and was about to take over the ownership of his father's successful grocery store. That had pretty much made food his focus in life, concentrating on that and that alone until the day the luscious Margaret Mary McDonell breezed in. Up to then Gene had lived with the unspeakable dread of possibly having to share his gastronomical habits with a woman who wasn't of the same comestible mindset. It would have been unthinkable.

In Margaret, Gene found the perfect food aficionado. And if that were not enough frosting on his cake (or in their case, marbling throughout the sirloin), Margaret was also, as celestial fortune would have it, a cook extraordinaire. There was nothing she couldn't turn into something delectable.

To be sure, Margaret's kitchen dwelled on a higher plane, never descending to the likes of TV dinners or canned spaghetti. But, had there been such a bourgeois invasion, she would have magically set them aglow with capers, wine and truffles.

> "Truffles are globose, whatever that is—
> brown, black, sandy and warty.
> The taste of truffles has been likened
> to that of strawberries, garlic,
> flannel and unclassified."
> Will Cuppy

Marrying Margaret was like hitting the jackpot. Actually in more ways than one! Despite being a rather demure girl, she also had a spirited seductive side. Before they knew it, her tantalizing and oft repeated words of, "Oh, Ge-eee-ne, where are you?"—or, on the other hand, was it, "Oh, no, Gene, not again!—produced four children in the space of less than four years.

> "Anyone who believes
> that the way to a man's heart
> is through his stomach,
> flunked geography."
> J. C. Collins

SIX

FOR JEFF, MATT, and me, life in Austin was sublime. All perfect, that is, except for one vexing snag. Gas. It was neither the car kind nor the furnace fuel kind, but rather that of the people genus: flatulence. 'Twasn't me. 'Twasn't Jeff. 'Twas Matt. Poor wee baby had world's more than his share. Not really his fault because he was a baby, after all, and, I suppose, really couldn't help the way he ate. Gulp, snarf, glurp … that's what large babies do. It is also why they're large babies.

Weighing nearly ten pounds at birth, Matt was already on the road to gastric distress. In his infant ardor to take in as much food as he could, as fast as he could, each swig and guzzle was accompanied by a chunk of air. Air added up fast. Like the bubbling yeast in rising bread dough, so, too, Matt bubbled and expanded. The resulting puffy disquietude was immense.

As Matt's mom and caregiver, I had the regular duty of administering relief to my suffering bambino. After trying many tricks, the one in the end (his end) that seemed to rectify (couldn't resist) the problem best was the infant glycerin suppository. Gently parting Matt's cushy soft-as-satin cheeks, I would insert a small birthday-candle-like cylinder … and wait. The outcome, and I mean just that, took only a few seconds in which time I hastily prepared myself, getting ear plugs in place and stepping clear of the highly volatile line of fire.

Let me tell you, when that slippery bullet left my newborn's yeasty bowels, the trajectory was impressive enough to get the military's attention.

The capsule zoomed out of my little boy like a waxy projectile shot from the muzzle of a fleshy gun. A bum's rush, if you will, hurtling itself across the bedroom. I could have sold tickets.

My old bedroom was long, no less than twenty-five feet. It looked like the phoenix rising from the asses when wee Matt propelled those tapered missiles across it. Why, you ask, didn't I curb those explosions by leaving his diaper on to contain the discharge? And miss the show, *I ask?* If you haven't realized it by now, I would never have blown, excuse the expression, the chance to see any performance discharged by my children. No if, ands, or butts about it.

After a while I began marking the suppository's long distance fall lines just as people rule high water marks after a flood. If I'd had my wits about me, I would have taken bets and earned a little spending money while we were in Austin. But then, I wasn't sure whether or not gas-passing gambling, much like shooting craps, was even legal in Minnesota.

But, even more disturbing than this baby hydrogen thing was the fact that its power made it impossible for me to stop thinking about Japan. The very place we were going! I wasn't just whistling Dixie here. Japan had no clue what new dyspeptic American weapon would soon be headed its way.

SEVEN

THE SNARLED ROPES from the sails entangled my legs, pulling me under the swell of the waves as the catamaran collapsed into the sea.

Earlier that day, Glen and I had accepted an invitation to go sailing in Tokyo Bay with our Army sponsor, Gordon Tyler. Gordon had a 21' catamaran, a boat which set Glen's heart to palpitating; a boat which for all the thumpings in his chest was for Glen a bejillion heartbeats away.

"In every man's heart
there is anchored
a little schooner."
Henry Miller

Of course, Glen jumped at the chance to sail in such an awesome craft, and of course, Glen jumped at the chance to bring me along for the drenching, terrifying ride, with the specific purpose of my falling in love with it, too. Not!

In my mind, the vision of that boat with me in it equaled self-flagellation! I must have been out of my mind. Heck, I knew for certain I was stark raving mental the moment I laid eyes on the thing! For the love of Mike, neither had I ever been on a sailboat nor I had ever been on a basin of water that opened out to an ocean. My only frame of water reference was the East Side Lake in Austin where you could almost throw a stone from one side to the other. In Austin, we did think that was an ocean. You know them: the Atlantic, the Pacific and the East Side Lake Oceans?

18

"The town was so dull that
when the tide went out,
it refused to come back."
Fred Allen

Furthermore, I soon realized that I would not be sitting down in the boat, as in a seat built into the hull, but rather on top of the hull itself! How lucky could I be? It was like this—Gordon's catamaran, an Australian design, was built with twin hulls held together by two crossbeams. Before I knew it, I, like a hopelessly deranged numbskull, was perched on top of the wooden platform straddling those hulls. There was nothing—not a handle, not a rope, not Glen's hand—to hold on to. Where, oh, where had my prefrontal cortex been when I needed it most?

In Latin there is a proverb which says: "Be on your guard against a silent dog and still water." That morning the perfectly mirrored surface of Tokyo Bay gave me no clues. Neither did the silent dog. Even so, quiet and serene as they both were in those early hours, I still couldn't believe I was going along with the insanity! My innards were mush; my mind a storm of panic.

But, who wants to be a skunk at the picnic? So rather than make pathetic mewling sounds which most certainly would have laid bare my stark terror, I, like a good dumb egg, played the part of the jovial, though secretly horror struck, girl sailor. Olive Oyl would have understood.

Let me point out that unlike us, Gordon Tyler was free as a bird. After all, he was a bachelor: an un-tethered spirit with no accountability to anyone. In contrast, Glen and I were inordinately tethered, the parents of two small boys. Two small boys who needed their parents! Our ties and responsibilities were stupefying.

EIGHT

BEFORE WE KNEW it, June had ended, and Glen's four months of training in Baltimore were up. That meant our extended vacation with my folks was also up. The boys and I had spent many days, indeed every last one of them, replete with good times, never once knowing a blip in our combined contentment (except for Matt's you-know-what-blips). We had, on all counts, been a gift to each other. But now Glen was on his way to Minnesota to retrieve us. From there we would travel to Loveland, Colorado, to say our goodbyes to his family and further spread the exaltedness of our boys, my job description exclusively. We would also pick up our small collection of household goods stored in their attic.

Next stop Tokyo.

Naturally, I had virtually no concept of what Tokyo was. Zilch, nil, nix! For all I knew, I could have been going to the moon—or even South Dakota. Heck, I could barely say the word, and then I said it incorrectly. It was, as Glen pointed out, not Toe-key-oh, but rather Toe-kyo, that "kyo" business being a tongue-rolling, lip-pouting pronunciation to which mouths in Minnesota could not and would not contort. But then, for gosh sakes, what did we in Austin know? And besides, what did we care? Put "kyo" in their Japanese pipes and smoke it. We had won the war!

Mr. Myers, the borderline intellectual codger who lived across the street from my parents, was one of those Minnesotans who, let me tell you, knew what was what. One day when I was out in the yard, he yelled across to me in his booming curmudgeon voice, "Peggy, whatever you do, do NOT eat that seaweed in Jap-pan. It'll make your hair turn black. That's why they don't have any blonds over there!"

Oy, what a goober!

"I can't believe that
out of 100,000 sperm,
you were the quickest."
Steven Pearl

I, a sort of blond, briefly pondered his prudent gooberly advice while imagining myself with raven hair. But really now, did seaweed honest and truly have that kind of power? And what about little kids like my Jeff who had snow-white tresses? Besides, I liked Jeff that way. And who says, Mr.-Know-It-All-Across-The-Street, that I would even feed black grass to my child?

No, I couldn't see that seaweed business. As unworldly wise as even I was, I could recognize the fact that the intellect of some of our Austin citizens was, in a word, pukey. It wasn't just their eyes that were myopic, it was their brains. Like gosh, Peggy, you don't want to go to Japan. There are Japanese there! Sheesh!

Just the same, I couldn't shake his words and trying not to get all hasty in my judgment, I supposed there could be some truth to his weird declaration. After all, in the National Geographic photos that I had seen since childhood, those folks in Asia did, unquestionably, *all* have black hair. Do you suppose there was some magical follicle force over there that turned hairs from light to dark? And, what about eyes? Mine were green! Could I even see out of black-brown eyes if their diet so changed me? I knew one thing for sure. I wouldn't want to be a sunglass salesman in Japan. Sales would have to be dismal with all those built-in Ray-Ban eyes.

What was Glen getting us into, anyhow? Jeez Louise! Things were feeling really creeped out.

It was about then that, like a ton of bricks, it really hit me. Hair and eyes weren't worth a lick compared to the big thing. You know, the really, really BIG thing ... *weren't the Japanese still kind of our enemy?* As in archenemy-hostile-foe? I knew it had been seventeen years since World War II ended, but even so, for some people crusty combatant feelings died slowly. Or, not at all!

"The war situation
has developed not necessarily
to Japan's advantage."
Emperor Hirohito
(after losing two cities to atom bombs)

As a black cloud of foreboding suddenly gathered overhead, I began to have serious doubts as to how they "over there" would take to me—to our babies—to our bleached-out hairs? Besides, I didn't even think we'd like seaweed! Criminy! What if it had driftwood slivers, sea shell shards or dried up eel bones embedded in it; way too chafing for our delicate honky innards!

Glen, savvy beyond good reason, had as an enlisted soldier already served a tour of duty in Japan. I met him shortly after his return to the States when we were both students at the University of Colorado. He had regaled me with stories of how much he loved the mystique of Japan, and how interesting his job had been there as a Korean translator. Yes, you heard me right. I said Korean. In Japan. It was my first lesson in how the military does things.

Glen had also learned Japanese and he spoke it beautifully. Course, he'd had help. Had even learned a few unusual terms that one would not ordinarily be taught in a classroom—words possibly spoken in a bath and massage parlor! You may ask why a cowboy from Snyder, Colorado, would be hanging out in a place like that, and I would answer—why the heck *not* would a cowboy from Snyder, Colorado, be hanging out in a place like that? It was cultural enlightenment, don't you see?

It seems that on his first and only visit to a bath house, a lovely young thing sashayed over to him and announced she would be assisting him in the bath, followed by a friendly rubdown. *Really?* Having not had assistance in the bath since he was three, and never a rubdown in all his nineteen years, this got Glen to thinking. Golly gee, as titillating as it sounded, he wasn't sure he was ready for this. Even though he was eager to learn about Japan, would his embarrassment—which was now rising faster than a thermometer in a batch of Calcutta curry—even allow this? Furthermore, would word somehow get back to his mother? Torn between two principles, fusty sweat began beading up in his tight, dark, unventilated places.

"Oh, Lord,
help me to be pure …
but not yet!"
St. Augustine

The lovely bath attendant, having seen his Snyder type before, began slowly by first removing Glen's shirt—just a mild rise in temperature to 99.9°. Next the shoes and socks—a tolerable 101°. When the trousers dropped to the floor, warning bells went off as a soaring hot streak pushed his fluctuating mercury up to an alarming 103°!

Just about the time the assistant (who Tallulah Bankhead would have described as "pure as the driven slush"), began peeling off his briefs, the incendiary heat index peaked at 107°. Sensing this unseasoned hayseed may not be quite ready, she stopped in mid-peel and left the room, a moment later returning with a long narrow cloth. Folding it over and over into a three-inch band, the vixen proceeded to tie it around Glen's head, covering his now bulging eyes.

With Glen no longer able to see, and therefore anxiety free, the Asian fox yanked the briefs down and began the kinky scrub-down. That year she got the Nobel for psychology.

> "A man has missed something
> who has never left a brothel at sunrise,
> feeling like throwing himself into the river
> out of pure disgust."
> Gustave Flaubert

Glen had also told me he'd had a Japanese girlfriend. Okay, okay, a bathhouse wench is one thing, but I can tell you he certainly could have left out that girlfriend part! Good grief! But, darn, much as I didn't like to admit it, if I tried really hard, I *could* see the merit in her. Yes, the companionship of an inscrutable tart probably was a swell thing for a lonely guy in a strange land. But, man, I could just envision it: the bewitching strumpet teaching the naïve country boy the ways of her inexplicable society, including exotic hands-on demonstrations. I'll bet you the bank that was when Glen really started to catch on to those cultural lessons!

Wow, things were getting quirky and unsettling ... and not a little bit snarky.

I had to get hold of myself, not get all riled up. Yet it must be said that I couldn't and wouldn't ever like that girlfriend—the pint-sized, epicanthic-eye-lidded geisha from hell! Holy craps, what if I met her on a Tokyo street someday? Was I supposed to be nice, gracious, even a teensy weensy bit friendly? Heaven help me, for I hadn't a clue how I would feign such a charade. Don't you see, in the deepest recesses of my soul, I was secretly planning on becoming America's first unappointed Ambassadress to Japan? That meant I needed to give peace a chance. Ha! Fat chance of peace blossoming with her hanging around!

> "If you haven't got anything
> nice to say about anybody,
> come sit next to me."
> Alice Roosevelt Longworth

DESPITE MY INCREASING misgivings, Japan was, nonetheless, insidiously beginning to tweak my fancy, causing me to itch, quiver and tingle deliciously in unexpected places. Wow, a new way of living! It sure sounded gorgeous. And honestly, more than anything I implicitly trusted Glen's sagacity and excitement. Therefore laying my disquietude aside, I allowed my expectations to bubble up—just as long, that is, as I never bumped into you-know-hussy-who, which would save me a whole lot of almond-eye scratching. But, not to worry. She was so yesterday whereas I was so today ... *and tomorrow!*

Yes, Shorty, don't you soon forget it is I, Peggy, Peggy *Married* Lady, who is wearing the wedding ring. Nanny-nanny-boo-boo!

Centered by this sound matrimonial logic, I embraced my commitment, took a deep breath, and began preparing my mind for the great unknown: the other side of the planet ... assuming, that is, that all my geography teachers had *not* been lying, and that the planet really and truly did have another side, as in a side on the other half of a spherical earthen ball!

NINE

GOING TO JAPAN in 1962 was not child's play. If you are to understand the entirety of this story, then you must also understand just how difficult this journey was. The entire procedure—from packing the first crate to the moment we stepped out onto the airstrip in Tokyo—was a back-breaking, grueling, nail-biting process, each step fraught with worry and irritation. Absolutely nothing about it was cinchy.

To begin, going with two babies was incontestably not cinchy. We would not be accompanied by the kind of useful items we needed on a daily basis, like cribs and highchairs, those familiar components conducive to a pleasant, orderly life with baby people. Such necessary items would travel on a slow boat from their attic storage in Colorado to Japan, and arrive, if we were lucky, in roughly four months. That was pretty much a lifetime in the infant scheme of things. A girl could be fifty-percent pregnant again by then. In the meanwhile, a military wife had to make do, creativity being the mother of invention and all that jazz.

My first order of business, before Glen ever retrieved us from Austin, was to get vaccinations for the boys and me. So, what was the big deal, you ask? In 1962, it *was* a big deal. The World Health Organization plus the U.S. Department of Health, Education, Welfare and the Public Health Service said so.

Imagine if you will, two toddlers getting shots for small pox, yellow fever, cholera, typhus, typhoid, tetanus-diphtheria, and polio, plus a tine test for T.B. By the time we finished, the boys and I were flesh and blood

Whiffle balls. Oh, and did I mention anything about all of the above needing to be later revaccinated on a regular basis? The military was dedicated to keeping us viable. Otherwise, we sure were a waste of your tax payer dollars.

There was also the passport, the wee document which all foreigners needed, then and now, in order to leave their country and enter another. Most people had one under their name alone. I decided that because I would never ever leave my children behind (especially alone on the other side of what I was still counting on to be a round world), there was no need for three passports. That decided, all three of us were photographed and documented as a single clinging unit; like simpatico Siamese triplets miraculously birthed in assorted sizes, genders and ages.

Our passports were not the usual tourist types, but rather *official* U.S. government passports. Rather than declaring on the first page that the "U.S. requests all whom it may concern to permit this citizen of the United States to pass without delay or hindrance, and in case of need, to give all lawful aid and protection," our passports read, "The bearer is a dependent of a person abroad on an official assignment to Japan and other countries for the Department of Defense of the United States of America." It said absolutely nothing whatsoever about any "lawful aid and protection." Once again I paused for more serious than usual reflection.

Whenever we traveled, all military personnel wore two identical stainless steel dog tags around our necks. These tags were strung on two bee-bee chains, one of long necklace length, the other very short. The tags were stamped with our names, social security numbers, blood types and religions so that in case of a disaster, we could be identified and transfused with the right kind of blood, if we were still alive, and preached over appropriately, if we were not. A small notch cut into the top of one of the tags allowed it to be wedged between our open jaws, thus in death labeling us at our heads. At the other end, the tag on the short bee-bee chain could be secured around our big toes for easy identification in the drawers at the morgue.

I never could figure out exactly what good any of this was—I mean dead is dead!—but, to my surprise, I did find the dog tags marginally comforting. It was the same kind of psychological manipulating that calms the conscientious prison executioner, assuring him that he's doing the right thing when he sterilizes the needle before giving a lethal injection. Neither does a lick of good, but it makes those involved feel better.

Dog tags were a kind of highly indestructible rabbit's foot where we were highly destructible. Stainless steel didn't even rust if we had to float in the ocean for days and weeks and years. It was, at the very least, something, sort of, kind of, working on our behalf, or so I told myself until I believed it.

There were also the official military orders. These highly coveted documents allowed us passage onto the many aircraft we needed to get to Tokyo. They were our tickets. There were reams and reams of them, as you know the government does not work in singles of anything. Without the passports, the shot records, the dog tags, and the stacks of orders, we were nobodies going nowhere.

Such a profusion of bulky documents required its own luggage. On top of that, I would have to take brimming satchels of snacks, glass quart bottles of milk, toys, cloth diapers, and several changes of clothing for the boys, because did I mention there were no direct flights? Well, I will now. There were no direct flights. In fact, once we finally left the U.S., we would stop and stop; two different additional landings, on two distant islands, before we ever laid eyes upon the the third stop: The Land of Seaweed Induced Pompadours and Pageboys.

Our itinerary was to fly from Minnesota to Colorado, ship our household goods, and say goodbye to Glen's family. Then following a lengthy drive to Denver, we'd fly to San Francisco, catch a taxi to Oakland, and finally a bus to Travis Air Force Base. As simple as this may sound, trust me when I tell you the snarly schedule was fraught with possible and probable delays and mishaps.

But, did I care? No! For this was the Keener's Big Adventure. Furthermore, I was looking forward to seeing California for the first time, especially Oakland. I had heard some compelling things said about the place. Gertrude Stein described it as: "The trouble with Oakland is that when you get there, there isn't any there *there*." Equally enticing was Herb Caen's description: "The trouble with Oakland is that when you get there, *it's* there."

But the most tantalizing of all was Johnny Carson's very short and succinct list of things to do while in Oakland: #1. Go to the Safeway parking lot for the roller skating festival called "Holiday on Tar!" Or, wait, was that Burbank? It didn't matter, because I hadn't brought my skates, anyway, and besides it would have been hard to skate while carrying all that luggage and the boys, too—even though it was on tar.

Gosh, for a girl from Minnesota, any place in California—Oakland, Burbank or how about Los Angeles?—would be wild and wonderful. Imagine having palm trees and movie stars and outdoor roller skating twelve months out of the year. I could hardly wait!

> "Fall is my favorite season
> in Los Angeles. I love
> watching the birds change color
> and fall from the trees."
> David Letterman

TEN

ONCE WE LANDED in San Francisco, we collected our stuff and caught a cab to Oakland. As predicted, Oakland was "just there" and little more. It turned out to be okay, though, because we had no time to sightsee *or* to skate. Instead, as soon as the taxi dropped us off, we boarded a military bus for the two-hour ride to Travis. Already we were wilted, frazzled. Each vehicular shift meant that along with the boys, all our impedimenta had to be shuffled by us on and off the different modes of transportation.

The sun was beginning to set as we boarded the bus. For the seventh time that day, Glen again schlepped our mountain of baggage while I got Jeff and Matt and their own mini-mountain of little boy baggage into their seats. When at last all the jostling had ceased, the bus began to move. I propped my elbow on the armrest and began wondering if during this leg of the journey we'd be able to relax. Even sleep. Now there was a concept.

As I was beginning to unwind, I was abruptly aroused by the huffing and puffing of the man across the aisle. He was making a noisy commotion hauling out a guitar case from under his seat. Wow, that was nice. The military had hired a traveling troubadour to entertain us en route!

Looking forward to this unexpected treat, I perked up. By golly, I could use a few tunes about now. With rapt attention I waited. The man opened the case. Expecting to see him reach for a guitar, I was disappointed when instead he pulled out a can of 3-in-1 All Purpose Oil. Not being particularly guitar smart, I assumed he needed to first oil down his instrument before he performed. Okay, I could wait. Wherever he was going, so were we.

Holding the can in one hand, the man proceeded to plop several blobs of rich, greasy lubricant into the other hand. Then putting the can down, he began rubbing the stuff between his palms. It looked to me like his guitar was about to get a massage. Nice! I could've used one myself.

Then, to my utter astonishment, instead of reaching for the guitar, he raised both hands up along the sides of his head and began rubbing the oil into his hair! Whoa, that was unexpected. Clearly not of the Brylcreem "a little dab'll do ya" mindset, he moved on to a second, then third and fourth application. By now his hair, where his fingers had raked through it, looked remarkably like stiff, stubby, demarcated rows of harvested corn stalks.

After the fifth slathering of the Ace Hardware pomade, he apparently felt his coif had at last reached perfection. I, believing he was now finished and would move on to our serenade, was surprised all over again when he didn't begin to strum, but rather to rub the ointment up and down his arms, giving special attention to his elbows and armpits. Did Helena Rubenstein know about this potion? Should I be the one to tell her? After all, anybody could see it was working as his skin, like an oil slick, was glowing with an iridescent luster.

As my shock ebbed, I began to see the merit in what the guy was doing. What a money saving scheme he had come up with: grease the car, the boat, the house, the motorcycle, the lawnmower, himself and any available musical instrument all at the same time! It was disappointing, albeit, that after he got his body all lubricated up like that, things just kinda fizzled out. No concert followed. What did happen, though, was that the toxic, over-powering stench of the 3-in-1 All Purpose Oil sucked up all the available oxygen in the bus, putting us passengers in a semi-comatose state, thus creating a rather restful, unconscious ride to Travis.

> "Anyone seen on a bus
> after the age of thirty
> has been a failure in life."
> Loelia, Duchess of Westminster

Lounging back in the bus seat in my noxiously induced sleep state caused my mind to drift. Thank goodness the many arduous weeks of preparation were behind us and we were finally on the threshold of our departure. We were exhausted, discombobulated and thoroughly in the dark as to what to expect next. Even Glen didn't know for sure. His first trip to Japan had been as a single G.I. on a troop ship with one duffel bag, a pushover compared to moving a home and family. Little did I know then that things were just beginning to heat up; that if only one of the prickly steps in the departure procedure failed, the entire string of transient dominoes would fall as fast as a bouffant hairdo in a sauna. Only divine intervention could put it back together.

Night had already settled when the bus dropped us and our heap of stuff off outside of Travis. Hailing a taxi, the driver took one look at that heap and at our frowziness, and immediately recognized who we were and what we were about. Without batting an eye he whisked us to a seedy motel. You know the kind of place. They surround all military bases. It didn't matter that it was second-rate ishy. The price was right, and we were too brain dead to assess its lack of embellishments.

The next morning, even before the cock had a chance to crow, we four were up, bathed, dressed, repacked, and once again smashed into the tight confines of a taxi. For some silly, misguided notion, goofy me in my innocence thought that we'd now simply hop on a plane. It was stupefying how unprepared I was for Travis. I had no inkling *it* was the big enchilada; that everything before this had only been a twitch in the migration madness. We were about to enter Angst Acres.

ELEVEN

TRAVIS AIR FORCE Terminal looked like the beer concession at a super bowl game, minus the beer and the fun. We immediately crammed into one of the many long lines of harried military parents, all jostling crying babies while trying to corral older loose-canon youngsters who had just discovered the joys of plundering and pillaging an airport before the sun came up. Each person's fraught-filled schlep to Travis was written all over his ravaged face. Struggling to keep things in some semblance of order, we were all juggling the family shot records, the bundles of passports, the tons of personal luggage, and the many Los-Angeles-telephone-book-sized stacks of official orders, all of which were required for *each* passenger. One missing paper, one missing signature, one missing injection and we were out. Kaput!

It wasn't as if any of us could change our minds and go back home. We had reached the point of no return. "Home" had either been sold, rented out, or vacated back to its landlord with all the furnishings disposed of, shipped off to storage or packed in a ship. We had no choice but to make this Japan thing work. Our lives, like bug spray, could not be put back in the can.

The first hurdle was the scrutinizing of the paperwork: "orders" in military lingo. Every last page was painstakingly examined with Uncle Sam's fine-toothed comb. Next the luggage search reared its nasty head as every bag was opened and inspected. It mattered not a whit to the inspectors that martyrdom had gone into that packing; that agonizing decisions had been made in selecting the most strategic of items for the long trip ahead, and that we, like contortionists, had somehow scrupulously squashed it all into the confines of our suitcases. All was immediately and systematically undone by Air Force Security, who I swear had been taught all they knew by Fibber McGee, the closet disorganizer. What a mess. It required all four of the parents' hands to put the ravages back in order, thereupon unwittingly unleashing testy toddlers, who had heretofore been restrained, to join their older siblings in the discovery of the Travis Terminal temptations. If they had not already commenced, throbbing migraines set in about now.

> "In America there are
> two classes of travel –
> first and with children."
> Robert Benchley

No doubt about it, the urgency for national security was real. The scene was one of mad, orderly, martial chaos even though, for crying out loud, this was 1962, a time of almost world peace. Even Osama Bin Laden—a guy who we would all later learn could really mess with our contentedness—hadn't yet been toilet trained! I felt a smidgen of the kind of trepidation the immigrants must have felt upon arriving at Ellis Island. But, jeez, this was *my country!*

Military travel was making child birth look like languorously licking down a Hershey bar. But, in spite of this first time wailing and gnashing of teeth, I would be remiss if I did not also describe my excitement. My insides were twittering with the kind of feel you have after your heart transplant is over and, by the rhythmic thumping in your chest, you know you've made it.

Finally, when all the above was stamped and approved, we were at last allowed to enter the passengers' lounge, a coveted place highly treasured, segregated and guarded. It was like we Keeners were the finalists on Queen For A Day, and we had won the refrigerator, the stove *and* the four snow tires. You see, once inside the tightly patrolled departure lounge, we were home free. Well, not exactly home or free because, as you are aware, we were categorically homeless, and owned lock, stock and body by our government.

At the very last minute, just when we thought the whole shebang was in the bag, an Air Force sargeant—a seemingly mild-mannered, pleasant enough fellow—began diligently riffling through our documents *all over again*. In mid-riffle he stopped, glared at us and with seasoned histrionics demanded to know where our shot records were.

Well, no problem, they were right here in Glen's briefcase ... somewhere ... in here. But, they weren't. Military shot records, those long, canary-yellow, accordion-pleated cards that were so very easy to spot—or not—were missing.

It was strange how at the precise moment I realized they were gone I also noticed the hairy knuckles and remarkably simian features of the airman. Why hadn't I seen them before? The mean spirited, churlish curl to his upper lip, and the way his red-rimmed eyes sparkled at our discomfort, told me everything. I knew then ... and believe me I know these things ... that yellowbellied louche of a miscreant was on loan to the military from a padded cell just down the bay in Alcatraz.

Through debased, misanthropic eyes he glowered at our little family as if to say, "Well, aren't you each just the most pathetic muck holes of inadequacy." I strongly suspected that in the scheme of things, he was little more than a paper tiger, but even so, he was the tiger holding the clipboard, and on this day that made him boss.

Raising his surly lips into a deriding smirk, he spit out his orders across the counter. I could feel the viscous droplets hit my cheeks like the syrupy fizz from an Orange Crush pop bottle. I, yes, I—Peggy, Peggy Kindhearted Lady—even wished him harm. And I was just the one who could carry it out. Little did this lout know that there in my arms I held a powerful weapon. All I had to do, if I so chose, was to aim gassy Matt at him. Backwards!

"You must find the doctor," he commanded (spit-splash), utterly indurate to our brittle feelings, "who administered your vaccinations, and tell him to telegraph the information to me *at once!*" Then with gleeful Schadenfreude, he added that if we could accomplish this (and it was implicitly obvious he hoped we could not and would therefore rot in Travis Terminal limbo forevermore), *he* would allow our family to enter into the sanctum sanctorum departure lounge.

> "The fly sat on the axle
> of the chariot wheel
> and sighed to himself,
> 'What a dust do I raise.'
> Francis Bacon

The guy had either a crusty callus for a heart, or simply a hole where it should have been. Surely Oscar Wilde had him in mind when he said, "Some cause happiness wherever they go: others, *whenever* they go." This malicious fiend was one of the latter. It would have come as no surprise to me to learn that as a baby his mother had regularly fed him Pablum laced with rusty razor blade shards.

My heart began beating as fast as the tambourine in a merengue band. Our migration, which only moments before had seemed to be congealing so splendidly, was instantaneously flipped into wretched pandemonium. Just when we thought we had it made, with all the weeks and weeks of life-sucking preparation behind us, we were reverted back once again into a froth of Keener action.

There are the frenzies and then there are *the* frenzies. Ours were those last ones, the really acute feral ones. Our behavior could best be described as maniacal as we began an agitation of urgent calls from a Travis Terminal phone booth. Naturally the pay phone required exact coinage and lots of it, both of which we did not have. This, then, caused us to scurry greatly, begging change wherever we could. Had I still had my virginity, I would have sold it. We *had* to locate the Austin doctor, the one and only person on Planet Earth who could save us from this displaced travel inferno.

> "Hello, hello!
> I'm in a phone booth
> at the corner of
> Walk and Don't Walk!"
> Unknown

Phoning took a ton of time, precious time, as well as a month's pay. For all we knew our plane was leaving without us! Crammed into the teensy booth (built to the age-shrunken dimensions of Ma Bell), Glen spun the dial, zinging the numbers around like a whirly gig in a wind storm. Meanwhile, spasmodic Saint Vitus-like dance twitches hitched the muscles in my lower limbs, causing me to jerk like Elvis when he really got going.

Finally, just as Glen's over-stressed finger collapsed onto itself like a wet noodle, the tension broke. There on the line were the reassuring tones of the doctor's voice. Why, *of course* he could help us. Why, of course, he *would* help us. With all haste he'd telegraph the immunization information to Travis. What a guy! Then and there I swore I'd name our next child—or rename Glen!—after him.

Gathering up the boys, we zoomed from the phone booth through the halls and back to the departure counter where the telegram would, we prayed, soon arrive. Tick, ti-i-ck, ti-i-i-ck, the imperceptible minutes crawled by. It was like waiting for sequoias to grow, the consternation of it severe enough to trigger a lifetime of incontinence. Meanwhile, a grimacing Sargeant Meany Pants openly luxuriated in our distress.

Neither Glen nor I can remember just how much time actually did elapse—was it hours *or days?*—before we heard the phone ring, both of us having blocked out this agony in our need to reconstruct our happiness. On the phone was Dr. Minnesota Nice with all the information. Praise his altruistic Scandinavian soul.

Re-confronting Sargeant M. Pants was a snap. This time we had every single official document in our hands. Begrudgingly, he embossed upon them a rainbow of rubber stamps, suddenly coloring our papers from top to bottom and announcing we had at last passed muster. Despite his contempt, we had conquered the system. Taking one last look behind me as we walked away, I caught a glimpse of a sulking Donnie Detestable choking on his own mucilaginous spittle. Concentrating fully, I shot a voodoo curse in his direction, hexing, I hoped, the rest of his insufferable life. May he spend it on a baggage-claim conveyor belt to Hades! Or a tar covered parking lot in Oakland with skates glued to his feet so they would never come off.

"To knock a thing down,
especially if it is cocked
at an arrogant angle,
is a deep delight of the blood."
G. Santayana

Many months later when our household goods finally arrived in Tokyo, we found in their midst our four canary-yellow shot records. An overly impassioned packer, in his zeal to not miss a thing, had sealed them in a box, and placed that box in the hold of the slowest ship to Asia. From that day on, like those Pepsodent ads of old, we never ever made a trip without first checking for the yellow.

TWELVE

AS IF WE were a quartet of star-crossed singers, the rest of our journey unfortunately continued on a discordant note. Just because we had crossed over into the hallowed departure lounge did not mean smooth sailing. And please do not get the goofy notion that once our names were on the plane's manifest, the plane was there waiting for us. Au contraire! For all we knew, the plane wasn't even in the U.S.! Hells bells, nimble engineering fingers could still be building it!

With this disheartening awareness, it became clear that the next most urgent step was to locate four seats because a sixth sense told us we'd need those seats for the duration. I soon learned that duration in military jargon meant "long" with extra ooooo's. Departure time was anyone's guess. Occasionally an announcement came over the intercom, but it was always spoken by someone whose teeth were stuck in the boggy bolus of partially chewed taffy. This made it necessary to keep one ear keenly attuned—or in our case, Keenerly attuned—so as not to miss any important information.

It seemed as though this trip would never end—correction, never get started. And, if you think it's long in the telling, you should have been there in the doing. We tried to unwind, but that was like corralling bats on caffeine, plus all eight of our arms ached like blue blazes from those life-saving shots. Collectively, we were a pooped-out mess; our brains slushy. With Matt clutching me, I slid down in my plastic contoured seat and closed my bloodshot eyes. Only seconds into my attempted repose, the number 24 suddenly popped into my reverie.

"Twenty-four hours of air time," it chided, "in which you will be cooped up in an oxygen-deprived, smoke-filled plane flying over the entire Pacific Ocean to the edge of the world that you could very well fall off of if the world is flat instead of round!"

"Furthermore," it taunted, "are you, Peggy Keener, absolutely sure you have the right kind of figure for a kimono?"

It was too much. With this last assault on my tranquility, I figured I had just completed basic training. No matter how nicely cropped his goatee was, how patriotic the stripes were on his designer suit, or how impressive his pointy finger was, Uncle Sam was an unaccommodating turkey who needed a reality check.

Squashed in all about us, were folks like us: the disintegrating families. We made a sharp contrast to the single soldiers who, antithetically, seemed to have it made. On the floor they lay deep in sleep, stretched out luxuriantly along the perimeter of the departure lounge. Their agonizingly short haircuts rhythmically rose and fell across the surface of their duffle bags in cadence with each snore. To me the decided upturn of their freshly shaved lips was proof they were dreaming of any place other than where we were.

I eyed them with consummate disbelief. Who did they think they were anyway? Was Travis to them some kind of resort and spa? Wasn't it I, the solipsistic mother of two, who needed the rest? Especially so after learning, at this late stage in the game, that I might be seriously kimono fashion challenged? Egads! But despite my accumulating distress, I put on a front that belied my inner commotion. Across my face I plastered a waxy Madame Tussaud smile.

> "You know it's not a good wax
> museum when there are wicks
> coming out of the people's heads."
> Rick Reynolds

Hours slugged by like the apathetic snowmelt of a Minnesota spring. Then all at once we heard the loud speaker kick in. With a heightened energy, the same fellow, having cleared his sticky back molars of the last shreds of taffy, was now all business. Our flight was ready. We snapped to a benumbed attention, grabbed our mélange of wee ones and stuff, and joined a dazed queue. Thereupon I learned for the umpteenth time that day the word "military" is spelled l-i-n-e-u-p. Figures! How else could they play Whip the Tail with us?

Ever so slowly the fagged out column filed through the last checkpoint, parading past the terminal doors and onto a hot tarmac. We looked like inmate families let loose from a lengthy stay in solitary confinement, which coincidentally, precisely described the strict constraints of that departure lounge! A short distance away stood a pea-soup green military bus, poised to shuttle us to the plane. Was I, I wondered, the only one musing over how long it would be before my feet once again touched the soil of this, my home?

> "Immigration is
> the sincerest form
> of flattery."
> Jack Paar

THIRTEEN

THE WIND PICKED up, fully ballooning the sails of Gordon's catamaran as we neared the center of Tokyo Bay. Our plan was to cross from Yokohama to Chiba nearly out of sight on the far distant shore. There was not another pleasure boat to be seen. In 1962, the idea of hobby sailing was barely a concept in a poor country like Japan, its economy many years away from inspiring such frivolous distractions. Only wealthy Americans like us (who were we kidding?) dabbled in such exhibitionistic monkey business. Still, on this day despite how glitzy we may have appeared, being pseudo filthy rich was turning into self-inflicted damnation, for now we were all alone out there in one heck of a lot of water.

Glen and Gordon were thrilled out of their gourds. It was incredible. How lucky could we be? We had the entire, huge, empty bay to ourselves! To their further joy, the winds were hurtling us along at thrilling breathtaking speeds. Conversely, I was looking at the very same winds through starkly different eyes. Okay, so I didn't know anything about sailing, but ... hadn't the winds just picked up? Dramatically? And weren't they suddenly way more frenetic? In fact, a lot more than they had been only moments before? Dang! By now not only were we alarmingly far from any shore, but we were also outrageously diminutive—miniscule?—out there alone in this colossal body of water!

"The snotgreen sea.
The scrotumtightening sea."
James Joyce

If you asked me, this was not having fun. This was downright idiotic. From out of nowhere the old comic book hero, the Lone Ranger, popped into my head. The haughty Ranger, surrounded by wild, blood-thirsty Indians all poised to do him in, yells, "Tonto, we're in serious trouble here!" On the periphery of the action, Tonto yells over his shoulder as he gallops off the page, "Whaddya mean 'we,' Kimosabe?" I, like Tonto, didn't want any more of these sailor cowboys and their treacherously asinine hobby, no matter what the heck kimosabe meant.

Years before, as a young child learning to swim at the Austin YWCA, I had been strictly taught about the necessity for the Buddy System. Our lifeguards were fervent in their implicit instructions: never go into the water without a buddy! Never!! Where was our buddy now?

Just then another powerful squall struck the boat. Painfully, I felt the sharp jolt of my head snapping backwards as I looked up at the straining sails. Then a loud, reverberating crack!

No, it wasn't my neck; something worse. To my horror, the mast was no longer there. The once tall, erect shaft of wood was now only a splintered stub with its freed lines and metal stays whipping around it like a giant unleashed weed whacker. Pressure from the fierce gales had been too much. The mast had snapped like a twig.

Next the crossbeams upon which we three were perched shattered and we were instantly tossed into the foamy water. I felt myself being pulled down; down under the wild waves.

Try as I might, I could not get back up to the surface. Something was holding me under. It felt as if an octopus had wrapped me tightly in its tentacles, binding my legs together and trapping me in water too deep to imagine. I couldn't free myself. I couldn't breathe. I couldn't do anything. I was imprisoned under water in what I knew was the most vulnerable, most deadly predicament of my life.

FOURTEEN

OUR WEARY, BUT exhilarated troop of military families and soldiers filed out of the Travis Air Force lounge lugging our accumulated gallimaufry, and with a sluggish quick-step-shuffle proceeded onto the steaming asphalt. In a wavering line, we boarded the pea-soup-green bus which drove us to an awaiting, also pea-soup-green plane, the trendy military being fashionably color-coordinated. Once there we again formed a queue (always the lineup), this time at the bottom of a tall metal staircase, uncannily resembling a project from a child's Erector Set. A lone soldier was single-handedly rolling it up to the plane. The stairs looked so … well … temporary. Not the kind of well-fortified, steel structure I associated with airplanes.

The column moved closer to the steps. It was my turn. I began to climb. It was scary as all get out. The steps were astonishingly uncharitable—very steep, uncommonly narrow, and terrifyingly jiggly with wide slots through which below I could see the ground abruptly vanish as I judged the alarming height of my ascent. The pressure of my recently acquired incontinence began to threaten my dignity.

Gingerly creeping up the tinny steps, Glen held two-year-old Jeff and the biggest of our carry-on luggage, as I, like an ungifted tightrope walker, balanced my share of multifarious bags in one arm while hauling ten-month-old, thirty-pound Matt in the other. I knew exactly how Sir E. Percival Hillary had felt. But then Percy, I now realized, was a cheater! He had had Sherpas!

41

I know, I know, we were ridiculously encumbered with overloaded satchels. Still I knew, as mothers know these things, that I would need every last one of them for the decidedly long flight. Besides, wherever one goes, there he is. Not necessarily so his stowed luggage.

> "The scientific theory I like best
> is that the rings of Saturn
> are composed entirely
> of lost airline luggage."
> Mark Russell

On this aircraft there were no seat assignments, and our stewardesses were male soldiers. I don't mean G.I.s in drag, but guys in soldiering gear. In civilian life—real life—stewardesses took care of people on planes. They were women doing women's work. But, here in the military stewardesses were red-blooded, testosterone-infused troupers who, when commanded to do so, did men *and* women's work. Okay by me, just as long as they brought food and drink, and reminded the pilot when the gas gauge got low.

Along with the eighty other passengers, we scrambled for seats. I asked Glen if we could sit over the wings as in my know-absolutely-nothing-about-airplane logic, figured that particular spot was the strongest part of the plane. Okay, so I wasn't exactly Peggy Earhart, but this shortcoming did not make me the weakest link in the aviation chain. I knew a thing or two about planes. Had I not in the last few days ridden on two? One to Colorado and the other to California? You'd better believe I had experience under my cinch waist belt!

But, to my dismay, our plane had few similarities to the two commercial flights I had just come to know and love. Our plane, besides being that yucky green, had not even been designed for human transport. This was a C-54 of Berlin Airlift fame, later reconfigured for people. Human cargo people. Us!

> "There are two kinds
> of air travel
> in the United States—
> first class and third world."
> Bobby Slayton

There was another big difference. Our plane did not have jet engines. Not necessary! It had four propellers. You know, those plastic things pinned to sticks that blow around in the wind when little children run with them? Peering at ours for the first time through my small window (for crying out loud, I'd really have to talk to the pilot about enlarging it so a girl could see), I did something I don't recommend to anyone. I tried to calculate just how many thousands of miles we had to go on this journey, and then just how many times those propellers would have to rotate without stopping.

Not even one itty bitty once! With that disquieting thought, my tranquility dissolved and the irritating Saint Vitus dance returned, this time unchecked. I whispered a prayer that the full-body rash I could feel creeping over me was not evident.

Wasn't it somewhere in the Ten Commandments that it said, "If God had intended for us to fly, He would have made it easier to get to the airport?" Jeez Louise! While He was making things easier for us, He should *also* not have pinned whirly gigs on a flying bus!

I knew right then and there it was my sacred duty to every passenger on that plane, crew included, to watch the twin set of propellers out my window. I had a perfect view over the wings (which, as I told you, could certainly have been improved with a larger window), and I'd tell—I'd shriek!—if the blades began to falter in any way. For all I knew the pilot couldn't even see the propellers sitting way up in the front like he was … and with his door shut. Plus (and this I really *could* not believe), I had noticed when we boarded there was not even one rear view mirror on our plane! I wondered if I still had Ralph Nader's number in my purse?

What *was* I thinking? Could I have been even one snippet more simple-minded? More dunderheaded? More green? Heaven help us all. I was like Johnny Carson who admitted that as a kid he was so green he used to sneak behind the barn … and do nothing!

In no time we lifted off from the western-most rim of our continent and whirred out over the ocean. My initial gasp of panic over the sudden loss of land beneath us, made me nearly suck myself outside-in. This was my first aerial view of water; nothing but water! Forget the East Side Lake Ocean. This was the Pacific-King-Pin-of-an-Ocean. Outwardly, I was able to maintain some semblance of composure (you know, that Madame T. airport actress thing), while inwardly, I was a raging tempest of shock at the immensity of the Pacific. Beyond my control, I felt my bottom begin to chew a hole through the C-54 reconfigured seat! Squeezy butt time for sure!

> "How inappropriate it is
> to call this planet 'Earth'
> when clearly it is 'Ocean.'"
> Arthur C. Clarke

Then, as if I had suddenly lost the elastic in my panties, my defenses dropped. Out of nowhere an intimately private thanatopsis began rolling through my brain.

Zap, zap, the flashes began to flip by.

There was a baby. Who was that baby? Me? Ye gads, there I was "down there" squishing out of my mother!

And now look. I'm marching off to kindergarten.

Zap, zap!

Are those braces on my teeth? And, is that my first training bra ... training those twin nubbies to do what, I was never sure? Could this be that thing called my moment of reckoning? My swan-song-finale-last-curtain-call-finis?

Zap, zap!

The rapid autobiographical scenes snapped past with a vengeance. Whoa, 1954! I'm sitting in geometry class. Sitting in geometry class taking a test. And, gadzooks, I'm doomed. I'm looking at geometry answers *written on the palm of my hand!* Okay, okay, so my parents had given birth to four children and three had turned out honest and upright. Those odds weren't so bad, were they?

For sure things were getting way too confessional. For the love of Mike, I wasn't even Catholic! And please say that cheating on one little math test eight long years ago was surely not enough sin to bring down a plane, was it? *Well, was it?*

> "I was thrown out of college
> for cheating on the metaphysics exam.
> I looked into the soul
> of the boy next to me."
> Woody Allen

This plane I was now defiling was chock-full of people, really nice people, innocents all, who were needed to stand up for America. Condemning them and their unblemished souls because I had been a bottom-sucking-high-school-cheating-bad-seed just wouldn't be right.

Get hold of yourself, girlfriend! Breathe in deeply. Let loose illogical logic. Sighhhhh ... exhaaaale ....

Slam! B movie blockaded. Conscience cleansed.

Absolved of my horror show, I was at last ready to enjoy the ride. Golly, this was the very moment I had been slaving towards. Savor the here, savor the now, brown cow. Silly old me, anyway, thinking I had that kind of omnipotence over four mighty steel propellers. Japan was just ahead ... just over the edge of the world. What was that – *the EDGE – as in flat?*

Oh, for Pete's sake, not again. Quell the swell, gal. Relinquish, abate, subside ....

FIFTEEN

UNDER US WAS water, nothing but water. This was a good thing, I was thinking. Landing on water would, in anybody's book, be softer than landing on dirt. Wouldn't you agree? I clutched my dog tags and held them as hopefully as the Pope fingered his rosary. Hours passed.

During that time I discovered that Jeff and Matt were born peregrinators. They slept, amused themselves, and without skipping a beat, smiled at the other passengers while accommodatingly spreading thick, gooey, cupid-like charm all over the place. Like Eleanor Roosevelt had done, it was immediately apparent to me that my sons were also on an international goodwill mission here. Yes, the connection seemed as transparently clear as Frederick's of Hollywood underwear.

I knew, oh, how I knew destiny had a plan for us. With the boys' intrinsic adorableness and my unrelenting encouragement of them (just try and stop me!), Jeff and Matt would soon be mesmerizing Asia, now that they had finished conquering a good portion of North America. I would have to arrange their schedules to find plenty of altruistic opportunities for this to happen. And, no, it was not an imposition on me, thank you very much indeed; simply one more of my patriotic duties to America.

Peggy, Peggy, Plenipotentiary Lady.

When the boys took time off from being irresistible, they had to be fed in order to refuel their charm levels. Now well into our second day, we were seriously in need of a warm five-course meal as we had eaten nothing but snacks since leaving Colorado. Instead, we were offered a basket of government surplus pretzels passed over the tops of our seats and down the aisle by us, the passengers. Nestled cozily in their crinkly cellophane wrappings, the honey-hued wicker basket gave them a homey, fresh-out-of-the-oven feel. In a feeble way, it soothed my sense of mothering.

Still, we sure could have used something more substantial. I looked across the aisle. There a G.I. was pulling out of his pocket a big, lumpy bag of Planters peanuts. He began dreamily chomping down, his jaws a metronome crunching in cadence with the growling of my stomach. I stared at him like a starved castaway. Good grief! This travel phantasmagoria had caused yet another psychosis in my overtaxed psyche. Peanuts envy!

It didn't seem fair! It was I who needed nourishment. I, whose body had twice given birth and then abidingly suckled those babies for world without end. And, it was I, too, who had moved my family for the fifth—get that *fifth*—time from hither and yon, while that young buck chewing his peanuts over there had done nothing more than ... well ... save his country from rack and ruin? Holding back my growing weltshmerz, I wondered where *was* the equality in this world?

Just as I was near swooning from weakness, a soldier stewardess came through the plane with some gunmetal-gray mess hall trays, their surfaces cordoned off by humpy dividers into various sized compartments. He was followed by another soldier stewardess distributing small, mud-green boxes: C-rations.

Each box contained little cans and packets dyed to match the mud-green boxes. Once again I was impressed with what lengths Uncle Sam went to in his color harmonizing. A tiny can opener and miniature tin fork and spoon were included. C-rations, I would learn, generally included such delicacies as one-serving size cans of government surplus beef, turkey, cheese and fruit cocktail, as well as packets of pound cake, peanut butter crackers, instant coffee and Chiclets gum. With an eye for the practical, toilet paper and waterproof matches were also included. On this trip, being fancy as it was, we were offered a trio of food ensembles to choose from: beef, turkey or not.

> "If this is coffee,
> please bring me some tea;
> but if this is tea,
> please bring me some coffee."
> Abraham Lincoln

To make our dining experience complete, resting at the bottom of each box was a slim mud-green package of five cigarettes. Cigarettes were *always* included in C-rations. Anybody could see that life-sustaining nutriments alone were not enough. Unfailingly, military dining came with more; a terrific bonus. Lung cancer! For the thousandth time that day I had my doubts about our caring and solicitous Uncle, no matter how good his color sense was.

But, what did we know? In 1962, smoking was not only permitted anywhere, anytime, any day, but it was also downright encouraged anywhere, anytime, any day. The surgeon general told us it was good for us. Calmed us down. You can only imagine how many G.I.s took him at his word and began their cursed, ill-fated affair with the weed when they were out on lonely patrols, heaven knows where, and friendly feel-good ciggies were included in their packaged meals three times a day. Cigarettes were what a soldier did after eating. They were his invitation to relax and forget the strain of battle. What an opulent feather in the caps of the well-heeled tobacco companies. I'd walk a mile for a Camel; straight into my grave.

"As ye smoke,
so shall ye reek."
Unknown

"I have every sympathy for the American
who was so horrified by what he read
about the effects of smoking
that he gave up reading."
Henry Strauss

Aside from the pesky cancer flaw, C-rations were almost not bad fare. Sometimes good, in fact. And on our plane they were served up with unmistakable style. But, don't in any way think we were forced to eat them. We were always given a C-rations dining option. Yes or starve.

Jeff's lap was too short to balance a tray, so I remedied it by having him kneel backwards on the floor facing his seat and using it as a table, all the while trying my best to ignore what war detritus was imbedding itself into my firstborn's peach-skin knees. This was a very workable idea and we used it for many flights in the years to follow. Not being one to let a good concept like this slip through his fingers, I believe Jeff finally gave up on this technique about the time he left Asia for the U.S. to begin his junior year in high school. Tragically for him, though, the trendy madras plaid Bermudas that were all the fashion rage then allowed his scarred and pitted knees to be on display. His new friends were at a loss as to how to understand his knee disfigurement … and Jeff wasn't telling.

Imperfect knees aside, no problem on this plane was more pesky than Matt's cloth Curity diapers. They were so large—each being a yard long and a foot wide—that they took up most of our suitcase space. Never was one or even two Curities enough for his thirty-pound-fed jet stream, making it necessary to use six, seven or even eight diapers all cleverly folded into an astonishingly thick pad, coming well down past his chubby knees. It's a wonder the lad wasn't permanently disfigured, somehow blessedly growing up with thighs that touched!

The unspeakable, extra heavy diapers posed the biggest problem. It wasn't as if I could just toss them out the window. Besides, it was stuck tight.

Must have been a messy paint job because I tried my best, but couldn't budge it open. Neither were there garbage cans conveniently located in the aisle. A soldier carried out what a soldier carried in. Extra deposits included. It didn't matter, anyway, because disposing of a Curity was a cardinal sin. No way would I have dreamed of doing such a frivolous thing, and it was just my tough luck that I'd have to contend with them for the next three days, the duration of this trip. Leave it to say, crappy nappies were something I would definitely have to work on for our future return flight to the States. And who knows, perhaps some inventive type—like, say, a Mr. Pampers back home in the good old U. S. of A.—might get an idea before then.

> "If an idea is not
> at first absurd,
> then there is
> no hope for it."
> Albert Einstein

SIXTEEN

ALL AT ONCE everything I had believed to be security was now churning about me as if I had been, without warning, hurtled into the agitation of a giant Waring blender. Abruptly set free, the dismembered ropes and pieces of boat were hurdling about on the tops of the stiff waves. Bobbing there beside them, my arms flailed uselessly going nowhere, as the once taut sails lay lifeless in crumpled, creamy heaps, swirling around in all directions like whirling dancing skirts.

It's strange what a person thinks about at a time like that. I was thinking of how utterly alone I was, like the startling isolation that grips a patient as she is being wheeled into surgery. All at once she knows that everything is happening to her and to her alone. But even a patient in that kind of trauma is assured she is surrounded by people who are dedicated to helping, saving her, for gosh sakes. That, and the certain guarantee that her gurney is rolling on a firm dry floor with a granite earth core beneath it. The aphorism "a good time to keep your mouth shut is when you're in deep water," was taking on a startling truth, its real meaning coming clear for the first time.

There was no question that I was snared in a death trap. I couldn't get free, I was sinking fast and I could not hold out much longer. For the first time in my life, I became conscious of the precise limitations of my lungs. I needed air. Air! That stuff in the—well, air!—that I had never paid much attention to before now.

Just when panic was about to overtake me, I felt some tugging on my legs. Someone, something was pulling on the lines; the lines that were still attached to the submerged mast and were encircling my legs, holding me deep under the water.

It was Glen! He was under me, pushing me up to the surface. With the force of his shove, I broke through the water's skin, gasping and breathing in convulsively. Trust me when I say, breathing is not overrated.

My gasping lasted only a moment before I was once again pulled deep under the water. In and out, in and out, I continuously gulped air and held my breath as Glen repeatedly dove down to free me from the lines that yanked just as hard as he did, only in the opposite direction.

Then slowly I felt my legs begin to loosen from their deadly bonds. Next, strong arms pushed me up, up to the surface. Glen and I broke through the waves at the same time, coughing and choking from all the sea water we had swallowed. Plain and simple, without question, Glen, my selfless husband, my brave protector, had just saved my life.

Through the waves, he towed me over to a piece of wreckage and yelled for me to hang on. I reached out to follow his orders only to discover I couldn't. I couldn't seem to hold on to anything. There at the lifesaving surface of the water, I found that even though my legs were now free, I was helplessly slipping down fast through my life jacket. As I descended, my arms were suddenly thrust skyward, forced straight up beside my head in the tight vise of the jacket, now a stiff girdle making it impossible to bend them. Bizarrely, I was like a football referee whose arms were permanently frozen in a touchdown signal.

Maybe it was a blessing, I'll never know, but a strange and very dangerous thing had just happened. Wet and fully engorged, and without a strap going between my legs to hold it in place, my life jacket had turned into a perilous canvas barrel with me deep inside it. In this swollen state, it was many times too big for me, and I had slid downward through it with my head blindly trapped inside, an arm's length below the shoulders of the vest. From above the water, it must have looked like a big, plump orange was floating on the rough seas. No one would have guessed there was a person inside it. Me!

The good part was that I couldn't see what was happening, if that is considered good. I was literally floating blind in a gigantic ocean basin while secluded in muffled darkness. Forget about clinging to the wreckage. With my arms stiffly extended above me and bound tight by the unrelenting jacket, the sole remaining thing I could hang onto was the top edge of the bulbous life preserver. With all the strength I had in my fingertips, I clutched it for dear life. The only other option was to let go and slip downward into the bottomless sea. No one on the surface would have even been aware it had happened.

It was scary inside. Trapped there, my eyes and ears were where my waist should have been. The darkness, the churning water and the blurred sounds struck me as the way it must be for a fetus floating in the swirling pool of its own amniotic fluid. But, rats, I had been born a long time ago and was used to being dry, seeing, and hearing, and it was decidedly unnerving to not be able to perceive what was going on around me with all of my senses.

Forcing my head slightly backwards, as far as I could in the confined space of my dark container, I looked up. There above me, as though peering through a pipe, I could make out the round circle of a noontime sky. To my horror, it had turned from a brilliant sunshine into a menacingly dark void. I knew then we were in the midst of a serious storm, unaware before of its approach. The agitated waves were tossing the three of us and the boat wreckage about like scraps of buoyant balsa wood. In the scale of things, we were completely insignificant in that broad expanse of sea; only small specimens of gulping flotsam. Or were we jetsam? I wasn't sure.

No matter, it was all extraordinarily surreal. Over and over one question replayed itself—"What in the world was I doing out here? I should be home hugging my babies."

SEVENTEEN

TWENTY-FOUR HUNDRED MILES and a ton of hours later, our plane began to tip toward its first descent, Honolulu, Hawaii, our first refueling stop. Mercy me, did I forget to explain that our plane couldn't carry enough fuel to get us across the ocean? Yes, it was true, and I wasn't about to argue the need. Certainly not. It was me, after all, who was so vigilantly supervising those propellers.

Oh, it would feel heavenly to get out and walk around. Besides my cramped legs, I felt as bloated as a methane popover. Peggy Zeppelin Keener that was me. Girdles and long flights to Asia, I was learning, were not compatible. But, what was a girl to do? This was 1962, and we ladies—we *traveling* ladies—dressed up. It was what we did. Crammed in our elasticized restraints, our facades were confined, re-shifted and concealed, akin to the hiding of the dangling double chin behind the fold of a turtleneck. The girdle was a must for every dame whose aim it was to tame her frame.

I know in my heart of hearts that women across the globe owe a huge debt of gratitude to the many distressed, but elasticized svelte trailblazers like us who went before them. Surely we were the ones who inspired the invention of the pantyhose. Better yet, polyester stretch pants! Holy moley! The divine give those generous benevolent threads would one day provide was almost illegal. But I, a pioneer, knew nothing of them yet. In the interval, I was singing "The Too Tight Girdle Blues."

We deplaned and I tooted—ahhh—into tropical rays that were as pure and bright as I never knew the sun could be. Hawaii, even the airport, smelled of blossoms and pineapple and coconut frappes. After the cramped, stagnant, smoke-filled plane, we had landed in paradise. A liberated Jeff scampered across the glinting, tropical sun-streaked floors, while Matt, who didn't know how to walk yet, struggled to break free to get his piece of the action.

"Look over there!" Jeff cried gleefully. Peering through red-rimmed eyes in the direction of my son's chubby finger, I saw what he saw. Was it a mirage? Jeff picked up speed as he ran towards a swimming pool right in the middle of the airport. Well, perhaps to a young boy's unschooled eyes it looked like a swimming pool, but in reality it was a fountain. It didn't matter. Before we knew it, Jeff was over the side and, in pure rapture, splashing about in the cool, revitalizing water. I don't believe there was a single bedraggled passenger who at that moment did not envy our ecstatic, leaping, splashing, dripping wet son. I know I sure did.

> "Never play leapfrog
> with a unicorn."
> Unknown

In the plane, parked somewhere off on the pineapple-infused tarmac, we had extra outfits for the boys, but it was mainly Curity changes, not a pool party, for which I had come prepared. Moreover, it would probably not be a good thing to put Jeff's soaking clothes in our carry-on bags next to the perfectly packed dry garments. With this in mind, I had to think fast. Well, actually not all that fast nor all that brilliantly, for there was only one thing to do. Strip the boy down to his buck nakedness and dry him out!

Glen plucked Jeff from the fountain while I peeled him down to his skin. From there we made a quick exit to the outdoors. Those were the days of flimsy airport security. Uncorrupted passengers, as well as those already corrupted, could come and go, inside and out, anywhere they pleased. No one cared. Just beyond the nearest airport door was a lovely manicured grassy area with, lo and behold trees, all exquisitely sculpted by proud professional horticulturalists' hands. What a perfect place to hang laundry and further enhance the dignity of the Honolulu International Airport!

While Jeff romped about like a little Adam without his Eve—or his fig leaf—I hung his ensemble over the flawless flowering branches and let the island breezes do the rest. No doubt about it, the Keeners were meeting Asia head-on with unabashed panache.

EIGHTTEEN

I STRUGGLED TO lift myself up through the life jacket. Hells bells, I was not only over a barrel, I was in a barrel! Trapped under the water, I desperately needed to see exactly what was going on. Finding that out I realized, would take more strength than I feared I had. Deep in my cave with water lashing at my chin, I solemnly studied the situation. I found that when a strong wave hit, I was pushed upward, and with that surge lifting me, I could perhaps momentarily see around me.

Thus, gearing for the next wave, I rose up with it. Pulling with all my might and holding on tightly to the neck of the jacket, I got my first good look above the water. In that brief, sobering moment, I knew at last the severity of our predicament. Pieces of the catamaran were all about us, the sails like thin crumpled ice floes, and everywhere there were ropes, tangled and drifting as far as their knots allowed them to stray. Beyond our debris there was only water. No land in sight. No other vessel of any kind.

It was too exhausting to hang on any longer and I let myself once again slip down into the inky, suffocating blackness. Again I thought about our boys, my babies. I remember being absolutely clearheaded, wondering again and again if the Japanese babysitter would stay until my folks could come from Minnesota. I calculated how long it would take for someone to find Glen and me missing, then for someone to notify my parents, and then for Mom and Daddy to organize their rescue mission from across the globe. Yes, Jeff and Matt would have a good life with them. They'd grow up eating lots of beamy Minnesota steaks and going to fun happy hour parties.

If only the babysitter would stay till my parents could get here.

NINETEEN

AFTER WHAT SEEMED like too short a time in paradise, a ukulele-timbred voice melodiously trilled over the address system that our long, but pleasant layover in Hawaii was over. Still, it had not been long enough to revive us, all except for Jeff that is, who after a nice swim was now outfitted in a freshly sun-dried getup. The rest of us, thoroughly exhausted, rumpled and considerably discomposed, lumbered ungracefully like a cluster of loobies out to the plane in a poor excuse for a lineup. Wobble, wobble.

What time was it, anyway? Real time. *Our time!* It was so darned hard to figure. By now, a day and part of a night had passed. During those long hours on the first leg of our trip, Glen and I had catnapped between baby watches. Well, if truth be told, Glen had done the napping while I remained on propeller-earth-edge watch. Additionally, Hawaii was in a weirdly different time zone, making everything screwy. Boy, they sure must have thought they were something having their own time zone. But then, I figured, the mesmerizing sway of swiveling grass-skirted hips could very well cause them to ignore their watches, so I guessed it was necessary.

"There is never enough time,
unless you're serving it."
Malcolm Forbes

With the plane's steely belly once more bulging with fuel, we lifted off the island with a deafening whir of its four spinning blades. As we rose, I looked out through my little window, still unable to open it due to that sloppy paint job. Holy smoke! From up here the Hawaiian Islands were dismayingly tiny. Little more than a chain of specks strung out on the immensity of an ocean. How did such microscopic things stay afloat? And, weren't the Hawaiians scared that their very existence might wash away—or sink—never to be heard from again? I was certain that all the oscillating hula hips, all the perfumed flowered leis (and why, for crying out loud, couldn't they just call them necklaces like the rest of the world did), plus all the clattering puka-shell castanets in their entire island chain could not save them if the ocean decided to swallow them up. Clink! Gulp! Burp!

Maybe, just maybe, Pineapple Land was not such a Shangri-la after all. Do you suppose this revelation, too, was up to me? You know, to report my findings to the Honolulu Tourist Bureau? So many responsibilities, so little time, so trapped in this seat—in this darned girdle! Out of nowhere the idea of a pragmatic Minnesota surrounded on all sides by solid, deep, subterranean earth came to mind. Gosh, Peggy, with the islands below looking like splattered bug spots on a wet windshield, it made a whole lot of sense to remain a Minnesotan, in Minnesota. What in blue blazes were you doing here, girlfriend?

> "I just got wonderful news
> from my real estate agent in Florida.
> They found land on my property."
> Milton Berle

TWENTY

WITH ANOTHER STRONG thrust from beneath me, I was shoved upward. As I cleared my vision, I was surprised to see Gordon straddled atop one of the over-turned hulls, struggling with something while trying his best to hang on. He seemed to be tying a white cloth around an oar that he had somehow had the good sense to grab from the fizzy sea. Tossed about by the bullish waves, the maneuver was taking forever. Finally, Gordon raised the oar in his right hand as high above his head as he could, while with his left hand he held onto his slippery, unpredictable perch. Then slowly he began waving the oar back and forth. An unexpected feeling of hope began to swell inside me.

Then just as quickly it faded. The cloth, immediately soaked and wind-blown, wrapped itself as tightly around the oar as bark on a tree. It looked ridiculous. Gordon looked ridiculous, like an amoeba holding up a micro Q-tip in the middle of an enormous pond. Though well intentioned, all his efforts were fruitless.

I sank once again into my chamber, bobbing wildly in the waves. Then out of nowhere, an idea popped into my head. Why hadn't I thought of it before? I could bargain! You know what I mean: "Oh, God, if you get me through this, I'll become … or I'll do … or I'll give …."

Though I desperately needed a faith lift, it, however, didn't last long. Right off I decided negotiating wasn't fair. Like it wasn't exactly God's problem, you know. He only made the weather. It was up to me to listen to the forecast. Anyway, I didn't like the idea of becoming an emergency room Christian just because I was in a tough spot. I knew God could part the waters, but did this include the seas of the Shinto/Buddhist Tokyo Bay? Years before in Austin, Mrs. Dovenburg, my Sunday school teacher, had never covered this particular situation, but now I suspected her Presbyterian thinking probably didn't include waters of the Asian persuasion.

Inside my jacket, I suddenly heard muffled sounds. It was Gordon and he was shouting, his words distorted through the jacket's sodden layers. "Ship," I thought he was screaming, "over there!" Hope instantly surged. Tugging as hard as I could, I pulled myself upward and peered over the edge of the neck opening. I could just make out a ship in the far distance. It, of course, could see us. And, wasn't it turning in our direction? From the water Glen began to cheer, while from atop the hull Gordon frantically waved his arms back and forth, shrieking with all the powers in him.

We were going to be saved. Glen and I would see our babies again.

TWENTY-ONE

IT WAS BEGINNING to feel as if this trip, like that glued-on roller skating curse I had put on the Army sergeant, would never end. Mind you, we were not going to just any old east here, but the *real* one. The Far one. The East with capital letters like where the sun came up—on the other side of West where it didn't. Then it dawned on me. That must be why the Japanese called it the Land of the Rising Sun. The world just began there! I'll bet they were sure hoity-toity conceited over that!

As the Hawaiian Islands disappeared from sight, I once again set up shop in our confined C-54 quarters. On hand were the glass quart bottles of milk I had brought, now ready to pour into baby bottles. I had come prepared for everything and anything. Our aircraft was not exactly what you'd call the Queen Sheba of the Skies and heaven only knew what we might need next. By now the families were completely befuddled as to whether to sleep, eat or play. As for me, I'd just go along with anything anybody decided to do. Meanwhile, the single G.I.'s snoozed, smoked and read to their hearts' content. Parenthood to them must have seemed a trillion lifetimes away. That or they were in a deep state of reflection debating the merits of the vasectomy.

I tugged at the uncompromising confines of my constrictive girdle and began my own reflection—a future spent entirely in saggy sweat pants.

TWENTY-TWO

DURING A STORM at sea, there is little a capsized person can do to be seen. While being heaved about on its surging waves, you and the wreckage around you are pushed up onto the crest of the swells and there, just when you think you are obvious to the universe, you get lost in the sudsy foam of the waves' ringlets. You are like a Tonka Toy boat in a tub of thick bubble bath with a child under you playing Bathtub Bluebeard. As the wave upon which you are riding reaches its final height, it breaks, tossing you uncaringly back under the water's surface along with the torrent of the forceful deluge. There is no opportunity to be seen … unless you are very large. I wasn't. But, I thought I was. Everybody thinks he is.

You think you're big because you're you: an ego. Not only are you sure of this, but by gosh, you're also unfailingly sure that anybody looking can see you. After all, it's you out there in the water. You, a person of import, recognizable as a friend to some, acknowledged as a presence to many. And yet the reality of your being spotted is as slim as that of a midnight jogger running in a downpour, dressed in black from head to toe.

Nonetheless, you grab with all of your being onto those straws called faith.

Our eyes were now riveted on the ship. Had it seen us? It was headed in our path. That meant it had. At once I understood what real joy and deliverance were all about. There wasn't even time to further contemplate deals and promises and atonements with God, because I was too excited

Peggy Keener

and scared and exhausted to creatively haggle. Besides, that could all come later. On dry land.

The ship continued on its course heading directly toward us. I let myself slip down once again into the murky black of my sodden enclosure, holding onto the neck opening with my fingers. It would soon be over. There would be no need to bother my mom and dad after all.

TWENTY-THREE

THIRTEEN-HUNDRED MILES AND a lifetime of hours later, our plane once again tipped downward in its second descent. I peered out the window. The dinky point of land we were headed for surely could not be our destination. I could barely make it out in the humongous expanse of ocean below. Wait, where did it go? It just disappeared! Darn! I'd be able to see it if only those pesky rotating blades would stop for just one minute.

Hold on! Did I just say that? I'd have to get a grip on myself. For the love of Mike, I was becoming too frazzled from this vigilant propeller watching. I must remain serene, jelly bean.

But, quite honestly, there was no way a cargo plane *this* size could land on a clump of dirt *that* size. Was the pilot even sure it *was* land and not just a great big glop of seaweed?

Klump! Praise the Lord! We landed and taxied to an abrupt stop, alarmingly near the water's edge. Hoisting ourselves from our well lived-in seats—by now the perfect contours of our individual rumps—we teetered off the plane onto an air field that looked deceptively like melted licorice.

Helloooo, Midway Island!

This was a place air had forsaken. A person, I immediately discovered, did not breathe on Midway; rather he cut out a chunk of oxygen and sucked on it. You could *feel* the weight and texture of the air. I didn't know this was possible. It was as if the entire population of the island had en masse taken a long, hot, steamy shower without anyone turning on the ceiling fan. In Minnesota the schools would have declared this a Fog Event and everyone would have been told to stay home. The gleeful kids, set free, would have played their hearts out, blindly crashing into each other the whole live long day.

Compared to Hawaii, Midway Island looked like a cornfield, minus the corn. I supposed that being a Pacific island there was potential for it to be another paradise, but on that day it was only a Hawaii in the rough. Real rough.

To explain, Midway, only five degrees north of the Tropic of Cancer, is a tiny part of a string of widely separated islands and reefs that stretch across one small area of the Pacific. The clump of land we were now standing on was one of the two main islands in this chain. It was sparsely populated and only three-square-miles in size. It was truly amazing that our pilot could have even stumbled upon it in all that water, to say nothing of landing this beast of a plane on it. As for the other "main" island, it was even smaller and inhabited only by wildlife.

The U.S. took formal possession of a deserted Midway in 1867. Then with the laying of the trans-Pacific cable in 1903, it brought in its first known residents. It must surely have felt to them like the end of the earth with its rugged volcanic outcroppings and sparsely vegetated land. Additionally, it must have been a stunningly lonely place. There was, however, company of sorts, for these brave souls shared the small island with hundreds of thousands of gooney birds (albatross), as well as an abundant variety of other bird species. In fact, there were so many birds the island was eventually declared a bird sanctuary. With one glance, it was obvious to me these birdies had a dubious taste in environs. Like a really sensible alternative would have been … let's see … the woodsy wealds of Minnesota? What a bunch of dodo birds!

In 1935, a cargo ship arrived at Midway carrying enough supplies to build a hotel and a restaurant, along with a power generator and the other necessary ingredients for a full tourist resort. Developers had discovered that the island, with its multitude of atoll lagoons, was perfect for scuba diving. Midway was about to be transformed into a vacation utopia. Within a year's time the island was touted by adventurous travelers as a tropical off-the-beaten-track Eden. Its fame was short lived, however, for only five years later all the activities abruptly stopped with the declaration of war by the Japanese—you know—the ones who would soon be our neighbors!

Consequently, Midway—because it was *mid-way*—was used as an American refueling stop for military trans-Pacific flights. Then in 1942, our victory over a fleet of Japanese warships took place just off shore and generated a turning point in World War II. The Battle of Midway became household knowledge in America, even though nobody knew where it was. Now I did, even though nobody cared.

Following that, Midway Island was closed to the public for fifty years. During this long protected time, the island evolved into a pristine locale and was reintroduced as one of the most fabulous dive sites in the world.

Additionally, numerous new species of fish and seaweed were identified and named. Approximately one-hundred-and-fifty people presently live on Midway, including a staff of forty U.S. Fish and Wildlife Service folks. A limit of only one hundred guests at any one time is allowed. (I'm thinking it might sink if there were more!) Virtually all food and manufactured goods must be brought in. With that said, you now know more about Midway than you ever wanted to know. Just being helpful.

During the interim, before all the rediscovered glory took place, the Keeners stood on this pinhead in the Pacific. I must say that as I gazed at its scruffiness, it would have been impossible to guess what it would become some day. All I could see were brave patches of sparsely feathered grasses toughing it out in the unfriendly soil. But, then, it was hard to see anything through my sleep-deprived eyes. Besides, most of my concentration had to go towards breathing. Suck, suck.

As Jeff toddled about in zig-zaggy lines, I carried Matt and took the opportunity to stumble off in my own personal plane-induced brume ... and toot ... also personal. Matt didn't seem to mind. As you know, he was used to that sort of thing. We passengers were not *like* zombies, we *were* zombies. Gone was any freshness we had ever known; gone were starched and ironed clothes; gone was the ability to speak in compound sentences; gone were eyeballs that simultaneously moved together. On top of that, we were unanimously experiencing the most significantly bad hair day of our lives.

> "Why don't you get a haircut?
> You look like a chrysanthemum."
> P. G. Wodehouse

It was a given that no one knew exactly what day it was. Had we gone forward or backward in time? I wondered if any of us four had gained or lost a birthday? But in the end, it was too complicated to figure out.

TWENTY-FOUR

THE SHIP SHOULD be approaching at any minute. We were about to be saved. With dogged determination, I pulled myself up through the life vest, my salt-soaked eyes peering over the edge of the canvas eagerly awaiting a first glimpse. There it was! Yes, I could see it!

Then just as the ship came into focus, something unexpected happened. As suddenly as it had appeared, it just as suddenly took an abrupt turn—away from us! I couldn't believe it. It couldn't be true. Our only hope for rescue was abandoning us!

Until that moment, I had not known how quickly hope can plummet from elation to dejection. This was nothing like the everyday kind of disheartenment when you find that your brother has eaten the last piece of your birthday cake, or that you didn't make the cheerleading squad, or that you had spinach in your front teeth during your wedding photo shoot. This was our lives here!

My eyes pivoted around to Gordon and Glen. They were staring in disbelief at the disappearing stern of the ship, their mouths perfect o's of denial. This would have been the quintessential moment for me to begin a nail-biting habit, if only I'd been able to get my nails to my teeth.

One thing was manifestly clear. We had no choice but to hold on; to start praying that another ship would come along, see us and not shun us. Unbelievably, I remained calm and let myself slip down again into the darkness; the darkness where the ocean sloshed and tugged at my upturned, gasping mouth.

I knew this experience was different for each of us. Gordon must have felt enormously responsible, even possibly guilty for being the one who got us into this predicament, if a finger of blame could be pointed. He must also have deeply regretted the extensive damage to his boat. On the other hand, I knew Glen, like myself, was thinking about our boys; how young they were and what their futures would be like without us. From where he hung onto a ragged chunk of the catamaran, Glen was also keeping a vigilant watch on me, making sure I wasn't pulled beneath the sea again by the tangled ropes, or that I'd not drift too far from the wreckage.

In a way, I suppose, I had a good deal being submerged and unable to see what was—and was not—happening. But, Mary, Mother of God, wasn't this the kind of deep that we Minnesotans said went all the way to China? Do you suppose that conversely the sea I was now suspended in went all the way to Minnesota? If I let go, would it be a cheap one-way ticket home?

"I Don't Know Whether
to Kill Myself
or Go Bowling."
Song title by unknown

I remained with these thoughts for what seemed an eternity. To be sure, all sense of time had been lost along with the boat. Two hours for sure had passed, although it could have been ten. The truth was that a count of minutes didn't much matter in our vulnerable circumstances. More important was how long I could continue holding on with the tips of my fingers.

All at once I again heard a muffled shout. "Ship! Ship!" Gordon was yelling. Struggling with all my might—you cannot imagine how difficult it was—I again slowly, painfully hoisted myself upward. Sure enough, there it was. There was no mistaking it. This ship was bearing straight down on us.

We waited. Slowly it drew nearer. As it came up beside us, for the first time we realized just how tiny we were. Beside us, it looked like a floating Empire State Building. Its metal side loomed above and across our field of vision, blocking out everything beyond it. To be sure, I could never have guessed that one of the most beautiful sights I would ever see would be a wet, gunmetal gray, steel wall.

As best it could, the ship stopped and chugged in place. I could see men way up at the distant top railing peering down at us. From my vantage point, they looked like toy figures scurrying about. But, trust me, they were much more than toys. They were heaven sent theophanies: ordinary men who without a doubt appeared to me as gods. Before we knew it, the men/gods lowered something over the towering side of the hull; something tied to a thick rope. In slow motion it descended. As it came closer, I could see it was a long wooden ladder.

Glen, grabbing from one piece of wreckage to another, made his way over to me. I was to be the first one up. There was no time to feel anything. My mission was to somehow, in the heavy swells, get myself over to the ladder. Glen snatched hold of my vest and towed me through the waves. As we neared the ladder, we both realized to our dread, that it had not sunk upright into the water. Rather, because it was so big and heavy and made of wood, the ladder was now bobbing and whipping about on top of the rough seas. Exhausted, I once again sunk deep into my saturated trap. It did not seem possible that I could hoist both my body and the weighty, unwieldy life jacket up onto the rungs of this floating stairway. Salvation lay before me and I didn't know how in the world I could grasp hold of it.

All at once I felt Glen drag me through the water and over to the ladder. Next he dove under me and with all his fortitude shoved me out of the water up to the bottom rung. It must have taken Herculean strength, the kind of adrenaline-fed energy that kicks in during an emergency, the rescuer only learning afterwards of his astonishing surge of power.

With the waves churning around me, still deep in the life jacket and unable to see, I felt the bottom rung with my fingertips and grabbed it, clinging with all my might. My deliverance would depend entirely on my ability to hold on until this heavy ladder, with me hanging from it, reached the men way, way, way up at the top.

I moved in slow motion, blindly sensing myself being hoisted out of the churning seas. As the ladder left the water, I felt a sudden sharp jerk downward. My body weight, along with my wet clothes and the ponderous albatross I was encased in, were all pulling together against the grasp of my fingers. Somehow I would have to hold on.

The movement up was interminable. Inch by inch the men, the gods, raised me skyward. Unable to see, I was being pulled up the side of a sky scraper to the very top penthouse floor while at the same time fighting the raging wind and rain that tore at me from all directions.

All at once I sensed the angle of the ladder shift from vertical to horizontal, followed by the feel of many toughened hands grabbing me. As my body tilted over the railing and onto the deck, I blacked out. I didn't have to do anything, anyway, anymore, so without being aware, I gave myself permission to blissfully slip into unconsciousness.

The next thing I remembered was being carried across the deck, descending a narrow iron staircase and finally being laid down in a small passageway outside of a room. Many hands removed my life jacket ... and then my tennis shoes.

Huh? My shoes?

Eventually, with no sense of how much time had elapsed, I was carried into a cabin and laid upon a tatami mat beside Glen and Gordon who had been pulled out of the water after me. Even in that befuddled, depleted state, I was still able to catch the irony of what had just happened. No matter that our clothes were soaking wet and thoroughly saturating the *rice straw mats beneath us, or that our tennis shoes were immaculately antiseptic after an extended soaking in salt water, we had just been rescued by a Japanese ship—and in Japan, shoes were always removed before entering a room!*

Had I had more energy, I would have howled at the absurdity of it all, but in its place I could only muster a sentient smile. Besides, it was no time to be looking (and judging) a gift horse (and his customs) in the mouth. Almost immediately Glen began vomiting. Salt water he had swallowed in saving me now gushed out of him, also soaking into the tatami mats. Bad as the damage was, though, it wasn't anywhere as bad as keeping our shoes on.

As we three lay there ruining the floor mats, the story of our rescue unfolded. The crew told us that, sure enough, we'd been hit by a severe storm, striking without warning. (Actually, we'd pretty much figured that out on our own.) The first ship, the one we thought had abandoned us, had after all been a Good Samaritan. Deciding it was too large to rescue us, the captain had radioed to the smaller ship behind it; the one steaming back into Tokyo Bay from a trip far out to sea where it had unloaded a hold full of trash. Glory be! Our guardian angels were seafaring garbage men!

But, call it what you will, to us it was a golden gunmetal gray chariot, and our sanitary sailors were nothing short of saviors. Besides, we were in no position to cast aspersions upon any of it. As Mark Twain once said, "A man with a hump-backed uncle shouldn't make fun of another man's cross-eyed aunt!" For sure, we were the ones with the humps.

Our rescue ship was as immaculate as a garbage ship could be—if you ignored the occasional maggot here and there, which I did. Furthermore, it had barely even the slightest olfactory hint of its function. As well, our benefactors were gracious and exceedingly kind, and they sailed out of their way to deliver us to a port in Yokosuka not far from where Gordon had an office. Upon docking, we arose on skittish sea legs, and poured out our "domo arrigato gozaimashitas" all over the place; "thank you" seeming so haplessly inadequate as payment for saving our lives.

Fragile as I was after our harrowing ordeal, I was still able to make out a sign posted in the hallway through which we were exiting:

> *"For safety of life cargo and ship body,*
> *it is prohibited to bring swords, guns,*
> *rifles, six-shootings and other inflammable*
> *inexplosives into cabin without permitted*
> *if you have such a things with you. Please*
> *apply to informant. Crew will keep them*
> *as long as you are among us."*

I paused, trying to remember if I'd had any swords, guns, rifles, six-shootings or other inflammable inexplosives in my pockets that I should now ask the informant to return before we departed. Unable to recall anything at all, including my name, I let it go.

We teetered down a very long dock and dripped toward an unsuspecting taxi where we laid waste to a perfectly good backseat. The ordeal for Glen and me was over. Not so for Gordon who still had to arrange for the towing of the wreckage and then decide if his boat was salvageable. But, that was his worry. I, Tonto, just wanted to get home to my babies. I was feeling dry land under my feet and it felt divine, and I could almost begin to give myself permission to relax. Almost, but not quite.

I needed a bathroom and I needed it now! I was ready to burst. All the time I had been floating in the water, I kept telling myself it would be perfectly all right to do "it" in the Pacific Ocean—bringing to mind that old moral debate over the appropriateness of urinating while in the shower. Indeed, it gave me something to think about down there in my dark tube. After all, I had argued with myself, wouldn't it be better to concentrate on wetting while fully clothed and in front of two men, than to concentrate on drowning? Additionally, would my personal liquefied contribution to such a gargantuan body of water really be noticeable?

"What a ninny," I had chided myself. "Just do it and get it over with. Nobody's gonna know. And besides, you certainly don't have to worry about a wet groin stain on your clothing!" But, try as I might, I had not been able to allow my bladder to relax. Therefore, by the time I finally got to Gordon's office, I was desperate. I began pulling off my soaked clothes as I stumbled towards the nearest restroom.

I pushed opened the door and looked at the toilet. Taped to the open lid was a sign in childlike block print: "PREASE FRUSH." A hoot of jubilation burst out of me. I was back in the land of the ridiculous. My nightmare was over. It had ended on solid ground, on a toilet, with a good guffaw. Glen, our boys, and I would have a future together.

"When you're safe at home," Thornton Wilder once said, "you wish you were having an adventure; when you're having an adventure, you wish you were safe at home." He must have, once upon a time, gone sailing with Gordon.

> *"It is unpleasant*
> *to go anywhere alone,*
> *even to be drowned."*
> *Russian proverb*

TWENTY-FIVE

MY EYES WERE glued to my tiny window as we descended into Tokyo. Down below I could see people; people everywhere! It seemed we were about to mistakenly alight on a really large anthill. And look at that! All the ants were the same size, all had black hair (egads, that gooney Austin neighbor *did* know stuff!), all had the same face, and all were scurrying about over and around each other in their haste to get somewhere in a confined space.

This, I thought, must be the true meaning of homogeneous. I glanced over at my fellow passengers. In a place such as this, we *gaijin* (guy-jean, foreigners or "outside people"), were going to stand out like albinos in a gospel choir! We were the anti-cloned! We looked nothing like those ants down below. We were too tall, too pasty faced, too big footed, too blond, too pale eyed, too fat bottomed, too round eyed, and heaven help us, we smelled (as I was later to find out from the Japanese), like butter; none of it being our fault, except for the butter part. Oh, and maybe the fat bottoms.

By word of explanation, dairy products were not all that common in Japan in 1962. Because we Westerners consumed lots of them, the Japanese claimed we also smelled like them. Who knew? I, myself, had never given it a thought, but had to admit those Asian folks certainly had a point. Why, I couldn't think of a single Minnesota recipe that didn't call for butter—pounds, tubs, churns of it. In time I found the Japanese smelled like mothballs and soy sauce. I'd like to say that by then I blended in with those aromas, but the truth is, once a butter girl, always a butter girl. Besides, I'd take the fragrance of a processed Bessie any day over camphor and fermented beans.

Deplaning in a near comatose state, our little family stumbled into the Tachikawa U.S. Air Force Terminal and lined up for customs inspection. The Japanese officers took one look at our unhinged condition and decided we weren't clever enough to smuggle in unlawful goods. They stamped our passports without hassle and waved us through, no doubt wondering at the pitiful plight of foreigners, while at the same time fanning away our offensive Land-o-Lakes stench.

About this time, young Jeff took a full circle look around and began to wail. "Where is he, where *is* he?" he cried in ever increasing sobs. What had gotten into the boy? And how, for the love of Mike, was I supposed to know he was expecting a puppet to greet him when he got off the plane?

Only later when he calmed down did I get the full scoop. During all those days leading up to our arrival (decades in a little boy's world), Jeff had been building himself up not to see Tok-ee-oo, but rather Pin-oo-chi-o! Yes, I could see the confusion alright. Like a movie fan gearing himself up to see Rock Hudson and then having a *Rick* Hudson show up. Indeed, I could feel his pain. Poor lad, he never quite forgave us for our unintended trickery.

As Jeff dried his tears, we boarded a bus. We were informed that we had a long drive ahead of us. (So, what's new?) They weren't kidding. Tokyo was huge. In fact, some time later an old friend wrote informing me that he would have a short layover in Tokyo on his way to Hawaii. Would I like to meet him at the airport and we could discuss old times? I had to decline. Little did he realize that after his plane took off, he would arrive in Hawaii before I could drive back home!

After several hours of weaving through astonishingly tight traffic on inconceivably narrow roads, we arrived at the Gajo-en Hotel. It was, by anybody's count, a suspect kind of place, otherwise known as a Japanese establishment contracted out by the American government. That is to say, it was a Japanese hotel reserved pretty much for the temporary use of U.S. military personnel, although a few Japanese guests, throwing caution to the wind, braved it, as well.

Upon entering the main lobby, I was immediately assured that all would be well; that I would never find myself alone in this strange land (to say nothing of this gamble of a hotel), by a sign posted over the front desk:

"You Are Invited To Take Advantage of The Chambermaid."

What a relief to know assistance was at hand.

We were told we would stay in the Gajo-en until we could find a place to live (however long that would take), as military quarters on post were not issued to lowly GS-7 civilians like ourselves. Our hotel room—a.k.a. new home—turned out to be as plain as a Japanese Jane could be, with just enough space to move around the modest, barely adequate furniture. A note taped to one of the beds seemed to me a bit rude—"No smoking in bed and other disgusting behaviors"—but I thought it probably didn't apply to us because none of us smoked, including the boys. What did apply, however, was the stern warning I found in the bathroom:

> "Is forbidden to steel hotel towerls,
> please if you are not person to do such
> is please not to read notice."

Since I wasn't such a not person, so I did not to read it.

The temperature inside the room was as hot as a strip tease in Hades; its fug nearly knocking me over. Still, uninspired as it was, it was our first Asian home and I was prepared to make the most of it, lackluster discounted. There was, albeit, some good news in our room. Even though it felt like the inside of a warmed-over casserole, it was as secure as Fort Knox. Yet another sign on the door reassured me of this:

> "Note for the swell safegourd of our gorgeous guestses.
> Though we have told already in regards to grime
> prevention of our hotel through the informed
> book equipped in your now room, we anew
> inform the followings – be careful!
> Never leave open the door full and half.
> This is to be care of viscous swindlers and
> not be cheated by their skillful enticement."

Boy, I'd remember that alright.

> "The chief merit of language is clearness,
> and we know that nothing
> detracts so much from this
> as do unfamiliar terms."
> Galen

TWENTY-SIX

WITHIN DAYS, GLEN and I met head-on with the local real estate game. Finding a house was easier said than done. There weren't many, and on top of that the Japanese rents were exorbitant. Wouldn't you know it? After the penny pinching it had taken for the four of us to get through college, now at last when we thought we were pretty hot stuff reveling in the $5,338 awesomeness of Glen's new annual salary, we learned that the outrageous rental rates were clearly beyond us. It would be imperative for us to learn the tricks: the underhanded, rascally bunko of the Japanese rental house racket.

As I said, Glen was a civilian working for the army. Because we were not provided quarters on post, the army was required to make up for this by giving us a monthly housing allowance to pay for a home "on the economy." This was called "a Japanese house." Do not, however, be fooled into thinking that folks like us could move right on in after paying one month's rent. Not this simple by a long shot. This was Japan, remember?

Upon signing a rental agreement, one also signed a "key money" agreement. This meant an *additional* six months' of rent was required at the time you signed the contract: one month's worth to the landlord, one to the realtor, another towards a deposit, and yet another to "key money," the most baffling of all the indecipherable real estate game bewilderments. The remaining two months' of payments were simply lost in red tape.

You do the math. If our house cost $200 a month, (remember, this was 1962), we needed at extra $1,200 just to walk through the door, making a total of $1,400! Recall, if you will, that Glen's new sumptuous salary amounted to just over $5,000 a *year!!* Now you understand why I called those landlords shamelessly unconscionable. And, while you're remembering things, remember again that we had managed to: pay for college by living in a half Quonset, then in a deserted mountain canyon, with two children—and all on the G.I. Bill. Get the picture?

Here's the way the housing scheme worked. The army housing inspector would come, evaluate the rental property and then set a price the military deemed it was worth. Each month we would receive a check from the army for that amount. With this money, we'd pay the landlord. It was called "the housing allowance."

But, alas and alack, the allowance was nowhere near enough to pay what the chousing Japanese landlords charged. Hence—and here is where we played the game—from our own shallow pockets, we were forced to slip the difference under the table. It was painful. It was also the twisted take of those rapacious racketeers on the Golden Real Estate Rule. It went like this: those with the gold (in this case, them and their properties), make the rule.

> "There's a deception
> to every rule."
> Hal Lee Luyah

Would you believe that I, the very same person who had fretted buckets over roasting in hell for some measly geometry answers written on my palms, picked right up on this unscrupulous money-slipping business? What choice did I have? We had to live somewhere. It is sad to say that one of the first things Glen and I mastered in our new culture was to be honestly dishonest in an okay Oriental sort of way.

> "In spite of
> the cost of living,
> it's still popular."
> Kathleen Norris

As civilians, we only got housing quarters when and if our rank became high enough to warrant such a privilege, and then only after all the military filled them first. That would be years away. So for now, off-base housing and the devious rental game were our only recourse. Actually, living on the economy was perfectly fine with me. It would force me to go native, learn the local customs, live with the Japanese, learn Japanese, eat seaweed and watch my hairs turn black. Time for a change. I'd been a blond too long. Let the party begin!

IN THE INTERIM, before any of this house glory could be ours, we waited and stewed in the Gajo-en. It was July. We were newbies in the Land-of-the-Rising-and-Never-Setting Sun. Boy, did we, the uninitiated, ever learn in a fast hurry about orbs and rays. Each morning the searing sun rose unrivaled by any cooling breezes, and it stayed and it steamed and it sweltered. Drippy humidity hung in the air like phlegmy chiffon. Along with it brought the discovery of new sweat glands of which, until then, we had no idea we were equipped. I wondered if I'd ever see the day when I would declare, "My, it's a little nippy outside." But then, I supposed, it was always a little nippy outside … they were, after all, everywhere.

Our insufferable hotel room contained only two windows of which neither opened, no doubt the fault of the same sloppy painter who messed up those windows on the plane! Even if they had opened, it wouldn't have mattered for I soon discovered there wasn't enough extra air in Japan to serve as superfluous window air. Rather, what little there was, was needed not for comfort, but for our very existence as we back-and-forth, in-and-out, drew in each other's condensation. It was a beautiful groupie kind of thing.

> "What dreadful hot weather we have.
> It keeps me in a constant state of inelegance."
> Jane Austen

Of course, Glen left everyday to go to work, leaving the boys and me behind. In his absence we did a little exploring. To my delight I discovered that the Gajo-en had a decent dining room. Actually the manager wouldn't stop boasting about it, proudly declaring they had "fine foods, and also Italian." To further impress me, he added that "all vegetables served in this mine restaurant is washed in water passed by mine head chef." Whew, was I glad to hear that!

Then he went on to say that "our hotel décor—unglazed tile, goatskin seat coverings, copper medallions and happy light softly falling from ceiling boards—contributed to one glittering atmosphere for grilling meat."

And with that additional information about the decor, I knew I was in the right place!

Not only did the manager make me feel welcome, but also the hotel staff bent over backwards to please me. Before you could say, "You're welcome to Japan," a note arrived at my door:

"We hold cocktails party for foreign
and Japanese participanters for purpose
of becoming intimate with each other.
You are welcome anytime. That time,
please phone your arrival otherwise
we may give you heavy trouble when
you come to us. Waiting for
your nice courtesy call."

Looking forward to becoming intimate any old time to avoid heavy trouble, I no longer felt alone.

TWENTY-SEVEN

OUT ON THE streets I noticed that all the folks, children included, carried special summertime hankies: layered gauze-like cloths just for wiping up sweat. Turned out these were used constantly as the need was incessant during the fierce diaphoretic summer months. Following each vigorous swipe of the face and neck (or dab-dab if you were a lady of refinement), the cloth was precisely folded—never balled up—and put back into a pocket, a satchel or tucked under the obi (oh-bee, the sash around the kimono).

In the weeks to come, I would also learn of a second necessary cloth, the oshibori (oh-she-bor-ee, a thin terry wash cloth presented in restaurants and homes before beginning a meal). Initially I was struck by this charmingly hospitable and solicitous concept. Then in restaurants, I began observing more closely. Ish! The male customers used the oshibori to vigorously scrub down their entire faces from hairline to chin, including behind and in the ears, as well as scouring the backs of their necks. Even though they stopped there (because they were out in public and all) and did not progress further down their torsos, I did begin to question the quaintness—and hygiene, for Pete's sake—of this custom. It sure did smack of indelicacies. They should have just called it like it was—*ishi-bori!*

Moreover, whenever I left a restaurant, I would often catch a glimpse of the waitress who had just served us, squatting over a small dishpan of water on the ground outside the door. She would be rinsing out the very same ishy oshibori that we had just used. Initially, this startled me, but then I realized—what the heck! I was in Rome here, and more than anything, I wanted to be a true Roman. So, I stopped thinking about microorganisms. Like the rent, why fight it?

Aside from harboring all the bacteria, protozoa, and viruses that must have been in the oshibori, I really did like them. They always arrived at the dinner table tightly rolled like fabric tamales laid side by side on miniature bamboo trays. Oshibori felt refreshingly good and smelled like room freshener. I surrendered totally, buying into the seeming purification of the execution, as well as the refreshingly moist, but cloying, flowery aromas. Keeping only these high points in mind, I closed my thinking to further bacterial scrutiny. It paid off, too, for never once in all our years in Japan did I ever hear of anyone coming down with oshibori-itis.

Quite possibly the most important cloth—its magnitude unappreciated by foreigners—was the indispensable, dispensable, nose blowing tissue. Whoa, this custom was radically different from ours in the West, and we were clueless as to its seriousness. Observing the very strict hanky rules of the Japanese, I began to wonder if we Americans weren't dwelling on the lowest rung of the evolution chain. Here's what I mean. In America when we wanted to blow our noses, we simply pulled out either a handkerchief or a tissue and honked away. My, oh, my, oh, my! This was sooo not done in the Land of Many Helpful Wipes.

I soon found out that in Nippon there was a special paper tissue designated only (I stress *only*) for the nasal passages. It was used once and then discarded, "discarded" being the operative verb. "How awful, how boorish," a disgusted native once disparaged of us foreigners, "to blow all that nose stuff onto a piece of cloth, wad it up into a lumpy squishy ball, cram it back into one's pocket, use it again and again, and then, if all that is not loathsome enough, haul it home and throw it into the laundry basket along with the clothes!" Insightfully, I saw at once a vision of my barbarian self, revolting and brutish, through her reproachful, obliquely-shaped eyes. I was thanking my lucky stars I had not used my sleeve!

To my further nasal dismay, I learned that in Japan even though you had the appropriate snoot cloth, it was deemed extremely rude to blow that same snoot in front of others and their snoots. Rather than perform this vile act, it was quite alright, on the other hand, to snort and schnurf to your heart's content in front of the world, for as loud and as long as it took until the nasally challenged could finally find a solitary refuge where an honest-to-goodness authentic blow could be consummated. During classes, meetings, movies, concerts and get-togethers of all kinds, it was thoroughly disconcerting to hear those calm-shattering, juicy inhalations being executed without one scintilla of consideration for the delicacy of others. And no one, *no one,* but me seemed to notice, or be concerned.

My goodness! Had I as a child back in Minnesota flagrantly suctioned my own nasal sludge in front of my mother, I would have been reprimanded to kingdom come for my egregious manners. And here these snorters were adults! It was all very incongruous in a society known for its overly polite ways. Okay, okay, oshibori I could go along with, but these niggling nasal things were turning my life into a risky trip down a slippery slope, if you catch my drift; certainly snot to be taken lightly. Who could have ever guessed that mucus—*mucous, for crying out loud*— would turn out to be such an international challenge?

I hesitate now to go here, but I suppose it must be said. Did you know there are cultural differences in the art of nose picking? I won't go into the subject deeply, for which I know you'll be relieved, other than to say that in Japan, the very best most eloquent pickers were, and probably still are, businessmen. Alluringly, it was their little fingernails which they grew to Hollywood starlet lengths. In the beginning, growing out nails was actually done to send a message to the public that these men were more highly achieving individuals employed in elevated white collar jobs; desk kinds of jobs that kept them out of the fields, thereby allowing their nails to grow. But, surprise, surprise, the act became functional, too. Their long pinky fingernails, as fortune would have it, made good nose tools. Like teeny ice cream scoops, the white collar workers grew and filed them down to the precise contours of their nasal canals—and went to town. I'll leave it there.

But, no way could I conclude the subject of cloths without the mention of the public toilet cloths. I'll begin by explaining that in the sixties, public bathrooms in Japan were few and far between. If you were lucky enough to find one, you really *weren't* lucky!

These abysmal cubicles were about as far from bliss as Prince the Singer is from Prince the Charles. In comparison, our Western public facilities looked pretty darned good, even though ours, too, could certainly be abysmal. This, of course, begged the question Americans have oft asked themselves, "Why, in heaven's name are our gas station toilets locked?" I mean, come on! Are the owners afraid some conscientious soul might just walk in off the street and clean them? Public toilets were not locked in Japan and no one walked in off the street to clean them either.

Not only were the public toilets wretchedly befouled (vile-abhorrent-atrocious, come to mind), but they were also not equipped with salubrious paper helpmates. Therefore, it was necessary for folks to bring with them extra tissues for toilet jobs, plus a portable terry cloth towel, or more paper tissues, for drying one's hands … if there was a sink and if it ran water. These inconveniences in the conveniences were a stunner to me, a girl who frequently frequented the facilities. In my book, snubbing such basic human needs made for not only incommodious commodes, but also significantly mangled international relations.

This, then, brings us to the toilet. Any foreigner who ever lived in Japan will tell you it was impossible to spend too much time warning of the travails of the benjo (ben-joe). Without being cutesy, I'll begin by telling you they were flush with the floor. Also, for whatever reason, the Japanese language had nearly one hundred polite and not so polite expressions for the word "toilet."

Picture a white porcelain, rectangular box roughly two-feet long by one-foot across sunken into the floor, its raised rounded edges much like that of a kitchen sink overhanging its surrounding counter. The front of the benjo had a miniature, curved porcelain awning resembling an outdoor concert band shell. That was the deflector. It rose a good six-inches high and attempted to thwart bad aimers.

On the wall next to the benjo hung a small water tank equipped with a two-way lever, offering a choice of flushes—"small" or "large." "Small" denoted deposits of a liquid nature, while large … well, you get the idea. There was often a sign reminding the user to "step a bit forward" if he planned on doing the larger of the two, which by all accounts was a swell idea. Built into the top of the water tank was a miniature shallow sink no larger than a medium-sized frying pan. This ingenious receptacle was an ecologist's dream, as after the participant washed his hands with fresh water, that same water drained into the tank and was used for the next flush. How smart was that?

The benjo sat in a Liliputian-sized closet, designed to contain only it and nothing more. The master plan was for the user to squat over the benjo and accurately get his/her business into it. Balance was key. Once you got that seemingly simple maneuver down, it was a breeze to follow the clear toilet instructions solicitously posted for clunkheads like me: "Use foot to handle the cock," or "To stop flow, turn cock to right." Not having one of my own—and highly suspicious both choices would be painful—I was never cocksure which of these commands worked best.

Squat, I quickly learned, was not an American posture. Our bodies didn't even come with a squat. As for aim, well, I ask you, what Yankee female ever learned to do that? Whereas this contortionist's feat was quite effortless for the Japanese kimono-clad, non-pantied lady who simply hoisted up her long garment (actually I was never quite sure about that non-panty thing and didn't dare ask … or look!), it was the undoing of many a female foreigner. I won't even bring up the harrowing struggle that ensued with my girdle, garters and nylon stockings. Let's admit it! I was an utter failure at squat. Had I known of the dangers accompanying this skirmish, played out in the tight confines of the teeny benjo quarters, I would have, before leaving the U.S., bought extra accident insurance.

In addition to these unmentionable unmentionables, consider the fashion scene in the 1960s. Take the circular skirt, for example, a spin-off of the prior wildly popular poodle skirt with its full three-hundred-and-sixty degrees of fabric. I had several. When wearing one, half of my skirt (one-hundred-and-eighty degrees worth), ended up without fail, either suspended a mere hair's breadth above the benjo or dipping deeply inside it. A thorough hem soak was more often the norm. Add winter to this scene with the supplemental long woolen coat over the circular skirt, and you, well, you get what I'm saying. Not good, not classy. Not only did a girl gaijin have to perform a hunkered-down balancing act while holding her bulky lower wardrobe bunched up around her waist (along with her purse and packages), but she also had to do it without knowing if her aim was true. Of course she couldn't see the target, and where, I implore you, were those blessed God-given free arms which would have and should have been a stabilizing factor? The whole thing was against the laws of nature.

Additionally, do not overlook the angst of the squatting/straddling stance, a pose (like those extra sweat glands), previously unknown to me. One dared not let any of her outfit—ANY OF IT—drape down to ground zero where at that sub-elevation lay pools of other people's deposits all around her recently dampened shoes! This brought to mind that perhaps, just perhaps, the Japanese had not yet perfected this benjo thing, even though they had been at it for at least a million years. Let's face it, benjo business wasn't worth squat!

Just when I thought I had mastered the pose and everything was under my control, I faced another hurdle—retrieving the toilet paper—that private stash I was forced to bring with me because none was provided, and which now was in the pocket of my long winter coat that was presently bunched under my arms. Why, oh, why had I not thought about this until now, the last stage of this bedeviling elimination game? With thoughts drifting towards the merits of being born a centipede, I began the execution of the tricky maneuver with one of the two hands I needed in the worst way to negotiate everything else that I previously mentioned. I tell you, the pathetic scene would have made a perfect Pee ... er, B movie.

Regrettably, I'm not finished for even after the toilet paper was retrieved, it was not over. I still had to get back up; to unsquat. Time after time—and depending how long I'd been down there—I discovered I might have to *stay down there* for the rest of the duration of our tour in Japan. For people named Keener, knee and thigh muscles were never meant to rise from such ungodly low crouches. It was not in our kneecap genes. Many a time I found myself quite unable to return to a standing position. Trust me when I say that holding "it," under the threat of uremic poisoning, was a far more pleasant experience than grappling with a Japanese john.

Men, of course, with their anatomical aimers had it easier. They were also the most likely culprits of the disgustingness pooled on the shared unisex floors, because, as we all know, creative spraying was a skill passed down to them from the cave men. I'll bet the dream of every male throughout the ages was to sear strips of marble off the cave walls ... or in modern times, paper off the drywall ... with nothing more than their pissy hot streams. Look, Ma, no hands! Zssssssst ....

If you ask me, every last man was guilty and deserved a sentence of pee-nal penitence in a place with no walls, only chicken wire. It would have driven them crazy! But then what do I, a mere squatting dame, know about such things? For the guys, I suppose it's a sort of duty to the brotherhood; fidelity, constancy and sky writing. Did you hear about the sign that, for all I know, still hangs in one of the men's bathrooms at Hebrew University: "The future of the Jewish people is in your hands!" One hundred bucks says there's not a shred of paint in the place.

Due to eons (peeons?) of poor male bulls-eyeing, the resulting slovenliness on the floors gave Japanese toilets a very bad rap. Even today go into any home, inn, public building, anywhere and you will find special plastic slippers for wearing only in the toilet. These protect bare or stockinged feet (because shoes are left at the front door entrance), from coming into contact with the unspeakable heartbreak lurking on benjo floors. If you do not at first recognize just which ones *are* the toilet slippers, look for the subtle hint. "TOILET" is stamped across each toe in bold, over-sized English letters, obviously intended to grab the attention of imbecilic outsiders who never know for sure *what* they're doing and *where* they should be doing it!

OLD HABITS DIE slowly in the Far East. The disreputable status of the loo remains nasty in the Japanese mind despite the current popularity of the modern Western toilet. Anything that might remotely come into contact with a toilet floor is still isolated from the rest of the building, no matter what mode the commode. All weirdness aside, we have to give them this: the Japanese do sit and sleep on the floor, so such prissiness about pissiness is permissible.

I remind you that shoes are always taken off at the door of a Japanese home whereupon special house slippers are substituted. Heaven help the uninformed gaijin who either wears the house slippers into the toilet room, or wears the toilet slippers back into the house rooms. I say "wear" with a smirk on my face because all house and toilet slippers come in only one size: 9 XXXXXXX wide.

Decades ago, the Japanese National Board of the Toilet Slipper Industry (JNBTSI), determined that these dimensions were the ideal universal size. Many a foreign devil has been annihilated since with cramping arches and pulled calf ligaments in their futile attempts to keep the blasted things on. Imagine yourself, the erstwhile gaijin lady-guest praying with all your might you are doing everything right as you, in your slippery nylon stockings, attempt to cross the treacherously over-polished-and-buffed-wooden floors leading to the tatami rooms. And doing so while wearing perilous plastic shoes designed for Yeti.

On the other hand, consider Glen who wore a 13 XXXX wide, which is the gospel truth. The slippers barely covered the front one-fourth of his feet and stopped there, encasing them in the vicinity where his toes met his metatarsal arches. Too enormous for me; too puny for him! We couldn't win. No doubt about it, this was exactly what I had feared. Under the guise of social niceties, Japan, still holding a grudge, wasn't going to quit until they got the outcome of that irksome war settled once and for all.

My in depth study of toilet slippers revealed they were programmed to fall off precisely at the point where I gingerly lifted one foot in a high arch over and across the benjo, to where, on the other side, I would attempt the unladylike straddling position, followed by the dreaded squat. The slick-as-glass slippers routinely slipped off at the summit of the arch, followed by a muffled smack as they landed directly inside the water-filled receptacle. I learned quickly that if my luck did not hold, this could just as easily happen when going backwards in the other direction. Speaking from experience, I would say the first direction was probably better than the second, for in the latter there was a good chance the bowl now also contained an assortment of undesireables in which you would have to delicately probe to retrieve the damn slipper!

Meanwhile, in my haste to fish out that damn slipper, I would be left hopping with both feet unshrouded because I had, by then, straightaway stumbled out of the other slipper causing both bare feet to now be in direct contact with the very benjo floor pathogens I was trying so hard to avoid in the first place!

Had all this occurred in secrecy, it wouldn't have been so bad, but of course it didn't. Exacerbating my humiliation was the knowledge that there was no way on God's green earth my klutziness could be kept under wraps. Whoever was the next person to be greeted by the forsaken drenched slippers, knew exactly what had just happened. Criminy! It was all a nerve-wracking, dicey game and invariably happened just when I thought I had, at the polished age of twenty-four, not only mastered my potty training, but also attained a state of grownup grace.

Many years later, when we returned to Japan for a second tour of duty, I gave lectures throughout the country. On one such occasion I was about to give a speech in front of an assemblage of several hundred employees of the Cannon Camera Company. As was my custom, I visited the benjo right before going on stage. On this occasion, Lady Luck was smiling down on me, just as my right foot reached the crest of the old familiar arch, the demonic plastic toilet slipper slid off and plunged into the benjo. On that particular day, having less balance than usual, my foot went in with it also.

Now, women worldwide know that when an invisible nylon stocking becomes wet, it magically turns dark brown. Thus, in the blink of a splash, I wore one brown sock with a perfect high water mark two-inches above my ankle. Hesitating for only a moment, I gathered my wits and did the only sensible thing to right the sock wrong. I stepped in with the other foot. That day as I took the long walk across the stage to the podium, I hazarded an extreme fashion risk, jeopardizing the chi-chi reputation of American women everywhere, by sporting two precisely matched mahogany anklets with my tailored dress. And here you thought I couldn't think on my feet.

Soon after, I began the first support group for displaced gaijin, who along with me, suffered from—no, not xenophobia—but rather the substantially worse, monumentally more abhorrent, toiletslipperphobia.

On a rare occasion I encountered a seat-style Western john in a public building. Invariably it was accompanied by a graphic pictograph taped above the toilet demonstrating how to sit upon it. This clear guide was, albeit, not so clear, because it neither convinced nor deterred the majority of the Japanese. It was not at all unusual to see two perfect footmarks on the seat! Now, just how any short Japanese person climbed up to that ungainly height and then balanced in such a precarious position ... *while wearing a kimono!* ... was something I was sorry to have missed seeing. They must have thought all Western folks were housebroken by P. T. Barnum, or we were just plum out of our minds. Why, they surely pondered, would anyone go to all the trouble of climbing and perching at such a dangerous elevation when they could just squat on the floor? Okay, so one point for the Japanese.

TWENTY-EIGHT

THERE IS AN ancient Japanese proverb claiming that pregnant women who keep their toilets sparkling clean give birth to beautiful babies. A stretch, I know. So, just what connection does one have to the other? Well, for starters, the Japanese word "kirei" (kee-ray) means both clean and pretty. But more importantly, in the past, the death of many mothers during pregnancy and labor did create a need for them to be well cared for. Since all brides moved into the homes of their husbands' parents, the begrudging mothers-in-law—even though they abstained from doing so the rest of the time—took vigilant care of their daughters-in-law when they were pregnant. Ultimately, in a society where females took the furthest back seat, babies were the most screaming evidence of a woman's worth to mankind. Absolutely no one could dispute the importance of their contribution. They were the factory outlet *for* mankind, and by damn, grandma, who had had a hand in manufacturing her son's seed in the first place, wasn't about to miss out on the kudos.

Furthermore, if the snarly mother-in-law had any brains at all, she surely recognized that one day in the future when she herself was old and the fight had gone out of her, the very same daughter-in-law to whom she had often been so surly, would now be the one who would wipe her nose and empty her bedpan.

I knew many Japanese women whose lives were made miserable by ruthless, bullying mothers-in-law who deeply resented another female moving in on their sacred turf, even though they themselves had moved in on another woman's sacred turf only one generation before. Even worse was the allegiance the sons had to divvy up between their moms and their new brides. Having been through such misery, one would think these women would vow to never repeat it, but as so often happens, goodwill was cast aside when their turn came, selective amnesia being handy when one takes umbrage.

> "No matter how
> cynical you get,
> it is impossible
> to keep up."
> Lily Tomlin

The word "oyome-san" (oh-yo-may-san, bride), spoke to the separation between her and her wedded family. Not only did it mean "newly married woman," but also "someone from the outside." With a label like that, the barriers were set in place when the filly left the matrimonial starting gate.

It was admirable how so many new brides bit the bullet and endured years and years of jealous mistreatment. But then, they knew it was how their society worked and questioning custom was futility in excess. Two women under one small tiled roof had to be a tough go, but each knew she would, in turn, dutifully take care of the other, no matter how deep the resentments lay.

For most daughters-in-law, the angst usually abruptly ended when the mother-in-law finally died. That was the moment of triumph when the now aged bride at last had her chance to run the house her way. How well I remember one friend's elation over finally, finally getting to put up the curtains of her choice after decades of having no say in anything. Of course, this brief respite lasted only as long as the interim between her mother-in-law's death and her now grown son's wedding when the cycle began all over again.

Despite those harbored grudges and testy rivalries, it was, as I said, the responsibility of even the most hardcore mother-in-law to care for her pregnant daughter-in-law. Also, the matriarch knew full well that in the end her reward was, of course, a grandchild whom she could unceasingly show off to the neighbors, as well as preach day and night to the new mom the ways in which the child must be raised. Hers!

Somewhere in all those nine months, though, the new mother had to, even for the briefest of moments, be given the opportunity to exercise. Enter toilet cleaning and beautiful babies. Getting down on all fours to scrub at ground zero with a ponderous belly hanging beneath her, the cramped space in and around the benjo would certainly have caused the new mother's blood and oxygen to circulate more rapidly than, let's say, lying on the tatami. Aside from being icky, such a flow of nutrients and energy to both the mother and fetus would have certainly been a bonus. As for a clean toilet resulting in comely baby facial features, it sounded downright bogus to me. But then, I had always kept my bathrooms sparkly, and I surely had beautiful boys, so maybe they were on to something.

You will notice, in all of this, that I have said nothing about the new father. He was pretty much left out in the cold. He may very well have been utterly unaware of the animosity between his mother and his bride because he was dutifully off earning a living six very long days a week. But, if he *were* aware, he would have accepted it as how the rice cracker crumbled because, gosh-darn, it was *his* mom's house. It made me want to open an artery. Hers and his!

Toward the end of the pregnancy, the bride left her matrimonial home, the one she had "come from the outside" to join. It was time for her to return to her real mother for the familiar and unimpeachable care she would receive while giving birth. With this arrangement, both new grandmothers shared in the all important re-run of motherhood. Often this meant a separation of a great distance for the husband and wife, resulting in the impossibility for the father to visit in the weeks following the delivery. It was for him a deep interruption of time and emotion. I heard many a couple lament that Daddy was unable to meaningfully bond with either his wife or his baby during these pivotally important months in their lives. You don't say! There is another Japanese proverb which states, "A good husband is healthy and absent." Not funny. His absence at such a crucial time, created an irreparable breach that left its mark for all their lifetimes.

THE GREATEST EVIDENCE in old Japan of the high rate of infant and child mortality was the fact that when a child did survive, he was publicly celebrated in a resplendent way. He still is. Every year on November 15th, the entire country celebrates "Shichi-Go-San" (she-che-goh-san). Translated it means "Seven-Five-Three," and it heralds the fact that a child has survived to those ages. Therefore, all the children who have reached their seventh, fifth or third birthdays during that year are recognized. I know you're thinking they're counting backwards, but keep in mind that things are read in a funny direction in the Far East ... or might it be, perish the thought, that we're funny in the Far West?

Children celebrating these milestone birthdays are royally fussed over. Gifts are presented, special food is consumed, and the celebrants are dressed in kimono with every embellishment necessary for the composition of bedazzling photos. All little girls are decked out in lipstick and rouge and have their hair swept up on top of their heads by expert cosmetologists who excel in making three-year-olds look like very short forty-year-olds, minus the wear and tear. These photos are mandatory. They are never taken at home, but instead in studios by vigilant professional photographers who excel in the bedazzling department. It is a must to do this; akin to Western wedding photos.

"Children are a great comfort
in your old age,
and they help you
reach it faster, too."
Lionel Kauffman

TWENTY-NINE

BUT NOW I must return to the subject of toilets. The only time I really loved—can I say that?—appreciated the miniscule benjo room with its flush-to-the-floor toilet, was when I potty trained our boys. I can still see them frantically rushing in from play with their ping-pong-sized bladders straining to be drained. They'd throw open the benjo door and let loose, aiming not for the toilet, but for the whole room!

What difference did it make? The benjo was the only thing in there, and besides, with the assistance of gravity, all liquids eventually drained down the four plain, undecorated walls and onto the floor. And don't overlook the beginning stages of that caveman complex that may well have been lost had our boys been forbidden to practice in a stifling pink and ruffled Western bathroom. I soon lost sympathy for American housewives who complained about cleaning their foo-foo bathrooms. I, on the other hand, was required to wash down the entire room, ceiling to floor, in order to rid the room of the hands-free graffiti.

Why was it that this elimination game, as old as Methuselah, was such a trial anyway? Because no one on the planet escaped it, I guess. But, still it had to be handled with delicate refinement. With this in mind, Glen and I bent over backwards to be socially correct in our new land. I believe we were politically correct eons before politically correct was even invented; over-the-top heedful of not being offensive in any way, shape or form. Primary in this goal was the desire for genteel bathroom terms to be used by Jeff and Matt. For reasons never quite clear to me, we settled on "chair-

chair" and "big chair-chair"—the "big" designating the weightier of the two. Goofy us! With our boys jumping up and down in front of us grasping their crotches—or worse their rumps!—our well-intentioned verbiage was of no consequence. The message was the same the world over.

"Big chair-chair," as goofy as it sounded was, nonetheless, not nearly as nonsensical as what my dad went through years earlier in his grocery store. It involved selling Kotex, one of the first and only sanitary pads on the market. The word was volatile. Could not be spoken aloud in public! Always mindful of his customers' comfort and discomfort, Daddy painstakingly wrapped, if you can imagine, every single Kotex box in plain brown paper. In spite of his chivalry, absolutely every person in the store knew what the customer was buying. When they eyed the only plain brown paper package in the cart sitting beside the other brightly arrayed foodstuffs, it could naturally only be one thing. Such a transparent smokescreen could, I guess, also have been said of us. "Big chair-chair" was our boys' plain brown paper package.

There was, for all my sarcasm, good news about the benjo. It was actually world's less scary for little children than was our elevated Western toilet. At least Japanese tykes felt in charge of the procedure when their own two feet remained in contact with Mother Earth, as compared to their erstwhile Western buddies straddled high up over a bowl of loud, swirling, disappearing water that resembled in every way the Bermuda Triangle.

Think about it for a minute. My gosh, elevated up there on their high-altitude toilets, terrified Western toddlers sat with their wee derrieres protruding down through over-sized seats. Like pixy trapeze artists, they hung above the roiling Amazon, their stubby fingers clinging for dear life to the rims. From these toilet cable cars, their little feet dangled perilously over the Grand Can Canyon as they pitifully crooned for their former lives spent in comfy and secure Curities, knowing from this day forward, the door had slammed on their old solitude. Furthermore, the brave cherubs did all this while being coached and prevailed upon to relax enough to perform, because busy-busy Moms were in a busy-busy hurry. Additionally, the younglings accomplished this petrifying feat while under the mothers' dire threat to never, ever, EVER touch the contaminated toilet seat. Pul-leeez! Toilet training on our side of the Pacific was dumbfounding. Some of us never got over it.

> "I was toilet-trained
> at gun point."
> Billy Braver

Occasionally I visited very old Japanese homes where the benjo was nothing more than a hole in the floor that went directly to a wooden wagon on the dirt ground beneath. It was like our outhouse, only an inhouse. Using these in winter was especially dicey, for if you were not speedy in your executions, the frigid draft could instantly render you sterile. Placed strategically under the benjo, a wooden wagon (one form of the endearing honey bucket), collected all the deposits. Whoever had the ungorgeous task of emptying it, pulled it out from under the house with an attached wooden handle and carted the contents off to a burying ground. This was, in all cases, the rice paddy where human chair-chair, big and small, had been used for centuries to nourish the earth.

Lucky ducks that we Keeners were, later when we finally got a real house, our "night soil" was pumped out by a small three-wheeled truck, a honey wagon, that never ever failed to announce itself by charging right up onto our lawn like Steve McQueen in a Hollywood chase scene. I'm not sure just why the drivers were always so frantic, but it may have been their futile attempt to outrun the cloud of putrescence that hung over their trucks. An early rendition of the collection agency, our honey wagon had a sign on it written in characters I was unable to read. I'm pretty sure, though, they said "Fetid R Us."

I don't know whether or not perfume always announced Elizabeth Arden before she actually arrived anyplace, but the stench of those trucks did. That, however, was only the introduction. The stink upon their arrival was but a trifling compared to the later assault of the rancid effluvium that escaped when they pumped the reeking stuff into their trucks.

As chance would have it, rather than having a pink plastic flamingo in our tiny front yard, we had instead an above ground septic tank placed there by a landscaper trained by Satan. We shared this with several neighbors, meaning that we were doubly blessed with a tank size Super Large. Habitually parking just outside our windows, the drivers siphoned out the contents of this snake pit through long coiling tubes. This, of course, released all manner of nasal discontent throughout our house, as well as the entire neighborhood. But, seeing as how they were in *our* front yard, *we* were the most discontented.

For some reason—or could it have been that revenge, being the can of worms that it is—I was pretty sure General Tojo owned the Honey Bucket Company. This was repeatedly made clear to me for the trucks invariably arrived at the most inopportune of American times. Like, for example, at the precise moment I was serving dinner to our fellow countrymen guests on our first Christmas Day. As I was about to pass the potatoes, you-got-it arrived. It was a whole new version of *Guess Who's Coming to Dinner.* The foul blot could not be expunged. Our holiday meal grew numb and viscous while we recovered.

Equally bad socially, but not as icky as the "Fetid R Us" gang, was what happened to a friend of mine. It didn't involve chair-chair, but rather a nose. One Sunday she had invited a Japanese man to dinner. No one in the family, except her, knew the guest, which meant that no one in the family, except her, knew the guest had a nose the size of a mature sweet potato. It was necessary for her to prepare the family.

After a brief explanation of his appendage, my friend severely warned her children that no one was to look, say—or under any circumstances—touch the mature sweet potato appurtenance. The Sunday meal was to be spent as if nothing were out of the ordinary, or those same children would never live to see another Sunday meal.

The good news is that everything did go splendidly. The children, scared out of their little wits, were perfection, swallowing all the things they wanted to say but didn't dare, because they liked Sunday meals to keep on coming. As the main course drew to a close and dessert was about to be served, my friend breathed in a delicious sigh of relief. The entire dinner—alas, the entire day—had been a grand success. Soon all strife would be behind her.

Leaning toward her guest in one final perfectly poised posture of politeness (while keeping her distance so as not to be mistakenly bludgeoned by "it"), she, in a syrupy voice that would have been the envy of Miss Manners herself, asked, "And would you like some cherry pie, Mr. *Nose*?"

There is a moral lesson in this story. Assumptions are dangerous things. Like we'll never know for sure, but what if Mr. Nose did not feel any sensitivity, or even regret, over his you-nose-what? And whose to say that he was not just gosh darned pleased as punch over his unusual snout? Furthermore, what if the whole issue was only in my friend's mind because *she* had the narrow-minded belief that a nose should look like a nose and not like a mature sweet potato?

> "Do not free a camel
> of the burden of his hump;
> you may be freeing him
> from being a camel."
> Gilbert Keith Chesterton

The result of her unfortunate faux pas was that the children did live to see many more Sunday dinners, as did Mr. Nose. My friend, however, did not—at least not with them. Her mortification was so great that she chose to move to Nebraska by herself where lots of folks had all manner of mature sweet potato noses; a place where it would be impossible for her to ever again fear repeating that same social blunder, because no one would notice.

BUT I HAVE drifted from benjo to noses, even though some would argue they are aromatically linked. I will end this subject with "night soil," a term which has always been a mystery to me. Why did the Japanese say "night?" It just never made sense. Correct me if I'm wrong, but isn't "it" done day *and* night—or perhaps they only brought it to the fields in the dark. But then, I guess, it wasn't my job to know these things. As far as I was concerned, using "it" for fertilizer was a touch of genius. Pretty darned terrific and a whole lot better than ... well ... right now I can't think of another good purpose, but just remember, you heard it here first.

THIRTY

THROUGHOUT THAT FIRST sweltering July in the upper floors of the Gajo-en Hotel, the boys and I soldiered on in our one-room encampment. Compared to all the marvels I knew were happening out on the Tokyo streets, the cramped, airless, inhospitable hotel room made for disheartening living. The only good thing I could see coming out of its malevolent confines was that the heat and humidity caused us to no longer suffer from the embarrassment—or stinging shocks—of static cling.

None of us was more affected by the ceaseless mugginess than dear baby Matt and his ten-month-old, cherubic, thirty-pound body, an early, though stunted depiction of the Michelin Man. My Lord in heaven, overnight his gossamer baby skin turned into raw hamburger. From head to toe, patches of industrial sized heat rash flourished like lichen. I spent most of my days striving to come up with ways to keep him dry, but in the stifling constraints of that smothering space, it was a hopeless, losing battle.

Of course, there was no air conditioner. God hadn't seen to that yet, at least not for military hotel contractees. Breathing at all times felt like drawing in oxygen through a tightly woven wet washcloth plastered over and inside our mouths, coming to rest just in front of our uvulas. I began doubting whether or not the Lord had even invented universal air. It was as if the creative juices He had spent putting all the bells and whistles into the western heavens and earth, just sort of pooped out when He finally started work on His Big Pacific Project.

95

> "The Lord created the universe
> in seven days, but the Lord
> had the wonderful advantage
> of being able to work alone."
> Kofi Annan

By myself during the daytime with two bored, sweaty babies in my care was, to be sure, not the best of times in which to explore Japan. Although I ventured out on brief forays near the hotel, I didn't have the courage to go much farther. I knew if I needed help out there on the teeming packed streets, I would have great difficulty, for almost no one spoke English, and I was beyond worthless when it came to Japanese.

Inasmuch as this was the first time I had ever been in another culture (except for a short stay once in North Dakota), I had no idea how far to take risks. I had a stroller in which I squashed both three-year-old Jeff and infant Michelin Matt, but stroller contentment lasted only so long, as any mother could tell you. What in all creation was I supposed to do if Jeff escaped? I cringed at the thought of being caught in that look-alike crush of strangers while I tussled to corral a child who had escaped his bonds, while weighted down on my left hip bone with another: the struggling Baby Atlas. Useless, of course, would be my remaining arm, which was needed to thread the now empty stroller through the mass of clones.

And then there was that other long-standing issue. Heaven forbid the perils of having to change Matt's dreaded diaper *out there!* What was I supposed to do with it, anyway? Neatly fold up the squishy mess and put it in my pocket along with my dastardly nasal cloths? Good grief. The visual of it did nothing for me; scratched at my good sense, while severely crimping my spirit of adventure. On top of that, there was that old war thing to consider. I certainly did not want, in the madness of it all, to crash the stroller into the shins of General Tojo or his honey bucket crew.

As it turned out, we had one of the few strollers in Japan, the other handful owned by foreigners like ourselves. All Japanese babies were tied to their mothers' backs—or any other available females' backs—and kept there for much of the day, indeed much of their lives, until they finally went off to nursery school. Like night soil, this was a pretty good idea. Another important plus for the over-burdened moms was reminding the public once again that the big fast growing humps on their mothering backs were sure proof of their contribution to society.

If the crunch out there on the streets were not bad enough, to make matters worse there were no signs to guide me. Well, actually there were, I just couldn't read them. And, my wretched sense of direction was hopeless in the twisty, narrow maze of streets that hypnotized me by the way they braided in and around and through each other. The pinched roadways were a dizzying array of engineering madness, laid out in the days when the samurai used them to confuse invading enemies. Now the enemy was me, and it was working!

Neither did I get a lot of clues from the endless, tiny, unpainted shops that each looked like a replica of its neighbor. They sat crammed along the winding roads like dominoes placed by uncoordinated giants. Those civil engineering samurai knew what they were doing alright and I—who couldn't navigate then and still can't now—was the perfect test case to prove their theory correct.

Furthermore, and much to my dismay, I, a flaming consumer, had somehow inexplicably lost my shopping smarts. Not only was yen a mystery, but so also were the products. Alarmingly, little looked familiar. And, besides, don't forget that I couldn't breathe. Also in the confusion of it all, wouldn't you just know that my sweaty, heat-rashed and bored babies were morphing before my eyes into dumplings with attitudes. Oh, yes, and we were homeless. Other than that, our first week in Japan was peachy Keener.

By the middle of the second week, I was ready to break out. Chained in that choking hotel, I knew exactly why Atlas had shrugged. I was consumed with thoughts of going permanently AWOL from the Gajo-en. There I felt as trapped as a famished lion seeing fresh meat on the outside of his glass enclosure. I, the lion, could see Japan from my window and was ravenous to consume her. With a full-blown, hotel-induced meltdown imminent, Glen and I hired a hotel babysitter (actually we took advantage of the chambermaid), and flew the coop.

I don't want you to think I was rushing into something that I had not prepared myself for. No, I had done my homework to be sure. I'd read every single travel brochure in the hotel lobby and I was ready to meet Japan. For starters the brochures taught me that:

> "Japan is a beauty Utopia Land where
> there is lots of party with simple-minded
> inhabitants who are bright as larks and
> blessed with sunny basking health and
> Japan have splendid air and eating.
> Peoples awake by dirds singing.
> Peoples can play at live in summer,
> go nutting in fall, and eat hot foods
> besides stoves. Enjoy best living and
> have good time at here! "

And, that's just what I planned to do. Still I'd have to watch myself, avoiding eating too much hot food *besides* stoves. Wow, in anybody's book that warning about stove consumption was really good, really helpful information!

As well, there was another brochure in the hotel lobby. It warned me of the dangers of unwanted weight gain.

> "New weight chart here. You are
> now over good and decent weight
> if accidentedly you step on a
> people's dog's tail and it dies."

Oh, my god! I'd have to watch closely what I was eating. For sure I wouldn't want the responsibility of my fattening flattening Fido!

THAT FIRST NIGHT, my fledgling foray into sundown Tokyo, was beyond enchanting. For a small-town girl, it was also my first time ever to trip the night lights fantastic. What a place to start! In the pulsing heart of Japan, I found a world different from anything I had ever dreamed. Where people back in hayseed Austin went to bed because the sun went down, the Japanese hit the streets *because* the sun went down.

> "A hick town is one in which
> there is no place to go
> where you shouldn't go."
> Alexander Woollcott

No centimeter of space was left empty without gray mortar, packed dirt, unpainted wood or drably dressed, tawny flesh filling it up. In a ridiculous contrast to the blinding lack of color, were the single sprigs of outrageous fluorescent pink, green and yellow plastic flowers (a summer enhancement), hanging over every merchant's doorway.

Equally surprising was my delight in discovering that the fierce, unrelenting fire ball in the sky had yielded to the night, the brief interlude from its glare bringing a sense of rebirth, the very reason folks were out and about. That is not to say the atmosphere had suddenly turned cool or dry, because the wet, gauzy, evening air still hung upon us like moist, filmy cobwebs. The difference was that at night, with the absence of light, we could only feel it, just no longer see it.

How to describe the hectic scene? Compared to this bustling chaos, the only similar experience I'd had was the feel and look of the August fairgrounds back in Austin. There the crush of carnival merrymakers strolled down the midway past row upon row of booths manned by seedy looking, gypsy-like carnies. In contrast, what I was now seeing made our summer fair seem paltry. Even though the Tokyo shops were not a whole lot bigger than the Austin fair booths, they were a million times more inviting. And, where in Austin I had had little interest in winning a dusty stuffed bear bigger than Lassie at the rigged Milk Bottle Toss, I was itching like crazy to get my hands on the enticing Japanese merchandise.

There was another conspicuous difference. Tokyo was starkly unlike the ethnic melting pot of the polyglot Austin carnival. On this Far Eastern street, every last one of the folks looked like Xerox copies of each other, all clearly having gone overboard in their consumption of sea weed. But way more enchanting than even them were those mysterious diminutive stores constructed of ancient, untreated boards, leaning against one another like rows of uneven, un-brushed teeth. They filled every lane without a break, radiating out, from and around our hotel. Nearly every shop was open to the street. That is to say, their front walls were missing. And, because of the tight spaces, merchandise from inside the shops overflowed out onto the streets. It was a consumer's heaven ... and bewilderment.

I LOOKED ACROSS the street. Wonder of wonders, there was a shop selling matches. In very big English letters it said so—"MATCHES." But, just a minute. Weren't matches free? I mean, even I knew that in Japan matches were given away at every turn of the head. I had to check it out. Pulling Glen, we threaded our way through the traffic and entered the shop. I expected to see itty bitty boxes all lined up on display. Instead I saw ... watches. Lamentably, the sign painter was unschooled in Basic English and had painted the "w" upside down. But, not to worry! It was only the family's blood, sweat and tears; only their subsistence for life. Sheesh!

> "If I had known that my son
> was going to be president of Bolivia,
> I would have taught him
> to read and write."
> Enrique Penaranda's mother

In a country whose language was made up of thousands of characters, you would have thought the Japanese would, of all people, understood the good deal to be had in the piddling twenty-six letters of the English alphabet. And, how really cinchy is was to get those few right. Brother! And here was this country confoundedly scratching its head over why its international trade hadn't taken off.

Upon exiting the match/watch shop, we found ourselves immediately in the street. There were no sidewalks. Shoppers, bicycles, carts, vehicles and store merchandise all shared the same narrow lanes forcing a constant alertness for one's safety. It did no good to look for vehicular danger to the left, because it was all coming from the right. Everything about the scene was not in the American safety handbook. But who cared? Not me. Caution be damned. I was spellbound!

"In some parts of the world,
people still pray in the streets.
In this country they're
called pedestrians."
Gloria Pitzer

As unexpectedly as a thunderbolt, Japan had struck me through the heart. Her charm and uniqueness electrified me as surely as Eve's magic had once magnetized Adam. With one simple passe-partout, I had slipped from one culture into another. The commotion and chaos of the ancient cramped passageways now churned my blood, while the riddle of the baffling shops' wares so captivated my imagination, I had to remind my heart to continue beating. To my further delight, I soon realized that Japan was one big Dollar Store where nearly everything in it was affordable, even for the likes of us, the newly annual salaried. Right and left, bewitching shoppertunities that I had never before imagined—and had no understanding of—caused my voice to trill up and down the entire range of my soprano vocal chords.

"Whoever said that money
can't buy happiness, didn't
know where to shop."
Unknown

Meanwhile, Glen, who was marveling at my marveling and pleased over my pleasure, was suddenly feeling a whole lot of relief in finding that I, too, had fallen in love with Japan just as he had some years before. Yup, we were both crazy mad smitten.

THAT EVENING AS we strolled in and out of the lanes, I got my first glimpse into the Japanese homes. There, in the back of the shops, I learned that the merchants and their families lived. This, of course, meant they could walk to work, making commuting a non-issue.

By glimpsing through the short, narrow doorways, I could see how astonishingly confined the living spaces were, and how one small area alone—tiny as it was—could by day serve as a living room, office, dining room, and study/sewing/laundry/craft area, but by shifting things aside and laying down futon (foo-tong, folding sleeping pads), it could become the family's sleeping quarters by night. At once the importance of the shoes became evident, for by removing them, the tatami flooring (tah-tah-me, woven rice straw mats), stayed clean, thereby allowing the easy switch from walking upon, to sitting upon, to eating upon and finally to sleeping upon. Before seeing the efficiency of it all, I had not realized what house hogs we Westerners were.

About the time it became apparent to Glen that I could not stuff one more smidgen of delight into my sensibilities, he grabbed my arm and led me through the crowds to a tiny restaurant. Pushing aside a curtained door, I entered. As my foot crossed the threshold, I was attacked by a vocal blitzkrieg. Deep, raspy, male voices assaulted me from behind a narrow counter bellowing, "Irrashai, irrashai! " (ee-rah-shy). I was so taken aback, fearing Pearl Harbor had begun all over again, that I froze against the door frame in stock still terror.

How was I supposed to know they were not screaming war cries, but rather shouting ebullient cheers of greeting? "Welcome, welcome, please come in! Have a seat and make yourself at home!" Imagine all of that in only one succinct word. I had just been initiated into my first sushi-ya (sue-she-yah, raw fish restaurant).

Steadying my knocking knees, I moved across the charming pebble-encrusted floor to a line of six stools. Before them was a counter running the length of the tiny shop where the yelling, but smiling, men awaited us. The counter space between them and us was divided by a narrow, glass, refrigerated display case. In it were individual piles of glistening sliced fish, each variety divided by strips of green plastic, cut to look like grass. It was as pretty a piscine presentation as I had ever seen; absolutely nothing whatsoever like the colorless Norwegian lutefisk back home.

Peggy, Peggy Small Town American Food Lady was about to sign on to the world of raw fish. It took all of one bite. Chomp ... sigh! Divoon with a capital D! Instant addiction.

The lovely fish and vinegared rice were like nothing I had ever tasted. Out, out McDonalds! I banish you forevermore! How could anyone not like this celestial manna? I mean, it was like if you didn't adore puppies, then you didn't have a heart, and if you didn't like sushi, then you didn't have taste buds ... or a gizzard ... or something germane.

To my astonishment, there was little taste of fish. In its place was a delicate slice of wondrousness that seemed to barely need chewing. It just sort of said on its own "Let's get going!" and glided down my welcoming gullet. And, how heavenly it was to be eating fish which only hours before had been plucked from the surrounding sea. With sighs of delight, I savored its pure nakedness, natural and uncontrived. The price was thirty-yen per piece; about a dime U.S.

Where had this ecstasy been all my life? I paused to wonder how it would play out in Minnesota. Probably not. Next to the noodle and canned tuna casseroles that the hair-netted Ladies' Guild served in the Presbyterian basement, sushi would undoubtedly have a barbaric, cannibalistic ring to it. That realization was all the proof I needed to explain why missionaries fail.

Over the years, I have alone consumed a small ocean's worth of raw fish. Glen and I even added raw horse and raw chicken to the list. All the varieties dazzled the palate, never once disappointing. My favorite turned out to be uni (ooo-nee, sea urchin), quite possibly the worst looking (resembling jaundiced phlegm) and certainly one of the most expensive (wouldn't you know!), but nonetheless, the loveliest in the mouth.

> "In Mexico we have a
> word for sushi: bait."
> Jose Simon

THIRTY-ONE

THREE WEEKS INTO our stay at the Gajo-en, I decided to take my new love of sushi into my own hands. I don't mean make it myself. Heaven forbid! Remember, I didn't have a kitchen. Besides, women were not allowed to make sushi. The men claimed (for Pete's sake, isn't it always the men?), that women's hands were too warm and, therefore, their heat tainted the flavor of the rice. Gimme a break! It was all just one more of the trillion ways in which Japanese men kept women in their place; the place *they* claimed women should be. Home!

Anyway, that day I once again took advantage of the chambermaid and decided to go to a sushi-ya all by myself. This took audacity. Heretofore Glen had been with me, the sushi-ya at that time being mainly a men's bailiwick. I waited outside the door till it opened at noon, and then went inside to the now familiar raucous greetings. I was the first and only customer. So far, so good.

I seated myself at the counter and put in my order by pointing out, because I couldn't say the words, the fish I desired. While waiting for the sushi to be assembled, sculpted and primped to perfection, I decided to go to the benjo. Remember that place?

I looked around. There it was, one tiny door clearly shared by all, ten feet away at the back of the restaurant. Sweet relief poured over me as I realized that because I was the only customer, I would not have to share the john with who-knows-who. I opened the door and peered inside looking about for a booth. At least I *hoped* there would be a booth. Sure enough.

Scrunched against the back wall was an even tinier door no wider than my body standing sideways with my stomach pulled in.

The problem was not, however, with the booth itself, but rather the entire room. It had to have been the teeniest, quirkiest latrine in all of Nippon. The only way I could get to the booth was to actually step down into a four-foot long trough that began just inches from the entrance. This handy walking lane also cleverly served as the men's urinal. I was pretty sure that the brainstorm behind this maniacal project was a coordinated effort by the designers of the Ford Edsel and the Champion Studebaker.

I stepped hurriedly into the trough (avoiding thinking Minnesota thoughts), and once again thanked my guardian angels that I was alone in there. Next I encapsulated myself inside the booth, whereupon I squatted over the benjo and began my business. In mid-hunker, I heard the door open. The alarming sound of entering footsteps nearly toppled me over. You must remember that I was only three weeks into this benjo methodology and still shockingly unbalanced in "the stance." Plus, in my staggeringly uninitiated state, I was stingily unwilling to dole out any toilet space to a complete stranger.

What to do? My overextended knee cap muscles, not yet acclimated to the elongated stretch, screamed for mercy while I contemplated my next move. This would be to stand up. I had been down there in an extra long squat due to the pondering of my dilemma and wasn't sure of any success in this effort. Like what if I tried and failed? Or even worse, tried and fell over? What if I splashed *into* the benjo or crashed *onto* the door causing it to fly open, leaving me and my lily white rear exposed to ... to ... a ninja, the local mayor, a serial rapist or Emperor Hirohito himself?

Think, think, Peggy, Peggy Ivory Assed Lady!

In the end (did I just say that?), there was only one thing to do. Go native! Of course! I'd simply steady myself and walk out of my booth supremely dignified as if I'd been eliminating with uninvited Asians all my born days. Yup, I'd sashay out of that room with my head held high, eyes glued to the exit ... and only the exit! Don't look down. Don't look sideways. *Don't forget!*

With a firm push, I opened the door and stepped out. That's when I remembered how I'd gotten in there in the first place. Through the Edsel-Studebaker urinal.

A man was standing in front of it. He was in deep concentration, meditating about heaven knows what. Oh, yeah, that's right—putting out fires, marking his territory, creating wall murals, practicing sky writing! What to do? With no other option, I proceeded with the only maneuver I had: step down into the trough, walk unflinchingly in front of this guy, and ignore completely his on-going art project by not critiquing it with either a scowl or a hand raised to cover my eyes.

In two bold steps I was beside him. Then with one smooth effort I raised my right leg in a giant arch over his stream. I was nearly home free.

Half way through the arch, when my leg was at the peak of its crest, the man abruptly jumped to attention, breaking his reverie. Had he just seen a Western she-devil in his urinal?

In a million years you'll never guess what happened next. The fellow seemed not at all surprised to be sharing his space with a female. Heck, no big deal. That happened everyday. He was, however, surprised, indeed utterly astonished, to have that female be a gaijin! Holy moly, what an unexpected opportunity had just fallen out of the sky and into his stream. As his left hand was busy (making sure his aim was true), he grabbed my shoulder with his right hand, never once stopping his flow—which for a man, I've heard, is tricky to do.

Now, I know, I know, you're thinking sinister thoughts about now. Erase those base images from your dark tinged minds. This was law-abiding Japan where few people owned a gun; everyone waited for the green light before crossing the street even when it was pouring rain at 3AM and no cars were in sight; and they all told you they were glad you came to their island even though they secretly hated your butter smell.

> "If you really want to be
> safe on the streets at night,
> carry a projector and slides
> of your last vacation."
> Helen Mundis

There I was awkwardly poised on one foot with the other raised as high over his arc as I could get, while he continued to peevishly pee under me. Suddenly, as I told you, he grabbed my shoulder with his right hand. On a cold day in hell I could never have guessed what came next. "Could I prease plactice," he blurted out, "my Engrish convahsation with you?"

It was the last thing in the world I expected. I froze in that raised-leg pose like one of those ridiculous nymph fountain statues surrounded by spray!

I don't recall just how I got out the door, but I couldn't leave fast enough. Hello and goodbye! Have a nice life, Pee Brain!

Never had I constricted a laugh so hard, and there was not a soul sister in sight to share it with. I almost herniated myself.

From deep inside my most innermost pit of poise, I once again reached in and pulled out my trusty friend, Madame Tussaud, the dependable guide I could count on when society tested me. With a frozen waxy face, I exited the benjo. Unsmiling, undeterred, I walked back to the counter where I ate my awaiting lunch, nearly choking on raw sea urchin and self-controlled glee. I never once glimpsed down the counter to check out my fellow eliminator. He was no doubt sulking, having missed his chance of a lifetime to speak Engrish. Forty-eight years later, I'll bet he's still pissed off.

105

THIRTY-TWO

AFTER A TWO month's stay in the Gajo-en, where the boys and I were quickly ripening into the kind of hybrid mushrooms that grow in hot, dark, dank basements, we finally found our first real Japanese home. It was in one of the bejillion suburbs of Tokyo; a second-floor apartment in Ogikubo (Oh-gi-koo-boh). The landlord lived down below. Taking full advantage of us the disinherited, he naturally demanded that we pay him mightily under the table for his fine accommodations. Exploitation aside, I did find the apartment's four rooms palatial after the confinement of the bleak, prison-like, oxygen-challenged hotel room. I would, however, miss the happy light from dining room ceiling boards falling on goatskin seat coverings, to say nothing of the security I had felt under their grime prevention program.

> "Last night somebody broke into
> my apartment. When I pointed
> it out to my roommate, he said,
> 'Do I know you?'"
> Steven Wright

Unfortunately, the apartment came with no chambermaid to take advantage of. In her absence, the most immediate task I had was laundry. Laundry! As I look back on it, I know my brain had seriously slipped a cog. Like weren't there coolies on every corner to do that kind of labor? Or was that in China?

Figuring that it would be way too expensive, to say nothing of inconvenient, for me to make the daily commute to China, I became my own coolie, jumping into the laundry fray by doing *all* our washing *by hand*, bent over a tall, oval-shaped, wooden bathtub, because, naturally, neither a laundry area nor a washing machine were featured in our second-floor manor. A flat stone and a beating stick beside a flowing creek would have been cushier.

Aside from the usual soiled clothing and mountains of debased Curities, there were also the sheets. Clearly I had become demented during our over-heated hotel stay. Have you any idea how much work it is to wash sheets for four people by hand in a bathtub built of wood? How clumsy it is to rinse and wring them out while on your knees? And then what a hassle it is to hang them, along with the rest of the laundry, from ropes demonically crisscrossing the inside of your bantam-sized apartment while everyone is living in that same bantam-sized apartment? It would have been Apoplexy City for Martha Stewart. My fingers bled from the effort. And I wonder why I have arthritis in my hands today? What a total crackpot I was, but honestly, I didn't know any other way, and I certainly didn't have DexKnows to guide me!

The other bad thing about that apartment was the aforementioned landlord. He thought he owned not only our home, but also us. Well, me, in particular. He never hesitated to burst through the door whenever he felt like it under the pretense of making a repair, delivering something, or hoping to catch me in a state of undress so he could get a glimpse of my lily white ass! In his nervy, unforgiving heart, I believed he was the Japanese version of Lucifer. Furthermore, I suspected he was getting his comeuppance by vicariously living out the life of the once famous General Tojo, the same one I was trying so hard not to crash into out on the street.

That said there was a good side to this apartment. It served as my hapless, but sincere, introduction to really living in Japan. The first weekend we were there, Glen decided to make my intro official. To seal it, we would mark the event with a toast. The drink of choice, for absolute authenticity, was sake (sah-kay). Now, I had never tasted sake. I had never seen sake. I had never heard of sake. The closest I had come to it was an advertisement hanging outside a bar near Ogikubo Station. It looked suspiciously like it had been printed by our friend, the match/watch sign maker—"Special Cocktails for Ladies With Nuts."

Glen's toast did not come with nuts, but instead, a carrot. If I would/ could chug-a-lug the sake, he pledged to give me ten-thousand yen. Ten-thousand yen! Why, that was almost twenty-seven dollars! Did he have any idea how far I could make that go back in Austin, to say nothing of what I could do with it on the streets of Tokyo? Why, I'd be filthy rich. And, shucks, all I had to do was drink some stuff squeezed out of rice. Rice, for crying out loud! That's what they made gruel out of for babies and old people. What a chump Glen was turning into. Jeez, it looked like a glass of water. Hoo-wee! This would be a snap.

Glen handed me a lemonade-size glass. Full. "Better get your yen on the table there, Daddy Warbucks," I winked at him, while murmuring to myself about what an easy mark he had become now that he had his new high falutin' paycheck. Drink it down, sloooow and easy, girly girl. Show him the kind of stuff you're made of.

Glug ... glug ... glug ....

Pow! Straight from my lips around my ears to the back of my skull it surged, then slammed directly into my brain, circumventing any digestive philandering that would have reduced its effectiveness.

Wheeee! Giggle! I felt so free, so light-hearted, so light-bodied. I was as dizzy as Liberace in a rhinestone mine. Everything was suddenly funny. I couldn't stop laughing, even though I was laughing alone. Glen and our wee boys were just staring with their mouths open. Where had Mommy gone?

> "You're not drunk
> if you can lie
> on the floor
> without holding on."
> Dean Martin

Up to that point in my life, I had made merry with other people. Suddenly I no longer needed them to have a party. I had my sake! Long after Glen, Jeff and Matt went to bed, I was still up reciting poetry and telling myself jokes, thoroughly enjoying them over and over, each repetition proving even funnier than first time. Yes, it was confirmed. I had at last discovered the truth in a proclamation made by a guy named Horace in 65 B.C.:

> "No poems can please for long
> —or live—
> that are written
> by water drinkers."

Don't get the wrong idea here. I was not a cheap date. Keep in mind, that one glass of sake had set Big Daddy back ten-thousand simoleons!

The next day was Saturday. The wrath of grapes (or, in my case, the rage of rice), was upon me. Had I experienced this agony first, I might never have imbibed. Without warning, some time during the night Big Ben had taken up residence inside my skull. Moving very slowly, I did a painful search through my closet (emitting multiple stabbing jabs to my head), where I located an undersized, very tight hat which looked like it had once belonged to an unusally small Amish child. After delicate positioning, it nicely bound together the two halves of my cranium where a fresh crack had split it open sometime after midnight.

With the hat in place, I then, in a faint but determined whisper, insisted that Glen take me and my ten-thousand yen shopping. Hand in hand, Glen and the boys, with me walking very straight, very steady, and very slowly, caught the commuter train to downtown Tokyo. Unable to bend over, turn quickly to my right, speak to anyone, or listen to any more bells, I nonetheless had the time of my life spending every last yen of those twenty-seven dollars, an enormous chunk of change in the Japan of 1962. I have since led a sober, monastic life.

> "One reason I don't drink is that
> I want to know when I am
> having a good time."
> Nancy, Lady Astor

> "I drink too much. The last time
> I gave a urine sample, there
> was an olive in it."
> Rodney Dangerfield

ANOTHER VERY IMPORTANT—dare I say life-changing event?—also took place during our stay in the Ogikubo apartment. It was there that I decided to buckle down and learn Japanese. By now we had been in Japan more than two months and I realized that for any quality of life (like, say, survival), I really had no choice. How to go about learning it was the problem. After much analysis, I came up with an idea. If I could somehow say in Japanese only this one sentence—"What do you call this?"—I could point to things in the shops, say the phrase, and people would respond with the answer. Then I would hear it and I would learn. Perfect!

Glen, who knew all, taught me, "Kore wa nan toi imasuka?"—"What do you call this?" The only catch in the plan was to pick out the right word from the answer when the people replied, and then to remember it. To my surprise, most of the time it worked like a charm. Not always, but, word by word, I was on my way.

> "I personally think
> we developed language
> because of our inner need
> to complain."
> Jane Wagner

Naturally from there I wanted to expand to sentences, as in conversation. I figured the best way to do this was by chatting with the neighborhood wives. I had often seen them walking with their children to a small nearby park, so I began taking Jeff and Matt there to play. As the boys frolicked about, I clandestinely watched and listened to the mothers. I even put on my most wistful face, inviting them, *imploring* them, to speak to me, only to have them turn away, snubbing me, the new white consumer-of-butter-products-she-devil-neighbor-invader.

It couldn't be my lily white ass, because I knew they hadn't even seen it. Well, not yet, anyway. So, not to be deterred, I made a bold plan. If I could gently approach the mothers, gaze down adoringly at their offspring, and then gloriously praise those children to the high heavens, the mothers would fall at my big size-seven feet, prostrating themselves in friendship. There was simply no mother on earth who did not eat up the adulation of her children. I oughtta' know.

I asked Glen how to say, "How cute!" That's all I needed; just one short, concise statement to get cordial relations started. "Kawaii," (kah-wah-eee), Glen instructed. Well, that was easy. One word only? "Kawaii." I could handle that.

The next morning I scrubbed the boys and myself until we shone like white marble bowling balls. In our most prepossessing Presbyterian outfits, we headed for the park. The mothers were already there congregated near the swings. Taking a deep breath and reminding myself of what I was going to say, and how I was going to say it, I silently chanted my way towards them.

Then just within steps of my target, I faltered. Kawaii, kawaii, kawaii—that's what Glen had said, wasn't it—or was it kawaii with an "s"? Oohhhhh ....

Drats, which was it? I wasn't sure. Settle down, I told myself. Stay on the safe side. Just say it all! Kawaii-sss-ohhhh.

Shaking off my momentary uncertainty, I moseyed over to the first mother, gazed admiringly down at the infant nestled in her protective arms, and sighed in a voice full of bonhomie, "Kawaii-sss-ohh."

There, I'd said it! I was enormously pleased with myself. To my utter disbelief, she was not. Her jaw dropped, her slanted eyes bugged out viciously in two slitted wedges, and she abruptly turned away. I moved onto the next mom, thinking the first had misunderstood me, or simply was jealous of blonds.

> "Picasso had his pink period
> and his blue period.
> I am in my blonde period right now."
> Hugh Hefner

Smiling down at her youngsters, I very carefully and slowly (so my pronunciation would once again be perfect), cooed, "kawaii-sss-ohhh."

Same response, same shock, same recoil! I didn't get it. Was it something I had said? How callous could these women be to my friendly, heartfelt gestures, anyway? And, how mean and short tempered they were, like every last one of them was going through a bout with early mental-pause. Oh, dear me, where *was* Eleanor Roosevelt when I needed her?

But, then to my dismay, I recalled that even Ellie hadn't always been such a hot shot success. I remembered reading about her once where she was lamenting over a rose that had been named for her. At first she said she was flattered. That, however, lasted only as long as it took for her to read the description of it in a gardening catalog, "No good in a bed, but fine against a wall."

Plus, wasn't it that erstwhile, impish Johnny Carson who reported, "In 1932, lame duck President Herbert Hoover was so desperate to remain in the White House that he dressed up as Eleanor. When FDR discovered the hoax in 1936, the two men decided to stay together for the sake of the children."

Oh, Ellie, Ellie, even you suffered as I was now suffering ....

After my third attempt, and with the same wretched results, (by now the women had gathered and were hunched over in a raven-haired heap, chattering sentence talk I could not understand, while looking looks in my direction that were also beyond my comprehension), I decided perhaps the boys and I should gather up our last shreds of dignity and sashay on home.

Sayonara to the sisterhood that never hooded.

Utterly stupefied, to say nothing of my humiliation, I couldn't wait to re-run the entire puzzling event past Glen, so when he walked through the door that evening, I replayed the scene for him, telling him how splendidly I had praised the babies to kingdom-come-and-back, only to be met with icy rejection. The scrunched up look on his face showed me that he was also bewildered.

"Tell me again, Peggy, just exactly what you said to them," he queried.

"Just what you taught me," I responded, "kawaii-sss-ohhh."

Now it was his turn to go into early mental-pause. His jaw dropped, then slammed back up as it bounced off the floor, nearly chipping a front tooth. Next *his* eyes bugged out, only unlike the playground mothers, his were real round.

"Peggy, by adding the 'sss-ohhh' to 'kawaii,' you changed the meaning of the word entirely. You didn't say 'cute.' You said 'pitiful!' "

I was so busted. With one slip of my well meaning tongue, I had just told my neighbors—my only hope for friendship and Japanese lessons—that their babies were pathetic. Way to go, Peggy. I was off to an amazing start with my first stab at international diplomacy. None of it boded well for my future happiness, or for establishing any hopes of sisterly love abroad.

> "A wittle wranguage
> goes a wrong way."
> Hinoku Kobota

Craps, it wasn't the locals who were pathetic, it was me! How would I ever survive Ogikubo? In the weeks to follow, I avoided the park like the plague that I was.

Fortune, however, gave me another chance. I was thrilled to my spleen when Glen came home with the news he had found us a house. It was in Kichijoji (Kee-chee-joh-jee), another suburb not far away, and even though I had trouble saying that name (it sounded like someone getting tickled), I couldn't get away fast enough. Yeah, I'd leave that icy, unforgiving Ogikubo clique—to say nothing of our voyeur landlord—in my dust. Just 'cuz they thought they were so high-and-mighty uppity special, I, the new Mrs. See If I Care, didn't agree. In my book, those over-inflated peons deserved each other.

> "If I were a grave-digger
> or even a hangman,
> there are some people
> I could work for
> with a great deal of enjoyment."
> Douglas Jerrold

THIRTY-THREE

ASAHI COURT WAS a complex of seven gray cement duplexes encircled by a dirt-gravel driveway. It looked ambrosial. In reality I guess it was a far cry from bliss, but my eyes were now seeing things differently. The shabby, scrubby concrete, which showed signs of having once been pink, had dust all about it—and absolutely no familiar faces. In particular, that last part looked inviting to me. I could start afresh with no landlord downstairs, with some new real friends, and with way better pronunciation. It would be my Shawshank redemption.

On the first floor were two rooms: a small living room adjoining an even smaller kitchen, with no wall dividing the two spaces. Off the kitchen was a storage area, about the dimensions of a medium-sized closet. Within this closet was another smaller closet: a miniscule toilet room that barely contained one benjo, one roll of toilet paper and one small-to-medium sized occupant. Surrounding the benjo were very plain walls; the place where our young sons would first begin dabbling (dribbling?) in chair-chair graffiti.

A faux granite staircase led up to the second floor, making an abrupt turn to an eight-foot-long hallway that opened on to two scaled-down bedrooms and one tight-quartered bathroom. In the space of only four short years, Asahi Court had become our seventh domestic rendition of Xanadu. In cinder block.

Quite possibly the bathroom was the most oddball space in the house. Actually it was the tub in the bathroom that was so screwy. Erase all images you have of what a bathtub should look like. Neither was this tub like yours nor was it like the wooden one we had just left behind in Ogikubo. Our new tub was concrete, four-feet-long, two-and-a-half-feet-wide, and three-feet-deep. It was shaped like a thick, boxy bunker with menacingly sharp corners and edges. In an attempt to enhance it (since not all occupants found raspy-edged, gray concrete altogether adorable), the entire outside and inside were encrusted with tiny blue ceramic tiles, each about one-inch square. Unlike American bathtubs, this tub was meant for soaking; soaking up to a Japanese neck. Not necessarily so an American neck.

The first evening we were there, Glen decided to take a bath. He was looking forward to the recuperative powers of a soothing soak after the fatiguing move into the house, so I didn't think anything of it when he stayed upstairs in the bathroom a long time. An inordinately long time. Meanwhile, as was by now my habit, I was doing laundry *by hand* (crazy-psycho-nutcase-weirdo that I had become!), in the new kitchen sink downstairs. Scrubbing away, I thought I heard a sound. Being in a new unfamiliar building, though, I wasn't sure, but I thought it was coming from upstairs. What was it? Someone calling my name? The boys didn't call me Peggy, so it must be Glen. But, why was his voice so faint?

Squeegeeing the soap suds off my arms and upper torso, I followed the noise up the stairs to the bathroom door. Ever so slowly I opened it and peeked in. There was my husband soaking in the concrete tub, not quite up to his neck, but somewhere just south of his nipples. My eyes drifted downward from them to the floor. To my alarm, I saw it was covered with water.

"Say, Honey, were you calling me?" I entreated in my most caring, wifely voice. "Is everything okay?"

At my words, Glen's head swiveled in my direction. A sheepish look sheathed his suddenly strained vermilion face. "Uhhhh, Peggy, I think I may need your help," he beseeched. "I'm ... well ... stuck. I can't get out."

Why, help was my middle name! Like a paramedic on uppers, I covered the distance from the door to the bath in two strong strides. I peered into the tub. What the heck? Where was the inside of the tub? I could see nothing but Glen *everywhere!* Holy Toledo, his body filled up the entire receptacle. Even the four square corners were full of his pale flesh. It was as if Glen had been melted down and poured into a rocklike mold. My Lord in heaven, in the time of only one long soak, my husband had turned into a block of living, gasping tofu!

Of course I couldn't help him. Not just then anyway. First I had to laugh! Falling on knees that could no longer support me, I cackled and chortled and exploded with crazed merriment. Glen, on the other hand, did not laugh. Nor smile. Nor see one damn thing funny about his predicament. I suppose you could say he had really gotten himself in hot water this time.

It took a while to recover my composure, but once under control, I gave myself over completely to the rescuing of my husband. After all, he had once done the same for me—and in water, to boot! With the help of the mightiest tugs I could muster, his crammed body began a prolonged un-wedging of itself from its concrete encasement. Slowly ... sluuuurrrp ... he came up the sides of the tub as strenuously as a stubborn cork from an aged wine bottle. Then with a final brute force thrust he popped, breaking the suction. It was clear to me that had he stayed in his bathtub vise even ten seconds longer, the life would have been sucked right out of him.

Modestly, I realized I had saved my man from a bean curd cube existence.

I glanced up and down his glistening, freshly abraded body. Trying my best to not lose control again by either tittering or blurting out words I would later regret, I barely stifled what my eyes perceived. There between the scrapes and scratches from those rough, malevolent tile edges, was my hubby's exposed backside now whimsically embossed with tiny one-inch squares. His rump looked like a slick, wet Rubik's cube.

It took a few moments to recover from this discovery before I made yet another. I peered into the tub. Gosh, it was almost empty. Just an inch or so of water remained in the bottom. "Didn't you fill this baby up," I inquired, "before you got in it?"

"Well ... er, yes, I did," he replied sheepishly, "but, gee, when I got in, the water sorta all came out over the top."

An hour earlier, as Glen had lowered himself into the full tub of hot water, his body so completely filled the concrete coffer that he instantly became a human bung. Like a giant biped toilet plunger, he caused the water to suction in a tsunami-like effect up and over the top of the tub. At this point, and unable to stop the swell in mid-flood, Glen simply sank to the bottom of the deep box. He knew then that he had just become one with his new bathtub. What he didn't know was how tight the bonding would be.

Phooey! Darn! Where was I when all the entertainment was going on? I'd missed the entire first act.

It was pretty obvious that Glen would have to come up with a new bathing system because we weren't moving just so he could avoid cubism imprints. Thus, with no shower option to turn to, he developed his own unique style of bathing. While bent in a tricky, semi-fetal position, he washed and rinsed with a fast, non-lingering crouch-and-plunge technique. He would have to wait almost five years until we would move to the next house, the next country, before he could comfortably sit again in a roomy bathtub. During the long interval, his embossing slowly faded.

THIRTY-FOUR

DESPITE THIS BATHING blip in our dwelling contentment, Asahi Court seemed so very fine to us. Our neighbors were Japanese, Americans and Chinese-Americans. Among them was the Japanese lady on the other side of our duplex who we seldom saw because she came down with tuberculosis shortly after we moved in and spent the rest of the time in a sanitarium. There was also the Japanese couple who lived to our right who had sex a lot and were proud of it, or at least their housekeeper attested to it because she was always having to pick up gooey, wadded Kleenexes from around their bed—an advertisement, if I ever heard one—for their favorite hobby.

> "Kinky sex involves
> the use of duck feathers.
> Perverted sex
> involves the whole duck."
> Lewis Grizzard

Down from them was a rascally American twosome. They were the oldest couple in the court: a high ranking American civilian and his over-heated wife who *wanted* to have sex a lot but couldn't because they were both—during the only two free days of the week in which they could hope to pull it off—dedicated weekend alcoholics. Dang it!

Next door to them was a Chinese-American family who was more Chinese than American although they were trying.

Another couple lived directly across the dirt-gravel driveway from us: an American woman and her spanking new Japanese husband. They were, hands down, without a doubt, the world's oddest couple. Believe me, long before Felix Unger and Oscar Madison ever came on the scene, these two pioneers had already defined the title. No couple since has held a candle to their level of mismatchedness.

Not to cast aspersions ... oh, why not! ... this couple was physically quite possibly the most unparalleled, atypical twosome anywhere in the Judeo Christian Buddhist Shinto world. They were against all dating rules of conduct. The woman, six-feet-tall and in her mid-forties, was a mountain of flesh. A mountain, I tell you! Rolls upon rolls of soft, bulbous corpulence spilled out of her in every corporeal direction. When she lumbered toward me to say hello, she blocked out the sun, the moon and the stars like a three-hundred-and-fifty-pound wall shrouded in billowing fabric bearing down on my life. I never failed to step aside and let her have the right of way.

Keep in mind that the sixties were the thin days when a one-hundred-and-seventy-pound American woman drew gasps of negative exclamations from disapproving on-lookers. An equally fat Japanese woman would have stirred up no response, because there were none.

Queen Kong's husband, in contrast, was a nineteen-year-old, five-foot-three Japanese who weighed all of one-hundred-and-twelve-pounds after a smorgasbord. Their identical-to-ours blue tiled bathtub was a soaking dream come true for him, whereas his meaty wife would have nothing more than sink sponge baths in the year they lived in Asahi Court.

One could only imagine the attraction between the two: her finding him an elfin Asian boy doll, and him finding her a delicious massive American chub. Surely never in his short homogeneous life had he ever seen so *much woman* stuffed into one bag of stretch-marked flesh. She was a wiggling receptacle of ripples; the antidote to "the *little* woman." And, she was all his.

"On Golden Blond"
(porn video title)

Now, I don't want to be Debby Downer here who always sees the negative side of things, but this union was just begging for a slide down the slithery slope of love. Woman big! Boy teeny! Imagining the two of them locked in the throes of phantasmagorical carnal magnetism was like envisioning a black-haired fly bestraddling a great big pink picnic ham. You've all seen those huge blow-up fun houses that are rented out for kiddies' parties? Well, that had to have been his experience on her— rolling, lolling, wallowing about over the hillocks of her commodious bulk. I wondered if their health policy covered sex injuries.

> "They made love only
> during total eclipses of the sun,
> because they wouldn't take off their clothes
> unless it was dark—
> everywhere in the entire world."
> Unknown

> "I'm not kinky, but occasionally
> I like to put on a robe
> and stand in front of
> a tennis ball machine."
> Garry Shandling

After a short, but scorching romance—completely ignoring the old advice that contraceptives should be used on every *conceivable* occasion—they got married because, you guessed it, they had to. *Picnic ham was with Spam!*

> "The late porn star,
> Johnny Wadd,
> claimed to have been laid
> 14,000 times.
> He died of friction."
> Larry Brown

Although the bride's family was far off in America and unable to join the rushed wedding ceremony, the groom's family attended. Following the nuptial vows, it was decided that the occasion should be celebrated. Thereupon, the new in-laws invited the couple for a celebratory row around one of the rare ponds (man-made) in Tokyo. First the new mother-in-law, father-in-law and groom settled themselves comfortably into the boat. Then it was time for the blushing bride to step into the matrimonial vessel.

Coyly she raised one nyloned ham hock and placed it into the rowboat. Then, heavily heaving herself off the dock, the other hock followed. As fast as the flushing action of a Koehler toilet, the small boat, with the newly joined family inside, was sucked under by the rush of lake water that instantly filled it. Sunk they were. Actually that was pretty much accurate, for it portended the destiny of their marriage.

> "The heaviest object in the world
> is the body of the woman
> you have ceased to love."
> Marquis de Luc de Clapiers Vauvenargues

Some months later, and by then fully dried out, they had a lovely little boy. When he turned one, and with no announcement of any kind, the couple just up and moved their separate ways. No surprise there. Mysteriously they faded into the chaos of Tokyo, never to be heard from again, proving once more the old theory that opposites *can* detract.

"Better to have loved and lost a short person
than never to have loved a tall."
David Chambless

It was beyond irony that the couple who next moved into that same duplex was physically the exact opposite. The Missus was a Tom Thumb version of a Japanese woman, diminutive even amongst her own kind. A lively little grig of a thing, she was appropriately named "Blossom." Her American husband, Norm, wouldn't you know, was a behemoth among Caucasian men. Unlike the first couple, they were a contented, loving twosome, *her* soaking in the tub this time while *he* struggled with sponge sink baths, their love obviously overriding their diversities and questionable hygiene.

It all seems so unfair how the matching of an over-sized male to an under-sized female is all hunky-dory, while switching the pairing around is too oddball to be socially suitable. It's like the albino squirrel we have in our yard right now. I can't tell if he/she in all his/her ethereal glow is acceptable or not to the brown-gray gang that hangs around our bird feeder. Like, is he/she dateable? Eligible for Rodent Club membership? Allowed a fair share of the acorn harvest? Or is he/she just simply too ... well ... squirrely?

"Love will find a lay."
Robert Byrne

THIRTY-FIVE

QUALITY WOULD PROBABLY not be the word I would use to describe absolutely anything about our Asahi Court duplex. The closest it came to it was maybe the staircase to the second floor. The architect's plan was for it to look like marble or granite or even solidified pea gravel, but instead it simply resembled hardened mucus decorated with the same kind of tiny spots you would find on quail eggs. It almost fooled the eye of the less discerning, but with a second glance, even they recognized its fabrication. As grand as it almost was, its mean, pointy corners and hard, slippery surfaces (no doubt also installed by the mean-spirited bathtub mason), made it a really dumb kind of staircase to have in a home with young children.

One day while toddling across the room, Matt fell and landed squarely on the spiky corner of the bottom step. The sharp, stony, point dug deeply into his soft baby flesh precisely between his eyes. Had he hit half-an-inch over in either direction, the point would surely have put out one of them.

Blood began spurting upward in a horseshoe curve, resembling a red drinking fountain. His life fluids were everywhere. I grabbed my baby and ran to the kitchen for a towel. Then I yelled to Sakae-san (our newly hired housekeeper), to get Jeff and run to the car, which by some miracle was at home that day because Glen was out of the country. The nearest U.S. military clinic was Green Park, twenty minutes away on a good traffic day. Jumping into the car, I instructed Sakae-san to press as hard as she could on the wound to stem the bleeding, as I steered the mini-car through the narrow, winding, congested dirt roads.

The traffic that day was as slow and congealed as old bacon grease, miring our progress and making the trip to the clinic stretch on forever. After what seemed an eternity, we arrived. I slammed on the brakes in front of the main doors of Green Park, grabbed Matt, and over my shoulder yelled instructions to Sakae-san to stay put with Jeff in the car.

The long hallway through the huge building went on incessantly, with the clinic at the far end. It was no easy feat carrying my heavy boy in one arm, while bearing down on the compress with the other, all the while running as fast as I could.

At last, breathless, we arrived at the dispensary. Once there, I realized it must be noon. The waiting room was completely empty. I called out for someone. Anyone! No one came. I called again louder; and again even louder. From a back room came a Japanese nurse obviously interrupted while eating lunch as she was licking off grains of rice from her lips. The relief I felt at seeing her was monumental. Someone would save my baby. I rushed towards her.

As I got to her side, she reached over and grabbed the towel from my hand. Uncovered, the blood once again regained momentum, spurting onto the floor in a high red curve. And just what did Florence Nightingale do next, you ask? Why, what all good angels of mercy do. She screamed, threw up her hands in alarm, turned around, and ran out of the room. My heart plummeted to the bottom of my bottom. I was devastated. Angry! Just when I had found help for my baby, there was no help at all.

I quickly placed the towel back over the injury, pressing down to again stop the blood flow, all the while attempting to corral and calm Matt's pain and fright. It's not like I had other alternatives. Then I paced the floor and waited, hanging in limbo there in the empty room, hoping and praying Florence would return; return with someone a whole lot more competent than she was.

She did. With her was an American doctor who immediately took over. With a hypodermic needle as long as Matt's forearm, he injected a painkiller into the center of the wound. Then while Matt watched cross-eyed, the doctor sutured across his nose from just short of one tear duct to the other.

Once finished, the wound needed covering. There were no ready-made bandages for that particular body locale, so with medical ingenuity, the doctor placed a gauze pad over the wound and then held it in place with two long strips of white adhesive tape stretching from his forehead down across his cheeks. The large, cross-hatched bandage looked for all the world like an X-marks-the-spot-bull's-eye, and it was now perfectly centered in the middle of Matt's sweet angelic face.

For weeks afterwards, our second-born appeared as though he had been marked for one—or all—of the following: a special purpose, a military recognition for young people, a target for darts, or a hex from a Haitian curse. The doctor informed me that the resulting scar would migrate as Matt grew. He said it would most likely go up or down, but said nothing about it going sideways, which I suppose would have dragged his nose along with it into one of his eyes. We were real glad that didn't happen.

I never again rented or bought a house with a quasi-granite, quail-egg-speckled staircase.

THIRTY-SIX

BY NOW YOU know the rooms in our Asahi Court duplex were small. The boys' bedroom was particularly so. I was lucky to have found a bunk bed at the Green Park PX, for two beds side-by-side would have been an impossibility. I was also lucky to have found a bunk bed with guard rails. This meant that, young as they were, both boys could safely sleep stacked on top of each other.

When Jeff was almost three and in the late stages of toilet training, we thought it was a brilliant idea to move his potty chair into the boys' bedroom each evening so that in the event he felt the call during the night, he would have instant access. Neither would Jeff have to awaken us for assistance nor would he have to find his way in the dark to the bathroom next door. The plan was foolproof.

Days went by without any need for the nighttime potty.

Then one morning Glen and I awoke to a powerful stink. "What in blue blazes is it?" we choked in unison, holding our hands over our mouths to keep from gagging. I checked in the bathroom. Nothing. There was only one other room upstairs: the boys' bedroom. Standing outside their door, I hesitated, stifling a retch. It surely seemed that the stench was coming from that direction. Inhaling as deeply as I could in the befouled air (suspecting that it was about to become even fouler), I held my breath and opened the door.

Pow! Thwack!

The rank malodor nearly vaporized me.

123

Holding onto the door for support, I looked into the room. I had been in it only hours before when I put the boys to bed, and I was sure ... no, downright certain ... that it had been all one color. Now the room sported a glistening two-toned paint job. Try as I might, I couldn't recall painting the bottom half of the walls anything at all. In particular ... brown?

As it happened, in the early morning hours while Glen, Matt and I slept, Jeff had been stricken with the call. Rising from his bed like the dutiful son he was, he executed his job in the conveniently awaiting potty chair, all the while knowing the pride his parents would have in his obedience, to say nothing of his more than impressive output! The sun was just coming over the horizon, peep-holing between the curtains where, like a well-placed spot light, it came to rest on Jeff's fresh handiwork now lying inertly in the bowl of the little chair. Of course the shaft of light caught his eye, just like all good spot lights do, focusing in on the targeted show stopper.

Wow, had he done that? *All* that? And had it really come out from the inside of *him*? Awesome!

Fascinated, and not just a little smug, Jeff leaned in for a closer scrutiny. It was amazing. He, *JEFF KEENER!*, had produced that thick, gooey stuff all by himself! Not one person helped him. Not one!

> "Very few people do anything creative
> after the age of thirty-five.
> The reason is that very few people
> do anything creative
> before the age of thirty-five."
> Joel Hildebrand

Up till that time, Jeff had never really paid much attention to "it," not having a private moment to himself quite like this one. But, now, there it was. His invention! Like an artist glimpsing his first creation, so did Jeff move yet even closer to gaze at his.

Gosh, it looked so interesting lying there, curvy like a snake that had just finished off a teenage anteater. And, such a nice rich color, too. In fact, a lot like chocolate pudding. Hmmm, he wondered ... how would it feel ...?

With the irresistible temptation getting the best of him, Jeff plunged right in. Oh, surprise, surprise, delight, delight! It was soft and warm and squishy. He squeezed it between his fingers and around the palms of his hands. Fun! Oh, how he instantly regretted having wasted all those other opportunities before this one. But, now seizing the moment, his rapture continued as he deliciously rubbed the pudding up and around both arms.

Then, all at once, Jeff remembered something. He wasn't supposed to make messes. Mommy had warned him about that cardinal sin more than once. He looked down at his brown arms which now contrasted starkly with the rest of his pale skin. He should try to clean them. But, how? Why, of course, he'd go in the bathroom and wash them.

He reached for the doorknob only to discover there the magic of instantly turning silver to brown. Who knew he had such power? Maybe, just maybe, he could create the same kind of magic on the door. And, then … let's see … why not the wall? After all, it was right there. With sweeping motions as high and as low as he could stretch, the newest Major Domo of Dung distributed his handiwork proportionately.

In time, he came to the dresser. The only drawers he had ever accessed were the two bottom ones because they were the only ones he could reach. Now, would you look at that … as if it had been ordained by the potty chair gods … the two bottom drawers were slightly open! Seeing that as a definite invitation, Jeff scooped from the pot more raw material, then excitedly proceeded to rub down the neatly stacked laundered clothing within. Cool! Jeff was ecstatic over the darkish, although somewhat cloudy, results!

With creativity now consuming him like an opera diva captivating and holding the audience with her high note, Jeff could not allow himself to stop.

"If that's art,
I'm a Hottentot."
Harry S. Truman

In the meantime, as the fresco was progressing, little brother Matt lay sound asleep on the bottom bunk only inches from the dresser. Dead to the world, he was oblivious to the workings of his big bro, the newly budding prodigy. Jeff paused in his labor and looked at Matt. You know what? There really was no good reason whatsoever to give up on a good thing now … like I'm right in the middle of my project, can't you see?

With that note of self-encouragement, Jeff proceeded. He began to paint Matt. To paint Matt *generously!* This should come as no surprise to anyone, for altruism, especially towards his own flesh and blood, was Jeff's middle name. His hands began to glide from Matt's wavy head to his well-fed tummy to his chubby toes, not neglecting the sheets, blanket, pillow and bedspread in between. Kawabunga! This was like the most fun Jeff had ever had!

By the time he ran out of supplies, Jeff had finger painted the entire circumference of the room (including his brother), in a solid mahogany mural, fashioned to the exact height of his up-raised arms. I opened the door just as he was standing back admiring his rectal rendering. The rapture on his face told me that everything in his world was copasetic.

Oh, shit! … *if you know what I mean?*

I tell you, it was one of *those* moments—and it *was* shit! If you've ever experienced either, you know what I'm talking about. Had I been the cussing sort, this would surely have been the time. I wasn't—well, except

125

for that shit part—but then, wasn't that accurate? Furthermore, had I, at that moment, been asked to name what my most demanding challenges had been up to that point in my life, this would surely have been a #2 (in more ways than one!), right after the #1 which was the three long arduous days it took me to birth that boy!

Code Brown! Code Brown!

I looked at the inglorious mess. This must be what people meant when they talked about being in deep doo-doo. My eyes stung in disbelief as that dangly thing at the back of my throat began ululating.

Oddly, at the same moment, I was hit with a flashback. With it came a connection, indeed a mental bonding, with who else but Michelangelo's mom? Wouldn't you know it? It had happened to her, too. Like me, she had also been pushed to the brink of exasperation by her boy's childhood art. I had read somewhere that on one particularly vexing day, she had lost it completely. Exploding in anger she screamed, "Michelangelo di Lodovico Buonarroti Simoni, (using his full name to emphasize her aggravation), can't you paint on walls like other children? Do you have any idea how hard it is to get that stuff off the ceiling?"

Holy cow! Do you suppose my firstborn was in that league of maestros? Okay, okay, so it was a little early to tell. Besides, Mickey's mess was bigger than Jeff's, being so high up and all, but just the same, I'd surely stash away that provocative thought for future rumination. I wondered, as well, if I shouldn't—and in a darn hurry, at that—consider giving Jeff a couple more middle names?

Two hours later, after I had completed multiple VERY BIG wash downs with multiple NOT VERY EFFECTIVE results, Sakae-san arrived. A craziness was in her. In her broken Engrish, she decried over and over again about detecting something—clear down the road—that was dis-stink-ly wafting from our direction!

Butter, as it turned out, was not our only disagreeable aromatic. I thought it was commendable, as well as un-bigoted, of Sakae-san to stay on.

> "If you have a job
> without aggravations,
> you don't have a job."
> Malcolm Forbes

THIRTY-SEVEN

SOMETIME IN THE early fall of 1963, just over a year after we moved into Asahi Court, a young fellow from Naperville, Illinois, joined us. Fresh out of teachers' college, he was about to begin a job at one of the U. S. Department of Defense high schools in the Tokyo area. Science teacher, Robert Fink (who on the first day of class always pointed out to his students that the "R" on his lab coat did not stand for "Rat!"), became our instant new best friend. He was chummy and fun, but more than anything, he tweaked my curiosity with the promise his new bride would be showing up any day.

The exhilaration Bob was feeling over Karen's approaching advent was like waiting for a Girl Scout cookie delivery. It also, in a personal way, became infectious for me—friendless me—who could sure use a girl pal. For her arrival, Bob and I eagerly put the Fink duplex in order with borrowed government furniture and commissary food, even placing fresh-cut flowers on the table. Then we began counting down the days before they wilted.

Feverish excitement built as the date drew near. At last, "Karen Day" arrived! With hugs and wishes for a speedy return, I waved a psyched-up, turned-on Bob off to Tachikawa Air Force Base where he would meet her plane. I was nearly as twitterpated as he at finally meeting his bride, the very one I was counting on to become my shiny new, closest compeer, and enduring bosom buddy.

But, before this could happen, Bob had to get to the airport and bring her home. You must understand that driving from Kichijoji to Tachikawa was a lengthy ordeal. Indeed, every destination in Japan was a lengthy ordeal due to the astonishingly twisty and gnarled dirt roads which were as narrow as many single car driveways back home. Also, to our never ending amazement, the pot holes in them were at times the same size as the car we were in. I kid you not. Japan was real big on pot holes.

Asphalt, I had read, was "that hellish black substance used to pave the earth so that it might be made safe for automobiles." Well, not where we were. As yet, penurious Japan had only gotten as far as paving some of its roads, while merely tamping the earth on others. This did not sit well in a monsoonal climate. Driving through the ravages created by those muddy torrents required at all times to have an alert brain, or was it having no brain at all? Either way, it was not for wimps. Much as I hate to say it, I believe the civil engineers who designed the roads in Japan must have graduated from the University of Sodom and Gomorrah.

On "Karen Day" the sun was shining. Bob left while I, back at our duplex, paced the floor in hyper-anticipation. I couldn't wait to get a buddy; somebody who would split her sides over my sushi benjo caper and sympathize with my pathetic attempt at making Japanese friends; somebody who I could depend on, and wouldn't notice, or even care, about my butter smell. Yes, a sidekick, a confidante, a playmate, a pal was what I needed, and my hopes were all rolled up into Karen Fink being just that.

I didn't expect Bob and Karen's return for at least five hours, but when seven went by I was nearly beside myself with consternation. I tried concentrating on housework, but little got done because of my constant running to the windows to see if Bob's car was coming up the gravel driveway. Finally when I was nearly prostrate with worry, he drove in. I flew out the door in a poor attempt at both containing my enthusiasm and maintaining good manners.

As the dust from the driveway settled around the automobile, I peered inside. To my alarm only one person was in the car. Bob! What was wrong with this picture? *No Karen!* Had she already ditched him—him, a really nice chap—for some lesser no-good rascal back home? Gosh, Bob had arrived in Japan only two weeks after they were married, and since then only a month had passed. Could Karen have gone astray in so short a time? Was Bob's bride—and my possible new best friend—nothing more than a two-timing conjugal skanky tart?

> "Absence makes
> the heart
> go yonder."
> Robert Byrne

Poor Bob Fink! He looked like something the cat dragged in, and I don't mean a rat! Where, oh, where was that frisky Mrs. Karen Cuckold, the cheating little minx? Dare I even ask?

"Dancing begets warmth,
which is the parent of wantonness.
It is, Sir, the great-grandfather
of cuckoldom."
Henry Fielding

I wondered how good a dancer Karen was … and how wantonly warm she got when she was doing it?

With the longest white face in the neighborhood (which wasn't at all hard to do), Bob very slowly and even more abashedly drooped out of the car, stuttering and sputtering his explanation. It seemed that in his haste and hunger for his bride, he had gone to the airport on the wrong day. Karen wasn't due until tomorrow!

It was all the fault of Bob's inbred Illinois chronometer: that pesky time/date thing that happens to all world travelers when they cross the International Dateline. Everyone must tussle through it one time (a decidedly irksome rite-of-passage), and then learn to check the dates on the calendar once, then twice, and finally three times, just to make sure.

"'Um, who's Bob?'
(this is what to reply
to a person who says,
'I'm so confused, Bob.'")
John Grimes

That evening I allowed Bob the space he needed to stew in the juices of his own chagrin. By the next day, however, I found myself once again going through the enthusiastic rigmarole of the big airport sendoff. This time, however, it was slightly tinged as all reruns are, but just the same I clung to the hope that for today the planets, the stars, the timetables—and Bob—would all be in alignment.

Having done nothing constructive the day before, due to my Fink vigil, I had work to do. Setting about my chores righting my home and preparing the boys for a sitter, I was at last ready to make the twenty-minute trip to the by-now infamous Green Park, home of debatable health care. I should point out that Green Park was not only a clinic, but also a very large, multi-leveled, U.S. Army housing compound. Under one roof was a commissary, a PX (where I could easily buy a nice Christmas gift for each of us with a single $20 bill!), a church, a library, a movie theatre, various schools, *that dispensary/clinic*, a barber shop, a beauty shop, a nursery, a dry cleaner and dozens upon dozens of family apartments. As handy as it was to our needs, I was deeply grateful that Glen's civilian status did not mandate our living there. Without question, it was a place to avoid once my shopping was completed.

At the commissary and PX (grocery and general store to the uninitiated), we could buy American things familiar to the American way of life. This was Uncle Sam's attempt at making our imaginary lives in

Japan—a world away from our quickly fading unimaginary lives in the U.S.—seem more normal and comfortable, as if, so far from home, such a thing were possible. Don't get me wrong. I appreciated the effort, but it was a real streeeetch.

Green Park was an all-encompassing, all-encapsulating microcosm of a world. It was possible to spend the normal four-year military tour there and never exit the building other than for the initial arrival and the final departure. Which some people did. I'll never forget the day I was there shopping and met a friend who lived in one of the apartments. In an amiable gesture, I asked her how things were going. I'll never forget her reply.

"Oh, it's been terrible! Here at Green Park we've had nothing but rain!"

As if the Green Parkites had a perfectly rectangular, nimbostratus cloud exactly the shape of their building hanging over them—and only them—while the areas just outside their perimeter were under a fire alert due to tinderbox conditions. I should have slugged her.

> "Some people are always grumbling
> that roses have thorns. I am thankful
> that thorns have roses."
> Alphonse Karr

> "You can be sincere
> and still be stupid."
> Unknown

BUT, NOW HERE I was in the Green Park Commissary grabbing food packages and throwing them in the cart in my haste to get home. To be there for Karen's arrival! Rounding the end of a grocery aisle, I happened to look down the row to the other end. Oh, m'gosh, there was Bob!

Standing in front of him was a tall redhead obviously in a high state of excitement. Her arms were gyrating like a New York traffic cop as she pointed at something. I watched Bob's eyes follow her gesture. Then as she, up close, and I, at a distance, both looked in the direction of her point, Bob's face detonated in an explosion of unchecked contortions, going from surprise to disbelief to joy to stark terror, all within a fleeting second.

The redhead was Karen, and she was facing a Gerber baby food display while announcing to Bob that in the near future, they would have need of that. Even from my remote vantage point, the more highly perceptive female in me had already caught on faster than had Bob, the still green, six-week-old husband and now new father.

Back at my end of the aisle, I bubbled over with the sheer delight of it all. As I saw it, it was a heck of a marriage deal; Bob, right off the bat like that, getting two for the price of one.

And, as for me, I felt decidedly privileged to learn about their microscopic cashew of a baby at the very same moment the father did. Whoa, those two randy Finks were fast! Even Glen and I had waited two whole months before our fruitfulness blossomed. Like rabbits, Bob and Karen must have been at it on their way out of the church! I was suddenly sorry I had not been invited to their wedding to see them grabbing and clawing at each other on their way to the get-away car. But then, I didn't know them then.

It's not everyday a person meets someone for the first time during such an intimate moment, but that baby announcement is exactly what happened. Unable to contain myself, I swept down the aisle. After a few mumbled words of introduction, I grabbed Karen, gave her that all-knowing maternity wink, and the two of us began squealing. Harmoniously, as if cosmically programmed, my pores commenced to squeeze friendship, Bob's oozed rapture, while Karen's sprayed hormones.

At last, stopping for an air break, I keened my effervescent congratulations. Karen was frothy with good cheer, and I knew on the spot that I had found a friend for life. The year was 1963, and even though we have always lived at great distances during the intervening years, Karen has remained dear to me, a profoundly real and meaningful part of my life. "An old friend is better than two new ones," says a Yiddish proverb. How true. Karen has consistently, through all this time, been my old proverbial piece of gum that never loses its flavor on the bedpost overnight.

IT QUICKLY BECAME routine for Bob and Karen to amble over almost every evening about the time we were finishing dinner. Uncannily, they knew to arrive just at the moment our two squirmy boys were finding it humanly impossible to sit at the table any longer. On the boys' swiftly vacated plates were leftovers that could, in all likelihood, go to waste if someone didn't benevolently eat them. Enter the benevolent Finks. Perfect meal planning! For dessert we had each other's company. Like Elmer's Glue, we four bonded with a ferocious stick.

Sitting around our Asahi Court kitchen, we never failed to comment on the uniqueness of the one and only table we had in our home, our dinner table. Actually, if truth be told, it was a card table that I had purchased back in Minnesota using my mom's S&H Green Trading Stamps. The designers never intended for it to have constant use, but only occasionally host a card game. That's why they called it that!

I don't mean to be a complainer here because, in reality, we really would have liked to have occasionally played cards on our table, but we had no choice. First of all we didn't know any card games, and secondly we needed to eat on it. Believe me, I had searched in vain for a long-legged, Western style dinner table, but there seemed to be none in Japan. Virtually every table I found was for floor sitting. Uh-huh, way down there. This was not yet our custom nor had it been our first priority for we were still preoccupied with that other low down thing: fine-tuning our benjo squats.

Our card table had a mahogany colored, lacquered paper top, and was supported underneath by two metal crisscrossing rods. As the months went by, the four unsupported sections, which happened to be exactly where our four dinner plates sat, began to sag. This contoured slumpage resulted in a small, individual valley in front of each Keener. To be sure, the four bowl-shaped gullies were definitely a tricky place in which to balance dishes, especially glasses. There was, albeit, one good deal about the dents and that was that whenever the boys spilled their drinks, clean-up was a snap. All liquids pooled to the center of each hollow.

We were in Japan for nearly four years before I found a real table. In the meantime, I was able to save a ton of money by not buying mops. All spilled stuff never once made it to the floor.

Another dining glitch was that there was very limited space for any table in our postage stamp of a kitchen. Only one tight corner was available. It was the place where the low-ceilinged kitchen met the equally low-ceilinged living room. A narrow transom created a dividing line delineating the two spaces. At the top of it, on the kitchen side, was a narrow shelf running eight inches down from the ceiling, and not visible from the living room. The shelf served as an out-of-sight storage area, acutely needed in our cramped home. My designated seat at the table was the only one directly under this shelf.

As we were eating dinner one night, I commented on my food having a peculiar taste. No one else found a problem with their dinner, so I ignored it. It happened again the next evening, and then the next. Each time I complained, the other three answered that nothing was amiss. Finally on the fifth day, when I could no longer tolerate the vile stuff on my plate, I asked them all to pause for a moment, concentrate, and see if anything didn't have a particularly off flavor. Glen and the boys—followed, of course, by Bob and Karen who were benevolently finishing off the boys' meal—found everything tasty as usual.

I glared at the group in disbelief. There they sat enjoying their food, while I felt myself descending into a blue funk of a hole, cogitating over whether or not I had turned into that rain-soaked Green Park ne'er-do-well who believed misfortune fell only upon her!

Why was it that my food alone was so horrible; really deplorably ghastly inedible? What was going on? For a moment I considered a psychiatric appointment at the Green Park Dispensary, but decided that in all the other areas of my life, I was pretty darned stable; even well adjusted. It didn't matter, anyway, because there was no taste bud specialist at the Green Park Dispensary. Thus, I soldiered on.

"Roses are red, violets are blue,
I'm a schizophrenic,
and so am I."
Frank Crow

During the second week of my plight, I, by chance, decided to clean the storage shelf above the table. As I dusted my way across it, I came upon a 3-in-1 All Purpose Oil can. It was lying on its side. The tip of the spout was hanging over the edge of the shelf and there was no cap. As I stared at it, one gleaming brown blob of oil dripped down to the table, precisely into the valley designated for my plate. Hellooo! Earth to Peggy! Don't tell me that greasy guitar guy on the bus back at Travis Air Force Base had followed us here!

Now, it's been said that the only tools a person really needs in this world are all purpose oil and duct tape. It's like this: if it doesn't move and it should, use the oil. If it shouldn't move and it does, use the tape. But, take my word for it, if it's meant to be consumed, use neither, or at least not the 3-in-1 Oil. As for the tape, I didn't know. I hadn't tried it yet. What I did know, indisputably, was that all-purpose oil and dinner made a contemptible mix. Sitting here now, all these years later, I realize there just may have been a silver lining to ingesting all-purpose oil. It might explain why today I have so few creaky joints.

As I continued to watch that shiny blob dissolve on the table, so too did my psychosis. It was pretty obvious to me that David Thoreau must have had a similar shelf over his plate for he knowingly professed:

"Some circumstantial evidence
is very strong,
like when you find
a trout in your milk."

THIRTY-EIGHT

EVERY NIGHT, AS all good moms do, I checked on our boys before going to bed. One such evening, things did not go as usual. That night, as I quietly raised myself up on my tiptoes to peer at four-year-old Jeff sleeping on his top bunk, he looked like his usual self: an alabaster angel enfolded in cowboy sheets. Then I bent deeply over into the bottom bunk to peer at two-and-a-half-year-old Matt. He looked like … what in the world? I looked again.

Darn! It was so hard to see; so hard in the darkness of the cavernous cubicle to make out his face. A third examination. Good Lord! The little boy in that bed was not mine! That boy belonged to someone else's mother! Who was he?

But, that child who was not mine *was mine*! Or at least he must have been because why else would he be in Matt's bed? Moving in for a closer scrutiny, I realized his head was half again as large as Matt's and his face looked distressingly like an inflamed navel. Furthermore, his lips protruded like those of a short Ubangi, his nose mimicked my friend's sweet potato dinner guest, and his alarmingly bloated, tightly sealed eyelids ballooned out like twin miniature bottoms sitting sideways. I screamed for Glen!

(For what it is worth, I have always screamed for Glen as a first immediate reaction to any emergency whether he is in the next room, downstairs, outside, at work, in another country—or not any of the above. It doesn't matter. It's just what I do.)

Breathless, and as scared as we had ever been, Glen and I stared down at the little stranger in the bed. Poor child! He looked like someone had hooked him up to an automatic tire pump and then in a fit of forgetfulness, gone off to a movie. I slowly and very apprehensively pulled him onto my lap searching for anything familiar that would tell me this child was ours. His ears, now huge and puffy, had collapsed upon themselves from the weight of their swelling. No beautiful blue eyes fluttered open in recognition of me, for in their tumescent state, it was impossible for the lids to open. And, no sound came from the Ubangi lips.

But, even though his face was unrecognizable, two things were clear: the sweetness of his familiar smell and the intimate feel of his sturdy body. Both told me this was our Matt. Panicked, I shouted at Glen to run over and get Karen. Karen was a nurse. Karen would know what to do.

Within minutes a winded, night-gowned Karen came leaping up the stairs and into the bedroom. She took one look at Matt and let out a gasp. Then she did a full body once over, turned, and ran down the stairs and out the front door. Holy cow, had Karen been taking auxiliary training from that excitable and inept Florence at the Green Park Dispensary?

Only one house in Asahi Court had a telephone. Karen sprinted to that house. She pounded on the door awakening the startled Japanese occupants who, coincidentally, were the same ones who used all that Kleenex on nights very much like this one.

"The phone, the phone," yelled Karen, "this is an emergency!"

Inside their door (carefully stepping around the moist tissues strewn about the floor), she dialed Tachikawa Air Force Hospital. When a nurse answered, Karen told her we were on our way and that *a doctor should be at the emergency room door to meet us!*

Of course, I didn't know what Karen was saying, nor did I know the way in which she was saying it. I was at home mewling over my son. Had I been aware of her urgent directive, I would have been doubly alarmed; as if such a thing were possible.

I gathered up Matt while Glen sprinted out to get the car. Karen stayed behind with Jeff. Clutching my baby to me, we tore through the blackness of the night on the long, never-ending, nerve-racking drive to Tachikawa.

Per Karen's instructions, a doctor was waiting for us at the emergency door. Upon seeing Matt, he was as aghast as we had been, and as equally mystified as to the cause. Eliminating possible diseases one by one, it could only be one thing the doctor concluded. An allergic reaction. But, allergic to what? None of us had allergies.

Glen and I were then assigned the urgent task of remembering everything out of the ordinary that Matt had done before going to bed. Our minds raced through the evening's events. For starters, Matt had watched Glen bathe, or at least attempt to bathe in that poor excuse for a bathtub. As Glen dried himself off and applied deodorant, Matt asked if he could have some, too. Glen affably swiped a dab under each chubby arm.

Deodorant! Was that the culprit? But, hang on. There was also the package Glen had brought home that evening from the army post office. Grandma Keener had sent each boy a cowboy outfit. Naturally the boys immediately wanted to wear them, so we had complied. Maybe it was the dye in the new clothes? Other than those two things—plus knowing the oil can cover was screwed on tight—no matter how hard we struggled, we could think of nothing new added to the evening's mix.

With a stern face, the doctor warned that if this kind of reaction ever happened again, it could be fatal. But, what was the culprit? What were we supposed to be aware of?

We left the hospital assured of nothing.

Back home, just as the sun was trying for another day to pierce through the perpetual layer of pollution over Tokyo, I tucked Matt into his bed. This new day would be long, full of speculation and worry. As the first weak stream of sunlight sliced through the part in the bedroom curtains, I could see some of the swelling had diminished. The medicine the doctor had given Matt was working. His eyes were still shut and his ears still folded over, but, yes, there was improvement.

Gradually, very gradually throughout that day and the next, Matt's face returned to us. As it did, something weird happened; something equally as strange as the swelling. I first noticed it on Matt's hands. Thin, bright, red lines that looked as if they had been scribbled with multiple ball point pens began appearing on his fingers.

I pulled up his pajama sleeves to check his arms. To my fright, they were both also covered with hundreds of squiggly red ink lines, as were his feet and legs and back and tummy and face and neck! I parted Matt's hair to discover hundreds more doodles covering his head. My baby looked like a road map of Iowa!

Mason City was just under his second chin, Des Moines somewhere left of his navel, and Ottumwa appeared to be heading straight inside the waistband of his pajamas. I tried to connect them to make sense of it all, but my lack of navigational skills stopped me in the vicinity of Davenport.

There was no explanation for these squiggles. For all I knew, maybe this is what happened to things like tires after they were blown up and then deflated. But, we'd never know because tires were so black that we couldn't see if they had any red lines. Besides, they kept turning around and around and it made us dizzy. Or maybe basketballs and balloons had them, but we didn't know because we never looked inside them because we couldn't see inside them?

For three more days Matt was the spitting image of a Rand-McNally Road Atlas. Thank goodness he was too short to see his reflection in the one mirror we had, as it would have scared the living daylights out of him. Poor, puffed-up dumpling!

Thankfully, in time, all Matt's parts shrank to their proper sizes, and the cartography on his epidermis faded. His ears flipped back up to alert mode, his nose shrank to baby button proportions, his blue eyes popped open, and Rand McNally faded into oblivion. Our beautiful boy returned. To this day, it all remains a mystery.

And, if truth be told, Iowa has, as well, remained a mystery.

"Young people are more hopeful at a
certain age than adults, but I suspect
it's glandular. As for children, I keep
as far away as possible. I don't like the
sight of them. The scale is all wrong. The
heads tend to be too big for the bodies,
and the hands and feet are a disaster.
They keep falling into things. The nakedness
of their bad character! We adults have
learned how to disguise our terrible
character, but children, well, they are
like grotesque drawings of us! They
should be neither seen nor heard, and
no one must make another one!"
Gore Vidal

THIRTY-NINE

DURING OUR SECOND year in Japan, quite on a lark, I was invited to tour a Japanese TV studio. It sounded fun; a break from my habitual hausfrau days. Oddly enough, Joan Olson, a friend of mine from Austin, whose husband was in the Air Force, worked there. She was about to finish her job and wondered if I might be interested in taking over her position. With my curiosity being way stronger than my work qualifications, I agreed to the tour. But, certainly not the job! It didn't matter, anyway, because there was no way on earth I could pull off something like that.

With this now decided, I hopped on a commuter train bound for the heart of downtown Tokyo. I was heading for NHK, the government owned TV network, much like our present day American National Public Television.

> "If it weren't for
> Philo T. Farnsworth,
> inventor of the television,
> we'd still be eating
> frozen radio dinners."
> Johnny Carson

I was greeted in the lobby by the program's directors. They were outrageously polite, guiding me down assorted hallways and opening doors here and there, while giving brief, but thorough, explanations of each room. Then all of a sudden they upped the speed, catching me completely off guard, and briskly whisked me through a door, firmly shutting it behind me. The entire maneuver happened in a heartbeat. Before I could catch my breath, I was ushered onto a set in front of a bunch of cameras and lights, and a script was shoved into my hands. I was to read it. I was to act it. I was to make my first program!!

What, for the love of Mike, had just happened? Wasn't I on tour here?

So, what did I do? Well, I, the ever-obedient Peggy, Peggy Ridiculously Compliant Lady, did just as they requested. *Demanded!* I made my first program.

I still can't believe I did that; that my job started like that. For criminy sakes, I was as qualified for that position as a ham sandwich. Obviously the directors didn't agree. Little did I know that from the moment we met at the front door, they had already begun scrupulously checking me out from all microphone and camera angles.

Let's see, my flesh was warm and young, I had not a single black hair, my eyes were round and green, I really looked foreign, I spoke English, and … this was BIG! … I was shorter than Tazaki-san, the star of the show. All these factoids resolutely clinched the deal.

Suddenly a star—me!—was born, my Austin High School Thespian skills at last going to good use. Admittedly, I always suspected in my heart of hearts that there was a secret ingénue in me just waiting to spew, but who could have guessed it would happen like this, with no warning? And, in Japan, at that! I had been swept off my feet, my life changing in the flash of a camera, and I hadn't even had to break a leg. Maybe, just maybe, this might be a really cool job. Like hadn't I heard just the other day that television was even more interesting than people? I believed it, for if it were not so, someone had said, we would have people standing in the corners of our living rooms.

> "The top TV shows in Russia are
> "Bowling for Food" and
> "Wheel of Torture."
> Yakov Smirnoff

The year was 1963, and the Prime Minister was Hayato Ikeda, a man with eyes glued to the future. The way Ikeda-san saw things, Japan would never be a true player in the world until its citizens wrote and spoke correct English, Seiko *Matches* being a good example of what not to do. This is not to say that the people of Japan did not know English, for they did. It was, after all, a required course in all junior and senior high schools. Unfortunately, the Japanese teachers of English did not *speak* English. This left the students with only marginal reading and writing skills, neither of which was conducive to an easy flow of meaningful international discourse—or another way of putting it (plus a whole lot more fun)—meaningful international intercourse.

Upon learning this, I immediately understood the eagerness which had been so explicitly demonstrated by the man in the sushi shop urinal when he glommed onto me. Of course! I had been a sudden, unexpected windfall-of-an-English-speaking opportunity right there at his (and my) wet splattered feet! How often did that happen to a guy—a guy in a urinal?

Prime Minister Ikeda's educational plan was sweeping. It involved the entire country; all ages, no one left out. And what better way to reach the multitudes than through national TV? It was a masterful concept. Furthermore, Ikeda-san knew the always dutiful Japanese subjects would obey him. They did.

The program was a sweeping success. The viewers, shy and unsure in public, were able to practice their pronunciation in the privacy of their own non-public homes, away from the critical ears of others who, in all honesty, were as equally shy and unsure. It all made good sense. I mean what realistic person would put himself out there like that—a sacrificial lamb on the language chopping block to be castigated by English elocution bullies—when help was so close at hand? Only a twist of the TV dial and fluency could be theirs. Privacy was the key.

We aired the programs three times a week in prime time evening hours. The public loved it. They could hear real English from a real live native speaker (me) spoken slowly and correctly, with accompanying explanations by Professor Tazaki (one of their own) who unraveled the elocution mysteries of it all. There was no embarrassment over trying to twist their reticent, nonmalleable mouths into unfamiliar configurations, because no one saw them; their ever-important Asian faces clandestinely saved. And what could be better, I ask, than being saved clandestinely, with no one knowing or, for that matter, caring?

The two main actor/teachers in each program were Tazaki-san (supremely qualified), and me who you will remember was the supremely unqualified ham sandwich. Unqualified, that is, except for that big deal of my being shorter than the qualified professor, thereby not making him look like a dwarf, which would have looked unmanly for the English-speaking-spokesman for Japan's newly promised, freshly budding international relations. My job was to speak and act out all the English lines, while Tazaki-sensei (sen-say, teacher), translated. All the scripts were printed in textbook form, mimicking the size and thickness of a *Reader's Digest*, and could be purchased weekly at bookstores or mailed by subscription directly to the viewers. In their own private space, students followed along with us at home as we acted out the skits on the TV screen. Covert linguistic harmony.

It is interesting to note how history later regarded Prime Minister Ikeda. He was considered the single most important figure in Japan's rapid post-war growth; the man who pulled together a national consensus for economic expansion. His overall plan was to double the GNP over a ten-year span, but under his direction, in only five years the average growth climbed to an astounding 11.6 percent. It is, as well, interesting to learn that Ikeda-sans was prime minister from July 19, 1960 to December 8, 1960, again from December 8, 1960 to December 9, 1963, and finally from December 9, 1963 to November 9, 1964, in three consecutive, although not equally proportioned, terms. Nine months later he died. Hmmm, wonder why?

> "Being head of state is
> an extremely thankless job."
> Bokassa, the 1st
> (spoken by the former Emperor of the
> Central African Republic
> while on trial for infanticide,
> cannibalism, and torture.)

Most of the time—except for those times when I reflect upon our current U.S. imbalance of trade with Japan—I am pleased with the small part I may have played in Japan's international success. Of course, I'll never know for sure, but I have to wonder just how much credit I deserve for the astounding growth of Japanese businesses abroad. Or should I, on the other hand, be publicly chastised, flogged, tarred and feathered because companies, the likes of Toyota and Honda, now monopolize the American car market *with negotiations carried out in flawless Minnasootah-accented English*?

Trust me when I say that back in 1963, who knew the impact our TV lessons might have? Gosh, was I like that tiny butterfly who gets credit for the "butterfly effect?" You know, where one imperceptible action—in this case the fluttering of her wings in a remote jungle in Africa—begin a broad chain of events which end up becoming a hurricane in Texas? And because this took place in Japan, would that make me a sort of business rendition of Madame Butterfly? Or, was I only the butter part?

All of our TV programs were shot straight through, with no stopping, on regular movie film. There were no reruns to correct mistakes which now makes me aghast all over again at the filming of that first program! Only two other foreigners before me had held this job: my friend Joan and somebody before her who we weren't sure about. The policy was to change the woman every six months so the audience could be exposed to different accents. A Midwest accent was considered ideal … as if anyone in the entire Japanese broadcasting system could have told the difference.

> "The human race is faced
> with a terrible choice:
> work or day-time television."
> Unknown

Joan, being of average American height (making her, in the Japanese eyes, roughly equal to a lady Amazon), must have sparked some significant insecurities in the diminutive Tazaki-sensei. Conversely, my short stature hit the mark, allowing his confidence to once again soar. I suppose he could have looked taller if he had gone the route of some of the other stars of the big screen—like Alan Ladd who used to stand on a box. Or Tazaki-san could have simply waited for human growth hormones. But, then I suppose, that would have meant a delay of another thirty years in which time he would have grown old and even more shriveled, thereby resulting in his contract being canceled because who wanted to watch an old, shriveled, three-foot-tall TV star speaking English—even though it *was* correct?

You have to wonder just what compensating tricks the famous have had to contrive to appear normal? Like John Wayne who struggled with pernicious hemorrhoids. Certainly explained why he walked that way.

As Tazaki-sensei stood beside me, he appeared virile and macho, just short of hairy-chested. Gazing up at his five-foot-three-inches—soaring above my five-foot-two-inches—nearly caused me a whip lash! Whoa, if I weren't careful, this job could be dangerous. Additionally, there was also that other problem: my name. Because Glen worked in a highly sensitive, top secret clearance, U.S. Intelligence job, I could not appear on camera as Mrs. Glen Keener. In fact, I could have no media connection to him whatsoever. At least that was his story and he was sticking to it.

Therefore I reverted back to using my maiden name, becoming Peggy McLaughlin-san. "San" meant any of the following: Mr., Mrs. or Miss, leaving the viewing audience baffled, but assuming that I was probably single. In their admiring eyes, I appeared as young, spouseless and pure as … well, Doris Day. (Hmmm, I wonder just how fourteen-carat pure she and her pageboy hairdo were, anyway? Hadn't Oscar Levant revealed that he knew her *before* she was a virgin?) I didn't think Oscar had told Japan about this, so I tried to be Doris for my fans, leaving out some of that over-the-top perkiness of hers, which was, frankly, just plain exhausting.

For close to three years I worked at this job. Everything went along smashingly, actually an unprecedented longevity record for the female star of the show. This all came to a near screeching halt, however, when I became pregnant with our third child. At first there was no cause for alarm—a wee bump of an abdomen easily disguised on the television screen by a strategically placed World Atlas. But then as I became more—and then progressively more misshapen—the NHK alarm bells began to clang. Such a shameful display of what I, Doris the Chaste, did on my time off being intolerably unacceptable. Cripes! If word of my fecundity got out, the world of TV English lessons would be rocked; the virtuous students shaken to their delicate cores.

As with all progressive things, overnight it seemed, my fruitfulness became alarmingly obvious. Just like that I'd gone from the sweet Minnesota-girl-next-door to the eight-hundred-pound gorilla in the studio. The NHK directors were barely able to control their twitchy antsy-pantsedness. They knew, oh, how they knew, that a not-so-fine kettle of fish was brewing, and they were it! Something had to be done about the pariah that Peggy had become, and it needed to be done before the reputation of the whole network was in question. In Japan, pregnant women stayed home. Now, here was one on display for the whole country to see! How, for crying out loud, were they going to cover up for the recreational pastime of their campy-slut-bottom-feeder-of-a-knocked-up-preggers-English-teacher?

> "She's the kind of girl
> who climbed up
> the ladder of success
> wrong by wrong."
> Mae West

While NHK stewed, the show, like all good theatre, went on. This left the weight of the predicament on the camera men, three guys now living on belly-avoidance tenterhooks. I proved to be their biggest challenge to date. If they forgot and went lax for even one second, the jig was up, for their drooping lenses would slide to my sub-bosom where the proof of my slatternly ways was in the pudding.

> "I used to be
> Snow White,
> but I drifted.
> Mae West

In the very beginning of my pregnancy, when there was only a slight possibility of the TV audience noticing (bless them and their abiding faith in my virginity), replacement lenses were easily adjusted to focus solely on my upper torso. And, if push came to shove, I could be filmed from a posterior angle. But late into the second trimester, matters took a decided twist when my burgeoning hormonal boobies blossomed. Kaboom! (Actually it was kaboom-kaboom!!) From there the consternation intensified as now there were three protrusions to avoid. Just like that, non-negotiable circumstances demanded that every camera angle, from that moment on, be shot only from my throat up, and not one centimeter lower.

In the end, much to everyone's relief, I took a leave of absence, bowing out of the job just about the time I could no longer bow.

> "Every morning I get up
> and look through
> the Forbes list
> of the richest people
> in America.
> If I'm not there,
> I go to work."
> Robert Orben

FORTY

THE VERY SWINGING Professor Kiyotada Tazaki was the most hip Japanese man I ever met. To keep up with all the happenings in the West, he made annual pilgrimages to America and Europe. There he gleaned fodder for his TV English lessons. But, he did not contain his coolness only to his professional life. No, his universal savoir-faire leached into all areas. For example, he named his children Mary and George. It was unheard of! Akin to a family in Austin naming their children Shizue and Kazuhiko!

To say the least, Tazaki-sensei was the ultimate avant-garde man. Thereby, it blew me away one day when upon visiting his home, he showed me his mother's umbilical cord trunk. Yes, you heard me right. Umbilical cord trunk! To my astonishment, there inside the trunk were the tangled, shriveled, twisty cords of all her children, plus all the generations of Tazaki children before them. Each desiccated vinculum was carefully packaged in rice paper, and labeled in jet-black, hand-ground calligraphy ink with the child's name.

Shall I give you a moment?

Okay, so that's a little on the icky side, I'll grant you, but you have to understand that in the Japanese society where in so many ways women were held not *on* a pedestal, but rather *beneath* it, this was the mothers' undeniable proof of their indispensability. Don't you see? Women held the power of propagation: the fertility-ability to reproduce themselves. Why, without females and their fruitful urns of prolificacy, how could the beloved

Nippon Empire continue? Each and every womb, by god, was important, and the owners of those wombs had the navel cord trunks to prove it!

> "My obstetrician was so dumb
> that when I gave birth
> he forgot to cut the cord.
> For a year that kid
> followed me everywhere.
> It was like having
> a dog on a leash."
> Joan Rivers

I'm guessing, and this is only a guess, that after enough centuries had passed, the packages and their contents must have turned to dust, making them bogus belly button bundles, to say nothing of the dread of sneezing upon them and mixing things up! But, then, who was checking?

Furthermore, I don't know if this practice of umbilical cord hoarding is still done today. Perhaps so, and now they simply call it icky scrap booking. But, I can tell you that when my baby was born in Japan, I didn't need a trunk. I already knew how indispensable I was.

FORTY-ONE

BACK WHEN I was still employed at NHK-TV, a sleek, black, highly polished sedan with a uniformed chauffeur drove me to and from the studio twice a week. It was shamelessly rhapsodic—and not a little ironic—to see such a glamorous, hot shot ride glide up to my scruffy duplex door. The motorcar would float to a stop, then the immaculately black-hatted, white-gloved chauffeur would alight onto the gravel driveway and immediately begin dusting off the roof and fenders for any accumulated dust particles that had dared to settle upon its gleaming surfaces. This he did with a gigantic two-and-a half-foot long feather duster contoured into the shape of a morbidly obese caterpillar. When the dusting was accomplished to his satisfaction, he next adjusted the blindingly white cotton seat covers, making sure the pleated ruffle-edged seams lay exactly in place. I felt as if the hand of Buddha had baptized me every time I set my fanny down on one of those pristine back seats.

Driving through the hideous traffic for the two hours it took to get to Tokyo, and then later during the two hours to get me back home, was a very inefficient way to transport me, but just the same, I greatly appreciated it. In our hopelessly small, hopelessly busy, hopelessly crowded duplex, there was little opportunity for me to learn my lines without interruption. Thus the backseat of the classy dust-free sedan served as not only my luxury transportation, but also my rolling office, rehearsal stage, and green room.

No one at NHK had ever seen, verily ever dreamed of seeing, anybody as white as I am white. The makeup people were at a complete loss as to how to do me up. Nothing in their arsenal of cosmetics had someone like me in mind. In the end, when every bit of pancake makeup had been tried and found wanting, there was nothing left to do but use that same pancake makeup that had been tried and found wanting.

In the beginning, each time they were finished (and I was done for!), I walked onto the set sporting an astonishingly authentic Mexican complexion. Through the magic of their cosmetic sponges, I had been turned into Carmen Miranda, unencumbered by the fruit salad hat. This would have been okay except that the Carmen part of me ended at exactly my jawbone. From that point down, I was my regular old translucent self. It's good the camera men did not favor up-close jawbone shots (which later, as you know, they got real good at), or the TV audience would have wondered at the sharply pied and compartmentalized skin tones of Caucasians.

As you can guess, changing my racial identity like that on a regular basis was a bit unnerving. But, even that did not bug me as much as what the NHK makeup crew did to my eyebrows. Now, I wasn't sure just how important eyebrows had been historically to the Japanese, but I was thinking not very. One strong hint was the way the geisha (gay-sha) painted over their eyebrows with white pasty stuff, and then applied only a single black dot to each center tip. Perhaps they were making the first in the history of mankind protest against the uni-brow, because believe me I had noticed plenty of those out on the streets. But, then, what did I know? Call me callous, but I'd take bushy arches any day over dots.

My unrest stemmed from my really liking eyebrows. Eyebrows were important to me. For gosh sakes, they were one of the few points of color in my otherwise bloodless face. Therefore it was important to me that folks saw them. But, then, I was also in Rome, remember? Enter the Papal NHK cosmetologists. Invariably, the first thing they did was brush over each eyebrow with some thick, butterscotch-colored powder which, at a pretty penny, NHK had specially mined, I was pretty sure, from the tombs of Montezuma.

When they finished, there was absolutely no defining hue, other than my two green eyes, left on my face. This, lamentably, was not particularly good news because in the Japanese culture, the scariest of all creatures is the obake (oh-bah-kay), or ghost. Guess what color eyes it has? Yup, you got it! Green as parsley. Green as mine.

Following the blanching of my eyebrows came the combing of them. Straight down onto my eyelids. Blessedly for the cosmetologists, the Montezuma gunk held each hair there firmly in place. Now, I'm not sure how you look when a cosmetologist does that to you, but I can tell you that I looked like I had a long-haired guinea pig hanging down into each eye, their pelts entangled in my eyelashes. How crazy dazzling was that? If you can believe this, it was the very thing I had dreamed of since earliest childhood! You know, to be a Miranda impersonator on national TV while two hairball rodents played footsy with my eyes! Was there any end to my good fortune?

But, harrumph! I didn't take the image lightly. As I, week after week, stumbled blindly down the hall from the makeup room to the studio all dolled up in my new image, I flagrantly and steadfastly flipped my guinea pig eyebrows back up to their rightful places, restoring my dignity—and my vision.

> "Eating an anchovy
> is like eating
> an eyebrow."
> Unknown

One day as I walked into the studio, Tazaki-sensei handed me a script. He told me it included a part for a young child and wondered if I thought our almost but not quite four-year-old Jeff could handle the job.

> "Never miss a chance
> to have sex
> or appear on television."
> Gore Vidal

This particular skit was designed to teach the kind of Basic English a person would need in a barber shop. I would be the mother, the professor would be the hair cutter, and the child would be the hair cuttee.

Well, of course, Jeff could do it I let him know in no short order! I wasn't about to let any son of mine miss out on an opportunity like that. Why, to spread my children's splendor over the Far East was my sacred mission; my original intent, remember? Besides, we'd both remain cleverly under wraps as far as Glen's delicate job was concerned, because no one in the vast viewing audience, except for our neighbors, would know that Jeff was birthed by me, or that I was married to Glen, or that—forced into it by the Army Intelligence folks—Jeff claimed neither of us as his parents. It was that simple.

Two days later with young Jeff in tow, we arrived at NHK in the sleek, black sedan. Not surprisingly, right off the bat his darlingness shattered the NHK cute meter. Furthermore, the crew was incredulous over his snow white hair. Those endowments, however, were just the beginning. When Jeff opened his mouth and perfect Japanese flowed out, the men were flabbergasted! It absolutely flew in the face of Jeff's Caucasian-ness. My boy, it was turning out, was a delightful aberration of nature. To hear their language spoken as flawlessly as they themselves spoke it, and have it come out of that little chalky face, was too much. It pulled the tatami mats right out from under their sense of sanctified sameness.

After considerable exaltation (to which I, in no way, objected), the directors got down to business. Jeff, they explained, had no lines, but rather needed to only sit in the barber chair and be effervescently opalescent and charming. Meanwhile, Sensei and I were to slowly and carefully enunciate our lines while acting out the skit behind Jeff. Piece o'cake!

In our zeal to get our words and actions executed perfectly, neither Tazaki-sensei nor I paid one bit of attention to Jeff.

Each skit was always performed three times: the first time very slowly followed by a translation of its English into Japanese, the second time a tad faster with fewer explanations, and the third time the big kahoona of a graduation—along with any remaining complicated elucidation. The day's filming ended with great satisfaction, everyone in the crew highly pleased with the splendid outcome; even better than they had hoped for. As for me, my maternal hide was quivering in tickly waves; the kind of visceral assurance only a mother can understand knowing the fruit of her loins has done it again.

With the filming now ended and the amazing performance in the can, I was barely able to contain my ecstasy. This was a really momentous, highfalutin' big deal—my firstborn on national TV! The crew gathered around Jeff, praising him to kingdom come. Since Glen could have nothing to do with it, I humbly took all the credit for the ovulating, fertilizing, birthing and raising of Jeff. Gosh, even before the cameras took their last footage, I was already unwavering in my commitment to not let anyone I knew escape without seeing Jeff in the performance of his young life. And, hey, Nippywood had better get their polishing mitts out and start buffing up Jeff's Oscar—or whatever it was called in Japan. Oscar-san?

With my plan fully in place, two evenings later I ushered the neighboring duplex folks into our postage stamp of a living room, the floor plan of which these guests were all too familiar, seeing as how it was identical to theirs. Everyone was atwitter, although I do think my twitter out-twittered theirs. How exciting it was for these humble folk to live so close to a budding star. This was their own personal brush with fame. Golly sakes, not one, but now two TV personalities could be called duplex neighbors!

The group clustered around our TV and instantly hushed as the show began ... or wait ... was this when I threatened them with my broom? No matter, the theme music diminished as the first scene opened. There on the black and white screen flashed Jeff sitting obediently in the barber chair, while Sensei and I began our best Hollywood renderings behind him. I could have swooned. Jeff looked so cooperative and flawless that I couldn't have been prouder, my only regret being that I wasn't able to share his quintessence with the rest of the world—including all of Europe, the Middle East and the African states. Oh, also Antarctica and the North Pole. But ... did Eskimos have TV reception in their igloos? Okay, skip them.

As the group watched, the first English skit finished followed by the usual long explanation in Japanese. During that time there was nothing for Jeff to do but wait for the second skit. I doubt he was aware of exactly what was going on around him. All he knew was that he was to stay put in the barber chair. His mom had said so.

> "If a child shows himself
> to be incorrigible, he should be
> decently and quietly beheaded
> at the age of twelve lest he
> grow to maturity, marry,
> and perpetuate his kind."
> Don Marquis

As Sensei and I performed the second skit, Jeff made a discovery. Wow, a TV monitor! Like pepper to mint, he was immediately drawn to it. What he saw was a really fancy mirror that reflected back to him all that was going on especially all that was going on with him. As any almost-four-year-old does in front of a mirror, he became fascinated with his own face and how remarkable it looked up there on the big screen. First he raised one eyebrow, let it back down, then raised the other. Golly, moving them was certainly more entertaining than sitting still in a dumb old barber's chair.

And, would you look at that! A nose! Well, wonder of wonders, it also moved! In fact, one side could be lifted while the other remained still. Or they could take turns! And get a load of the size of those orifices! Why, Jeff gasped internally (so as not to noncompliantly burst out externally), I can make them big! Really big flaring nose holes! Audacious!

At this point, the cameras switched from Jeff to Tazaki-sensei and me who by now were seated on a different set, each at a desk, and each explaining the script word by word to the viewing audience. Completing that, the two of us once again moved back to the barber shop set, stood behind Jeff, and repeated the skit for the third and final time.

Nearly thirty minutes had by now passed and Jeff was consumed with the twitches. It was unnatural, verily I say impossible—not even in the cards!—for a little child to sit still that long.

I noticed that the neighbors in our living room were no longer looking or listening to Sensei and me, but rather were fully concentrating, focusing, glued entirely on Jeff. You know what they say about kids and dogs? Why, that little pint-sized-opalescent-haired-perfect-Japanese-linguist-of-a-ham was stealing our show!

It seemed that at this point in the production, Jeff's two big discoveries—the raising of the eyebrows and the flaring of the nostrils—had swiftly grown tame, children's focuses being the fleeting wisps that they are. Now with the fresh taste of exploration fueling his curiosity, Jeff was prodded on to root out even more treasures. His eyes slid down to his cheeks. There to his great amusement he learned that they could be elevated by simply raising the lips ... which then showed the teeth ... which then showed the tongue.

The tongue!

Clearly the tongue was the most intriguing, inextricably captivating body part yet! All blown up to gigantic proportions on the TV monitor, it looked glorious, like a living, writhing slice of luncheon meat! Why, up until that moment, Jeff had had no idea his tongue could be mockingly wiggled up and down, side to side, in and out. Who knew a kid didn't need store bought toys? He'd sure have to keep that a secret come Christmas time.

"I knew I was an unwanted baby
when I saw
that my bath toys
were a toaster and a radio."
Joan Rivers

Jeff continued to ponder his reflection. What ... he wondered ... just what would it be like ... to combine all of the aforementioned face parts ... and join them in one orchestrated action? Why, it would be grand. Nothing short of spectacular! Oh, if only Matt were here to see the glory of it. And for sure he'd have to show Mommy and Daddy! Thus, with riveted concentration, all his muscular gesticulations were brought into play. He began first by flicking his eyebrows, then flaring both nostrils, and finally twisting the lips and tongue in snakelike grimaces. Whoo-hoo, this was great! Indeed, too entirely satisfyingly entertainingly wonderful to stop!

"A child is
a curly,
dimpled lunatic."
Ralph Waldo Emerson

From his extraordinary efforts, Jeff's face was now in a flush of pink bloom, all rosiness lost, of course, on our black and white TV screen. As the third and last skit wound down, his little boy face became a choreography of grimaces, smirks, jeers and sneers which altogether led up to the final facial climax where he lunged his entire upper body at the camera, his tongue poking out as far as he could possibly stretch it from his suddenly not so angelic face. Naturally, I hadn't had a clue that any of this was going on, but had I known about this nonsense—flying in the face of all that his mother had taught him about good behavior—I know I would have seen right then and there into Jeff's blighted future: a glimpse of my child getting free room and board at Rikers Island!

Perhaps, just perhaps, I should not have bred.

"I was going to buy a copy of
The Power of Positive Thinking,
and then thought:
What the hell good would that do?"
Ronnie Shakes

Jeff's contorted face and tongue were now frozen in mid-scowl. It was over-the-top glorious, as close to hog heaven as a kid could get! And to think he had accomplished it all without ever once getting out of the barber chair. Mommy would be so proud.

About that time, my living room combusted into hysterical laughter. People slapped their knees then slapped their neighbors, all the while howling their heads off with the delight of it all. Remember, I knew nothing about Jeff's shenanigans until I saw the show along with those folks. I was stunned. Our civilized program had somehow metamorphosed, flipped, twisted into something totally different from what we had intended. I was certainly no accomplice in the misconduct, and I was suddenly no longer a fan of this Jeff Fest!

My son, the Child Noir!

"All children
are essentially criminal."
Denis Diderot

As it turned out, had Tazaki-sensei and I *not* been so utterly oblivious to Jeff's antics, the show would *not* have been so funny. There the two of us were as serious as Billy Graham, prattling off our lines, while upfront Jeff's monkey business was hijacking the show. But rather than feeling elated, I was now all at once worried about my job. I felt a stinky cloud floating down from the performance, then settling upon my sense of TV-star well being. It was a good thing we didn't have smell-a-vision.

I dreaded the next time I would have to report to work, and the terrible confrontation I knew was waiting there with the directors. How could I explain my son's poor upbringing? And, what, God forbid, would Tazaki-san—the egregiously short, but still famous professor—have to say about being so up-staged?

To my relief, it turned out that everyone in the crew, *except Tazaki-san and me*, had known exactly what was going on. They had, of course, witnessed it all from the other side of the cameras. Furthermore, they were all in the same hog heaven as was Jeff over his natural, little boy performance. Wasn't it, after all, exactly how any young child—the world over—would have behaved in front of a mirror? What they originally thought would be a routine program, had turned into a slam dunk of a success, way better than anyone's wildest expectations.

Jeff was an overnight hit. As NHK's newest media darling, he received nearly as much fan mail from that one episode as I did in all the time I worked on TV. As the producers satiated him with their indulgence, he had every right to be jaded, even though he didn't understand any of it.

"Babies on television
never spit up
on the Ultrasuede."
Erma Bombeck

FORTY-TWO

AS I SAID, Jeff was fluent in Japanese. Of course, he was. It was inevitable. A few months before his third birthday, we had enrolled him in the local nursery school, Musashino Chuo Yochien, only a fifteen-minute walk from Asahi Court. With children's brains being the oozy sponges that they are, and not needing complex compound sentences to get their points across, it only took about one week before Jeff could say everything he needed to say. Little did I know that yochien (yo-che-en, nursery school), would become such a cultural education for Jeff ... and for me.

Twice daily I walked to school to deliver and retrieve Jeff. As I passed by the tiny houses that were butted up against the dirt-packed road, it was a perfect built-in excuse to *peer in their front doors*! Honest, I tried not to, but ... well, okay, so I didn't. But, see, I couldn't stop myself. It wasn't my fault. Those houses were right there next to the road. My shoulders literally brushed past them leaving scratches on their doors, while their doors scraped up my shoulders. Okay, a bit of an exaggeration, but you get the point. I was close. I had to look!

Peggy, Peggy Can't Help It Peeping Tom Lady.

The first thing that one always saw upon entering a Japanese home was the genkan (geng-kahn, a diminutive entry where all the shoes were removed). One step up from there onto the wooden main floor and you were inside the building. The houses were dinky and constructed of very old untreated cedar. One main room functioned as the living-and-everything-else room. Its compact simplicity made me realize that our plain, four-room (plus closet and bathroom), gray concrete, two-story duplex must have seemed stately to our neighbors. More than anything, I grasped how our home set *us* starkly apart from *them*. In every respect—physical, material, cultural and philosophical—we were an enclave of "different" in the midst of their unmitigated sameness.

> "There is no they,
> only us."
> (bumper sticker)

Being different was the most dreaded of all possible states in which the Japanese could find themselves. Nobody, but nobody, wanted to clash with the norm. The most strictly adhered to proverb in Japan was, "The nail that stands up, gets pounded down." In my way of thinking, that sounded like "only dead fish swim with the stream." But then that was me talking, not Japan.

In virtually every respect, the Japanese strived to blend in, in thought, appearance, word and deed. In time, when I was more certain of my cultural footing, I told them that we Americans went out of our way to be the nail that stood up. In fact, for many of us, our goal *was to be* different. Even Garry Trudeau agreed. "America is the only country in the world where *failing* to promote yourself is regarded as arrogant!" he said. Naturally, the Japanese never believed me, any more than they believed Garry. But then, they also didn't believe I was the same height as them, even in some cases shorter. There was no way I could be shorter, they argued—even as they measured me to find out it was true—because I was an American. In the face of such screwy logic, there was no point in my trying to convince them of anything.

> "Logic is
> in the eye
> of the logician."
> Gloria Steinem

Forget about all the other philosophical variances that separated us, I believed this fear of individuality was the single most driving contradiction in our two cultures, and I never stopped learning how hopeless it was of our ever coming to an understanding of it. We were different from each other, and that was that.

I LEARNED JUST how strongly our differences were felt one day when I arrived home to find a crudely painted sign in bright red characters posted at the entrance to Asahi Court. Naturally, I had no idea what it said, but in my flaming naivete chose to believe it was an ad selling something, or a lovely spring poem shared by a neighborhood poet, or—why not—an entire neighborhood greeting of welcome? Therefore I was shocked, and not a little unnerved, to learn it demanded, "Go home, damn Yankees!"

It was a fine how-do-you-do.

As it was translated for me, the hairs on the back of my neck bolted upright. There was absolutely nothing opaque in its meaning. My stomach lurched in fear. Suddenly the lovely red calligraphy no longer looked as if it had been penned in ink, but rather in blood.

"There are more
of them
than us."
Herb Caen

Who said the school of hard knocks was an accelerated curriculum? Right then I felt as if I had been forcibly enrolled in a crash course in International Relations 101. The whole thing was so dumbfounding, so downright unfriendly. Didn't the neighbors know we were the Keeners, the really nice people? Gosh, having this happen for real—as opposed to reading it in a silly damn-Yankee cartoon back in Austin—was a whole other ball game. Lamentably, I now realized what blatant sitting ducks we were in this other world.

"All the people
who are like us
are We.
Everyone else
is They."
Rudyard Kipling

Clearly, I now realized that we were divided into two distinct camps. The sign made it evident that my family was unwelcome; definitely dwelling in the Camp of They. We, on the other hand, were the tiny group of We! It made my flesh creep. Not knowing who or where the artist—or artists!— were, I couldn't help but start looking over my shoulder. I figured it would not be as simple as watching out for someone carrying a brush and a can of red paint. And, it sure didn't help that I worked on national TV. I mean, could I in my innocence have broadcast our presence any louder? It was itchy butt time for sure!

Disappointedly it had come to this; my fears back in Austin now realized. The war *was* not over. In the moments, days, and weeks to come, I had a hard time wrapping my bonhomie around this gesture of ungoodwill. I realized that not everyone had been told about World War II ending ... and ending with a conspicuous clear-cut victory. Just because we, on the winning team, had adjusted to the outcome did not mean that they, the defeated, had also. To be sure, our efforts to be the amicable peacemakers, rather than the suppressive conquerors, were the very and whole reason we were now bending over backwards, striving to live in our former adversary's midst.

Unable to shake it off, I finally reached the consolation that perhaps this antagonistic gesture was the work of not a group, but rather one sole disgruntled native. Right, that must be it! In a twist of desire, it wasn't *us* he wanted out; it was *him* he wanted *in*! His only wish was to have us leave so he could move into one of Asahi Court's drab, cinderblock, tiny, two-storied duplexes! But because we were already there with a sealed multi-year lease, he couldn't move in. That had to be it. The guy's real problem was that he lacked diplomatic skills. His sign was his way of telling us he wanted to be neighbors. That was it! Well, wasn't it?

> "Diplomacy is no more possible
> than dry water
> or wooden iron."
> Josef Stalin

Or maybe I was just making too much out of one little old sign. What if it was as simple as this: our buttery scent was wafting down the street, in and out of his protesting olfactories, and he didn't do dairy?

In the end, I added it to the growing list of thorny vexations I had to deal with ... someday. Still, increasingly, things were feeling a little nippy outside.

The good news is that aside from this one demonstrative malcontent, whoever he was, the rest of the folks along the road treated us with kindly respect. Just the same, seeing us living next door must have been a resuscitated, painful reminder of Japan's failure, and I had to continually remind myself of this fact. Of course it couldn't be possible that everyone regarded us as welcome guests, even though I smiled till it hurt. Unable to work out a solution, I decided not to take it personally. We were like the smell of garlic; some found it irresistible, while others simply called it bad breath.

AFTER THAT INSIGHT, my fears were somewhat mitigated. Still I had to continually remind myself that I was only one very small fragment in the very big scheme of international things, and in my simple-mindedness, the only trick I knew for furthering global relations was to smile and be a nice person. It's a good thing it stopped there, too. Dabbling any deeper into world affairs that were way over my head would have been downright dangerous. This was dramatically brought to my attention by a letter I had recently read. Written a few years after the Occupation began, it was re-published in the Japan Times Newspaper. The letter was addressed to Douglas Mac Arthur:

Dear Dagrass MacKather,

Peggy Keener

Dear Sir!

Petition:

We named "No lie Party" has born at Numazu City, Shizuoka Prefecture, fine landscape the foot of picturesque Mr. Fuji. This party is consulting with Mayor and chief member of Public Peace Committee at Numazu or others, & on back of Numazu Christian Party. The members of "No lie Party" are not only Japanese, but foreigner at any province in his world as if "Rotary-Club" & make up friendship, to trade every and then exchange the tourist Party etc. The spirit is same as Christism, included personal or international love. At any rate now happens bloody affairs about every days & dark & darker and the statements or leads of our Government as if no effect & people put on unsafty, such anxious has begin to this plan.

We premirily, are not religionor or holyer & only business men, however must keep "lie no tell," holding good interview in members. This shall give great "Mesu" in Japan, if our idea can realize in world, visit eternal peace to every states & nonecessary. "Then International Legue of Peace," but such am idea not soon, so we wish get members, by & by, & larger & larger.

Can you permit this plan as one of your good conducts in now Japan? Please give us all approval & O.K. as soon as possible. We believe that this plan is big tock in Japan, if you please give us O.K.

"Notice" we think. In case permit colonize, such a circle shall be get specialy. "Bible" teach us. "The Lier shall get rewards in burn pond & sulphor." "Don't lie make up as like as real"! "Bat fellow & false is always together."

your is sincerely,
S. Shimada

All I could say was the silver tongued, say-it-like-it-is Shimada certainly had a way with words. It was no mystery why the No Lie Party had selected him to be their spokesman. Why, a loquacious cat like him, full of the gift of gab, could have talked his way out of a paper bag—after he talked himself into it. With only a few deftly turned phrases, he had masterfully delivered their ardent appeal.

Boy! Dagrass must have exhaled an enormous sigh of relief when he, the busy guy that he was, realized he would not need a translator for that supplication. No lie!

In the end, despite Shimada's heartfelt appeal, I feared there must have been a dearth of applicants for Rotary that year, to say nothing of the downturn in Christism.

"Aaeeeyaaayaaayaayaa ..."
Johnny Wiessmuller
(alias Tarzan)

FORTY-THREE

WAR BUSINESS ASIDE, the folks at Musashino Chuo Yochien seemed genuinely tickled pink (well, sort of a tawny yellow), to have Jeff enroll in their nursery school. It gave the principal, a lovely gentleman with an astonishingly perfectly orbed face, the spitting image of a khaki, suede-covered basketball, the chance to practice his you-know-what: Engrish convahsayshun.

Thrust in their midst, Jeff, was the spitting image of a shock of nature. In the school's sea of identically matched, bowl-coiffed, coal-haired, black-eyed students, there was no guess work as to whether or not he was one of them. One had to wonder, in that group of three-year-olds, just how differently the children actually saw Jeff. Surely it must have registered somewhere in their young, though not yet bigoted minds, that he was a full-blown, flaming oddball.

It brought to mind an incident that had occurred some weeks before when I took Jeff to the now infamous Green Park Dispensary. We'd had to wait thirty minutes before seeing the doctor. During that time only four of us—a mother, her son, Jeff and I—sat directly across from each other in the waiting room.

Oh, did I mention they were black? And we were not?

It was Jeff's first time to see black people at close range, if he had ever been aware of them before. We did, after all, live in Asia, not the Congo. I wondered what his three-year-old cognitive ability was cogitating. As I turned to look at him, I was startled to see that his blue eyes were fully

160

expanded in spherical mode. He was staring. Really staring! I held my breath for what might come out of his mouth.

Note: this happened before he had become the actual TV Child Noir ... but I had my suspicions.

In mid-hold, the dreaded happened. Jeff leaned over and whispered in my ear, "Mom, do you see that boy over there?"

"Ye-es," I replied hesitantly."

"That boy is an Indian."

Completely caught off guard by this observation, I stuttered, "H-h-how do you know th-a-at, Jeff?"

"It's easy," he informed. "I just heard him say 'ugh'!"

That got me thinking. Perhaps the yochien kids thought Jeff was an Indian, too, as I'm sure he, from time to time, also said "ugh." But, bless their pure, not-yet besmirched souls, they did not hold it against him. Like a potato in a rice bowl, he became instant friends with the other children. Within days, Jeff remolded himself into one of them ... except, of course, for the eyes, the nose, the hair, the skin, the parents, the citizenship, and the potato that he was.

I can tell you, it sure wasn't like I was any kind of guiding light for Jeff in the Negro department. Growing up in Austin hadn't helped. You see, Austin thought it didn't have a racial problem because no blacks lived there. What Austin didn't realize was that Austin *did* have a racial problem because no blacks lived there! To make matters worse, no blacks even wanted to live there. I was so out of the racial mainstream that I remember once seeing a little black boy (obviously outside of Austin), pulling up his shirt. I was shocked. He was black under there, too!

> "I'd rather be black than gay
> because when you're black,
> you don't have to tell
> your mother! "
> Charles Pierce

I asked—no, I pleaded—with the yochien principal and teachers not to treat Jeff differently because he was, well, different. Whatever was expected of the other children must also be expected of him. They agreed. Or at least I think they did.

> "We will march forward to a better tomorrow
> so long as separate groups like the
> blacks, the Negroes, and the coloreds
> can all come together
> to work out their differences."
> Steve Allen

To my surprise, overnight the nursery school became my social headquarters. I was swept into its tight community unaware. Like all the other mothers whose one and only social activity was yochien, it was now pretty much my only social activity, too. Actually, strike me dead, for that wasn't completely true. I was occasionally invited to glitzy, resplendent and even unreservedly gala military soirees, but the Japanese mothers didn't know that. I would have felt like an inveigling, carousing rotten-to-the-core-party-girl-cheat had they found out.

Born under a luckless social star, aside from the infrequent weddings or funerals (unless, of course, they were theirs, and that only happened once around, if you know what I mean), nursery school PTA was the solitary communal deal these women had. It was the whole shebang and their esprit de corps was staggering. Because of this, the women made the most of the opportunity to fling, for once their babies turned six, it was all over. Elementary school did not include moms. I soon found out that to attend monthly meetings, it was a PTA requisite to not only dress up in one's best duds, but to also rev up into one's wildest party mood. If a gal wanted to mingle with the sisterhood—and what gal in that social sea of loneliness didn't—it was PTA or bust! Of course, as was my destiny, I hadn't a clue about any of this; absolutely no inkling what a major landmark event PTA was until the day I went to my first meeting.

> "Partying …
> is such sweet sorrow."
> Robert Byrne

Following my usual fashion credo, I put on what I thought was an appropriate Parent Teachers Association outfit (all parts complementing the others), applied my makeup (a modest dab here, another there), and contrived every last one of my hairs into a perfect coif (which took some doing in those high humidity days before hair spray). I felt good and ready to face the mothers, none of whom I knew. My confidence was bubbling. After all, this time I knew the difference between "kawaii" and "kawaii-so-ohh." I was in like Flynn.

My self-assuredness ebbed, however, then quickly plummeted into a downward spiral when our housekeeper, Sakae-san, arrived some moments before my departure. Tucked under her arm was an over-sized parcel. Without a word of explanation, she gave me a discerning once-over, shook her head in unconcealed disgust and tore open the bundle. Inside were garments folded in neat piles; garments belonging to her which she had brought from home. Was Sakae-san going to PTA with me?

Before you could say, "Boy, you sure look tacky!" she was redressing me in her own finery. It was clear that I was deeply flawed, and would certainly not be leaving the house until she was finished—and satisfied. It was also clear that I was not in any way to embarrass Sakae-san in front of the nursery school ladies, her reputation being on the line now that she was tightly linked to me as the poorly-dressed-devil-alien's new official housekeeper!

Her irrefutable message—delivered without uttering a word, but with a whole lot of heavy breathing—was made palpable by the fervency of Sakae-san's actions. After much fluttering and flitting over my body, she at last stepped back, did a thorough head-to-toe inspection, and finally, with some slight tweaking here and there, sent me off down the dirt road all decked out in *her* burka-sized crocheted stole, *her* shamrock green crocheted gloves, and *her* extra-ferociously crocheted handbag, all layered over my ultra-conservative Scottish tartan wool pleated skirt and matching lambs wool sweater.

> "Don't hate me
> because
> I'm beautiful."
> Unknown

With Sakae-san's skilled assistance, I had, in a heartbeat, been turned into the world's biggest fashion clash. Still, I was thanking providence that she didn't own a snood.

Despite my discomfort, though, I dared not do a thing about my ambushed make over, lest I incur the wrath of *her,* the all-knowing PTA fashion maven. Somehow in a pirouette with karma, she, our chambermaid, had taken advantage of me! Still, I would never have dreamed of tarnishing Sakae-san's haut monde reputation in the neighborhood, even though in my eyes, I could not have been more aesthetically challenged. Additionally, I also had the good sense to heed the unassailable and reappearing warning of the when-in-Rome-thing that was increasingly holding sway over me. Yes, more and more, monkey-see, monkey-do was getting the best of my Minnesota reasoning.

"Okay, Dorothy," I murmured to myself as I looked down at my shamrock green crocheted gloves, "I'm not in Kansas anymore."

"You got that right, sister!" Dorothy sneered back.

On the trek down the road to yochien, I made a mental note to enroll in crocheting classes.

> "Beware of any enterprise
> that requires
> new clothes."
> Henry David Thoreau

Sakae-san knew. Boy, did she know. Being perfectly put together equaled self-assured tranquility—just what I needed as I fretfully approached the mothers for my premiere appearance. As far as I could figure, I was only the second foreign mother to have ever joined their hallowed ranks. It happened some time before me, and I had no idea whether or not that woman knew how to crochet.

At the last second, just as I was nearing the school, I froze. What if Sakae-san was *not* the expert for *this* yochien? Like what if her ungodly sense of style only applied to *her* son's yochien? After all, did Harvard folks dress exactly like Yale folks? Did Baptists dress exactly like Episcopalians? Or, take people. Did Janet Leigh dress exactly like Janet Reno, and did Jackie Kennedy dress exactly like Jackie Chan? Did a floozified crocheted stole go with a conservative wool tartan pleated skirt? Somehow I didn't think so.

That's when I knew without a doubt that I was fashion road kill coming around the bend. Style a-go-go, gone a-went-went.

By the time I reached the school gates, I was a tormented, over-accessorized wreck. I stopped to sweep into my fist some of the yardage from the crocheted stole. Using it to dab up my angst-induced sweat, I realized I couldn't even get that right. Dang! The sweat went right through the blasted holes!

I paused, took a breath, then with one stouthearted thrust pushed open the gates and stepped inside. There before me stood a mob of mothers. One quick survey told me that ghastly needlework was in, every last one of them swathed in it. Yes, yes, I commingled perfectly! Bless Sakae-savvy-san! How could I, of the unclean doubting soul, have ever doubted her fashion sagacity?

The mothers rushed toward me like they were sweeping into a banquet hall and I was the featured entree. It was scary as all get out, but also (dare I say it?), quite wonderful. With undisguised sincerity, they gushed their goodwill at me in spit-fire Japanese. I didn't understand a word. I had only advanced, for Pete's sake, to four-word sentences. From deep in my soul's cavity, I again felt the rustlings of my patron saint, Madame Taussaud, who was always there to answer my calls of desperation. In the nick of time she saved me.

"Put on a waxy smile, Peggy," she whispered into my psyche, "that's all you need to do."

I did. I smiled. I smiled to beat the band. I smiled till my cheek muscles bunched up, rising into stiff, elongated lumps. I looked like I had taken Viagra for the face. This was good for my opening debut, a big smile like that looking blissfully wonderful, but—oy vey!—if it lasted more than four hours, should I notify someone? (Sorry, couldn't resist that last part.)

> "Start every day off
> with a smile,
> and get it over with."
> W. C. Fields

Whew! It seemed to be working. Madame was right. A smile *was* all I needed.

All I needed, that is, until dance time. *Dance time*? No one told me about dance time! It begged the question of how a person could, even a PTA member in good standing, execute a dance while enshrouded in all those knotted strings?

I was so trapped. There were absolutely no outs, no feeble Yankee excuses for not knowing Japanese hoedowns when, in fact, the mother mob assumed that like them, the entire, veritable rest of the world, did know.

When in PTA, do as PTA.

Joining hands, I linked with the women. I was about to face the music of my life. There I was a pure, guileless, unsullied (well, maybe a little bit of that), trusting, virginal (er, skip that) lamb going to nursery school slaughter.

The music revved up. Quick as a wink the moms with me in tow, formed tight circles across the cramped, dust-packed playground, while the delighted children clustered around the perimeter, cheering us on. Then slowly and with sublime exaltation, the psyched-up group began to spin to the rhythm of the loud speaker music, every last one of them a prima-PTA-donna, their shuffle-hop-steps honed to perfection.

Before I knew it, the playground was a sea of swaying, synergized booties, the clouds of dust nearly engulfing us. (Cough, cough) Oh, those moms were good alright. Soooo (gasp, choke) good.

And—I was soooo not. I was clunky—my feet now leaden appendages encased in mukluks full of day-old oatmeal; my head—a whirl of torments not knowing in which direction to next pivot my body; and my sense of okay-up-till-now-Caucasian-rhythm—gone. With all my high school dancing skills having now deserted me, I was nothing more than a bumbling mastodon on a nursery school dance floor. Had I been Ginger Rogers herself, I still would have sucked.

> "To not know
> the correct dance steps
> is to be alone."
> Unknown

It was becoming clear real fast that being unable to perform the right pirouettes, dips, twirls, hand inflections and glides was about to become the most notable transgression of all my PTA shortcomings. But, what could I, the clumsy sallow-skinned Gila monster on the playground, do? There was no way out of this snake pit fling.

My thoughts turned to that lady who I'd recently heard about. Yes, that one. The one who had been kicked out of her ballet class. Like was it her fault she'd pulled a groin muscle, even though it wasn't hers? Heaven help me, I was now her! I knew then that my misplaced dread of PTA had nothing to do with PTA. It had everything to do with my not being able to two-step. Heaven help me, I had turned into the man who thought the band was no good because he couldn't dance!

Yet, despite my dancing distress, I also realized to my surprise, that I was feeling truly happy for those mothers. Even in my discomfort, I could see they were basking in their moment in the sun. Furthermore, each mom was hell-bent on holding onto her moment with all the fervency in her. As if life itself depended on it, the ladies danced their hearts out, obviously their PTA reputations being on the square dance line. Meanwhile, I stumbled behind, around and into them like Dumbo in needlework.

"There will be a rain dance
Friday night,
weather permitting."
George Carlin

I guess, on that first day, the one thing that saved me from being a complete maladroit was that I was short; not standing a whole lot taller than the other mothers, and therefore not being the nail that stood out too blatantly (yeah, sure!)—plus of course, my inability to relinquish my scintillating, frozen rock-hard-international-relations smile due to my Viagra cheek cramps.

The biggest PTA lesson I learned that first time was what was expected of me the second time.

I wondered if, when she wasn't busy crocheting, Sakae-san also gave dance lessons?

None of this deterred me from attending PTA, however. But, quite honestly, every time I went to one of those meetings, it was the abject pits. Still, my goal was set and I was determined to blend into the society of those women and be just as much a Japanese mother as they were. I could do it, by golly, except for—well—just about every thing that made up me.

On the other hand, it was perfectly clear that Jeff was already one of them. He knew all the moves; he knew all the words. He knew all the all. He even knew how to use the nursery school toilet. So, what's so special about that, you wonder? Well, for starters, do not think benjo here! Do, instead, think toilet like no other. Think a bloody-marvel-of-practicality toilet!

The yochien's one and only toilet was an engineering marvel: a narrow wooden trough that ran the length of the short toilet room. What an ingenious latrine! (Oh, that word! It reminds me of a girl I once met whose name was Latrina. It always nagged the question of where she was born? *Or conceived!*)

"For birth control,
I rely on
my personality."
Milt Abel

Along the trough, at every eighteen-inch mark, there was a sturdy steel rod serving as a handle. It was bent up and over the trough, coming back down on the other side. There were many handles, and from the toilet room entrance they looked like small running track hurdles spaced out evenly over a long, narrow, wooden box.

Going to the toilet was a class event. Everyone did their business together, no gender silliness even remotely addressed. In amazingly tight choreography, each class of twenty students filed in, dropped their drawers, took hold of the handles, flipped one leg over the trough, squatted, did their business, wiped themselves with their own supply of tissues, stood up, redressed, washed their hands in a single long cement sink, wiped them with a small towel their mothers had pinned to their uniforms that morning, and finally paraded back to their classroom like itty bitty, empty-bladdered soldiers.

One teacher remained behind. Her task was to turn on a hose at one end of the trough and wash the contents out the other end into the school's septic tank, otherwise known as the ditch that ran beside the road. Whoosh! The whole procedure took only moments. A masterpiece of efficacious elimination!

By word of explanation, the roadside septic system/ditch was a narrow concrete gutter. Sometimes it was covered with a series of individual concrete plates, sometimes not. If we were lucky, the eighteen-inch long covers were in place. If we were not lucky, they had shifted off the gutter, or had slipped into the gutter, or were simply broken. More often than not, it was you who broke them. This happened because you trusted those covers to hold the weight of your car because you were forced to drive over them because another vehicle was coming down the very same narrow road and you were going to hit it if you didn't get all the way over to the far side where the gutter was! One of the greatest misfortunes that could strike a Japanese motorist, aside from vehicular death (or something close to it like being the nail that stands up), was to get stuck in one of those ditches. It was ridiculously easy to do.

To begin, the roads were outrageously incapacious. This caused the drivers to go to the very outer edges of the roads in order to pass one another. The ditches were just a hair wider than the width of a tire, and if the covers were not in place—as they so often were not—it was a sure bet you'd find both tires on one side of your car wedged perfectly inside them.

This predicament was made considerably more irksome for people who drove a foreign car, meaning that they, with their steering wheel on the left side of the car, were also sitting on the sewer side of the road. Abutting the sewer was almost always a tall cinderblock wall that served as a fence in front of the homes sitting up against the road. Because the drivers were seated on the left side, exiting from the driver's side was near impossible, unless of course, you were Gumby. Therefore the driver, who we will pray was in reasonably fit condition, had to somehow get himself around the driving gear, across the seat and out the passenger door. But before any of this could be executed, the driver would quickly realize that he was not only crammed inside (as in stuck until the next time it snows in Calcutta), but his tires had become an instant dam around which now flowed all manner of humanoid organic matter.

To top it off, once the driver got himself on the outside, he immediately discovered that it was not possible for a single person to get himself out of this mess. And I do stress mess! If it happened to you, you made an instant pact with yourself that it would never *ever* happen again, for clearly crashing into an on-coming car was way simpler—and more hygienic— than scrabbling with tires that were wedged in a Japanese septic system.

One time Glen had such a mishap. Now we know he knew a thing or two about being immovably wedged, so when it happened again, he was instantly aware of the seriousness of his predicament. At that time we owned a small Japanese car. Glen fit in it tightly, much like an apple in its skin. I deeply regretted not being there the evening it happened and missing the sight of Glen making a quick exit from our car, just as I regretted never having seen an apple exit its skin. It must have been quite a feat of large body trickery.

Looking about, he beheld the abhorrent fix he was in. Just as he was about to start whimpering—standing there alone in the middle of the road with the pariahs of plumbing pooling around his feet and trying like heck to remember if it really did or did not snow in Calcutta and if so, how long it took to melt—from out of the front doors jammed right up against the same skinny ribbon-of-a-road, men suddenly appeared. It was so odd, as if this had happened before. Ya think?

Without uttering a sound, they, like a skilled racing car pit crew, went to work, each knowing his assignment. Instantaneously they hoisted Glen's compact car up from the ditch and set it back on the road. Then just as quickly, they uniformly bowed and disappeared back into their houses. It was over in minutes. Potential night soil once again flowed freely down its chute, sliding along to the next unintentionally made dam built by another ill-omened motorist. As it agglomerated somewhere down stream, Glen drove off. He and the neighborhood were again at peace.

> "What a beautiful fix
> we are in now:
> peace has been
> declared."
> Napoleon Bonaparte

KNOWING THE PERILS of the elimination game as I so well did, whenever I went to yochien, I not only avoided the ditches, but I also made sure to go to the bathroom before leaving home, somehow the joy of mixing into the Japanese melting-toilet-trough-pot only going so far. Besides, what was I supposed to do in there wearing those Shamrock green crocheted gloves, to say nothing of Sakae-san's ridiculous burka shawl?

Furthermore, in defense of my wardrobe, I must tell you that in time I was able to muster up enough backbone to select my own PTA outfits. This did not happen overnight, mind you, but piece by piece the borrowed layers peeled off and I turned back into myself, a bit less fashionably precarious than I had been before Sakae-san's assistance. It didn't matter, for by then the mothers were used to me—and my outfits.

Later on when I started working at NHK, the nursery school mothers didn't even care what I wore. They just seemed to like dancing with me, a TV person, and I, in turn (not knowing just exactly what a TV person was and feeling pretty darned bogus about the whole thing), played my convivial role of liking to dance with them, too. By the time second son Matt enrolled in yochien, I was finally getting the gist of the fashion and the frivolities, although for me those school events were remarkably akin to having a root canal ... executed by one of the yochien kids ... using a chop stick!

> "You're ugly.
> Not only that,
> but you also
> need a root canal."
> James J. Garrett, D.D.S.

FORTY-FOUR

WITH THEIR FRESH spongy brains, both boys learned Japanese right off the bat. Indeed, they did not even realize they were learning a different way of speaking. Unlike us adults who usually study a foreign language in a classroom, children learn languages at play. They also learn in full phrases as they hear them spoken, as opposed to our word-by-word memorization. Children do not need to say as much as we adults do, and their fresh, unsuspicious minds are open doors, while their supple lips easily curl and contort into new mouth shapes.

Seeing as how I was not in a classroom, I, too, learned Japanese in phrases as I heard them, although the doors to my brain were neither as fresh nor as spongy as the boys'. Just the same, I put forth an earnest effort and, to my surprise, rather quickly had a good working knowledge of Japanese. If one good thing had come out of those Ogikubo park mothers' snubs it was that I was inspired to shape up my linguistic past. What also drove me was being piss-and-vinegar-bold, highly talkative and crazy mad to fit in. Was that a sin?

One day, many years later, I met a blind Japanese woman. We spent time chatting together. As we were departing, someone mentioned to her that I was an American. I was really surprised when she was even more surprised. She had not realized I was not Japanese. The realistic part of me questioned whether her ears were as deaf as her eyes were blind, but I, being *Vaina* White, chose to ignore the truth and believe, instead, that her hearing was perfect.

"I don't want any
yes-men around me.
I want everybody
to tell me the truth
even if it costs them
their jobs."
Samuel Goldwyn

FORTY-FIVE

CALLIGRAPHY IS ONE of Japan's most treasured art forms. All school children must, of course, learn it, and then continue studying it throughout their lifetimes. In other words, it is an endeavor without end. There were only a handful of artisans who mastered calligraphy well enough to be recognized as "Japanese national treasures." Glen and I were extremely honored to meet such a person. In fact, to receive a dinner invitation to his home! How such unforeseen fortune happened to us is still beyond us!

Our host, it turned out, was the calligrapher who had only a few years earlier been handpicked by the Rockefeller family to privately teach Michael, their son. Michael, some of you may recall, was the very same son who later disappeared in the headhunting, cannibal-infested jungles of New Guinea. To this day his remains remain an unsolved mystery— *like he was just swallowed up!!!* I reminded myself not to bring this up during dinner.

I would also not bring up a similar case, The Donner Party. I never could figure out why folks didn't just call it like it was—The Dinner Party. Sheesh! I can just hear those famished people chit-chatting while they carved ... "Guess who we're having for dinner?"

For the love of Mike, did I just say that?

"Cannibals aren't vegetarians.
They're humanitarians."
Unknown

Glen and I arrived at the calligrapher's very humble home, were greeted by a gracious middle-aged woman, removed our shoes in the genkan, and were ushered into a small adjacent tatami room, the home's living room, dining room, bedroom and everything else room. There we seated ourselves on the floor beside a small low table. Within moments the host arrived and seated himself on a zabuton (zah-boo-tong, a large square floor cushion) across from us.

Food began arriving. It was especially delicious and all served by the same woman who had greeted us at the door. Oddly she never once made a sound, her greatest effort being, it seemed, to try on all counts to make herself invisible. The artist gave her no recognition of any kind. In our ignorance, we were not sure if the woman was his wife or servant, or both. (What am I saying? This was Japan! Of course she was his wife/servant! They were synonymous!)

The meal was lengthy and beautifully attended to by the woman. Throughout, she remained "unnoticed" before our eyes, in no way making herself a part of the group. Like the Good Fairy, she silently kneeled and served, kneeled and removed dishes; kneeling and serving one course after the other. It was excruciatingly difficult for me not to recognize her efforts by striking up a conversation. It went against every politeness I knew, to say nothing of the natural sisterhood our sex habitually engenders.

When the meal concluded, she, like a mature Tinker Bell, cleared away every bit of eating evidence. Then much to our surprise, she proceeded to fold up the table, carry it off to one side, and lay in front of our folded legs on the tatami floor, a full set of calligraphy supplies.

Show time!

Glen and I were completely taken aback, expecting nothing like this. I mean what great artist performed his work in front of a pair of two-bit inconsequentials like us? It was totally uncalled for.

Or ... holy craps ... was he setting a trap? Feeding us like royalty and then creating something he expected us to buy payback style? Us, of the lean budget and monthly under-the-table payments to the landlord?

With studied drama—and not one bit of effort expended in hiding his need for showiness—the artist (clearly having done this innumerable times), leaned forward from his zabuton and rose half-way onto his knees. Then stoically, in one fluid whoosh, he imperiously unrolled a six-foot long piece of white, handmade paper, unfurling it gently across the length of the tatami room. The mute woman, who by now I figured had to be his wife, carried in a tray with an assortment of brushes and an ink stone, placing them at his side.

She kneeled upon the tatami and with masterfully polished movements, and nary a peep, began grinding the ink stone, mixing the powder into a black thick paste. When this was completed, the artist, with consummate aplomb, floated his hand over the selection of brushes until, for me, the suspense was static. After what seemed an eternity of ostentatious hand floating, he finally selected a fat, thick brush with kinky, stiff, uneven bristles which resembled exactly a teensy witch's broom. Throughout this drama, the two performers had moved like a surgeon and nurse team in a well-scripted, practiced, operating room procedure.

Having cooked, greeted, served, cleared away and prepared the calligraphy supplies, the woman now permanently melted away by removing herself to the adjacent kitchen. In the meantime, Glen and I waited, fascinated by the thriftiness and exactitude of this crackerjack duo. Throughout the entire show, from the last gulp of food to now, no one had spoken a word. Actually, Glen and I hadn't dared to.

Believe me when I say that everything that had transpired up to this point would have been plenty of show for the likes of us. But, no, without warning, our host next bowed his head to his chest and fell into a deep meditative state. It seemed a bit over-the-top showy to me, just short of swami-ism, but then I knew the Japanese were big on drama.

We two foppish Yankees stared at him, then at each other, not certain of what our part should be—like that awful unknowingness a Presbyterian feels in a Catholic mass. After what seemed to be an inordinate amount of contemplation—had the artist, I suddenly feared, gone comatose? But, no, he just as surprisingly snapped out of it. In one graceful motion the maestro again rose from his cushion onto his knees and leaned over the long paper. There he stopped, hovering with his kimono-clad back bent, and his kinky inky brush poised in the air.

Hitting his intended target with exact accuracy—his target, naturally, being Glen and me!—we now fell completely under the maestro's spell. The two of us, barely able to endure another second of suspense, were drawn hook, line and sinker into his galvanizing performance; the bewitchment he cast, suffocating us with anticipation.

Theatrics perfecto!

> "My niece was in
> *The Glass Menagerie* at school.
> They used Tupperware."
> Cathy Ladman

The calligrapher remained hovered—suspended in time, space and awkward position. It was as if we were watching Houdini with the chains and locks in place about to be lowered into the water tank.

Without warning, the brush then flew into a frenzy of action. It landed with a blob of viscous ebony ink two-feet down from the top of the scroll. From there it went into an unhinged discharge, dragging up, down, and across, zigzagging without hesitation to the bottom of the six-foot long paper. The entire procedure took no more than a moment, and the brush *never once lifted off the paper!*

We had just witnessed the preeminent artistry of a national treasure. Still no one spoke. Nor inhaled. It had all happened too fast to do either. Dumbfounded, Glen and I were stunned to the core, by now uncertain if we had permanently lost our ability to aspirate.

As we struggled for air, we thought the show had ended. It hadn't. Just as suddenly as the frenetic writing had begun—and then ended, the sensei froze once again into suspension mode. This time, however, rather than having a large brush in his hand, he had replaced it with a very small, one-inch square hanko (hahn-koh, a red inked rubber name stamp used by all Japanese to officially affix their names to documents).

This sleight-of-hand maneuver was accomplished with such dispatch that my eyes were flipping, my heart was pounding, my expirations were dangerously shallow, and I was at a complete loss as to what would happen next.

The sensei began incrementally moving the hanko over the scroll. First he held it in the air over one spot then moved it to another, doing this several times. Naturally, Glen and I in our oafishness didn't have a clue what was going on, and we weren't about to touch it with a ten-foot pole.

With time between hanko shifts, I moved my eyes from the hand that held the hanko to the eyes of the kneeling artist. It was pretty clear I wasn't supposed to do this—like the name of this game was keep-your-eye-on-the-bouncing hanko—but, I did it anyway. That's when I happened to notice that each time the master changed its position, he also, ever so slightly, shifted his eyes to the right ... as far as they would go.

It was so discreet, so utterly secretive, he was able to accomplish it without moving a single hair on his maestro body. Indeed, so surreptitious was it that one would never have been aware had they not been looking directly at his eyes. Like I was doing! I followed their path. Every time the cunning twin orbs crossed the room, they went straight to the kitchen door—and stopped. There to my surprise—my astonishment, my delight!—was the woman hiding behind the frame of the door with only the top of her head and her eyes visible. I was glued to the elusive scene. What in heaven's name was I witnessing here, and would I go straight to hell in a hand basket if I let on I had noticed?

I had made a discovery, alright, of that there was no doubt. Each time the artist moved the hanko, he also, very slyly and with great stealth, shifted those famous national treasure eyes of his over to his partner. I could never in a hundred lifetimes have let on that I knew.

For the umpteenth time, he moved the hanko, and again secreted a peek toward the kitchen. His wife did nothing, not moving a muscle. Then another shift of the hanko: number umpteen-plus-one. This time when his eyes rolled in her direction, she nodded. It was done so imperceptibly, it was barely noticeable. But, with that tiny inclination of her head, he brought the hanko down onto the paper.

Done deal!

It's still baffling to me. That famous artist who in his long lifetime had created all manner of glorious calligraphy, relied, in the end, for the final stroke of genius—verily the placing of his mark—to not be decided by himself, but rather by his wife-alias-servant. Such a mystery was art. And where, alas, would artists be without their mates?

> "He was the world's
> only armless sculptor.
> He put the chisel in his mouth
> while his wife hit him
> on the back of his head
> with a mallet."
> Fred Allen

I should explain that in Japanese art there is no set spot where the hanko must be placed. It is not like the conclusion of a book where "The End" must come at the bottom of the last page. The genius is that the hanko may be positioned just about anywhere, *but anywhere perfectly!* In so doing, this final stroke in the completion of a project—the coup de grace—must be the placing of the hanko perfectly where it will exactly balance off the entire piece of art. Apparently the maestro's talents did not lie in perfect hanko placing.

Imagine the acclaim his calligraphy had received over the years while his wife stayed hidden behind the kitchen door. Imagine the wonder of her artistry in its pure and absolute modesty, as she complemented the revered talent of her husband. And imagine how difficult it must have been for her that evening to even see the long scroll from her hiding place, so that she *could* perform her artistry. And, yet, she knew, and she did.

With the final stamp of the hanko, Glen and I both, at last, allowed ourselves a good intake of air, pinking up our suddenly ashen cheeks. My, we agreed, it had been a show on the grandest of scales, and we let the master know with an abundance of sincere praise.

Soon after, the evening came to a close. Still hanging in our minds, however, was that nagging question of how much payment would be exacted from us if, in all seriousness, the maestro planned to sell the scroll to us—us of the financially embarrassing penurious government salary. Tension was high. Would Glen and my destinies be to survive drowning in Tokyo Bay, only to forevermore rot in calligraphy debtor's prison?

As we bowed our heartfelt thanks and moved into the genkan to retrieve our shoes, we dreaded the moment when the bill would be presented. Just as we bobbed our final obeisance and were on the verge of making a clean escape, the woman appeared. In her hands was the rolled-up scroll, gift wrapped. She handed it to her husband. He, in turn, handed it to us. It was a present, he told us, which he had created just for us.

Oh, ye—*we!*—of little faith! Shame, shame! We should have known better. Nothing, NOTHING, compared to the generosity of Japanese hospitality. How could we have questioned their motives? How could we have been so ... well ... so American? We felt overwhelmed by their benevolence. Many years have passed since that day, and I tell you with pride that the scroll has remained one of our treasured objects, hanging with honor in every one of our many homes. .

During all that time, I have often kicked myself for not asking the maestro that evening what exactly those beautiful brush strokes of his said? What was the mystery in their meaning? I was pretty sure they had to be something extra deep; surely charismatic—even otherworldly—and no doubt, well beyond my Zenless understanding. Of course, I have guessed at what that might be, and figured it must be along the lines of: "Bountiful Autumn Harvest" or "May Buddha's Fortune Rain Upon You" or "May Your Loins and the Loins of Your Children Never Be Purloined" ... but, wouldn't it just be our luck for it to say, "Go Home Damn Yankees!"

FORTY-SIX

SOME YEARS LATER, and still unable to get the importance of the hanko out of my mind, I decided to have one made for Glen. I thought it would make a unique gift. Make him feel like a graduate of Japanese-transplant school. There were many shops to choose from because virtually all the Japanese (even our little Jeff and Matt in yochien), had to have a hanko. It was used, you see, in place of a signature. I had heard of one particular shop that was making them especially for foreigners; in other words, making them for people who did not have the kind of name that could be pulled off in complicated, beautiful, Chinese characters. Mac-oo-roff-oo-rin (McLaughlin) would be a good example of this.

Each time a Japanese needed to sign something, he reached into his kimono sleeve or purse, and pulled out a small leather covered case about the size of my little finger. Inside was a tiny stamp, hand carved out of ivory with his name in characters, along with a dinky case (about the size of a generous M&M), of red ink paste. Not owning this device, we foreigners had to use our pinky fingers, dipping them into the red paste and then stamping our prints on all official documents. This included dealings such as banking contracts, large purchases, and even post office receipts. To this day it beats me how a name stamp is any better than an original signature, but then who was I to question a system that had worked in Japan for twenty-thousand—or thereabouts—generations?

I thought the new foreigners' hanko gimmick was an awesome idea. Boy, somebody sure had their thinking cap on when they came up with

178

that! Just because we gaijin did not have the sort of names that were easily penned in wondrous brush strokes did not mean we had to go without stamps of our own. No siree. We didn't have good names, but we did have ... faces! Yes, faces which could be carved into ivory. How ingenious! I loved it. I knew Glen would, too. I presented the shop keeper with a close-up photo of Glen's face. This was going to be my best birthday present ever.

The hanko was ready just in time for the big day. Excitedly I presented the small package to Glen. Opening the gift, he couldn't believe his eyes. "Would you look at that," he exclaimed, "my own personal hanko!" He opened the case, removed the hanko, pressed it into the red ink and stamped it on a piece of clean white paper. I looked, anticipating the perfect reproduction of my husband's face. I looked again, this time re-focusing for clarity. Why, that wasn't Glen. Not him at all.

There on the paper was a perfect likeness of Elvis Presley!

Seemed that the hanko carver thought all the Caucasian faces he'd ever seen wandering around Japan looked pretty much alike; as did all the Asian faces wandering around Minnesota look pretty much alike. If he'd seen one, he'd seen them all, and Elvis' face was hands down definitely his favorite. I think Glen took it as a compliment.

> "What can you say
> about a society that says
> God is dead
> and Elvis is alive?"
> Irv Kupcinet

Unbeknownst to Elvis, before anybody knew it, legal papers all over Japan popped up with his bright red kisser on them. It didn't matter though, because we were simply no-account foreigners. Even so, after every stamping transaction, Glen always crossed his fingers that he would never be asked to sing ... or, Mary, Mother of God ... dance, swivelly hips not being in his DNA.

> "Help!
> I'm being held prisoner
> by my heredity
> and environment! "
> Dennis Allen

FORTY-SEVEN

ONE MORNING I awoke in the early hours with the mother of all flu bugs. I felt as if someone had over-zapped me in a microwave, although microwaves were not yet known. (But, if they had been, that was how I felt!) Unlike my predictable self, for the first time in my married life I stayed in bed that morning, unable to drag myself up at the usual crack of dawn. Four-year-old Jeff had never seen me in bed when the sun was up. Jeff had never seen me horizontal *on anything* when the sun was up. He was at a total loss as to my startling and dismaying behavior.

Standing beside my bed, Jeff looked deeply into my eyes (twin pools of misery), and asked, "Mommy, did you die?" When I told him I hadn't, he was reassured, but still confused and concerned, worry lines creasing his winsome face. That was when he got an idea. He knew something that would make his mom rise up from her bed, walk again, and be whole.

With an abrupt turn, Jeff marched out of the bedroom and down the faux, quail-egg stairs to the kitchen where he set about his task. He was not yet really what you would call a master chef, and he knew little of recipes, but he did know how finished food should look and taste. Although uncertain of the method to get it to that point, he was resolutely sure of how it should end up.

I, in the meantime, alone and grievously afflicted, was upstairs fighting off waves of hostile nausea and giving no mind whatsoever to what Jeff was doing downstairs—let alone what *anyone* in the free world was doing *anywhere*. An hour passed.

Upon hearing some up-close bedside breathing, I forced my eyes open to find my firstborn once again standing beside me. On his face was a radiant smile. He was holding something out to me. I looked at it through rheumy eyes, not quite able to clear the blur. Struggling, I scrutinized the object. There was a tall glass, I thought, and in it, I was quite certain, was a frosty vanilla milkshake!

But, how could that be? We were in the middle of the Orient here. Not only was ice cream barely a wisp of a notion then in Japan, but it was also a moot point because there were no home freezers in Japan in which to store it. But, of course, that was not the case for us. As Americans, we had a regular American-type refrigerator full to bursting with American-type foods, all purchased from the Green Park Commissary where it never stopped raining.

Being the Mom Emeritus that I was, and totally consumed with consummate care giving, I kept our refrig well stocked with the really good foods; those from the health pyramid. Ice cream was the biggest bottom level.

Genetics were to blame. I was born with three ice cream genes. To folks back in Austin, I was immediately recognized as Margaret Gene the Zesto Queen, Zesto being the broadly loved, enticingly soft frozen treat that was sold there, as well as cities as globally distant—I'm pretty sure, though not positive—as Sioux City.

> "I prefer Hostess fruit pies
> to pop-up toaster tarts
> because they don't require
> so much cooking."
> Carrie Snow

I illegally became the un-crowned Zesto Queen when I was only fourteen. Child labor laws, being what they were in 1952, made this a tad dicey. You see, the Zesto Stand had just opened in Austin and the owner was my dad's very good friend. Since I was convenient and eager, I was his only choice for the only job, thus I had no competition for becoming the first and only ever in the chronicles of soft ice cream queen. Who knew that you didn't need blue blood to become royalty? That you didn't even need a blood test? (Harrumph! They should have demanded a pint from Prince Charles' to see just how genuinely authentic his blue-blood was. Along with it, it might have explained those ears!)

But, I'd be lying through my teeth if I didn't admit to having had help in obtaining my crown. Back then, even though I probably didn't deserve the honor, I had the Zesto fairy watching over me. It was like this. Once the folks from Child Protection Services experienced in their own gullets the rapture of the frozen custard, the case was thrown out the window before it ever became a case.

That aside, and way more important than the law, was the fact that I was excellent at my job—modesty never being my strong suit. Like a suction-footed gecko on a glass wall, I clung ferociously to my august ice cream career, dressing everyday in a freshly laundered, white, heavily starched nurse's uniform (sans the peaked hat which got in the way of my crown), and bleached, white tennis shoes. Professionally attired, I know I looked fifteen.

> "I got a job at the
> International House of Pancakes.
> It was my dream ...
> and I made it happen!"
> Paula Poundstone

NOW, JEFF KNEW all about my sweet Zesto history. It was hard not to when your mom was royalty. Therefore, he knew exactly what brand of medicine would pull me out of my sickly blue funk, and in so doing, return his mom to him.

"Where did you get this, Jeff?" I gasped through a cloud of queasiness, completely flummoxed by his gift.

"I made it myself!" Jeff sparkled back (the sparks nearly triggering a seizure in me).

"Why, this is wonderful, Jeff, but ... but ... how did you do it?"

Always a stickler for details, Jeff began. "Well, I went down to the kitchen. I took a chair. I carried it to the refrigerator. I climbed up on it. I opened the freezer door. I took out the ice cream. I closed the door. I climbed down from the chair. I carried the ice cream to the card table. I went to the drawer. (We had two.) I got a big spoon. I carried it to the card table. I got a chair. I carried it to the cupboard. (Also two.) I climbed up. I got a glass. I closed the door. I climbed down from the chair. I carried the glass to the card table. I opened the ice cream. I stuck in the spoon. I put a big bite of ice cream in my mouth. I squished it back and forth. I spit it in the glass. I took another big bite of ice cream. I squished and spit it into the glass, too. I did that for a long, long time until the glass was full."

The three wise men with all their gold, incense and myrrh could not have been more proud of their gifts than was Jeff. Glinty shimmers of luminosity flashed from his resplendent, jubilant countenance.

What did I do next, you ask? Well, a true mother's love being what it is, I, naturally, drank it—bottoms up—straight down!

From somewhere near the ceiling, melodious angelic voices began instantly harmonizing. I felt a sudden supernatural laying on of hands as the area right over my heart began to heat up in a mini circle, like one of those warming packets you put in your mittens when you shovel snow on a twenty-below-zero day. It was a pure and simple miracle! My child's love had healed me.

Jeff, the shaman, could have patented that medicine: Rx Squish n' Spit.

"Orthodox medicine
has not found an answer
to your complaint.
However, luckily for you,
I happen to be a quack."
(Richter cartoon caption)

FORTY-EIGHT

A RAUCOUS CLAMORING outside our window awakened us very early one morning. It was followed by a relentless pummeling on our door. In the darkness a voice was screaming, "Wake up, wake up! The President's been shot! Kennedy is dead!"

(Although the assassination had happened on November 22, 1963, due to the time difference, we did not hear about it until the morning of November 23rd.)

The voice belonged to our American neighbor, a first class Darrell Doldrums, self-appointed harbinger of terrible news who, like Henny Penny of the perpetual sky is falling in fame, relished nothing quite so much as spreading, on a regular basis, dismal tidings. He was banging and screaming at our door in his urgency to get out the hideous announcement. The enormous import of his dispatch had to have been the all-time crowning coup in his bad news delivery service, because little else could have been worse. Hearing such heinous words, especially from him, was dreadful. But then, hearing them from anyone would have been dreadful.

As D. Doldrums continued to assault us with his message, we stood there in our pajamas, galvanized. I remember it being nearly impossible to take in his words. Somehow in that setting, along with being bombarded with the coarseness of his delivery, the gravity and weightiness of his news barely got through to us. Rather, should not such words have been whispered in anguish and disbelief? Furthermore, hearing it as we were on the other side of the world in a place so utterly un-American, and so far from our President—*our President who had just been murdered!*—made the message all that more grotesquely surreal.

When an event as devastating as this one occurs, people need to be in the company of those who share with them the ownership of the catastrophe. In that moment, this did not include Japan. Kennedy belonged to us; he was ours! What we did not realize, in those early morning hours, was how much the world also claimed him as theirs. We would quickly learn in the days to come what a citizen of the entire globe John F. Kennedy had been.

But in those first hours, with only a handful of American neighbors with whom we could commiserate our grief, we felt lost and uncomforted, and very, very far from home. While our hearts silently screamed, "Who *did* such a thing; who *could* do such a thing; and most importantly, why would anyone *want* to do such a thing?" our actual words were few, because within us there were no answers to those questions. None.

History would later prove there never were any real answers.

For the rest of the weekend, Glen and I moved about in a cheerless fog. Nothing, no matter what we could come up with, made any sense. In Kennedy there had been such promise of hope for us, for the world. Now that promise, in a fleeting second, was gone. How could it be that someone so insignificant could rob the world of someone so extraordinarily significant?

On Monday, as usual, I walked Jeff down the road to yochien. Then I returned home. Within the hour one of the teachers came running back to Asahi Court to tell me I had to come—and to come now!—to get Jeff. He wouldn't stop crying. They didn't know what to do. Hurrying together back to school, I found an inconsolable Jeff with his head on the table, sobbing. I took him in my arms, settled us in his small child's chair, and held him until his weeping diminished.

While his classmates and teachers looked on, Jeff raised his grief-filled eyes and implored, "Why, Mommy, did someone kill my President?"

It wasn't until later, when Jeff was finally able to talk about it, that I found out it was not President Kennedy for whom our four-year-old was grieving. It was John-John. Jeff had seen him on TV and realized with shock that John-John, like himself, was just a little boy. Jeff was crying for the sadness he knew was in John-John.

FORTY-NINE

I WAS ON a city bus one morning on my way to Kichijoji Train Station when through the window I spotted something. It was sitting on a narrow sidewalk in front of a small, astonishingly ancient shop. Much as Imelda Marcos had been magnetized by shoes, so was I equally drawn to the object.

> "I did *not* have
> 3,000 pairs of shoes.
> I had only 1,060!"
> Imelda Marcos

I couldn't quite make out what I was seeing other than being sure it was a small piece of furniture. Oddly, its seduction so hypnotically captivated me that I was compelled to interrupt my mission, get off the bus, and promptly walk back to get a closer look.

As I approached the shop, my heart began to flutter, setting off an uncontrollable quiver in what I hadn't known until later was my aesthetic core. Like a bolt of lightning, I instantly got it. This must be—though not quite the same—how Sakae-san felt in the presence of crocheting.

Standing there on the sidewalk, I couldn't explain what had stirred me so, but I knew I was being touched in the deepest part of my being. And, what I didn't know then was there was a word for this: "shibui" (shh-boo-ee). English had no equivalent term for this, nor did America have an equivalent concept. The Japanese, however, understood it completely.

Keep in mind I was a girl whose fanciest home décor had come from her mom's S&H Green Stamp Store. I had also, not that long ago, lived in half a Quonset hut and I now lived in a cement block duplex. That said, I suppose I was easy to blow away. But, this thing going on now was way beyond a simple seducement.

How to describe shibui? Shibui is the ultimate in subtlety. For the Japanese, it is the height of elegant sophistication. It is quiet. It is elusive to anyone who is consciously setting out to create it, although to achieve it would be their greatest desire. Shibui cannot be contrived. Rather it is natural, a marriage of material, design, craftsmanship and natural aesthetics. In furniture it may be seen in the grain of the wood, in the design, or in the patina acquired over years of use; all created by accidental happenstance or simply by time. Objects with such a character, speak in a noiseless, velvet voice entering into one's consciousness with a tranquil explosion. You only know what I'm talking about if it's happened to you.

Shibui is never cute. It is never souvenir-ish. You do not collect shibui like a set of Madame Alexander dolls. Rather it stands alone. It speaks without words. It is the Japanese epitome of beauty. Indeed, you hold your breath in its presence for it causes you to forget about breathing. That morning for the first time, shibui unexpectedly took hold of me. I would never again be quite the same Peggy McLaughlin Keener from Austin, Minnesota. Even though I could not explain what had transpired, I knew my consciousness had instantaneously expanded. I had fallen under its spell.

Japan, as you know, is an astonishingly ancient country, and unlike Western cultures, until the Edo Period (1603-1868), the Japanese used only a sparse amount of furniture. The wooden dressers and chests which they began then to incorporate in their homes and work places, were called "tan-su (tahn-sue).

Talk about love at first sight. Out in front of that tiny, leaning, bone-dry shop, I saw my first tansu. Up to that point, my heart had only been wooed by Glen, my children and Zesto turtle sundaes. Without warning, it was now tugged in a new direction. One look at the small tansu and I was hooked; utterly consumed. I snatched it up.

You must realize that in 1962, and even on our tight budget, these treasures were sometimes affordable to me. And working in my favor was the fact that I was living in a place of such antiquity that furniture only one-hundred-and-fifty years old was considered secondhand. The Japanese had very little, or no regard for these used relics. After all plastic and veneered wood now piqued their fancy. By the time we finally left Japan (including our second tour there many years later), I had acquired more than one-hundred tansu. Many were shipped to friends, some were sold, but the bulk I kept. We have nearly fifty in our home right now.

> "Our furniture goes back
> to Louis XIV,
> unless we pay Louis
> before the 14th."
> Unknown

Admittedly, when it came to tansu, I had very definite likes and dislikes. Consistently I was drawn to those—and only those—made during the Meiji Era, a forty-four year span from 1868-1912. Many times I suspected—to the point where I was nearly a believer—that I once lived an earlier lifetime in Japan during that period of history. Could that explain the ease with which I learned the language? Could that be the reason why I felt so absolutely at home (except for PTA), in a culture so very strange to me? (But then I didn't suppose there was any PTA that many lifetimes ago, was there?) Though I had never been in another country, things about Japan which seemed so inscrutable to my fellow foreigners, seemed scrutable to me. Almost.

> "There's nothing
> wrong with you that
> reincarnation won't cure."
> Jack E. Leonard

As much as the Meiji Era tansu overwhelmed me, tansu from the following era, the Taisho Era (1912-1926), underwhelmed me. I was totally put off by them. Beyond unlovely, they were boring, uninspired, wall-flower plain and about as un-shibui as edible underwear. This was likely due in part to the fact that during the Taisho reign, the emperor was teched in the head. Uh-huh, a mincing nutcase, the result of repeated inbreeding amongst the imperials. It was obvious to me that all that cousin-begetting-cousin business made for not only pointy heads, but also badly designed furniture.

But, now all this talk about tansu has my heart pounding and my blood coursing to the point where I cannot yet move from the subject. What may surprise you is that many of these astonishingly beautiful pieces of furniture were never meant to be decorative furnishings, but were rather regarded as only storage containers. There were, of course, certainly some that were needed on an everyday basis. Many of these tansu were designed with two or even three stacked sections of drawers, utilizing the wall space *above the floor* where they stood, rather than spreading out across it and taking up crucial living area. In small rooms, this was a supremely economical use of space.

Attached to the sides of each tansu section were long, rectangular iron handles. When raised above the height of the chest, these handles provided a bail through which a bamboo pole could be threaded, and then carried on the shoulders of two people out to a storage building called the kura (koo-rah).

The kura was one of my all-time favorite buildings. Every old Japanese farm had one for it was the repository for things not kept in the house. Of course, the big old farm homes also had attic-like lofts under their heavily thatched roofs. This space, however, was not used as storage. Rather it was the exclusive place for large, circular baskets layered with mulberry leaves upon which silk worms were raised. The heat from the open cooking fires below rose up through the slatted wooden ceilings, keeping the worms warm. I would add, too, that in some farm homes, a dirt-floored stable of sorts was also attached to the farm house. Here their small grouping of large animals was kept. In winter, the body heat from the animals helped keep the house warm, while the room sheltered the animals from the cold winter temperatures. Round-ups were not necessary; not even a remote concept. That, I suppose, explained why there were no Japanese cowboys.

Nothing produces creativity more than need, and in this the Japanese have always been experts. One prime example is the kaidan dansu (kai-dahn dahn-sue), step dresser. This ingenious piece of furniture was in actuality the staircase which provided access to the second floor attic. Rather than waste the space by using it simply as stairs, under each riser were ingeniously built drawers which one by one became progressively smaller as the staircase ascended to the top. Craftiness Numero Uno!

With the attic being occupied by silkworms, another storage space was necessary. Enter the kura. Think of it as the original POD. Unlike that later metal and plastic creation, the kura was constructed of sixteen-inch mud, bamboo and plaster walls. At the top of one of the overhanging ends of the gabled, heavily tiled roof, was the only window in the building: a tiny porthole placed either above or below a strikingly dignified family crest. The crest was painted black, contrasting dramatically with the always white-washed kura walls. (The family crests are the artwork you have seen throughout this book. There are thousands of them in Japan, each representing one of the thousands of families.)

The kura was a strategically important part of old Japanese family life. Aside from earthquakes, the next greatest fear the Japanese have known down through history (besides in-house rampaging samurai, out-of-town rampaging samurai or, finally, other-worldly rampaging American G.I. samurai), was fire. Why not? For hundreds of years the homes were built out of untreated wood, woven straw flooring, and walls made of wood and paper sliding doors. Living in close proximity to their neighbors, and with everyone cooking on open hibachi (hee-bah-chee), fire was an ever present reality. Hence, the need for the thick mud-walled kura where the family's valuables could be safely kept.

Do not get the idea folks were rich. "Valuables" meant little more than one black silk kimono per adult worn either to weddings or funerals, those two main events in most people's lives, remember, whether it was someone else's or their own. One kimono could serve a lifetime as it was quite possibly the planet's most accommodating outfit while still remaining form-fitting. When necessary it could, without even the hint of a grunt, adapt to fluctuating body sizes, regardless of how much fluctuation the fluctuating needed.

My aged Japanese friends, who had been born and raised in the countryside, told me many stories about their family kura. Its one room interior, they reported, was blessedly cool during the blistering summer heat, it was totally dark with only the one small window, and it was full of fun stuff much like our own American grandmothers' attics.

There was a good reason these folks knew about the kura's interior for it was the place to which their mothers banished them when they were naughty. Yes, even the ever-obedient Japanese children were sometimes not. Interestingly, my jailbird informants confessed that once they had become used to the pitch blackness, they actually enjoyed their punishment, for acclimated by the single shaft of light coming in from the sole, tiny window, they could just make out the intriguing objects stored inside the tansu drawers. Not a bad way to spend a hot, boring, TV-less afternoon.

Japan's old fire departments were all-volunteer forces. Rushing to a fire, one of the volunteers was specifically assigned the task of carrying a bucket of mud. His sole responsibility was to slather that mud into and around the edges of the single kura door, thereby sealing off the contents within. His efforts were highly effective. Because of him, many of the glorious old tansu survived. I'm also guessing he was the world's first sanctioned mud slinger.

In the late 1800s, my Victorian ancestors—those whose goal it was to see who could collect the most knick-knacks, paraphernalia and personal trappings—would have surely pulled out their hair in despair over the aesthetic waste of hiding such enthralling tansu out of sight. Had it been them, they would have pompously displayed the chests for all to see. (Actually, to make up for this terrible waste, that is what I am presently doing!) But then, minimalist Japan was not a culture of stuff. They would have suffocated under the overly-festooned, pretentiously cluttered, peacockish parlors that flourished on the other side of the ocean.

Unexpectedly, along with the acquisition of my first tansu, came a surprising bonus. Little did I know it was not only a place in which to store my own overly-festooned stuff, but it was also a handy emergency warning system. As I previously described, tansu came with thick hand-forged iron handles. Lacking a back plate behind them to protect the wood from dents, a small, slightly protruding nail head was placed directly behind each handle. It worked perfectly, saving the gorgeous dressers from scarring.

The iron handles made a sharp rattling noise whenever they hit the iron nail heads. It sounded like the kind of door knocker a mouse might have if it had a door and mouse visitors to knock on it. Imagine, if you will, an entire apartment building of mice who, coincidentally, all get company at the same time. The resulting door-knocker cacophony would be like that—or another way to put it if you don't like rodent guests—the raucous chatter of heavy coins in a tin cup. Both were the kind of racket a multi-handled tansu made when shaken.

Up until I brought my first tansu home with me, my life in Japan had been relatively smooth (if you discounted absolutely everything you've read up to this point), so I knew nothing about tansu possessing this unique door-knocking ability. Not, that is, until one morning. I was home alone when suddenly out of nowhere the tansu handles went to town, rattling to beat the band. I'd never heard such a clamor, and couldn't decipher where it was coming from.

Seconds later, the floor shifted beneath me.

Criminy! Floors don't shift! Oh, my god, this must be an earthquake!

What people learn very quickly during their first earthquake is that earthquakes are nothing like other natural disasters. You cannot run from them to seek shelter. "Earth," as you can see, is the first part of the word. It is also what you and everything else in your immediate world are standing upon—or at least trying to. "Quake" is the other part, the part that keeps you from standing upon your world. Furthermore, the jolts, you will immediately discover, are magnanimously non-discriminating, and on all levels, the pits.

Have you ever stopped to wonder just how all-fire democratic natural disasters are? For crying out loud, when they're happening, they don't give a tinker's damn about who and what you are. All creatures are equal. When it's over, however, the democratic coin flips. That's called the clean-up and rebuilding. Marginal folks know about this best of all.

> "Those who cast the votes
> decide nothing.
> Those who count the votes
> decide everything."
> Josef Stalin

As I swayed there holding onto the kitchen counter, flashbacks of our plane ride to Japan began pouring into my head. Trembling, I was feeling the same trepidations I had felt when I looked down at those dinky islands of Hawaii and Midway through my tiny, C-54, painted-stuck window. Seeing how precarious they looked, with the least little jiggle I knew they would be history. Poof!

The island I was now tilting on felt as if it, like them, could also soon be history.

Leaping lizards! That was me alright. Leaping! And to think I had once paid good, hard-earned Zesto money at the summer carnival fun house for this kind of insanity. Little did I know! And, never having been without it, little did I appreciate how firm the terra firma of Minnesota was. Hmmm.

191

Maybe those wacky fun houses were only fun in places where there *was* terra firma. Probably not such a big hit in the jiggly places.

One of those jiggly places, the one on which I was now swaying and rocking upon, was terrifying. Rumblings vibrated under my feet as I staggered to right myself. And where now, I wondered, when I needed it most, was all that caring concern I'd read about in those Gajo-en brochures? "Welcome to here with dirds singing and nutting in fall," my foot! Not a danged thing had been said about earthquakes. Nuts was right! They were the unspoken skeleton in the Japanese closet.

That's when I vowed to never allow my family to live in a place like this again. If sharp-tiled bathboxes, shared public urinals and open sewers were not enough reason to fly the coop, this dizzying teetering was sealing the deal.

Of course, what choice did we Keeners have but to continue living under the impending doom of an earthquake striking at any minute? And, of course, we knew there wasn't a thing we could do about it when it did. Talk about feeling helpless. The only thing I knew for sure was that the rattling tansu handles would be the first to announce our doom.

FIFTY

AS LONG AS the earthquakes stayed away, the days passed contentedly. Meanwhile I watched Jeff and Matt grow and blossom like sea monkeys in a glass of water. Japan was turning out to be not only the Land of the Rising Sun, but also the Land of the Rising Sons. Besides gloating over their wonderfulness and making sure nothing would cause this to trarnish, I continued to teach myself Japanese, share our leftovers with Finks, learn a few more PTA dance moves, tape numerous NHK-TV programs, and further develop into an almost-but-not-quite military spouse, as well as an almost-but-not-quite Japanese housewife.

Since our arrival in Japan, Glen had worked at Camp Drake, a very long drive from our home. I seldom went on post except for parties, and because of the distance, never mingled with the other Americans who lived and worked there. Make no mistake about it, the children and I were *not supposed to* hang out there; we were *supposed to be* invisible. Military intelligence was, above all, Glen's first all-consuming occupational life. We were his second part-consuming non-occupational life.

This was made crystal clear to me in 1962, on the day following our arrival on Japanese soil. Glen's commanding officer asked (ordered!) me to report to his office. There he laid out very clearly what the army expected of me and what I was to expect of the army. I quickly got the message. Glen and the army were synonymous; the children and I were not. I was instructed to never, *ever* ask my husband what he did at work. This was forbidden, off limits, nixed! Army Intelligence was business of which I had no business.

The commander also counseled that I was not to envision pleasant evenings spent at home where Glen and I would cozily—like two married bugs all snug in a rug (or actually in this humidity, two married bugs all snug in a fug)—shared our day's activities. Absolutely nothing would be forthcoming from the Glen side.

Additionally, I was not to become jealous or embittered over the many evenings Glen would be away from us doing whatever military spooks did. Also I was not to feel indignant over things like tobacco, liquor, perfume and all other sensuous hints that I might detect on him and his clothing when he did finally return home. I was never to question those evenings, nor was I ever to query any of the numerous weeks and months Glen would be away from us in the future.

I got the commander's drift in no short order. The name of this game was "No Questions Asked—Never, Never, Ever!" Biting my tongue, it was all I could do to not sarcastically reply, "And, Commander General King, I suppose this means that Glen will also not be appearing on 'What's My Line?'"

Forgive my jesting, Commander General King. I have sinned.

"Tell the boss what you
think of him, and the truth
shall set you free."
Unknown

I TOOK THE commander general king at his word. I never asked a thing of Glen. To this day, now many decades later, only bits and pieces of information have dribbled out, every one of them being, by now, too out-dated to matter. For many wives, this would have seemed debilitating, aggravating, downright shattering to the very core of their marriages. It could have been. Yes, it could have been *if* I had chosen to ignore the commander's words by attempting to pry from Glen information which I not only had no business knowing, but also no business dealing with. For sure I would have blabbed stuff I shouldn't have, in places I shouldn't have, to people I shouldn't have. Loose lips sink ships and all of that. It's just the way I'm built and I recognized that fact. It was better that I zipped my probing lips and stay in the dark. I followed those instructions while Glen stayed dutifully mute for thirty-five long military years.

I remind you again that I did not have a phone, there were no computer e-mails with which to stay connected, I had only one American friend (Karen), no car, two wee children, and a husband who was often out of the country. My only way of linking to the world outside of Asahi Court was the slow boat mail dispatched through Camp Drake, a place geographically out of my reach.

It's true that I could rely on help from Sakae-san, but that was only sometimes. Nevertheless, even in this isolation, I remained happy and very busy. Don't forget that I had the pleasure/bother of needing to walk to the food shops everyday because, of course, when Glen was in Japan, I seldom had the use of our car. Keep in mind that in the sixties, even American women back home in the prosperous U.S. of A. did not have the family car at their beck and call. The husband needed it to get to work. Which paid for the car. Follow me?

FIFTY-ONE

LAUNDRY ALWAYS KEPT me busy. Do you recall that aggravation? It didn't go away. My hands could prove it. One day kismet smiled on me as big as a toothpaste ad on Times Square. With it I took a gigantic leap into the world of modern homemaking. The Green Park PX got in some washing machines! For the love of Mike, like toilets that were sat upon, what had taken them so confoundedly long?

Upon hearing that news, you'd have thought I believed Glen's government paycheck grew on the local ginko trees. Shamelessly profligate! After contemplating a whole ten seconds, I bought myself a plug-into-the-wall electric washing machine. For the briefest of moments I felt as if I had started us on the path to pernicious ruination—maybe even to the bottomless pit of pauperdom!—but I allowed it to pass for now, in the palms of my pruney hands, I held a world of laundry promise.

Certainly the washing machine was the major player here. But there was more to this event. In fact in the bigger picture, this other part may have been way more significant. You see, I had cast weakness to the wind and made the decision to buy the washing machine *all on my own*. (Yes, you may clap.) I did *not* consult Glen! (Okay, okay, keep it down.) I know, I know, *I know*! It took courage to step out like that, but I did it. I made the $45 purchase all by myself.

I was the veritable image of moxie … with sweat stains.

Peggy, Peggy Big Bucks Lady.

Before you conjure up an image of sleek and modern, just stop now. I should explain. Actually, it would be best if you did not in any way excessively excite yourself over my purchase. And, gee willikers, do not picture the kind of washing machine you now have in your laundry room. Yes, my machine washed, but it needed a whole lot of help to do so.

It was like this. From the small storage area next to the kitchen, I had to first lug, strain and drag it into the center of the already jam-packed kitchen, plug it into the one kitchen outlet, and finally from the tin metal box that was our sink, fill and empty the tub. Each time it washed and rinsed, the water ran through a hose clamped to the sink faucet. A second hose, the drain hose, hooked over the edge of the sink, allowing the tub to empty. In other words, when I did laundry there was no click of a magic button to do the job for me. Also when I did laundry, the kitchen could absolutely not be used for anything else. The machine consumed the entirety of the small space.

Still, I loved it. No, I *adored* it! For me, my washing machine was a thing of splendor: a ten-carat diamond I could show off to friends and neighbors, and feel good about my station in life.

In my eyes, it was a thing to behold; a round white porcelain tub on wheels. On top was a wringer that uncannily swiveled to the inside or outside of the tub depending upon the task, the technology of that swivel being state of the art. There were no words to express the impact my washer had on my existence. I was no longer that hunched-over woman, beating laundry with a stick, on flat rocks, near the river's edge!

I can hear you. You're thinking it was not all that great, huh? Not so ultra up-to-the-minute awesome. And I suppose you're also thinking that it was not nearly as portentous as, for example, the discovery of the wheel. Well, all I can say about that is this: somebody should have clubbed those do-do bird cavemen right on top of their small brain skulls for being so dumb. Even I could have figured it out. I mean—sheeesh!—what knuckleheads they were driving their cars around with rocks on the axles. Spare me. The rocks weren't even round!

> "The guy who invented
> the first wheel
> was an idiot.
> The guy who invented
> the other three
> was a genius."
> Sid Caesar

No way, no how, were those blockheads me. Molly Modern had just walked through my door.

The first time I plugged in my pricey new appliance, I was deluged with delight; near reeling from the capriciousness of my wondrous acquisition. From the moment the electric current first surged through the cord, a guttural purring began. It was the motor. Let me repeat—*the motor!* Mary, Joseph and Waldo! Electricity! Don't you get it? Those guttural sounds would never again come out of me!

Next I attached the hose to the sink faucet, filled up the tub and put in some dirty clothes. Swish, whoosh, splatter ... the paddles began moving. I did nothing; did not raise a wrinkled finger; did not move; only watched the action. I was as entranced by the mechanized splish-splash of it all as Betty Crocker was by her doughboy, as Alfred Hitchcock was by his crows, as Cleopatra was by her eye liner. I reached out to touch my new marvel, stopping just short of genuflecting, and found I could not stop my chapped hands from caressing its lustrous, silky-white tubby sides. It looked like Humpty Dumpty on casters ... before it had its big fall.

> "If you fall out of a window
> and break both your legs,
> don't come running to me."
> Groucho Marx

I can still remember the sound of the motor on that first morning. It crooned. I swooned! No music ever sounded as rhapsodic to my ears, and that is the gospel truth. As it galvanically sloshed its suds—some of which landed on the kitchen floor, I pulled up a chair, sat back, and listened to it as others would to the strains of the New York Philharmonic. It was the purest, most idyllic melody I had ever heard, if you, that is, discount Glen's "will you marry me?" and our boys' delivery room cries. By a mile, Dick Clark missed out when he failed to include the strains of a washing machine motor on his American Bandstand top-hits list. But then, he probably didn't even know what a washing machine was. He was too busy trying to stay young.

When I judged the clothes had washed long enough, I drained all the water into the sink, filled the tub again with the hose, and after rinsing once, then emptying and filling it again a second time, plucked out each article of clothing, one by one, and cranked them through the wringer. Everything came out as flat and pleated as a wad of aluminum foil run over by a semi-tractor trailer. Naturally, this required rigorous shaking before I could once again recognize what article of clothing it was. But, in the face of modern technology, I put this niggling bit of inconvenience aside.

Peggy, Peggy, Maytag Muckety-Muck Lady.

Unfortunately, in all of this, I had somehow blithely forgotten that the clothes still needed to dry. Wasn't it just my luck that nothing yet existed in my world that could electrically accomplish this? But then, that is why we had the great out-of-doors! Well, some days we did, because don't forget we lived in the Land of Many Gully Washers.

Oh, and did I mention anything about the annual rainy season where the clouds, night and day, day and night, gushed, cascaded, vomited rain for two months non-stop? This is what we had to look forward to each spring. It was when everything we owned grew a green, fuzzy layer upon it: mold as thick and furry as moss. It was not unusual to flick a bit of viridescence off a friend's shoulder as you stood and chatted. It's what we did to show we cared.

The rainy season usually lasted (still does!) sixty-three days. And it really and truly did come down in non-stop buckets. I won't go into detail here, but you can only guess what this did to the volume and flow of the open sewers along side the roads, even without Glen being stuck in them. Counting down the days till the clouds ceased disgorging, was like checking off the days of a Gulag life sentence. In the meantime, we all became mildewed and fusty.

> "The rain it raineth every day,
> upon the just and the unjust feller,
> but, chiefly on the just because
> the unjust has the just's umbrella."
> Lord Justice Bowen

With or without the rainy season, each night after Glen and the boys went upstairs to bed and we no longer needed the two rooms downstairs, I hung the laundry on ropes which I threaded across them like juxtaposed fishing nets. In other words, the air space on the first floor was as thick, heavy and complicated as a rain forest. In the morning, everything had only progressed to damp. Dry was a word unknown in our Far Eastern environs. Here, dry was spelled w-e-t.

But, before you get the wrong impression about the efficiency of living in Japan, let me remind you that sometimes the sun *did* come out. Well, sort of. Unfortunately, the rays were thwarted by a layer of pollution hanging over everything. After being outdoors only a few minutes the unhealthy air actually became tangible. A nose blown into a white hankie came out slimy black; a comb raked through clean hair came out edged in charcoal. Even though few people owned cars, pollution from factories and buses was out of control. It would be years before Japan righted this horrendous wrong. It would also be one of the main reasons we eventually left Japan.

FIFTY-TWO

YOU MAY WONDER how we got hot water and heat for our duplex. Well, wonder no more for I'll tell you. In the kitchen to the right of the sink, was a wall-mounted, on-demand water heater. It was awesome, one-hundred percent reliable; honestly something to write home about. Of course it took up space, hanging off the wall like that—and I sure could have used a third cupboard in its spot—but, in exchange for such a trifling, we never ran out of hot water.

Heating the house was not so gorgeous. In winter, Tokyo became bone-chillingly frigid with an accompanying gray, dreary dampness which on some days felt colder than Minnesota. It was weird how that happened as the temperatures were never that low, so it must have been the insulating properties of Minnesota's deep, beautifully crystallized snow that lifted spirits there.

When we moved into Asahi Court, it was the end of our first sizzling summer. The last thing we did at that particular time was waste our sun-sapped energy on thinking about more heat. We were doing everything in our power not to think about it. However, as autumn advanced, we realized we'd have to do something. Hence, we bought a PX space heater furnace. Do not conjure up small or inconspicuous. In fact, conjure something more along the lines of blatant, in-your-face rotund! Also do not entertain the idea of good looking (scurvy comes to mind), or having one single redeeming fashionable feature. It looked like a shaved wooly mammoth, or his cousin the great silverback ape, had taken up residence in our minikin of a living room, the only place we could put the beast.

I took one look at it and immediately considered having Sakae-san crochet that snood I had formerly dreaded, but then upon reflection decided it might be risky—space heaters housing that raging inferno and all.

Our furnace was dark brown and shiny. (Jeff instantly related.) It was a big metal box that came up to my shoulders. Oddly—and this was an aberration as bizarre as is the singer Madonna being named Madonna— the symbol of the furnace company was a bronze, sixteen-petaled chrysanthemum. That, my dears, was/is the official, sanctified, canonized symbol of the *Emperor of Japan!!!*

You figure it out. We couldn't. But there the symbol sat, like a bronzed imperial belly button in the middle of our furnace's front panel. And, don't you think for even one minute that I wasn't worried His Majesty might find out we had it and want it back. Who knows how chilly his palace chambers had become without it? And, what was I supposed to do if he *did* walk in one day and demand it back—kiss his ring—and then help him load it into his chariot?

Without a hitch, every time a Japanese came to visit, he was awestruck—blown away!—over finding himself in the company of folks who obviously knew Emperor Hirohito on a first-name basis because they had his furnace in their living room! Glen and I never failed to expansively blush the appropriate amount of humility. I worked at fine-tuning this in the boys, but they, of a more honest bent, never quite caught on to pretentious theatrics, no matter how much we rehearsed.

How did the heating system work? Actually, I can't answer that, but it did. That is if you liked Hades-hot or Arctic-blast.

But, more importantly ... *always to me more importantly* ... was it aesthetic? Well, perhaps so in a perhaps so kind of way. In truth, what you saw crouched there in our living room and taking up one-eighth of our entire habitat was only half of the story, because like the Incredible Hulk, it had to be fed. Just outside on our small patio, and directly in line with the furnace, Glen had installed two over-sized steel barrels that rested side by side on a pug-ugly, rough, shoddy, unpainted, heavy wooden cradle. The first time I saw this collection of heartbreak, its repulsive dreaminess nearly knocked me flat. Actually as I recall, Glen didn't think it was all that bad, but then you may remember, he had also once worn *those socks.*

As for me, I considered it an abomination, an odious repugnance; an eyesore that took up much of the space on our very tiny, very narrow patio. Additionally, to soften the curse of it, we were further graced with full-length glass windows in the living room through which we could take in this wretched view day or night. Night or day. World without end!

The Lord heats his earth in mysterious ways.

Protruding out the back of the furnace was a large metal stovepipe. It looked wonderful with the décor of the room. In order to get the pipe through the glass in the full-length window, we ever so cleverly, ingeniously—down right masterfully!—removed the window. In its place, Glen installed a very good looking piece of untreated plywood with an appropriately sized hole cut through it. Quite possibly even more enchanting, were the two supplementary pipes that stuck out of the barrels through which the heating oil was routed into the silver-backed ape. We were, by the grace of God, able to also thread these pipes through the plywood by using their own set of attractive holes. The vision of this egregious eyesore, in our otherwise pleasing living room, had the same effect on me as a lovely young maiden reaching up in a sleeveless sundress who didn't shave.

Every week the fuel was replenished. I particularly loved it when the kerosene trucks pulled up to the front of the house, crossed the lawn, parked next to the patio, and filled the barrels with their long twisted hoses. If Dame Fortune smiled, that truck arrived at the very same time the honey bucket truck also arrived. It was magical how the two, while asphyxiating us, enhanced our curb appeal.

By now you might have guessed that it was a bit tricky to install this kind of heating system. You might also have guessed that this kind of heating system was not entirely risk free. You would be right on both counts. It was a bitch to install and it was freakin' dangerous to use! I mean, we had a raging forest fire in a tin box burning six inches from our faces at all times. And here I had worried over whether or not I looked good in a kimono?

The summer following our first winter, we decided to take out our furnace for the hot months, relishing the thought of a once again restored, clean, uncluttered living room. In doing this, we were blessed—darned blessed—to be able to pile the entire monster on top of those steel barrels, on their unsightly cradle, in a gigantic metal and wooden whimsical heap. It did wonders for the enhancement of our small patio, plus we had the heart-stopping, never-stopping, beauty-stopping view of it through the living room windows. Good taste never failed to follow us. When, however, the next autumn rolled around, the trial of re-installing the beast was so horrendous, we decided to just put it in and leave the blighted thing there for the duration of our stay in Japan.

Okay, okay, so I shouldn't be such a petty pill, and certainly shouldn't natter on so, unchecked. Above all, I of the permanent goose bumps appreciated above everyone else the warmth our furnace gave us. But honestly, seeing it every darned day through my darned discriminating eyes was like a darned on-going death from a thousand darned paper cuts.

Rare is the union of beauty and furnaces.

FIFTY-THREE

DURING OUR SECOND year in Japan, Glen came home one evening with big news. Of course he had been unable to inform me by phone, because—well, you know. That was still on the to-do list ... along with air conditioners, cars for wives, 3-in-1 All Purpose Oil cans with drip-proof caps, panty hose, tables with long legs, and children born potty trained.

He told me he would be going to Vietnam. *War time Vietnam!*

> "The time *not* to become
> a father, (*or be born!*)
> is eighteen
> years before a war."
> E. B. White

Up until then, Glen had taken periodic trips back to the States, to Vietnam, and to other countries in the Far East. But this time, he explained, he would be gone a long time. This wouldn't be like it was after college graduation when he went to Baltimore for training and the boys and I returned to the bosom of our Minnesota loved ones. We were to stay put in Tokyo, while Glen went into a combat zone. As Targeting Officer of the 500th Military Intelligence Brigade, his job would be to write up operational plans for the build-up to the 1964 Gulf of Tonkin incident. Nobody knew then that it was bogus—that we had not really been attacked—or that it would turn out to be L.B.J.'s folly.

As usual, I, above all, did not know any of this. I wasn't supposed to. I was completely in the dark, as I always was when it came to Glen's work. I was simply following orders as instructed: do not get involved. I was also not one to regularly kvetch, but the reality was that for Glen, this separation had danger written all over it. As for the three of us left behind (can you really be left behind if you're already in a foreign country?), it would be a separation without communication from Glen, without the sheltering arms of an extended family, without a network of friends, with very slow U.S. mail, with almost no military contact (remember we were invisible), and without any of the securities that wives and children back home had when they were un-moored. Furthermore, like the sword of Damocles, there still remained the unresolved mystery of the go-home-damn-Yankee malcontent who lurked somewhere down the road.

Jeff was four and Matt was two; I was twenty-five. I had Karen and Bob, Humpty D. the washing machine, Sakae-san's sagacious fashion expertise, and what I hoped was good sense. It all boiled down to this: Glen was the Keener tent; I was the center pole that held the tent up. That was about the sum of it.

Glen was gone for six months. Of course, I carried on as usual. My biggest break from the routine was going to NHK twice a week. The handsome chauffeured car regularly brought me home well past midnight because filming the shows took many hours. In no time at all a rumor slithered throughout the area that in my husband's absence, I had a paramour on the sly.

He was certainly someone filthy rich because he owned a sleek, black, chauffeured car, and always brought me home in the wee hours of the morning! It was easy for such prattle to germinate. Why not? And, why, for Pete's sake hadn't they noticed that car all along? But it was way more fun to make things up, and to be sure, I was a foreign sitting duck. Besides, there wasn't one other blessed thing for those neighbor wives to do but gossip ... and wrap up their newborn's umbilical cords.

Not to disappoint them, one day I gave anyone who cared an unexpected treat. What began as a normal day turned into a real provocation for their wagging tongues, for I had a surprise visit (the extremely rare visit I had was always a surprise visit!), from an American lady and her ten-year-old son. While drinking lemonade, the boy spilled a glassful on himself, thoroughly soaking his clothes. This was not a problem for me, as by now you know I was well versed in the art of hand laundry. I washed and hung them outside to dry.

The problem was finding something for the boy to wear while they dried. Matt's diapers were much too demeaning and Jeff's underpants way too small. What else to do but go into Glen's drawer and pull out a set of his skivvies. With a few critically placed safety pins, the over-sized underwear did the job. The lad passed the rest of the afternoon playing with my boys indoors while his clothes dried outdoors.

A radiant sun arose the next morning. I did the laundry, as usual, feeling pleased as punch that I could hang it outside on the clothesline rather than nauseatingly across the living room. Wet clothes and sheets, by now, had quickly turned into the most major ornamental blight on our home. It had also become hazardous for the boys. When they played Blind Man's Bluff in Mommy's Laundry, blinds were not even necessary. With their eyes wide open they could see nothing, because of the soggy, hanging, impenetrable layers. Perilously, this left them free to whack into each other, cracking their little skulls like ripe coconuts. Whee! What could be better than little brothers seeing each other's mutilated cracked skulls?

But, as I started to say, on this day the sun was shining and the living room laundry was closed. Amongst the things hanging outside on the line was Glen's underwear. He had been gone for five months.

Whamo!

It was as if someone had erected a flashing neon sign on top of our house. Gleam! Glare! Flicker! Flare! Underwear!

MAN'S UNDIES ON PEGGY'S CLOTHESLINE!
TOLD YOU SO! SHE'S A SKANK!!

I really hadn't given Glen's skivvies a thought when I hung them out there, but now seeing the excitement they were causing, I was rather glad I had. I did feel remorse for Sakae-san, however, as she had every reason to flip out—which she was now doing on the kitchen floor. After all, her reputation was also on the line being connected to us like that and all. Never one to hold back her emotions, Sakae-san was in the throes of a major hissy fit.

"Lumors are frying!" she cried.

And she was right. The word was out. I was nothing more than a low down, cheating, floozified-neighbor-lady-slut. Great! I was making their day.

Peggy, Peggy, Clay Pigeon Lady.

Out in plain sight, hanging on the line, was all the proof the ladies needed of my suspected late-night trysts. Why, the scandal of it all was causing the spiritless, droopy faces of each Mrs. Dryasdust to lift, as blood began to once again surge through their parched veins. The long dry spell was over; the drudgery of their boring routines finally taking a hike. I had become their instant soap opera—before Japan had soap operas; even the instant kind.

Peggy Keener

> "I will never
> repeat gossip,
> so listen carefully
> the first time."
> Unknown

As was my custom, I took the clothes down at noon before too much pollution could collect in their folds. But on that day, I purposely let two items remain on the line: Glen's underwear. By my proclamation, they were to stay there until the very last arch of the sun disappeared behind the horizon. Why curtail the ladies' enjoyment, I explained to Sakae-san? They needed a full eight-hour day in which to yackety-blabbermouth-yak, and I, being the noble sort that I was, was the very one who could bring it to them. In my heart of hearts, I knew it was the neighborly thing to do.

I thought it would end there. I planned it would end there. Crapola, it didn't! Following right on the heels of this occurrence was another totally innocent event, further convincing the mealy-mouthed neighbors that they were right about me and my slatternly ways. I really was a crumb. Even worse, a crumb-bum!

A week to the day later, a motor scooter with a dry cleaner delivery man on it brought some clothes to our door. No one was home. What was he to do? After puzzling over this dilemma, he decided to hang them outside on the front door ... *in plain sight* ... *for everyone to* see.

Wonderful!

In the meantime—behind *almost* closed curtains—slanted eyes were checking the days off the calendar. They knew exactly how long Glen had been gone. They also knew he had not returned. And now hanging there in their unfettered field of vision—if they squinted hard enough—was ... oh, m'gosh ... was that a man's suit?

A really nice man's suit! *Delivered to the wrong address!* But they didn't know that! Talk about neighborhood good times! Where, oh, where was Mrs. Dovenburg, my old Sunday school teacher, when I needed her to vouch for me? Oh, yeah, she was back in Austin preaching about how hell-bent-crumb-bum-wayward the Asians were!

Recognizing the insurmountable task of Japan-proofing myself, I just let it fizzle out. Why fight a system that couldn't be won? So, at the end of the day ... it was just the end of the day.

> "There are many
> who dare *not*
> kill themselves
> for fear of what
> the neighbors
> will say."
> Cyril Connolly

FIFTY-FOUR

AT LONG LAST the six months were up. This time it was my turn to go to Tachikawa to meet a plane. Right on time I was there to watch the passengers come through customs. Even so, I didn't spot Glen. He was nowhere to be seen. I was sure of the schedule, so where was he? Then out of the blue a stranger put his arms around me and gave me a big slurpy kiss. Slut that I was, even I was offended for I didn't know this man! Yet, his lips felt familiar ….

It was Glen! All the time I had been searching for him in the crowd, he had knowingly been walking right past me, waiting to be recognized. He was as thin as a bread stick. That is not to say he had been fat when I last saw him, but this was thin—haggard, gaunt, hollow-cheeked thin. I had to hear his voice to be convinced he was the man I lived with; the same one who had fathered my children.

I drew him to me. One close look, one close feel, and I knew my work was cut out for me. Unexpectedly, I was overwhelmed with the need to protect him. This was new. Glen had always been my protector. On our ride back to Asahi Court, there was no gushing reunion talk; only a studied, tired, very loud quiet.

As we drove up to our duplex, we saw over the door a big sign: "Do Not Disturb! Just Got Married *Again*!" (Karen's doing.) It was perfect. Just what the moment needed to jolt us into realizing this was all real. Glen *was* home!

Jeff and Matt poured out the door and into his arms.

In the days to follow I cooked all of Glen's favorite dishes in the hope of enticing him to eat—and to eat a lot—and I loved him thoroughly. Still, Vietnam had taken its toll. Glen remained distant and withdrawn. I knew he needed a kick start back to his old life. I contacted his commander and asked for a home leave to the States. Within two months, we were back in my parents' home in Minnesota.

That and … oh, yes … I was pregnant again.

Shazam! Just like that! As Glen slipped out of his Fruit of the Loom, I bestowed him with his Fruit of the Womb! We were both happy. I probably more than Glen because I really wanted another baby—the precious kind we were so good at making—and it even possibly might be a little girl. It also meant, and I know this was pathetically lame, that for nine months I would once again not have to worry about holding in my stomach, no matter who walked in the room. Only another female would understand.

> "I have an intense desire
> to return to the womb.
> Anybody's!"
> Woody Allen

FIFTY-FIVE

JUST LIKE THAT we were once again in Minnesota, ensconced in the special warmth that only Austin provided me. Jeff and Matt had not seen my parents for more than two years, an eternity in the lives of youngsters. It was as if they were meeting them for the first time—all over again. From the beginning, for some crazy reason we will never understand, rather than calling my mom Gramma, Jeff insisted on calling her Mrs. Wong. He couldn't have learned it back in Kichijoji. Good grief, Wong wasn't even a Japanese name!

At first we thought it was pretty cute and little-kid funny. Until it persisted. That's when I decided that two, three or even four Wongs did not make a right. It was time I said something to Jeff about Mom's real name. For what it was worth, "Margaret Mary McDonell McLaughlin" did not sound to me a whole lot like "Mrs. Wong," but then those were only my ears. I even went so far as to suggest that, ridiculous as it sounded, he might consider calling her "Grandmother"!

> "In order to influence a child,
> one must be careful to not
> be that child's parent
> or grandparent."
> Don Marquis

After pondering "Grandmother" (which apparently held no appeal), Jeff decided to call her no name at all. This continued for several days. On the

209

fifth day, Jeff overheard someone talking to Mom about honey. That was it! He liked the sound of it. Honey! *Gramma Honey!* That's who she was.

While Jeff liked it, Mom relished, cherished it! The name was so unique, so cute, so Jeff—so all hers and nobody else's! It was also fitting that Jeff, her first grandchild, should have naming rights. As I reflect back on that day, how grateful I am Jeff had not overheard a conversation on trusses or goiters or latrines—like my old pal Latrina! Yes, it was Jeff who anointed Mrs. Wong "Gramma Honey," and for the other seven grandchildren who followed, she was never known by anything else.

> Su Wong marries Lee Wong.
> The next year the Wongs have a new baby.
> The nurse brings out a lovely, healthy, bouncy,
> but definitely Caucasian-white baby boy.

> "Congratulations," says the nurse to the new father.
> "What will you and Mrs. Wong name the baby?"

> The puzzled father looks at his new son and replies,
> "Well, two Wongs don't make a white,
> so I think we will name him ...
> Sum Ting Wong."

Matt had been an infant the last time we were in Austin. Now he was a three-year-old who looked no joke, like a six-year-old. He was trying his best to measure up to that image, but the yardstick was just too tall. Take for example, manners, those testy things all children find irksome and unnecessary. As for me, I couldn't stress their importance enough because I realized this was our big chance to impress the folks back home. And, you'd better believe I was in the business of impressing the folks back home while I had the chance!

> "Manners are especially
> the need of the plain.
> The pretty can get
> away with anything."
> Evelyn Waugh

My mother had a dear friend, a very gentle and dignified woman named Nanna Tiegen. If ever there was a lady, she was Nanna, Austin's top choice for Miss Manners. During this trip home, Nanna invited us over for tea.

Tea! Just the word rattled me. This would not be a potato chip and Kool-Aid soiree. No way. This would be classy. I needed to prepare the boys for their first big etiquette hurdle. Tension was high. Lessons began at once.

On the day of our big to-do, I scrubbed, polished, primped and preened the boys, stopping just short of chafing. Then while I performed a last buffing, I did a final re-run of the deportment lessons. I knew in my bones if I did it right, the message would sink in forever.

Finally when I could think of nothing more to vamp up, we got in the car and drove to Nanna's house. Parking at her curb, we stepped out. By then I was pretty secure about Jeff's deportment, but still significantly shaky when it came to Matt. On the long walkway up to Nanna's front door, I did one last dry run with him.

"Now," I prompted, "be sure to say please and thank you to Mrs. Tiegen." I continued to repeat this as often as the length of the sidewalk allowed, just in case Matt had not gotten it the first, second, or forty-seventh time.

Just then Nanna opened the door. In a lovely, cultured, perfectly timbered voice, she said, "Why, helloooo, Mah-thew."

Matt stopped in the middle of the first step, puffed out his chest and in his full-throated Matt voice blurted out, "Please and thank you, Mrs. Tiegen!"

It just about blew the numbers off the cute chart. Or at least I thought so.

> "Few things are harder
> to put up with
> than a good example."
> Mark Twain

ON THIS TRIP back to the States, Glen and I decided we would take our time returning to Japan. We would rent a car and give the boys a chance to make an authentic connection with their real homeland. Therefore after a week in Minnesota, we drove to Colorado to visit the large Keener clan. Then we headed towards the West Coast and our flight back to our other homeland. The unreal one.

This was a drive that would cover more than a third of the United States. It was fun showing our country off to the boys. Jeff was convinced no one lived in America because he never saw anyone outdoors. He couldn't figure out where all the Americans were. The roadways were empty of people either walking in or beside them as they did in the bustling, over-crowded Japan. It was an interesting observation, something I had never really thought about. But, it was true. As we moved from place to place, we Americans were almost always encapsulated in our vehicles. Who needed feet when they were American?

Over the border into Nevada we stopped at a very nice dinner club. It was late on a Sunday afternoon and the place was packed with fashionable diners. Once inside, we were surprised to see that the entire back side of the restaurant was a wall of huge windows overlooking a lovely lake.

It was serenely beautiful, which of course explained why the place was packed. There was even a small sandy beach.

As we sat around the crisp white table cloth, the sunset began lighting up the horizon with luscious oranges and reds and yellows. It was more than inviting. We asked the boys if they'd like to go out on the beach and play while we waited for the waitress. No going near the water, however, I warned! Well, of course they would, and of course they wouldn't. Out they skedaddled looking forward to the feel of sand in their fingers. In the meantime, Glen and I studied the menu.

Like a good mom, I checked repeatedly on the boys through the big picture windows, while trying to concentrate on our dinner choices. Finally the waitress took our order. When she was finished I turned again to catch a glimpse of the boys. As I shifted in my chair, I noticed everyone, *everyone,* in the dining room had swiveled their chairs around and was looking out the windows. Must have been the lure of the magnificent sunset, I told myself. Well, I sure didn't want to miss that! I swiveled around, too.

But, wait a minute. What was going on? Not only was everyone looking, but they were also laughing. Laughing hard! Just what was so hysterically funny about a sunset, I wondered? But then, never having been in Nevada before, how would I know what amused the folks there? My eyes scanned the horizon. The colors in the sky were spectacular, but not particularly what I'd call comical. I searched the beach for Jeff and Matt. They were exactly where I told them to be. Good boys.

But ... uh ... what was it those good boys were doing?

Back in Japan, the men and boys never had the irksome task of finding a public toilet, because that is what the great outdoors had been created for. I mean, God was a male, so He made it easy for His kind! The men usually made an effort to be discreet by ducking into alleys, spraying trees up close, or at least turning away from on-coming foot traffic. Boys, on the other hand, just let it rip—yet another sorry example of that boys-will-be-boys (and not girls) thing.

Thus, following the lead of the Japanese males, and believing as the gospel truth that the outdoors had been specifically designed for their male needs, our boys followed their example to a pee. It didn't matter when the urge struck because the world was not only their oyster, but it was also their comfort station. And that was just what was happening now. Side by side with their little pudgy bottoms hanging out, they were spraying towards the lake in perfectly matched, high curving streams that, I will add, would have made men the world over proud. And like men the world over, I bet they thought they'd make the water level rise.

The diners, looking on with glee, found it hilarious.

It was nobody's guess who those boys belonged to. Glen and I, with our shoulders hunched over studying the weave in the table cloth, were the only ones with our backs to the windows.

"Men are superior to women.
For one thing,
they can urinate
from a speeding car."
Will Durst

OUR DRIVE BACK to Travis Air Force Base where we'd pick up our return flight to Japan, took us through lots of farm country. One noon we stopped at a busy roadside cafe. All the tables were full with only four stools remaining at the counter. We settled upon them, the boys' feet dangling in the air, and ordered lunch. Before you could say trans-fatty-licious, we were munching down on lardaciously red meat burgers and tallow-dripping, over-salted French fries. The boys thought they'd found Nirvana! Perfect bliss had finally joined hands with the dinner table. American food was so good. And so good for us!

Halfway through the meal, and just about the time their tummies reached full capacity, a farmer came through the door, ambled across the cafe and plopped down heavily on the stool next to Jeff.

Now, people who are unfamiliar with young children may not know about young children's noses. They may also have no idea that noses don't just start working at birth. It takes a while for them to kick into gear, usually peaking at around age three or four at which point everything— trust me *everything*— has a smell. Preoccupied with this budding sense, these youngsters are like high-strung, overly sensuous bunnies, their little noses crazily tweeching and twitching over everything in their paths.

That summer Jeff's nose just happened to be peaking.

"I cannot smell mothballs
because it is so difficult to get
their little legs apart."
Steve Martin
(Oh, Peggy, that was bad! Please don't tell Mrs. Wong.)

Our farmer friend, off to Jeff's left, had come in straight from his field. It must have been Fertilizer Friday. No, *for certain* it was Fertilizer Friday! As you well know, manure is not shy. It does not fool around. It tells it like it is. It was no secret that a clumpy layer of rich, rank, feculence was compacted deep in the treads of the farmer's boots. Also a swipe of it here, and a smash of it there, clung securely to his overalls. Moreover, oozing from his rural bulk was a heady mixture of toil and sweat, all combining at once to crash head-on into Jeff's newly waxing sensitivities.

With his nasal passages delicately primed to detect even the minutest trace of a scent—and hopelessly unable to stop himself from this newly evolving habit—the innocent Jeff took two deep breaths of the malodorous,

213

gamey sodbuster. Swiftly the noxious stench rode the airways through his undefiled, over-impressionable olfactories, and landed squarely in his stomach on top of the all-American lunch. I looked at my boy just as his face re-cast itself from creamy white to disgorge green.

Next his body started that slow motion heaving—the one we all know so well—swiftly building up to the moment when I knew the juicy hamburger and greasy French fries would be catapulted into time and space. No doubt about it, they were on the way. Imminent! I had to get Jeff out of there. Hells bells, we were at a lunch counter, if you follow me—as in one long connected dining table with hungry people seated at it!

I spotted the restroom to my right as I grabbed Jeff to my left. Then just as my arms wrapped around him, he erupted. Out came everything he had so recently consumed, flowing outward from his rosebud lips and his hyper-impressionable nose onto the counter top, along the counter top, down the side of the counter top, and onto the farmer next to him, swerving in a thick swath across the floor, past the tables of patrons, and all the way to the restroom.

To a whole new level, it upped the jargon "blow lunch."

As I said, it was noon and the place was packed. We'll leave it to guesswork just what transpired in the lunch room behind us, because once I made it into the ladies' room, I sure as heck was not going back to find out. Besides, I was preoccupied with Jeff in there for a protracted length of time. What I really hoped for was that if we stayed in there long enough, everyone would clear out of the restaurant before we exited, and we would not have to face the upchuck music. One thing I knew for sure was that I positively was not going to waste any sympathy in fretting over the likes of that foul, fetid farmer. As far as I was concerned, he and his stinky middle-of-nowhere-and-not-bother-to-freshen-up existence had asked for it. I had dibs that Farmer Eau de Dung had finished his lunch without noticing a gol darned thing.

> "Why should we take up farming
> when there are so many
> mongongo nuts
> in the world?"
> African bushman

FIFTY-SIX

OUR VACATION BACK home was just what Glen had needed. It brought him back to us. You know, when you have a fresh look at what it is you're fighting for, it gives a whole new perspective to the battle. That is not to say that Vietnam was behind us, for Glen's involvement there lasted more than two decades. The Vietnam War was a very long war and one, by the way, which the Vietnamese ironically called the American War. Whoever it belonged to, it was Glen's job to fight it by gathering intelligence data. Many times over the years to follow, Glen returned there for weeks, months and even a year at a time. Where other kids' dads went to the office, my kids' dad went to Indo-China.

But, now, with Glen back on track, I had extra concerns of my own. New worries and new responsibilities. This third pregnancy was not one to be taken lightly. The doctor who delivered Jeff told me I should probably not have more children. The doctor who delivered Matt said it even louder—absolutely I should not have more children! Their admonitions somehow flew out the window on the night Glen returned from that long stay in Vietnam. The expected date of the new baby was exactly nine months to the day of his homecoming! I called it Planned Parenthood.

Within five months my mid-section was already a shelf upon which I could set things, giving a clear signal something was amiss. At that stage the baby's health was not such a worry; it was me who was the problem. Already I was the size most women were at eight months. Crazy as it sounded, it seemed there was nothing holding the baby in me. I tried wearing a maternity girdle for support, but outgrew it in no time. Then I learned the Japanese women always bound their pregnant bellies in long obi-like cloths, so I tried that. It didn't work either. The bindings seemed to press downward which was already the direction my abdomen was going. What I needed was an under-prop that would raise my baby up where she was supposed to be.

Notice I said "she" even though we had no idea "she" was a she. No one knew the gender of their babies back then. It was all a sweet, talcum-powdered crap shoot. The nine months of tricky speculating, feigned prophesying, old wives' prognostications and, of course giddy anticipation, were all part of the maternity game. Don't you see? When parents could not depend on the certainty of either pink or blue, that's when yellow was invented—so they could immediately start purchasing layettes and get their decorating done early.

At an appointment during the seventh month, the Green Park doctor became alarmed. The baby's head was deep into the pelvic area, much too low for that early a time frame. He and his nurse went to work. They got some sheets and tore them into long strips. Then they wrapped the strips around and around my mid-section as if I was some kind of out-of-season May pole. On one side of my back they left a piece long enough to go from my waist up to my shoulder, down the front of me, under my abdomen, back up and over the other shoulder, down my back on that side, and finally landing at my waist where its journey ended. They secured this suspect invention with safety pins, strategically sticking them all over the place. Like a sling for a broken arm, my baby was inside me in her own makeshift hammock.

The next few weeks were a trial. The device felt good. It felt bad. It felt up-lifting. It felt down-pressing. It was my deliverance, my torture. I could barely breathe in. I could barely breathe out. I needed Karen's help to get it on every morning, and Glen's help to get it off every evening. It was a devilish contraption. And, I was running low on sheets.

In the midst of the disquietude, our Hawaiian neighbor, who lived in the duplex off to our right, had an accident. While using a knife, he nearly cut off his finger. By chance, Glen and I were the first ones on the scene. Lickety-split we got George, along with his bloody mess of a finger, into our car and rushed him to the military hospital at Tachikawa Air Force Base. I say "rush," but as usual it was a long, tedious, pot-hole-pitted drive on frightfully narrow roads. Finally when at last we arrived at the emergency room, I got out with the traumatized George while Glen parked the car.

George's golden Hawaiian skin had turned a deathly gray. He was obviously in great pain, to say nothing of the terror he was feeling at the possible loss of his finger. Together he and I shuffled through the big entry doors. They opened onto a long hallway with a nurses' station at the far end. George was slumped over, stumbling, in much distress, and holding his seriously injured, towel-swathed hand to his chest.

From the end of the hall the nurses spotted him. Three of them immediately began rushing down the hall toward us. By then I was no longer at his side. It wasn't that I wasn't trying to be. Even though George was bleeding to death, I was so burdened by the weight of my under-slung belly that I couldn't even keep up with a traumatically afflicted, nearly dead, nine-and-a-half fingered patient!

Already halfway down the hall, the women in the starched uniforms swept towards us gathering speed as they, at full run, began discerning the urgency of the problem. Closer and closer they came.

Finally they were in front of George. They stretched their arms out to him.

And moved right on past ... to me!

Gadzooks! What had just happened? In the blink of an eye they were on my belly likes flies on a colossal, overripe pumpkin, firing off a myriad of questions about contractions and minutes, and trying their best to assist me with the delivery of my child. Actually with my *children*, they were now insisting, because they knew I was carrying multiples! The chaotic foofaraw was so fast and consternating that I could not get a word in edgewise to explain I was neither Octomom (before artificial insemination) nor the patient.

Meanwhile as the commotion continued, the long-suffering George stood hunched all alone and verily ignored, dying slowly from his self-inflicted fingerectomy.

I tell this story only to illustrate how dreadful I looked. My belly was huge, blown way out of proportion to the rest of my body, sagging down to where no abdomen had gone before. Or since! It wasn't good. It was also not nearly as attractive as a lopped off, blood soaked, gory finger stump.

I know, I know. Every woman thinks she's huge when she's pregnant. I'm here to give you numbers. When I started this baby business, my waist measured twenty-one inches. When I delivered, my waist was sixty-five inches. It sounds unbelievable—wider than I was tall! But, it was true. On top of that, I was extremely, abnormally, uncharitably short-waisted. (Actually, I still am.) And, no, I wasn't fat, but rather a commendable size seven when I wasn't wearing a Ringling Brothers maternity tent. When I sat down my stomach surpassed the end of my knees by four inches. It was egregiously bizarre. I was thankful we didn't live in a nudist camp. They, *en masse,* would have forced me to put my tent back on.

The good dismembered-finger news is that finally one of the nurses spotted the blood pooling on the floor under the forbearing George and went to his aid. The other two followed. As I was now the ignored one and no longer of interest, Glen and I returned home, our responsibilities over. In time George did recover with his finger intact, while I continued for the next two months to sheet-strip my stomach into its shoulder braces, and look like motherhood gone bad. I was the poster child, if ever there was one, for GAWA—Girls Against Wild Abandonment.

Sleeping posed another challenge. Glen and I slept on a futon (foo-tong, a thick foldable sleeping pad), which we laid out each night on the bedroom floor. Using a futon instead of an ordinary bed gave us an empty, usable room during the day, and who needed a bed during daylight hours? Or for that matter, who needed an empty room at night? In our small home, it was one part of the Japanese mindset we embraced totally.

My problem was getting down to the futon, a tricky, slow motion maneuver. Getting up, however, and going against gravity, was considerably worse. It was a painful and even more drawn out procedure. Going in either direction required Glen's help. It was his job to hold my huge belly while my job was to move the rest of me. The two parts ... which, for crying out loud, should have been one ... were like individual separate units encased in and held together by not a girdle of muscles, but mainly by skin. My baby and I were living symbiotically like Chang and Eng!

Too late to go back, I had made my futong and now had to sleep in it! To lie down on my side (the only option I had), took precise teamwork to get me and my belly successfully moving in a conjoined fashion. In other words, both parts had to progress in tandem. Finally, when I was at ground level and resting on the futon, the baby was literally lying beside me. Glen and I could see the faint outline of the baby's body where my skin draped over her. Throughout the night whenever I had to move, I had to first awaken Glen, who would then in a slow simultaneous movement, lift the baby (which was my belly), while I moved the body around the baby (which was me). Yes, it was very unnatural, very weird, very much something you would want to avoid at all cost, and certainly nothing to write home about. Which I didn't! Mrs. Wong would have been beside herself.

On the other hand, there was something during those long nine months that was very nice. The boys, in their charming way, fell in love with their new baby. They talked to my stomach endlessly. This was done in polite stages. First, like true gentlemen, they rang the baby's doorbell conveniently located in the middle of my colossal pumpkin. Actually, this was not as evident as you are probably thinking. Do not envision a navel doorbell here, for my belly button had long ago reconfigured itself into a vague mystery. It now resembled either a pancake, a tortilla, a crepe, a chapati or a lefse, depending upon your nationality.

Next—after ringing my pancake/tortilla/crepe/chapati/lefse—Jeff and Matt talked softly and up-close to my belly in boy chat, enlightening their baby on the activities of their boy days.

Furthermore, Jeff and Matt had early on convinced themselves that the baby could see them by looking out my nose. This concept broadened as the months went by when they decided that my navel—or whatever that thing was—was not a doorbell after all, but also a special window to the world. Every time we went to the army movie theatre, they insisted I pull up my maternity tent so the baby, too, could look out and enjoy the movie. A womb with a view, if you will.

The boys also had a baby-arrival calendar they made and taped it to the front of the refrigerator ... the same one that contained the all-important ice cream stockpile. Each morning one of them alternately X-ed off the day in wavering crayon lines.

Like a precise Swiss watch, exactly nine months to the day Glen returned from Vietnam, I went into labor. As predicted this did not go smoothly. The doctor was very concerned. The baby, he asserted, had been dangerously low in the pelvis for weeks, and he expressed a genuine fear there would be brain damage due to a compromised oxygen supply. Hearing his concerns in my agitated state, I could not get over what an extraordinarily benevolent bedside manner he had. That information, coming at such a disquieting time, was just what a distraught, hurting, straining mother needed for comfort!

After many hours the baby finally arrived. There was absolute silence in the delivery room. Dr. Too Much Information didn't speak, no nurse spoke, no baby cried. The soundlessness hung like clashing cymbals. This was my third time at this and I knew what I should be hearing. I was hearing nothing. I was also unable to see anything. All the warnings the doctors had given me over the years now came screaming back in my head.

I waited and I waited. At last, when seconds had turned into centuries, I heard a squall. It was fantastic! Wondrous, melodious, baby squall music! With it I knew my baby was alive. I began to cry; then sob. Nine months of worry and pain poured out of me even though I had yet to see my baby or hear any uplifting words from the doctor.

Just then, into my wet, swollen eyes appeared the face of a corpsman (military nurse). He leaned right up next to me and spoke these exact words: "Why are you crying, Ma'am? You have a beautiful baby girl!"

Had he just said "girl"? That's what I'd heard, and with that, I completely lost it. I knew this would be my last baby, but I had not dared to let myself dream it could happen. It was more than I had hoped for. Way more. Two sons and now a daughter?

A daughter. A daughter!

> "When I was born
> I was so surprised
> I didn't talk for
> a year and a half."
> Gracie Allen

There is an old Malaysian proverb that states: The turtle lays thousands of eggs without anyone knowing, but when a hen lays an egg, the whole country is informed." That was me, the hen. Cluck-a-doodle-doo!

The corpsman stepped away and returned with a bundle of baby, enchanting and magnificently robust. My eyes, my hands, my mother's heart examined her—*my daughter*— in that unbelieving moment. Every part from the white down on her head to the tips of her wee ten toes was perfection. So, I marveled, this is what baby girls are?

In that moment, even though she was my third child, I was still dazed all over again by the immensity of her significance. What gift in life could be more prized than this, another child? And what responsibilities could be more awesome; what rewards more limitless?

"A baby is God's opinion
that the world should go on."
Carl Sandburg

Erin Mary, Her Royal Specialness, was born on June 8, 1965. She weighed just short of nine pounds, and you should know *there was not a single thing wrong with her brain!* NOTHING! In fact, having your head stuck in your mother's pelvic girdle for two months may just be the recipe for brilliance, because that is what *Dr.* Erin Mary, *M.D.* turned out to be. We should all be so lucky to have such a low-down start in life.

I turned her over. There across Erin's exquisite porcelain bottom were the words, "Made in Japan."

Just kidding!

"I was born in Australia
because my mother
wanted me to be near her."
Unknown

FIFTY-SEVEN

WHEN JEFF WAS born, I was stupefied over the depth of my love for him; awestruck by the fierceness of its intensity. When I became pregnant with Matt, I couldn't imagine how I could ever bisect such profound feelings and divvy out portions to two children. I found I didn't have to. It didn't work that way. There was as much passion for Matt as there had ever been for Jeff.

With Erin, I truly learned the elasticity and equality of a mother's heart. It never needs Sanforizing nor does it ever become diluted. No one of my children ever maxed out my love space, and a divided heart simply did not happen. Instead of my becoming one-third of a mom to each child, I became a whole mom in triplicate, for each child received the expansive, exuberant, inexhaustible whole of me.

I know this will sound like a crazy lady talking, but here it is. As with all new mothers, the night feedings, with their repeated interruptions, came just when the mom's furnace most needed re-stoking. This was necessary to build up the strength she needed to face another day of the clawing needs of a loving, but demanding family. Yet it must be said, those night feedings were the very times I liked best. In the dark of night, when there was nothing else bidding for my attention, I could concentrate all of me on whichever of my three babies I was holding. With only the two of us locked together in our rocking chair capsule, it was complete serenity.

Many years later someone told me about La Leche League. I couldn't believe it. How ridiculous was that! Like you had to take out membership in a club in order to nurse your baby? If they'd asked me, I would have dropped that Frenchy business and renamed it just what it was ... "Tits for Tots!"

AS ERIN HAD been stuck in one position inside me for so long, one of her ears had been pressed against my pelvic bone and folded over along the top rim. This I couldn't ignore. It wasn't just the discomfort she would experience wearing earmuffs everyday to hide it, but it could also curb her possible chances of becoming Miss America—or Miss Kichijoji, if it came to that. In my maternal all-knowingness, I was sure I could fix the problem.

During feeding times, as she nursed all snug and warm against me, I massaged her ear over and over, opening it up like a softly bent flower pedal. In no time, her little ear turned into a perfectly shaped contour. Such is the suppleness of a newborn.

> "As Miss America, my goal
> is to bring peace
> to the entire world,
> and then to get
> my own apartment."
> Jay Leno

BABIES REALLY INTENSIFIED the business of love. The truth about it was this: loving a mate was taking a risk, like plunging headlong into a huge gamble. As one little boy put it: "On the first date, people just tell each other lies, and that usually gets them interested enough for a second date." After enough of this epigamic gaming, you one day took the leap by making the decision to go for it as your studied, slowly building confidence assured you everything would be okay. Yes, it'd probably ... no, it *would* ... work. You *would* bind yourself to this person for the rest of your life.

You dove in. "I do!" Plop, it's done!

On the other hand, loving your baby was entirely different. It just happened. No games were played and no previews were shown to see if you wanted him. You didn't get to check out his I.Q., flirt with him, investigate his background, his build, or his bank account; you just incubated him until show time. When people talked about love at first sight, no way were they talking about sweethearts. They were talking about mothers, fathers and babies.

More suddenly than a hiccup, love struck. Nothing about it was negotiable. Even before baby's arrival Mom and Dad were so baby charmed, they fell goofy mad in love with the bump on Mom's stomach, knowing the preciousness within was the most perfect, most wanted child ever.

One final gigantic push + one first glimpse = unreserved love everlasting. It just was.

"Woman in Hurricane Has Baby Three Times!"
(Tabloid headline suggested by Tracy Ullman)

Right off the bat, Jeff and Matt felt the love, too. They were flat out smitten with their new sister. Matt, however, took smitten to greater heights than did Jeff, the elder Jeff needing to concentrate on his finger painting and cooking—swish-spit. As expected, during the first night Erin awoke crying. Shocked by the unexpected wailing in the middle of the night, Matt rushed into our bedroom. There he found Erin and me in the rocking chair. His adorable three-year-old face screwed into an agony of consternation as he crept up to my lap and peered down at his new baby. Even at that very young age, Matt had a compassion for others that was way beyond his years, and he now recognized something serious had happened to Erin. That's what crying was all about, wasn't it?

I assured Matt that Erin was only hungry, but he didn't buy it. He was on the case. Taking one of her tiny feet in his hands, he vigilantly stood guard beside the chair holding it throughout the feeding, no short amount of time for a newborn. Then he switched feet as I switched breasts. Only when Erin was at last returned to her bassinet, and he was fully assured his baby was alright, did Matt finally relax and allow himself to slouch into parade rest. Then, officially off duty, he marched back to bed.

Three hours later, Erin again awoke crying. A repeat performance ensued. Matt rushed in, held one foot, then the other, supervised the feeding, and did not relinquish his duties until he was sure she was once again back asleep. Words cannot describe the sincerity and charm of his actions. The world has never known a dearer child than Matt.

Night #2 played out in the identical way. Matt, the centurion, rode shotgun over the night feedings.

On the third morning, Matt did not awaken. Nor did he awaken in the afternoon. About supper time he showed up, just long enough to refill and return to bed. That night he did not appear. From then on, Erin was on her own.

FIFTY-EIGHT

FOR ALL OF the above reasons, I did not return to work at NHK, even though they had left the studio door open for me. As the mother of three young children who were rife with life, as well as a husband who was frequently out of the country, I knew it was time to give up on that job, fun as it had been. My new full-time gig was being Mom. Anyway, returning to work after Erin's birth simply wasn't reasonable. Besides, the strain of continually trying to fool the public into thinking I was a virginal maiden would have been difficult with spit up on the shoulders of everything I owned, as well as the seeping milk stains across my bosom. What I had now, instead, were *real* duties—far more important than teaching English as a bogus uncertified-teacher-actress-ham-sandwich. What I really needed more than anything was to get back into my physical groove. I was very far from the same body I had been nine months before.

To be sure, I was a mess. It wasn't anything an onlooker could see, and my weight had returned to normal in no time at all. It was my abdomen that was the disaster. We're not talking a few dozen stretch marks here. We're talking one gigantic, all-encompassing stretch mark: the entire front of me! The limits of its elasticity were shot with no resiliency left to reshape it. What did you expect when a mother swallowed a Volkswagen Beetle— whole?

My belly had absolutely no beguiling appeal. I could pull the skin away from it like the flaccid skin on a raw chicken, and it hung down, no joshing, around the tops of my thighs. I had this big empty bag hanging off the front of me like Chang had finally, once and for all, gotten rid of Eng; only in revenge, Eng left his skin behind.

We're not talking fat here. This was skin and only skin. In order to get dressed, I had to scoop up the whole sagging lot of it with my left arm while pulling on my clothes with the right. It was tricky and not beguiling. Furthermore, my skin from breast bone to pelvic bone, from hip bone to hip bone, was as black as soot. It looked like the remains of a fire ... dry, scarred, and dead as a doornail.

After five months and no improvement, the doctor became alarmed. He said there was no remaining girdle of muscles to hold my insides inside, and I absolutely must not continue like that. Surgery was scheduled to repair me, and for him to understand what had happened. Because he didn't.

During my pregnancies with Jeff and Matt, I regularly fainted from pain. I learned that Mother Nature, our ever present protector, allowed us a compassionate way out when we could no longer handle extremes. I used to describe it as a searing, tearing pain, as if my muscles were being torn apart. Guess what? That is exactly what had been happening. Once the doctor got a look inside, he found the muscles were nothing more than little shredded pieces, all disconnected from each other and floating around like goldfish in a bowl. He said it was a congenital problem as the abdominal muscles I had been born with had not been substantial from the start. They should have been stout, wide bands of elastic fibers, but instead were nothing more than thin, stringy things that (his words), "looked like baby hair ribbons."

So that was it. No muscles. It's no wonder I had that waist! The only thing that had been holding Jeff (nine-and-a-half-pounds), then Matt (nearly ten-pounds), and now Erin (just short of nine-pounds) had been my skin! Eeeegads! You'd have fainted, too!

With hundreds and hundreds of tiny silk sutures, the surgeon painstakingly pieced together scrap after scrap of torn muscle. He was quite the seamstress. Just before surgery, he told me he wanted to have a chat.

"Mrs. Keener," he began, "I have an important question to ask you."

"Yes, doctor," I replied.

"Would you like to have a navel?"

"Hmmmm, give me minute, will you, please?" I replied.

(Let's see ... I supposed this meant he would be removing all that chicken skin, taking my pancake/tortilla/crepe/chapatti/lefse with it ....)

"Well, gee, doctor, that sounds like you're talking about a pre-fab belly button here—unless, of course, I received one from a living donor. But, then she'd have to get a replacement for hers from someone else, and there'd be no end to it. You know what, I'm not sure if I'm interested. To be perfectly honest, I've never particularly liked navels and I have no recollection of what mine looked like, so, I think I'm okay without. Yeah, I guess we'll just skip it. But thanks. I think ...."

"However," I added, "my prying, inquiring mind wants to know just what in the world you have in mind?"

"Well," he replied, "I'd make one! I'd whip a strip of your perfectly good thigh skin around and around in a tight coil"—his pointy finger whirling around in smaller and smaller circles—"then I'd sew it to the middle of your new abdomen."

"And, stuck there in the middle of my new abdomen it would look like I had a cinnamon bun held on with decorative embroidery!" I exclaimed. "Don't bother with a bogus belly button on my behalf."

"Okay," he nodded, undoubtedly relieved to be relieved of the pesky time-consuming Cinnabon test of his surgical skills. "I shall," he theatrically continued, "expunge any trace of your old doorbell! To it, I say goodbye!"

Then to impress me with how much he had learned while living in Japan, he bowed and colloquially added, "Sayonara," except that he pronounced it "Sarah Noya." Now, I can tell you this was the last thing I wanted to hear. I knew those Noya kids—and that Sarah was the worst one of the lot!

It occurred to me right about then, that I if I were really smart, I should probably be saying a fervent prayer of supplication, asking for my doctor's surgical skills to be superior to his linguistic competency. As I began my silent appeal, the doctor took out a blue magic marker and wrote "Tab A" on my left hipbone and "Tab B" on my right hipbone. Then he wrote "Tab C" right under my sternum and "Tab D" right above my pelvic bone. I looked like a Vogue dress pattern.

These were the tabs, he explained, that he would bring together. Everything in between would go. "Be gone, dead-derma! Vamoose! Get lost! Hit the road!" He had such a scientific way of explaining things.

Meanwhile, I prayed he also knew the order of the alphabet.

IT WAS DOWNRIGHT ironic! Of all the places on this earth I could have ended up living, I chose the one place that was fixated on navels. Can you believe it? You already know how sacrosanct the umbilical cords were, but did I tell you the Japanese were also consumed with the remaining attached lumps? Yes, those protruding bumps—or cavernous caves, depending upon your inny or outty persuasion—were equally obsessed over. Jeez! I couldn't think of a less attractive part of the body with which to have a fetish except maybe old elbows. On old men.

Here's the scoop. In Japan, if you left your navel uncovered, evil spirits could breeze right on inside you and take up residence. The Japanese knew these things. Every morning they took heroic pains to make sure their stomachs were layered over with underpants and undershirts, alternately stratifying and tucking whatever next layers went on top. Many people wore wool knitted stomach binders for protection, especially babies, the pregnant, the sick, the heavy duty laborers and the elderly. Guess they figured they didn't need any more bogey men bogeying around inside them than they already had.

There was also a more pragmatic side to all of this. The Japanese were convinced that one of the fundamental purposes of the sarashi haramaki (sah-rah-she ha-rah-mah-key, belly band), was to keep the abdomen warm to prevent them from getting sick, similar to Western moms insisting their kids wear hats in cold weather, which by the way, the Japanese thought was bologna. Both were dubious prophylactics, yet both were dutifully obeyed. I soon learned there was much more to the simple belly band.

During the middle of the Tokugawa Era (a.1730), kyokaku (kyo-kah-koo, workmen) such as hard working fishermen, peddlers, carpenters, laborers and firemen began wearing them, no doubt, as back protectors. But, besides laboring, these good, brave and upstanding workers also chivalrously served as village peacemakers. When a dispute was threatened, the kyokaku would cleverly soak their heavy, thick, cotton belly bands in water and wrap them around their midriffs. This prevented them, during the impending scuffle, from having a knife or sword pierce their stomachs. (That's what they called a "scuffle"?)

Since that honorable time, belly bands had also been worn for other reasons. While we were in Japan, the laborers (who still caught fish, sold stuff, built stuff, dug ditches and put out fires) also wore them to stop themselves from overeating—you know, to avoid their fattening flattening Fido—as well as the binders being darned good and comfy sponge-like sweat bands. As for the rest of the population, the non-laborers, they simply clung loyally to the old primary belief that the binders kept them warm, thereby safe from harmful bacteria. This logic was all I needed to convince me their thinking was founded on the same principles as the Clean Toilets Make For Beautiful Babies Association.

Unfortunately, these revered stomach bands took on a tainted image when, in the 1960s, the local hoodlums also began wearing sarashi haramaki. Their binders, however, were stamped with membership symbols of the various gangs. Diabolically, these smart-alecky low-lifes had also discovered something else. The very same sacred bands which heralded their gang choices could be used as handy dandy bandages, too, and if the skirmishes turned out to be deadly enough, tourniquets! No doubt about it, the gangland sub-bottom dwellers were disgracing the time honored tradition of belly binders being worn by respected, intrepid, laboring warriors. It was unacceptable.

"If you can't beat them,
arrange to have them beaten."
George Carlin

Upon reading a newspaper account of this unrest, I immediately took a mental survey of Asahi Court, quickly coming to the conclusion that we had no gangland low-lifes living in our cloistered midst. I was, as well, pretty sure there were none in the boys' classes at nursery school. Therefore, not knowing any of them personally, I never did find out how the issue was resolved. At the same time, I did know that everyday out on the street I saw ordinary non-gangland types assiduously covering their navels from evil. It was as plain as day how superabundantly serious the Japanese were when it came to their belly bands. They believed, as sure as that sweet potato nose on my friend's face, that those protective bands warded off all manner of danger lurking about, for the belly-binders were everywhere. I, of course, the outsider-butter-smelling-living-in-darkness-ignoramus, harbored a deep suspicion as to their effectiveness. It somehow, to me, had the ring of original sin.

One day I went too far with my skepticism. It was not by any stretch of the imagination taken lightly when I suggested to some Japanese friends that they should occasionally uncover their navels to allow a few of the bad seed spirits to escape. Even more importantly, I added, was that quite possibly the unrepentant, degenerate, irascible, sub-bottom gangland dwellers (who must have been filled to the brim with depravity), also should do it, and should do it with all haste. By the looks of distain my friends shot my way, I quickly learned that clever witticism like that only goes so far in a believing culture.

"Analyzing humor
is like dissecting a frog.
Few people are interested,
and the frog dies of it."
E. B. White

But, this being Japan, of course belly button importance did not stop there. It seemed that navels—you're never going to believe this!—were also a sort of safety deposit vault. (I know. Another streeeetch.) For reasons I'll never quite comprehend, (so, what's new?), belly buttons were a rough equivalent for a place to stash what we in the West called mad money or rainy day money—you know emergency secret funds. This, of course, made no more rhyme or reason than our money being "mad" or being spent on a rainy day any better than it could be spent on a sunny day. It was what it was; some things in life forever remaining unfathomable.

The thought of hesso kuri (hess-oh koo-ree, money hidden in the belly button), probably sounds a bit ishy—to say nothing of how little could be stashed there ... or its inconvenience—but here's how it worked.

Hesso kuri was used to pay small household expenses or to occasionally buy trinkets for the woman of the house. It (and this is strictly my personal input), could also be used to hold the cash a fretting Japanese mother gave to her daughter just in case the poor girl got trapped by the date *everyone but her had planned for her;* the one which they all hoped would culminate in her arranged marriage, bless her soul. If things did not go well on that forced date, the daughter could make her escape by paying for a cab (or a rickshaw in the old days).

Obviously, not having a belly button in which to store cash, as I did not, meant any future dating for me would have to be a happy experience. Either that or stay married to Glen.

In America, we had not yet designated a specific body part in which to stash secret money. It really wasn't all that important because our pants had pockets, as opposed to the kimono which did not. With this lack in mind, it was sort of, kind of easy to see how the Japanese had come up with such a fleshy hiding place, along with that ... ugh ... lint.

Who's to say what the original intent had been, but when I thought about it, hesso kuri must have been more like a piggy bank, because no maiden would have ever gone alone on an arranged marriage date without either the accompanying matchmaker or a chaperoning relative. Couples meeting for the first time weren't even allowed a private moment together, thereby stymieing the need for an unhappy virgin's quick bolt. Hence, hesso kuri probably neither got an unhappy virgin home in a taxi from her coerced dating, nor did it provide an escape from an arranged marriage gone bad. This begged the question: what if after all the lengthy nuptial planning, the poor girl ended up with an unspeakable guy for a husband? And wouldn't it be just her fate for him to be the taxi driver!

Joking aside, hesso kuri had a serious meaning for Japanese women. Most of them, you must understand, owned little or nothing at all as nearly everything belonged to the husband or his family. If she could somehow secret away a few yen, they became her very private, very cherished fund from which she could buy a pretty handkerchief (remember, for dabbing sweat, not blowing), or a knick-knack for herself.

You'll be happy to hear that a housewife actually did have an alternative to hiding money other than putting it in her navel. No, it was not always necessary for her to conceal her cache there, because many tansu came with secret drawers: drawers hidden behind other drawers, where she could also put it. But, even better than squirreling away coins in the big tansu, were the small hari bakko (ha-ree bahk-koh, the needle or sewing boxes), for they were one of the rare items which belonged exclusively to women. Inside these treasured boxes were always one or two tiny hiding places in which a small amount of yen could be secreted away.

The only catch with the secret drawers—as I saw it through my pragmatic Minnesota eyes—was that *all* hari-bakko had secret drawers, which is to say they were not secret at all. Like my Dad's plain brown,

229

paper-wrapped Kotex boxes, everyone knew about them. This was about as birdbrained as something I once did. A friend was going to arrive at our home before I was able to get there. Naturally I wanted to be a good hostess, so I put the house key under the doormat and taped a note to the door telling her I'd be home soon and the key was under the doormat! Pray for me!

FIFTY-NINE

BUT, I HAVE drifted from *my* umbilicus to the *Japanese* umbilicuses.
Suddenly I found that I not only spoke an alien language, had an alien
wardrobe, and looked as alien as all get out, but now I also had to add to
that list navelessness. Sakes alive, how much more could a girl pile on her
plate? If push came to shove, now I couldn't even prove I was a member
of the humanoid pool! Where, in this Bellybutton Hub of the Universe, was
the evidence someone had birthed me?

Understandably, I was in the dumps about this (darn, I should've gone
for the thigh-skinned Cinnabon), until I saw the rainbow in it. You see, if
you looked at things my way, I had definitely turned a bad into a good.
Now, had I been the bragging sort, I might have even rubbed some noses
in it. Imagine the envy I could have incurred amongst the natives with my
new, smooth, unblemished, *entrance-free* belly. Why, I , perhaps I alone—
and here comes the rainbow—was free to not layer and tuck, for there was
a fat chance in hell the evils would be entering me. Cool! My contentment
made a comeback.

I did stay away from the public baths, however, so as not to freak
anybody out. In my reconfigured but almost original birth state, I didn't
want to start rumors about Caucasians, just in case I was the one and only
one they ever saw.

After the surgery, the doctor told me he had removed five pounds
of dead black skin. He said I had very little fat on my abdomen. And so,
just like that, aside from lacking the proof of my parturition, I was back

to normal, nearly. In the years to follow, I realized I had other congenital anomalies which were each as quirky and painful as this one. My mother's body must have been plumb worn out when she had me, her third baby, within ten months of having my older brother. Oh, and you should probably know she had had my sister only thirteen months before that brother. Also, I won't be the one to tell you—just ignore me—that she had my younger brother thirteen months after I was born! Is your head spinning? So was Mrs. Wong's.

> "Somewhere on this globe,
> every ten seconds,
> there is a woman
> giving birth to a child.
> She must be found
> and stopped!"
> Sam Levenson

I tell you, that randy Gene and Margaret were like a stove on a perpetual kitchen timer. Holy cow! Loaves popped out of Margaret's over-heated oven at precisely spaced intervals for four years running. How does a female body even survive a thing like that? Pow, pow, pow and pow! July, 1936 was Mary; September, 1937 was David; July, 1938 was me; September, 1939 was Neil! Or, come to think of it, maybe the finger of blame should not be pointed at their inability to control their animal instincts, but instead at that particular four-year-long cold snap that hit Minnesota right after their nuptials. Gosh, darn, they couldn't help it, don't you see? They were forced to repeatedly slip upstairs just to keep warm. Talk about keeping the home fires burning.

I'm thinking that after my little brother was born, Daddy must have been ousted from their bedroom, exiled two stories down to the basement. Either that or *he* wore the chastity belt and *Mom* kept the key. Alas, birth control for the masses was, as yet, light years away ... you know, those tiny little pills that finally allowed people to savor the mirth without the birth?

> "Last time I tried
> to make love to my wife
> nothing was happening.
> So I said to her,
> "What's the matter,
> you can't think of anybody either?"
> Rodney Dangerfield

SIXTY

WHILE I WAS in the Tachikawa Air Force hospital having my mid-section reinvented, I found out that having no navel was not nearly as aberrant as what the girl did not have in the bed next to mine. She was twenty-one and after suffering years of intolerable pain in her toes, decided to have them all removed. No more toe bones! You heard me right. All the bones in her toes gone. Sarah Noya!

This did not, however, include the toe skin which she elected to keep. She knew there was no fix for her then in 1965, but bravely took the gamble that in the future someone would invent fake, bendable toe bones which could be inserted into her toe skins. In the meantime, her feet looked like someone wearing gloves with no fingers in them ... closely resembling those floppy-bodied hens and roosters on the boneless chicken farms.

I make light of my surgery, but during my lengthy stay in the hospital, I honestly allowed myself to wonder if dying wouldn't be an easier alternative to living, because living with that kind of torture was not a life. There is no way you can imagine the agony, the world of hurt, of having every one of your abdominal muscles torn into little pieces, then patched and sewn together like the hundreds and hundreds of two-millimeter stitches in a homemade quilt. If you've ever thrown a baseball really hard after not throwing a baseball really hard for many years, or taken a long uphill hike after spending many moons in your La-Z-Boy recliner, you have some idea how much muscles can hurt. And those were only trifles.

After surgery I could no longer breathe normally, speak or move any part of me. Doing any of those things required an intake of air and a tightening of abdominal muscles. This in turn caused my newly stitched abdominal muscles to move, creating searing, unbearable anguish. I stayed frozen in only one position for ten days, sunken into a deep, wretched, over-medicated existence, roused only when a team of nurses slowly moved one part of me at a time. Since then, I've had nearly a dozen surgeries, some big, some small, but nothing holds a candle to the torment of that one.

"My doctor gave me
two weeks to live.
I hope they're in August."
Ronnie Shakes

My spirits, nonetheless, were momentarily lifted when a letter from a Japanese friend was delivered to my hospital bed. She was clearly distraught over my situation, but quite honestly, even more distraught over her own:

Dear Mrs. Keener,

How do you feel these some days? I have heared of your illness. Please take care of yourself goodly. Heartily I wish that you wold be safe and right.

Now I am cryed so long time. Because my up teeth is only four. Another teeth wear false teeth. False teeth is not so good. And not so fixed. So I am cry and grumble at my mother-in-the-laws and many around people. And I have no confidence. And be hasty.

But be hasty is not happy for me. When I be hasty my heart is the big earthquake. So I can't think good idea. So I decided. Don't be hasty. Now I have time because my sons and daughters is students. But they nead my help a little. But another time I have.

So another time is my relax time. And enjoy time. By and by false teeth to be good for me. I am sorry to write only about me. But I hope good time after your operation and I do hope you do get wall as soon as possible.

Sincerely,   M. Ariizumi

Whoa! And here I was complaining about a few million sutures holding all my vitals together when I still had all four of my up teeth—plus more! And ... they were all fixed.

> "You don't really
> know a person
> until you've had
> a letter from them."
> Ada Leverson

After a dozen long days, I was released from the hospital. A team of nurses helped me into the back seat of our small Japanese car, propping bed pillows all around my mid-section. They instructed me to press them firmly against my stomach in order to hold my new homemade quilt in place as we drove around and into the holes in the roads. The trip back to Asahi Court took exactly sixteen years.

Once home, Glen helped me walk step by agonizing step into the house to my awaiting rocking chair, the only real chair we had. With the utmost of caution, I tortuously settled myself into it. The doctor had given me a stern warning to not lift anything heavier than one of my shoes, and certainly, unalterably, not my new baby! As you already know, our living room was small, not much over ten-by-twelve feet. Our dining table sat just over the line between the connected kitchen and living room. I now sat there dazed, looking at it, waiting for the children and hoping I had the strength to respond to them.

During my long hospital stay, we had hired a woman named Hideko-san to alternate child care with Sakae-san. It was obvious Hideko-san was ruffled when she brought six-month-old Erin down from upstairs, for she immediately laid her on the table to change her diaper. Of course she wanted me to find Erin in a state of perfect hygiene, but I had unexpectedly arrived too early for her to accomplish this.

I knew the narcotics slugging through my brain were dulling my thought processes and that my vision was equally cloudy, but what was it I was seeing from across the room? The diaper was off, but there underneath it was a pair of red panties. Red panties? My muffled faculties kicked into gear. Erin didn't own any red panties, so how could she be wearing them?

Good lord! The red I was seeing was her. *Her skin!*

From the circle of her waist down to the tops of her little thighs, Erin looked as if someone had airbrushed her with crimson paint. As thickheaded as I felt even I realized that, to my horror, Hideko-san had gone for hours and hours without changing her diaper. My heart stopped, as if a spike had been suddenly pounded through it, leaving a gaping hole of sorrow. Then just as abruptly, my despair turned to anger, followed by outrage. How could anyone do that to a baby? Any baby! *My baby!*

Adrenaline took over. In very slow motion I pulled myself out of the rocking chair, agonizingly constricting every last one of those bits of hand-sutured muscles, and torturously—though determinedly—shuffled across the short space to the kitchen. Nothing could have stopped me. As I got closer I could see the skin on Erin's bottom was bleeding. Bleeding! My compassion and love for her at that moment hit me like a ton of bricks. As well, my fury at that woman set me to boiling. All at once I was no longer a helpless patient. Things were about to dramatically change. I, the safeguard of my children, was back on duty.

Still, I knew overwhelmingly that the reality of the situation was this. I needed Hideko-san. For the time being, my role would only be that of a sideline coach, overseeing and instructing from a distance. Even though I wanted more than anything to throw her out the door and never lay eyes on her again this, unfortunately, was not possible. I couldn't get through the upcoming months without her or without Sakae-san. But, at least from now on, I'd be there to supervise.

It would be many weeks before I could lift Erin. What am I saying? I could not even hold her on my lap for if she leaned over and I grabbed her, it would undo much of the doctor's handiwork. This did not mean, however, that I could not run the show. Now, bent over and holding onto the edge of the table, I gasped in a whisper—all I could rally—for Hideko-san to fill the kitchen sink with warm water, place Erin in it and wash her gently, but thoroughly. Then back on the table, I somehow dried my crying baby ever so delicately with a clean soft piece of flannel. My heart anguished over the unnecessary misery she was suffering.

Even now, as I retell the story, I can feel the heartbreak. I can also recall the strength that began to surge through me. There was no time for me to be incapacitated. No matter what was going on with me, I would have to disregard it as best I could. I was needed back at my post. The captain had returned to the Mother Ship.

I learned a big lesson that day; a lesson that would serve me well in all of my future surgeries. By getting out of yourself, you recover a whole lot faster.

"We're all in this alone."
Lily Tomlin

SIXTY-ONE

IT IS NO secret that in speaking English, the Japanese have a problem with the "r" and "l" sounds. There is no "l" in Japanese as we know it, so of course it's a thorny issue. We English speakers, on the other hand, have just as much trouble with the half-trilling of the Japanese "r." Linguistically speaking, I guess you could say we're even Steven-san.

In the game of Japanglish, I witnessed on a regular basis some inevitably quirky, funny, even lamentable mistakes ... the jinxed Match and Watch Store being a case in point! It went on for years. I'll never forget my excitement much later during our second tour in Japan, upon hearing about a new restaurant opening in our area. Hype had it that it was going to be French and something pretty darned upscale special. Being pretty darned upscale special called for a classy, dignified name. Sure enough, a large expensive French sign was hung in front of the building. "Le Gland." Yum!

In the same gland (er, vein), I was also known from time to time, to make my own verbal nightmares, and to make them often. Quite possibly, my darkest linguistic day was—if you discounted the time I introduced my friend, Kaoru, as Kaeru ... like, was I to blame that kaeru meant frog?—the time I went into an osushi-ya with a fierce hunger for uni (oo-nee). From the very first time I had eaten it, this raw sea urchin was my favorite.

By now I had, all on my own, learned quite a bit of Japanese and wasn't shy about using it, but because I had learned it only by listening, I was illiterate—absolutely clueless as to any knowledge of actual characters.

Therefore, I had to picture in my head the sounds of the Japanese words as they would be written out in English letters. Now you must understand that no self-respecting Japanese would ever wish to see his language spelled out in plain, unadorned English letters. What a comedown that would be. After all, why would the Japanese ever want to make their language convenient to learn? Such a thing would wipe out the years upon years of self-inflicted angst required for the poor little Japanese school children to learn it, to say nothing of the anguish of the tormented foreigners? How much better could life be when your exclusive mother tongue had an elusive ostentation of thousands of pretentious, over-wrought brush strokes? Harrumph! What exhibitionists! As it turned out, the cows would come home and stay there for the rest of their bovine days before I learned any characters.

Having now explained all this, the word uni looked in my head space like u-n-i. No mystery there.

About that same time in my quest to learn Japanese, I learned the word for dog—inu, i-n-u. No mystery there either.

And, so, just what I'd like to know was so god awful earth shaking bad about going into an osushi-ya and ordering inu sushi when what I really wanted was uni sushi? Other than the transposition of those two little i-dotted letters, they both looked pretty much the same to me. But, I can tell you this. By the whatthahell look on the osushi-ya-san's face, you'd have thought I'd asked for ... well ... raw dog instead of raw sea urchin—akin, I suppose, to the dyslexic who instead of regularly chanting "Praise God," regularly chanted "Praise Dog!" after which he walked into a bra instead of a bar! Picky, picky! The Japanese could get so worked up over the smallest things.

Still, my teensy error was peanuts compared to Le Gland. Jeez, I'd only asked for two little pieces of raw dog whereas those guys had doomed their entire fiscal future. What was, I wondered, so almighty difficult about saying, "Could I please borrow your dictionary?"

But, if things could get even worse, let me tell you about another representative illustration. This one I stumbled upon one day during our second tour in Japan. There I was, as casual as you please, walking down the road when I came upon a shop with a large sign emblazoned across its front. In over-sized English letters it read, "The Pimple Store." Whaddayaknow? They sold *those*?

Golly gee, I never realized a person could make money selling objectionable body parts. Why, I for one would have gladly parted with mine any old day—and for free! With such an illimitable source, who cared, for I could always make more? Holy cow, this was way too good to be true. I could see myself rolling in dough. And, gosh, do you suppose they also sold heat rash? (How grievous it was to think what wealth had slipped past Matt all those years before. Double dang! He totally missed out on becoming a toddler millionaire!)

Hmmm, I wondered what The Pimple Store paid? I could easily be bought ....

"New invention!
Snap-on acne for people
who want to look younger."
Johnny Carson

With visions of the world's cinchiest yen floating in my head, I had to investigate. I marched inside, ready to negotiate a deal. To my surprise, and not a little disappointed, I found a shop full of clothing for teens. As I noticed the manager standing nearby, I moseyed over and struck up a conversation in Japanese. "Why," I inquired, after a courteous interlude in which I built up to the big question, "did you name your store *that*?" except the way I said it was much more polite, even though I wanted to slug him for being such a store-naming blockhead.

Instantly he became animated, clearly wishing to share with me his ingenious talent in the world of commerce, to say nothing of his trendy be-bop English. With those points made, he then gestured expansively for me to look around and see the obvious: his shop sold anything and everything for teens. Next he added (lest I still neglected to recognize his brilliance), that all teenagers had pimples! I was flat out flummoxed over his gormless, tactless logic, too much cleverness being just dumb. But I'll leave it to say that I followed his lame explanation by asking if he, by any chance, liked the way his sign sounded translated back into Japanese—"Nikibi-ya (nee-kee-bee-yah)—The Pimple Store?"

Without warning his eyes fulminated into twin explosions, protruding much further from their sockets than Buddha had ever intended. Upon later reflection, I felt badly for planting the seeds of unrest like that in his cocksure marketing soul. I should have just dropped it. Well, that, or followed my original intention and sold him some of my own. Darn, I missed out so big time! What an opportunity I'd lost when I didn't peddle off my *imported* zits.

Peggy, Peggy Not Prosperous Pimple Lady.

"I didn't want to be rich.
I just wanted enough to get
the couch reupholstered."
Kate (Mrs. Zero) Mostel

"I don't know much
about being a millionaire,
but I'll bet I'd be darling at it!"
Dorothy Parker

BEFORE ERIN WAS born, I, too, like those fashionable teens who later shopped at the Pimple Store, did my best to stay in vogue. Problem was that I wasn't sure just what exactly was in vogue. At such a loss, I was thrilled one day to receive a package from my mother. In it was a pair of beautiful black slacks. To my amazement, they stretched! Honestly, other than the stubborn give of my Warner body-armor girdle, this was my first encounter with such a compromising, caring fabric. It was love at first bend.

I was astonished, upon holding them up, to find that the pants were only a few feet long! But even more unexpected was that at the bottom of each leg was a wide cloth stirrup. These, I soon discovered, were highly necessary in order to anchor the tautly stretched fabric in place. Before long I realized that once the pants were fastened around my waist, the fabric's impressive tensile strength had to elongate itself in a descending order: around the hillocks of my bottom, over my thighs and down my calves. With shock it dawned on me that if one of those stirrups slipped off of one of my feet, it would be like a sling shot to the crotch, killing my sexual buzz and rendering me forever sterile.

Whoa, American fashions were getting volatile. But, at the same time, wasn't my mom quite the fashionista finding such hot haute pants for me? Or could it have been that she thought two over-sized Keener newborns were enough for me to bear, and she was taking matters into her own hands? Snap!

Holding up my new pants for the first time ... dangling all thirty something inches of them in the air before me ... I decided to throw caution to the wind and take the risk. As I slipped one foot inside and then the other, the stretchy fabric accommodated me resiliently. It was an awesome, snazzy experience pulling them up to my waist—and then fastening them expeditiously before they seized-up and snapped back down to my ankles!

I looked down. Oh, sister, I looked good in those pants, the humble, you know, being so sure of themselves. I looked like, well, Barbie!—even though I'd never heard of her because at that time she was only four years old. But, in my new expand-a-pants, I'm quite certain I could have been the inspiration for at least her cousin, Beulah.

I was in love with my contractible slacks. Who wouldn't be? With one ziiiip, I went from whoa to wow! I wore them whenever I wanted to look my absolute ritziest, which as it turned out was nearly every day. And, yes, I could tell I was making an impression on people. But then what did the Japanese know? All anybody had to do was look around at the plaid skirts coupled with flowered blouses, or checked pants paired with striped shirts to know most folks here dressed in the dark. I could so easily imagine them selecting their outfits each morning, opening their closets and turning *out* the light.

> "Once you can accept
> the universe as being
> something that expands
> into an infinite nothing,
> wearing stripes with plaid
> is easy."
> Albert Einstein

But then, the strict Japanese were under their own fierce fashion dictate. How could I have expected them to know how to also coordinate Western style clothing? Observe the kimono and obi combinations and you will immediately see that fabric coordination is determined by color and season, not by geometric design—i.e. stripes, plaids, checks and polka dots.

I would be a lesser person if I did not admit to my own failure at matching up a Japanese ensemble. This was never made more clear to me than the time I was invited to a doll making class. The dolls were to be in traditional dress, outfits faithfully repeated since memory began. I felt like a hopeless spaz, woefully inept at harmonizing the various fabric designs required for the multi-layered undergarments, kimono, and obi. I did finish my doll and love her to this day, but by the end of that class, my eyes were crisscrossed with the clashing conflict of it all. To me it seemed that each additional fabric created an even more egregious fashion collision, crashing into my well-ordered sense of what pattern should be partnered with what. Every time I added a new piece of cloth (under the no-nonsense insistence of the teacher), I felt like I'd been made to scratch all ten of my fingernails across a blackboard … while chewing tin foil … in a niacin flush.

EVEN WORSE WAS my first ikebana (ee-kay-bah-nah, flower arranging) class. I had grand illusions of myself pairing posies, of which the world had never before paired, into unspeakably glorious arrangements, knocking the socks off of every one of the students including the astonished teacher.

Imagine their surprise when somebody with a face like mine (who let that transpacific pagan in the class?) would end up bedazzling them so! Yes, I would make Austin proud, holding up our global end of the floral world. I mean, let's face it. A flower is a flower is a flower. Well, isn't it?

Upon arriving at the class, I was completely abashed to learn that each student was given the *exact* three flowers and the *exact* single leafy plume, no more, no less. The teacher began by telling us to what precise length each must be cut—no ifs, ands, or cuts about it. Right then I could feel myself begin to huff. Next she demonstrated to which exacting angle each stalk must be severed. The Japanese students—unlike I who was starting a slow stew—immediately hunkered down and began to follow to the nth degree the sensei's instructions. I couldn't believe it. Wasn't a class in the arts—any art—supposed to be a chance for each student to demonstrate her own unique talents and abilities?

How could I have been more wrong? This was my first intro into how virtually everything in Japan was learned by unerring copying. Everything must be done exactly the way the teacher said it must be done! Not until a student had spent years of studying—painstakingly mimicking the teacher's every move—did she dare to step out on her own, audaciously building up to at last, with quivering hands, cutting in secret her identical-to-everyone-else's flower (or whatever medium it was), one centimeter shorter than the dictate. There, she'd done it. At last! She'd made *her* statement.

Well, I did *not* have years and I *did* have an imagination! Two major counts, I knew by now, were hopeless strikes against me. The thought crossed my mind that perhaps, with an independent spirit like mine, I wasn't the best fit for this class. But, it was too late. I was trapped. Pushing aside all notions of being the ultimate misfit—and with the hope that all the instructional part had finished and I could now strike out on my own—I began. Okay, I'd eye-ball my flower lengths, but, for Pete's sake, not measure! For crying out loud, any teacher in any art class I had ever known would at this point let her students fly.

How quickly had I forgotten where I was?

The students set to work. By now I knew, as surely as I knew that Rembrandt had not created his masterpieces by the paint-by-number method, that I was expected to join in with the robot-like imitators. I could feel my consternation rising. Hold on, I told myself, and don't, whatever you do, make a spectacle of yourself. Simply do the Rome thing and forget the way you're built. I looked around. All the students were well into their arrangements, measuring accurately their cut lines and angles. Each one was unequivocally following the sensei's instructions, and I might add, as happy as could be at being identical copycats of each other—all spit out in unison from the same homogeneous mimeograph machine. Good grief! Didn't any of them know their arrangements would end up exactly, meticulously, spot on, just like hers?

Well of course they did! I, with my finger still stuck on my own creative pulse, was the only one who hadn't figured out that this was their ultimate, most sought after goal. Sheesh, Peggy!

I reached for my scissors. There were two. One was what I would call regular, familiar to my experience and touch. The other was a short-bladed, heavy iron contraption with two over-sized handles that flared out into opposing matching ovals, then completed their loops by circling all the way back up to the top. Now, how unnecessary was that? Not only were those scissors ugly, but they were also heavily unbalanced, and with their harsh forged iron, unfriendly to the touch. I reached for the "regulars" just as the teacher sidled up to my table. As I forced a smile in her direction, ever heedful of spreading benevolence, I saw her upper lip curl into a snarl, causing her face to suddenly crease, pleat by pleat, into an uncomely ikebana grimace. Next her hand shot out thwarting my hand from making my unimaginably stupefying scissor choice. I must *never*, she hissed, *ever* use any scissors other than these (the "uglies"—my definition, not hers) to cut my flowers!

With that, the camel's back broke. I revolted. Gathering up my imagination, I excused myself and departed. I was darned if I would be an exact replica of her ... or of anyone else.

I believe she was the one—still experiencing the bitter taste I so long ago lodged in her self-esteem—who later planted the first kudzu vine in the southern American states. Her revenge was, and continues to be, extremely sweet.

I must confess that my exit from the class had been such a Peggy thing to do. *How could I have?* Wasn't ikebana the very essence of the delicate Japanese spirit; a path directly to the intimate soul of the mysticism I was so desperately trying to demystify? What a clod I was. Right then I knew just how rigidly—and how necessary—it was for my nail to stand up. I was what I was. They were what they were. East was East and West was West, and ne're the twain shall meet. That was pretty much it.

> "Personally, I'm always ready
> to learn, although I do not
> always like being taught."
> Winston Churchill

BUT, I HAVE digressed. I was telling you about my gorgeous stretchable pants. A couple years passed before we next travelled back to the States. (This was the trip, you may remember, where Jeff spewed his All-American lunch on Farmer Eau de Dung.) Arriving back in Austin, I was in the local J.C. Penney's when one of the clerks (Miss Smarty Pants of Pants), pointed out—and, I would add, not all that politely—that I had my hot-shot trousers on backwards! The zipper, didn't I know, went in the front?

And just how was I, on the Kichijoji side of the world, supposed to know that? Jeez Louise! I had never seen a woman's zipper in the front. That's what men had and it was called a "fly"—or in the case of Jewish men "a circumvent." The idea bordered on scandalous. Cripes, the world was heading towards ruination, bashing fashion commandments left and right. And what could we expect next? Earrings and eyebrow waxing for men? Well?

Furthermore, how could someone like myself, who lived on the Dark Continent instead of in the Emerald City, be expected to know about *both* stretch fabric *and* proper zipper placement? Okay, so I was clueless in those departments, but for certain I knew one thing. No one—not a single Kichijoji-ite—had noticed, or at least had pointed and laughed. Still the brooding thought remained with me. Was I to suppose that because I could wear body-cleaving pants either backwards or forwards, that it said anything untoward about my figure?

Peggy, Peggy Beulah Lady.

Alright, I'll be the first to admit that I wasn't exactly slack savvy. Big deal! I did, however, for sure know how to wear a bra. Yes, I could tell the front from the back. In fact, bras were making big news right then in Japan. It was all over the Tokyo tabloids. Some local genius discovered that for brassieres to fit correctly, they required not one, but two measurements. Imagine that! What in heaven's name had the Japanese women been wearing before that breakthrough? Two rice bowls on a string?

Not everyone agreed, however. An article written by the Kanto Foundation Industry Cooperative Union (whew!) stated that brassiere size must be dictated *only* by the measurement of the under bust and not the top bust. With that statement I knew—as sure as I knew you could not squash all of your life savings into your navel—that everyone in the local bra industry was a man.

Furthermore, I learned that a crack had appeared in the rigid mindsets of some of the KFICU members, splitting them apart. Between these know-nothing-numbnuts, a heated argument had begun over whether a woman should perhaps *instead* measure at the peak rather than under the swell. I could picture it, Delilah-Doughnuts-Around-Her-Middle having to buy a huge under-the-swell bra when she had only wee twin nubbies above it.

Another organization, The Japan Brassiere and Girdle Association (who I'll bet you dollars-to-donuts was headed by someone who knew a thing or two about taking risks—like, say, that brainiac who ended up at the Pimple Store)—insisted that bra size should, yes, indeed!, be determined only by where the bust was fullest.

Reasonable minds knew it took two to tango, but in this case it was clear neither side knew how to dance. At loggerheads, both groups unapologetically skirted around the issue of whether or not the bra might function better if it had *two* measurements. Was, by chance, an intervention needed? After a multitude of preceding centuries in which no one gave a hoot, a sudden urgency over computing correct brassiere size was suddenly now of the essence.

> "The universe is full of magical things,
> patiently waiting for
> our wits to grow sharper."
> Eden Phillpotts

As this was Japan, a committee was formed to mull over the two sides of this sticky quandary. Sixteen-to-seven they voted in favor of under the bust. A middle-aged woman was asked to testify before the committee as a representative of a true, honest-to-goodness, woman-on-the-street consumer. During her testimony she was heard to mutter, "I really don't understand why they ever picked me? I never used a brassiere in all my life!"

Yes, they walked among us.

> "The chief obstacle
> to the progress
> of the human race,
> *is* the human race."
> Don Marquis

𝔖𝔦𝔵𝔱𝔶-𝔗𝔴𝔬

ONE THING I knew for certain was that it really paid off to know a few emergency words when you were in a foreign country. I was the living proof of that. On a beastly hot July afternoon, only days after Erin was born, the five of us Keeners were home melting down to blond buttery oil spills when I was called upon to drop Glen off at the Mitaka Train Station. We would use our recently purchased car: an almost new, diminutive Toyota Publica that had been driven two months only by a little old lady, car salesmen using the same spiel the world over. But, of course, the bare truth was that no grandma, or any other woman for that matter, had driven it because almost no Japanese women drove back then. In particular, old ones.

It's important here for you to know that Glen and I were not exactly car boneheads. Like we did recognize a good bargain when we saw it! For our "new-only-two-months-old" car we paid $600, and it was gorgeous; a pale luminescent blue, like a jumbo pearl. We could have parked it comfortably in a large jewelry box.

In order for me to leave our duplex and deliver Glen to the station meant that, naturally, I had to take all three children with me. Erin was a tiny newborn, Jeff was five and Matt three. Somehow we five, along with Glen's big briefcase, all stuffed ourselves into our pearl. Inside, it was stifling. In fact, remarkably comparable to the life-sucking velvet lining inside a jewelry box! On this day it was sweltering, as only a July day in Japan can swelter. Smashed together in the innards of that car, we knew firsthand how stuffing felt as it baked on Thanksgiving Day.

You must understand that parking in front of any Japanese train station for any length of time longer than a swift pick-up or an even swifter drop-off, was absolutely forbidden. The constricted, over-crowded, maniacal space in front of all train stations was sacred turf. Only taxis could linger long enough to wait for a deposit or refill of passengers. With that in mind, here's a re-run of the scene.

Let's see ... blistering heat, insane confusion, berserk traffic, tiny twisted roads, strict parking rules, three fretful, fidgety children packed body-to-sweating-body, and ... oh, yes ... my lack of drop-off competence. That pretty much painted the picture. It was yet another perfect time for Glen to be leaving us.

As I maneuvered through the crush of cars up to the station curb, Glen opened the door, leapt out, waved goodbye, and tripped off as lightly as an XL-sized fountain nymph disappearing into a pond of black hair. Just like that he was gone, off on yet another covert mission of military intelligence gathering where he was no longer Glen Keener. To prove it, he was wearing his own sports jacket with another man's name embroidered on the inside pocket. Actually, I suggested using the name of Herbert Philpot, currently a secret agent of considerable American TV fame, but Glen did not find it amusing. Nor did he laugh when I offered to change my name to Mata Hari. In fact, as I recall, his response to my helpful suggestions was something like, "Put a lid on it, Peggy!"

As I watched him leave, the thought ran through my mind that just because *he* wasn't real didn't mean that *we* weren't. Heck, we— the children and I— *were* real. Real real! And to prove it, I was looking at them smashed together in the pearl's backseat. Furthermore, hadn't I just a few months before finished a job on national TV where most people would agree that I was bloody visibly real? True, I had used my maiden name to do so, but so what? I suppose Glen, in contrast, with his false name and documents was, I had to admit, probably really not all that real. But then, who was that fountain nymph I had just now in plain sight dropped off at a train station? Our life was so confusingly screwy.

Like Scarlett, I determined to file away that thorny conundrum for another day, for now I had to get us on out of there. My foot pressed on the gal pedal as I revved up the idling engine for our departure. Sputter, hiss, clunk. The engine conked out. I turned the key. From under the hood whining, whirring spurts burst forth, none of which graduated into a full-throated roar (actually, in the Publica's case, a full-throated putt-putt).

Just as this was happening, newborn Erin stirred, took one quick assessment of the inhospitable environs and began to wail. This caused a chain reaction in the boys who became immediately angst ridden over their baby crying, neither of them yet completely versed in the ways of babies, and believing in their hearts she had somehow been stricken with something calamitous.

Of course, there was no car seat for Erin as Misters Fisher and Price were still in utero along with Mr. Pampers. Thus, Erin was on a blanket in her plastic bathtub in the backseat, a place which I could not reach because I was—and still am—too short all over including my arms!

At this point Erin made the decision to dedicate her young life to seeing how high her voice could climb into the soprano range. The boys, joining in, caterwauled in the lower octaves. Somewhere in the middle, I mewled in a pathetic alto monotone.

As the unhappy traffic behind us began to clog up, I turned the key over and over. No response. Jamming my foot repeatedly on the gas pedal, as I was now doing, only produced the sound of my foot jamming itself on the gas pedal. The Publica, you must realize, was a really simple, really basic two-cylinder car; only one level up from the motor scooter; ten levels down from the motorcycle. There were no high-tech head-scratchings as to how it ran. Which probably is what had appealed so much to that little old grandma-san *who hadn't driven it long enough to have anything go wrong with it!* Sure!

By now the combined breathy, but musical inhalations/exhalations of our distress had caused the inside car temperature to rise into the triple digits. We were in Death Valley here! I was without water to save us ... or any semblance of control.

Having virtually exhausted all of my mechanical options (key and gas pedal), I resorted to the only other thing I knew. Leaning out the window and screaming at the top of my lungs, I shrieked, "Tasukete kudasai (tah-sue-ket-tay koo-dah-sigh)!" I knew this meant something similar to "help." I did not know it meant, "Help, *save my life!*"

From every corner of the station, like bats descending on belfries, men in police uniforms rushed towards us in full attack mode. To their disappointment, they found no crime to conquer (to make their families proud), but rather a pasty-faced lady and her even pastier-faced brood, all wet-cheeked and moaning unintelligibly, while holding up droves of traffic behind them.

It was amazing how swiftly the force was with us, upon us, under our hood, behind us, pushing us, starting us. Slam, bam, thank you ma'am for letting us be of service, even though you are a subnormal ding-a-ling-stalled-in-front-of-a-sacrosanct-station-fool! I flashed a TV-star smile as they bowed in unison, threw them a kiss, and off we tooted.

> "The difference between the right word
> and the almost right word is the
> difference between lightning
> and lightning bug."
> Mark Twain

Or, I would add, powder and powder keg? Or dumb and even dumber?

AS THE PUBLICA hummed towards Asahi Court, I couldn't help but wonder if one of my NHK fans had been on the rescue squad. He was a young policeman who had recently surrendered his life to the safety of mankind … and to the study of Engrish. I had, he informed me through fan mail, been selected to be his *teatcher*. Once again, my lucky star was shining with all of its lights burned out.

The policeman, to convince me of his dedication to this double effort, had enclosed a series of photographs which he'd taken of his police equipment. Each one was meant to introduce me to him and the dangers of his job, along with the hope of electrifying me out of my gourd.

The pictures started out simply. There were shots of his policeman's pants, his shirt, his hat, and his belt buckle, all laid out on his policeman's cot. I was still in my gourd.

The next batch—moving up a notch on the bedazzle scale—showed his policeman's pants, his shirt, his hat and his belt buckle *with him in them!* The wow factor was beginning to build.

Toward the middle of the stack, things turned markedly more seductive, even deadly. Glossy photos appeared—knight-type stuff laid out again one by one on his cot: his night stick, his badge and his handcuffs.

Just as he had plotted and prayed for, my heart was now beating as fast as that old stick I had once used to pound laundry on flat rocks. It would have broken his warrior's heart to learn it wasn't from lust, but rather from laughter. The absurdity of it all was consuming me.

That was not the end, however. There was more. Two pictures remained. My hands trembled with anticipation as I flipped over the first. Through cackles of awe and disbelief, I looked at it. *His gun!*

Boy, oh, boy! Here was a guy who—as sure as uncovered belly buttons attract abominable abdominal disease and disorder—knew how to charm an Engrish teacher. Could anything—*anything*— I ask you, have impressed me more?

He was certainly betting the store there was! One more snapshot remained. It was sure to utterly undo me in the impress department. The final climax photo lay in front of me. I swear there was steam coming off it. Or could it have been the gas bubble from hell that I suddenly felt I was trapped in—and couldn't get out of? I turned it over.

Wow! Definitely WOW!

There it was (be still my beating heart), the grand-slam-daddy-full-Monty photo: him in his pants, his shirt, his hat, his belt buckle, his handcuffs, his night stick, his gun … *and him shooting it!* With that, I flipped, flat-out clinical.

It was like this. In his most recent fan mail to me, he had explained that in his endeavor to conquer his twin quests, he had gone so far as to put in for a transfer to the police station nearest my home. In this cozy proximity, he would be close to me and able to watch over my existence. It was amazing. How in the world did he know that was exactly what I had been yearning for? The guy was not only good at photographing personal property, but he was also sincere, creepy, and now clairvoyant.

Keep in mind that the TV viewing audience had thought I was a single girl. Apparently he did, too. Cripes! Was I, a married-with-three-children-single-virginal-girl, being stalked? It sure had that ring to it. Could this be pay back time for the price of fame? Then I knew what the long suffering Marilyn Monroe had gone through. Egads, this kind of vigilance suffocated girls like Marilyn and me! Besides, I didn't want or need a Mr. Pervert Policeman-san, because ... remember ... I had my own fountain nymph. Glen!

More importantly, I certainly did not want this guy spying on me while I was outside in clear view hanging up wet diapers *without* my NHK Carmen Miranda Mexican makeup on. Moreover, knowing that he was out there meant I would have to hold in my stomach twenty-four hours a day just in case he was looking? Could this very thing have been what drove poor Marilyn over the brink, eventually to her demise?

> "Always look out for Number One
> and be careful
> not to step in Number Two."
> Rodney Dangerfield

I needed to do something, and do it fast. Holy smokes, the record had to be set straight, and it had to be done by me. Conjecturing over what Marilyn would do, I sat down and wrote him a letter. In it I explained that I was not really in life as I seemed on TV. There was more to me than met his eye. The more was called Glen, Jeff, Matt and Erin. I never heard from him again.

> "I have never seen a situation
> so dismal that a policeman
> couldn't make it worse."
> Brendan Behan

5IXTY-THREE

AT CAMP DRAKE, Glen worked with a fellow named Sam Tabouchi. Sam's parents were born in Japan. Later they emigrated to the U.S. where Sam was born, making him an American citizen, though his heart was a solid mix of East and West because he had returned to Japan for his college eduation. Like Glen, Sam was a civilian working with army intelligence.

Both Glen and I adored Sam. Sam adored us, too, but he especially adored Glen. In fact, he was the Head Glen Groupie. He looked up ... and up ... to Glen, actually in more ways than one. That's because Sam was short, built like a blocky 4' 10" lump of Playdo standing on end. In his eyes, Glen was G.I. Joe, Paul Bunyan, and Tarzan melded into one tall, hairy-chested hidalgo.

In the Japanese culture it was very common, *indeed necessary*, to give gifts. Sam took this to heart regularly presenting Hidalgo with kitschy collectibles. No gift, however, was a match for the one he brought over one evening shortly after the children had gone to bed.

Struggling through the door, Sam wrestled with a large parcel under his short left arm. (The right one was short, too.) Being so close to the ground himself, the package nearly overwhelmed his gift-giving composure. After sipping green tea and chatting pleasantries—the prelude to the main event—Sam announced he had brought something for us. What a surprise! We hadn't noticed. Oh, yes, now we saw it ... that behemoth of a parcel covering one-fifth of our living room floor!

Inhaling deeply, Sam reached for the package. His presentation, he hoped, would be like that of a sleek magician, building his audience up to a crescendo of frenzies. Smiling, knowing confidently that his pageantry was well rehearsed, he slipped one finger through the string and began the unveiling. Slowly, like a seasoned stripper whose every intention was to prolong the suspense, Sam began to undo the tie.

Piece by piece the papers fell to the floor, one sheet at a time. Glen and I could catch glimpses of red and green and brown and gold ... *and feathers?*

With one final flourish of his sorcerer's hand, Sam flung the last remaining wrapper to the floor. There before our unbelieving eyes stood a magnificent stuffed bird. Gee whiz, when Sam told us he had a surprise for us, he wasn't talking turkey. Or wait! Make that he *was!*

As events unfolded, he explained that as an avid sportsman, he had recently returned from a short safari to the outskirts of Tokyo where he ambushed and bagged this creature. As I listened to his tale of gallantry, feeling utterly transfixed by the chivalry of it all, I secretly wished I had been there to see just how he had done all that while carrying a shotgun that was every bit as long as Sam was tall. Damn! Would I ever get to see a big game hunter—even a little big game hunter—in action?

> "Reminds me of my safari to Africa.
> Somebody forgot the corkscrew
> and for several days
> we had to live on nothing
> but food and water."
> W. C. Fields

The Chinese Ring-Necked Pheasant that now stood before us, immobile, proud and extremely dead, was Sam's trophy catch, and he was about to bestow it upon us. As you can imagine, it was near impossible to take it all in, an overwhelming gift like that. I personally was so touched, I could hardly stand it, for I had actually not spent a single moment of my life desiring to own a Chinese Ring-Necked Pheasant.

Furthermore, it was utterly ironic that I happened to know all about hunting these birds! Only days before a Japanese man had told me that "Japanese shoot *peasants!*" At the time he said it, his statement caught me by surprise, suddenly fearing for my life, but now I realized he was just one of that group of sloppy English students who didn't care about "pffhh" sounds.

"Isn't Muammar al-Gaddafi
the sound a cow makes
when sneezing?"
Dave Barry

After the taxidermist finished stuffing Sam's conquest (with whatever taxidermists stuff conquests with—rice husks? feathers from lesser fowl? dried acorns? used pantyhose? ... oh, wait, those last things hadn't been invented yet), the bird was so unspeakably magnificent that altruistic Sam decided to present it to us. After all, anyone could look around at our poor excuse for a parlor and instantly see the need.

You see, absolutely no respectable Japanese home was without something from nature ... stuffed. It was considered a genuine feather in one's decorating cap to have a reincarnated weasel, ferret, squirrel or other assorted large-toothed rodent, sitting in the art alcove of the most important room of the home. I'm not certain if it was to herald the affinity the loving Japanese have for nature, in a twisted, macabre, misguided sort of way, or to just let everyone know the office-worker man of the house was also a woodsman of great prowess.

"Follow me, fellow warriors! Onward! Shoulder your blunderbusses and spears. Let's slay the ferret! "

On occasion I was invited to visit a Japanese home where I was always, to my never-ending bewilderment, considered an honored guest. Usually this esteem warranted sitting on the tatami floor around a dinner table, in the seat most directly aligned with the art alcove: the tokonoma (toe-ko-no-mah). Such an arrangement guaranteed the best view of the family's art treasure which was always either displayed on the floor of the alcove or hanging in it. Usually this art was in the form of a scroll, changed throughout the year in harmony with the seasonal shifts. Conjointly, this was almost always paired with the housewife's ikebana—a precise, of course, duplicate of her teacher's.

On one such day there were several of us who were honorable, so it was impossible for all of us to face the tokonoma honorably. Hence, it was serendipity that I was sub-honorably seated directly in front of it with my back to the alcove. Now, this was a family whose art affinity ran not so much to flower arrangements as it did to wildlife. Hence, I found myself seated in a very small, very crowded room, up close and tete-a-tete with a you-know-what.

Sharing my visitor's space was a defunct, dusty, permanently comatose woodland creature who had miraculously been reborn. Jeepers creepers! It freaked me out! Like what was I supposed to do—pet it, ask its name, secretly stuff food scraps into its frozen mouth, call the dog catcher? I don't know, call me fussy, but one of my most unfavorite things is having a stuffed, glass-eyed woodchuck, who needs a bath in the worst way, brushing against my arm while I'm eating. Silly, I know. I'm just goofy that way. If I had been looking for an objectionable dinner companion, this was it. The meal was uncommonly long.

> "Stuffed deer heads on walls are bad enough,
> but it's worse when they are wearing dark glasses
> and have streamers and ornaments in their antlers,
> because then you know they were enjoying
> themselves at a party when they were shot."
> Ellen DeGeneres

SO NOW HERE we were, Glen and I, the hapless owners of our very own Phasianus colchicus. Call us ungrateful, but really it was too much. I mean getting a wringer washer *and* a stuffed chicken-in-drag all in the same year was goodness gone awry, if you know what I mean. The two of us, sensing we were getting snared in too much of a good thing, glared wide-eyed at each other from across the short expanse of our living room, traumatized hook, line, and sinker by the gory—er, glory—of Sam's gift.

To be honest, it must be said that the bird truly was majestic. It hadn't yet had a chance to become cobwebby or moth eaten, for it had only recently given up its life for the home decorating cause. From its spiky, needle-sharp beak to the tip end of its elongated tail feathers, it was tall and expansive (as in taking up a lot of space), and unspeakably arrogant in a pompous pheasant sort of way, standing there frozen and devitalized on its two-foot perch. It was obvious Sam had gone to great expense to have this masterpiece immortalized. Just for us.

Nearly overcome with astonishment ... er, gratitude ... we bombastically thanked Sam, using all our powers of grandiloquence. Boy, oh, boy, did Glen and I lay it on thick. There was no doubt that Sam, having outdone himself in the gift giving department, was entirely well pleased that we were entirely well pleased. As the accolades began to run out, like the last crumbs of a celebratory feast, the three of us sat there staring in wonder at the beast.

After enough of this deadly silence (Sam believing we were too struck dumb to further comment, while we knew for sure we were too dumbstruck to further comment), Sam made his departure. Unrivaled in our hosting skills, Glen and I bowed gigantically and repeatedly as we graciously escorted him and his modest "oh-it-was-nothings" out the door.

After Sam left, Glen and I just stood there. Had what just happened happened? Were we now the custodians of two boys, one girl and a mummified, flightless fowl? And where, in high heavens, in our tiny house ... the one in which every square millimeter was cordoned off and charted ... were we supposed to put this ostrich?

Sometimes when it really counts, two minds can come together. Sort of like—if you'll pardon the expression even though it does apply—birds of a feather. Portentously, at the very same moment, Glen and I had the identical brain flash. Why not surprise our little boys with it ... like it could be their new dead pet?

Excitedly, Glen carried "it" (because I wasn't yet up to touching), as we tiptoed up the steps, stopping in the short hallway just outside the bedroom where Jeff and Matt lay peacefully asleep. In this idyllic scene where could we put the fowl? "It" stood in its entirety, a proud, three-feet tall from its base to its stately feathered crown, and was nothing short of three-feet-long. In truth, such an expanse of wildlife required its own designated zoo cage. Lamentably, we didn't have any extra zoo cage space, except for ... oh! ... and this idea was beyond swell ... how about putting it *inside* the boy's bedroom? Just think! When they awoke in the morning, the wee unwitting things would be delighted out of their wee unwitting little boy skulls.

For two tykes living in the over-crowded, natureless wasteland of Kichijoji, what could be more sublime than finding a glass-eyed falcon next to their cozy beds?

Now it was Glen and my turn to be well pleased with ourselves. Thus inspired, we pattered inside the room and placed the pheasant in the only available place, the narrow space between the bunk bed and the door. Then we crept out, closed the door, and went to sleep with happy thoughts of how splendidly this would, after all, all turn out. We had a new family member who, unlike our children, did not have to be fed, clothed, disciplined, housebroken or educated. Excellent!

About two o'clock the next morning, I was awakened by some extremely heavy wheezing beside my pillow. Startled, I opened my eyes to find five-year-old Jeff standing there hyperventilating real, real big time. Even in the dark, I could tell he was whiter than Casper the Friendly Ghost.

Unable to answer me when I asked what was wrong, Jeff stood there bolted to the floor, aspirating indecipherable mumblings. I put my arms around his shoulders and pulled his stiff, anguished body toward me, then put my ear up to his trembling lips.

"M-mo-mo-my, there's a gr-r-e-at big bi-r-r-d in my be-bedroom! "
Whoops!

The poor child had innocently awakened in the night not to finger paint, but to escape a bad nightmare. On his way to find me, his mother, to comfort him, *was* his bad nightmare, blocking his way in the pea-sized bedroom. A buzzard as big as he was! There is no earthly way Jeff could have been more terrorized. And how, there in the dark with my unhinged firstborn in my arms, was I to explain this creature ... why it didn't move because it was deader than a doornail ... why its eyes looked like glass because they were glass ... why it was unresponsive because its little beating heart had been plucked out and probably eaten with soy sauce and rice ... why it didn't speak because its long, ropey gullet was stuffed with somebody's old underwear ... and why it was next to his bed because two moronic lamebrains had put it there!

Ever since that night Jeff has not been quite the same, pheasantphobia, being the curse that it is.

ODDLY ENOUGH, A few months into his therapy, the pheasant did really and truly become Jeff and Matt's new best, rather stiff and not particularly playful, dead pet. They took a fancy to dressing it up in their own clothes, especially in different festive outfits in synch with the various holidays. This, undoubtedly, not only ruffled its feathers, but there was a good chance it also ruffled the ghost of the once proud, but now benumbed fowl.

As the days went by, the avian continued to take up an inordinate amount of inanimate dead animal space which we seriously needed for our animate live human space. This problem was partially solved one day when I went upstairs to find extra long tail feathers strewn about the second floor. My darling boys, the little copycats that they were, had struck upon the clever idea of cutting short the bird's expansive tail so it would be right in the groove with the current popular buzz haircuts I had given them the day before. Three identical coifs, by golly, would unmistakably link them forever! There might even be a rock and roll group in their future ... Two Tykes and An Asian Vulture.

The three of them would be as tight as the *Little Rascals*. You heard me. Those old films from the late 1920s, with voiced-over Japanese, were shown once a week to an amused, though thoroughly baffled, local TV audience. Instead of, however, the viewers calling them the rascals that they were, they called them Chibiko-Gangu (chee-bee-koh-gahng-ooo, The Cute Little Children Gang), because "rascals" was both too judgmental and way too tricky to pronounce.

Although there wasn't a single Asian in the gang, the rest of the cast was a rich mishmash of racially divergent children with whom Jeff and Matt, being the potatoes in the rice bowl that they were, instantly affiliated. On the other side of the coin were the homogeneous Japanese, who were flummoxed by the mix.

Even more bamboozling were the children's names. Let's see, Spanky and Porky and Chubby and Farina could all, without too much pulverizing, be rolled off their reluctant tongues, but what was it with a kid named "Buckwheat?" And why, for gosh sakes, would anybody *want* to name a kid "Buckwheat" after the millions of ubiquitous buckwheat noodles that were slurped down every minute in this country?

As for me, whenever I watched the show I was always on the lookout for a guest appearance by Sarah Noya, who, you will remember, was the worst one of her lot. In my book this surely qualified her to be a gang member, but apparently she was either not bad enough or too bad, for she never showed up. There was, however, Stymie who, true to his name, stymied the Japanese, thoroughly. But even he wasn't mystifying enough to claim the first-place stymie prize. That belonged to the most baffling of them all, Alfalfa. His name, alone, set the Japanese hearts and tongues to fretfulness, turmoil and stuttering. Just how, for the love of Mike, were they expected to deal with this odd, unaccountable child? Like wasn't he black, and was that pile on the top of his head hair—or a tumbleweed? Moreover, what kind of a name was Alfalfa, anyway? With its two l's and two f's, it was a deathtrap for the local linguists. Giving up in despair, they resorted to a complex "Ah-roo-fah-roo-fah," or in some cases, a more simplified "Hah-roo-hah-roo-hah," both again being much easier to pronounce than "rascal."

CUTTING OFF THE pheasant's tail feathers actually turned out to be not all bad. Other than our never being able to invite Sam over again, the pheasant now took up considerably less space. Its short haircut resulted in my being able to find a final resting place for it: a stingy eighteen-inch landing at the top of the faux marble stairs where they made a sharp right turn upward to the second floor. With the new crew-cut butt, the bird was able to snuggle nicely into the niche. But way more importantly, Jeff and Matt were unwavering in their insistance that the hawk kept them safe at night, never moving ('cuz he was dead) from his sentry guard box. Whatever ....

The story, though, does not end there. The day did come when we finally left Japan. We were limited in what we could ship to the next country. The by now nearly bald, disheveled, de-tailed pheasant was not among our chosen items, if you can fathom that. Word must have gotten out in the neighborhood that we were clearing out, for late one afternoon a man pulling a large wooden cart behind him came up the circle driveway to our house. He was nearly bent to the ground from the task of pulling his heavy load. Piled three times as high as the cart were pieces of junk, disenfranchised castoffs, and a smattering of undesireable desireables which he had collected throughout the day. He wondered if I had anything I didn't want.

Well, it took me about one-hundredth of a nanosecond to come up with something! To the top of the stairs I raced. There was the inert pheasant perched on its petrified legs (as it always did unless it was either getting a haircut or being dressed up for St. Patrick's Day), standing in its corner like a punished child. I snatched it up and ran back down. Would the honorable junkman-san (huff, puff) be interested in this item, I asked, presenting it to him in my two politely outstretched arms?

Up until that day, I thought I had seen joy on a human face. I had not. The junkman-san took one disbelieving look and began to swoon with rapture, the exaltation of it turning his strained, weary face into a radiant smile. The transformation was as big as Michael Jackson one day turning as white as Queen Elizabeth! It was as big as Queen Elizabeth one day *not* turning as black as the original Michael Jackson!!

"But, of course," the man sputtered between gasps, "if the honorable lady-of-the-house no longer wanted it, he would be pleased (actually thrilled, elated, in hog heaven), to take it off my honorable hands. But ... how ... how ... much (his voice trembled with trepidation and lust), would I be asking for something of such incomparable grandeur?"

Why, it was his for the taking, I assured him. Upon hearing those words, he nearly broke out of his strict Japanese mold. Coming very close to hugging me (a behavior as foreign to him as blowing his nose in public rather than snuffling, wearing toilet slippers into the living room, and—this was the ultimate—uncovering his navel *outdoors*), he bowed so deeply that his stiff, sweat-spiked hair left furrows in the dusty driveway!

The last view I had of the happy camper was of him pulling his monstrously overloaded cart out of Asahi Court, not bent over any longer, but erect and proud as a phea—make that peacock—our bob-tailed pet tied securely to the crest of his heap like the figurehead on the bow of a ship. He was making damn well sure that no one, NO ONE, missed seeing his newly acquired, defunct status symbol!

I know even today, as certainly as I know there was no toilet paper in a Japanese public restroom, that our bird is still adorning one of his descendant's homes, a treasure of that quality ferociously clung to and cherished down through the generations. I just pray none of them ever lived next door to Sam.

"We are here on this earth
to do good to others. What
the others are here for,
I don't know."
W. H. Auden

SIXTY-FOUR

BY NOW I should be telling you about Japan the country, its sights, its smells and its sounds, but how can this be done without your own eyes, your own noses and your own ears doing it for you? Words on paper are just not adequate substitutes. Besides, if I told you, you wouldn't believe me anyhow. Neither would you believe how quickly I fell in step with a culture I knew virtually nothing about. For sure, it wasn't Minnesota, but that was as good a thing as Minnesota not being Japan. Why, in heaven's name, would I have gone to all the fuss of moving to the other side of the world only to learn stuff I already knew?

But, I must make one thing very clear. I did not leave Minnesota because she was not a glorious place, because she was. And still is! To prove it I can tell you some interesting facts about my state. Did you know that for many decades downtown Minneapolis has had an enclosed skyway system that covers dozens of city blocks, connecting the buildings like glass walled ant tunnels? During the frigid winters this allows people to live, work, eat and sleep without ever going outdoors. The only downside is that I've heard a Norwegian occasionally turns up missing. Or how about the cartoonist Charles M. Schultz, who was born in Minneapolis and was the only artist, I also heard, to ever accurately depict the perfectly circular heads of the local Scandinavian natives? And finally, did you know that water skis were invented in 1922, by the Minnesotan, Ralph Samuelson? Sadly, he drowned shortly thereafter because the motorboat had not yet been invented. To be sure, Minnesota was/is quite a place to be from.

On the other hand, our home in Japan was really not our home. That is not to say I was not enjoying our life there, because in an ambiguous, nonsensical way I was in love with Japan. She filled me up. She gave me the joy of knowing that every single day of my life there, I would experience something I had never heard or thought of before. But, still despite my blind trust in her, Japan was a place with few of the comforts I had grown to know and love. It was, after all, a place still recovering from an economy that had been very poor before the war, was certainly worse after it, and didn't seem a whole lot better now some years later. She was over-crowded and her comforts were minimal. By Western standards, her homes were small, run down, unadorned, unsatisfactory and undesirable.

On top of that, Japan was afflicted with an *interiority* complex. She was simply too, too small.

Despite all this, I recognized a certain charm in the cramped together homes, for as was true of all cultures, the Japanese home was the very soul of the society. By all means there was a certain charm; a warmth if you will. No getting around it. The spirit of the Japanese home was one of undeniable togetherness. Lest you depict a Norman Rockwell painting, do remember there was togetherness because in such diminutive spaces, there couldn't be anything else. The Japanese family could not get away from itself. It was much like the cohesiveness of America's pioneers where families lived in two or three room log cabins, although I do not believe the pioneers had plastic toilet slippers, but you can correct me if I'm wrong.

Do you know the one invention that really broke up the togetherness of the American family? I bet your answer would be the TV, and you would be wrong. It was the furnace. This central heating system with its distributing tentacles, allowed the family to disperse from around the single coal stove or fireplace, and move to the other rooms in the house because it was warm *everywhere*. Like those bygone days, the Japanese homes also had no furnaces nor were the houses insulated. In fact, one side of the small homes was usually entirely made up of sliding paper doors from floor to ceiling.

For those of you unfamiliar with a shoji (sho-jee), it is a sliding panel door built with a very thin, unpainted, wooden, latticework frame, over which is pasted a single layer of white rice paper. It was the bane of every mother's existence to keep her toddlers from sticking their little probing fingers through them. But, of course, they did, and Mom couldn't stop them. Therefore, it was not uncommon to see shoji with small, perfectly applied paper patches, or in the case of one artistic friend, maple leaves, which she meticulously pasted over the punctures.

This sliding door system worked well in summer when air circulation was needed to withstand the sultry, searing weather, but the winters were another matter entirely. The only protection the families had in winter were the thin wooden pocket doors that slid over the paper shoji doors. And the homes had only one source of heat: the kotatsu (koh-taht-sue).

The kotatsu was placed in the main tatami-matted room. There a pit, roughly a yard square by sixteen-inches deep, was cut into the floor. In the center of the pit was placed an iron or pottery hibachi in which charcoal was burned. An elevated wire cage sat over the hibachi. On top of this was laid a wooden top with open, latticed squares resembling a giant tic-tac-toe grid. Through this open grill, the heat could flow. Next, a large, thick quilt was laid over the top of everything, just high enough above the wooden grill to not ignite. Like an over-sized bedspread, the quilt extended on all sides beyond the box and out onto the tatami floor.

But, you say, why cover up the only source of heat with a heavy quilt? Because the kotatsu was not meant to warm the entire room, but to warm only the people sitting around it. Placed on all four sides of the heater were zabuton cushions. Family members sat on them and put their feet down into the pit in the floor next to the warm kotatsu. Like a baby joey in a mother kangaroo's pouch, the quilt was then snugged up around their waists, keeping the entire lower half of their bodies toasty.

During the torrid months when the kotatsu was not needed, it was covered with a removable tatami hatch. As the houses were so small, most of the waking hours were still spent in this same spot no matter the season. Seated on their zabuton, Japanese women sat with their legs folded under them, while men, being men, were allowed to sit cross-legged. I don't ever recall seeing any round shouldered Japanese, due of course, to their having to hold up their own backs. We in the West should be so smart! And do not overlook the supporting qualities of the wide very stiff obi which often propped up a back that was listing towards a slouch.

The winter heating system did not end with the quilt, however, as the ever efficient Japanese incorporated one more use for it. Placed on top of the quilt was a solid square table top minus the legs. This served as a dining table, work table and desk. Encircling the kotatsu the family ate, studied, sewed, talked, read, did projects, drank tea with their guests, and watched TV, even sometimes learning English from Tazaki-sensei and me! It was kind of like sitting around a Girl Scout campfire minus the outdoors and the S'mores. One's upper torso stayed chilly and required several thick layers of clothing, while from the waist down a person felt as warm as a womb.

This, naturally, brings up the question of why people did not die of carbon monoxide poisoning from the charcoal that burned inside the closed-up homes. Well, they did! Glen and I distinctly remember often having headaches and feeling sick after visiting Japanese friends in the winter. The one saving grace was that because the houses were so drafty, air still circulated somewhat, no doubt saving many a Japanese life.

During frigid winter days when the bone-chilling temperatures were not caused by sub-bottom Minnesota-type digits, but rather by the kind of dampness that chilled the homes so thoroughly your blood turned into a serumy Slushie, the kotatsu was a lifesaver. Just how cold were these houses? Well, many a time, I found that the standing water in the benjo had turned to ice.

When it was time to retire, the family (yet again masters of efficiency), fanned their futon out and around the kotatsu with the foot ends under the quilt. Then laying their individual blankets both on top of the kotatsu and on top of themselves, they fell into a cozy sleep with the heat captured under their covers. Sound dangerous? You betcha! But it worked for hundreds of years. In the 1960s, a handful of really trendy folks began using the newfangled electric kotatsu, still a threat, but no longer the schlepping or smell ... or, way worse ... menacing fumes of the charcoal. Many a time I sat around the kotatsu with a Japanese family and enjoyed immensely not only the heat, but also the camaraderie. The only serious drawback was that eventually I did have to stand up, at which time I was once again reduced to a shivering, sniveling wimp.

"Strife is better
than loneliness."
Irish saying

Keeping warm in winter did not, however, begin with the kotatsu. In the evening before the family ever gathered around it, they first went to the sento (sen-toe, the public bathhouse). The sento was usually the largest and tallest building in the neighborhood, easily recognizable by its tall chimney, the only chimney around. Every neighborhood had a public bathhouse within walking distance. Keep in mind that most people had neither a car nor a bathtub, so the efficient bus and train systems, coupled with the public baths, took care of everyone's transportation and hygienic needs. The sento, built of unpainted wood like all the other buildings, stood three or more stories high with carved supporting beams holding up a heavily tiled roof. The roof had to be high to make a space for all the hot air inside.

On raw winter nights, before I became navelless, I frequented the bathhouse with Glen. We would enter the sento carrying our own towel, a yard-long washcloth, a pan, soap and shampoo, and pay our money which was equal to a dime. From the pay booth the men and women divided, each going to their own gender specific side. Out in the country, the earthy rough and tumble folks didn't bother with these silly inconsequential divisions, but the ninny citified Tokyoites, who were of a more modest bent, did. To that ninny citified list, I would add one gal from Minnesota.

In some bathhouses there was a sentry whose duty it was to sit above the dividing wall where both sides could be overseen. This person was usually a female, thereby quashing the problem of a man ogling the women. As for this woman ogling the men, she didn't give a tinker's damn. In fact, in my heart of hearts I'm thinking she was the very same woman who had earlier been interviewed by the Japan Brassiere and Girdle Association.

Not only did she not give a tinker's damn about the men—she also did not give a damn about their tinkerers!

In the dressing room we stripped down to nothing, then laboriously rolled our clothes into tight tubes and placed them in individual cubicles covering the walls, much like our U.S. post office boxes, sans the little doors and twirly locks.

Disrobed, with our big pink hairy bodies (Glen's, not mine) for-all-to-see-and-feel-embarrassed-and-overwhelmingly-sorry-for-us, we must have looked to them like mobile chunks of cured ham. In this handsome state, we presented ourselves to the communal bathers who were washing and soaking in the large bathroom. Now, if a girl like me was silly enough to feel bashful over her pink, cured ham body, she would use the long washcloth to cover her lower frontal privates—breasts being of no consequence. This worked fine for me because mine weren't.

I should also mention this. Whenever we were at the public bathhouse, the most highly improbable psychosis was Caucasian envy.

The interior of the bathroom was at first impossible to see. Thick cumulus clouds of steam created a visually impenetrable wall. Therefore we entered with great caution so our pink fuzzy bodies did not either cause someone to bounce off of them or we did not squash someone with them. Groping to find an empty spot on the wet, treacherously slippery, tiled floor, we began by seating ourselves on awaiting stools. I say "began" because we foreigners had to plan with great care for a descent that low to the ground. The wooden stools stood only eight-inches tall and had a seat only nine-inches across, obviously pork rumps like ours having never been considered by the Japanese National Sento Stool Planning Committee.

Once seated way down there, and still unable to see clearly through the vaporous fog, we somehow found one of the wooden scoops (about the size of a large mixing bowl) that was scattered throughout the room. This we filled with the water that gushed from spigots, also scattered throughout the room. Feeling the hot water, we became immediately aware that it came straight from the smoldering core of the earth, making it necessary to just as immediately cool it with the cold water spigot. Finally, when a bearable temperature was blended—often after scalding all of our fingertips and feeling darned fortunate those were the only tips we had scalded!—we poured the water over ourselves again and again.

When we were thoroughly dowsed, we washed from head to toe using our soap, our shampoo and our long washcloths. At first I found that hiding my lower torso female charms, while simultaneously scrubbing and rinsing, was a bit tricky. But soon I concluded that what the hey, my charms looked pretty much like everyone else's charms!

Finally at last, when we were way, way beyond squeaky clean, we were finally antisepticised enough to enter the tub.

The tub. I suppose many years later we Americans stole the idea from the Japanese when we put it outdoors on our decks and called it a hot tub. Believe me when I say our hot tubs are not hot. Not sento hot. Try to imagine, if you will, lowering your body into water in which you have just boiled potatoes. That is hot.

The pain was nearly more than I could bear. I knew this must be the way a French felt on its way to becoming a fry. Each time I went to the public bathhouse, it took me at least a week to inch my way, centimeter-by-centimeter, into the smoldering cauldron, beginning first with my right big toenail, next the flesh around it, toe by toe and on up my body. If I went on a Wednesday, it was the next Wednesday by the time I got submersed.

The tub, you see, was not a tub at all, but rather a box of hot lava the size of a small community swimming pool, or in some cases the size of a small community. It was chock-full of females of all ages and sizes. On the other side of the half-wall, we could hear the soaking men grunting and ahhhing over the splendor of their agony.

How can I make you understand? Try picturing a group of American tourists stripping down to their nothingness, and then gleefully jumping in unison into one of Yellowstone's scalding geysers. There they proceed to joyously parboil together. Doesn't that sound like fun? Actually, this is not an exaggeration because the Japanese do that, too. Not in geysers, but in simmering hot natural springs called onsen (own-sen). One of the biggest travel destinations is to go up north where you can be cooked alive in the great out-of-doors, while surrounded by banks of snow which could prevent you from being cooked alive, if you only had the good sense to get out of the crock pot and roll in them.

Finally when I was at last painfully immersed in the inferno, I could only take the fiendish temperature for a few moments before I, having unusually low blood pressure, felt myself go faint. Even the vapor went black. But, for those few minutes, I must admit that every pore of my foreignness opened and was meticulously flushed out, causing me to hope beyond hope that my saturated Land-O-Lakes epidermis was not leaving in my wake any of those embarrassing iridescent oil spills. But, even if it did, it was worth it because every ache in my body immediately vanished, and I was absolutely no longer cold to the bone.

It was obvious why the Japanese loved the bathhouse. It was a mini vacation every day; something, for gosh sakes, to look forward to each and every evening of their lives. Furthermore, while being simmered alive, there was no room in their minds for the travails of the day because it took all their brain cells to deal with the ungodly temperature. As I peered through the haze at their enraptured faces, the transported looks told me loud and clear that being poached on a daily basis was really a very agreeable pastime.

Certainly one enormous advantage of being fricasseed was that the Japanese, like hard-boiled eggs, stayed warm all the way home. And once there, they found an awaiting kotatsu and dinner, with the family clustered about. Expansive as it was, the Western furnace paled in many ways beside this chummy, forced familial closeness.

Meanwhile back at the sento, we foreign chickens, not fully appreciating the bliss of this blistering Nirvana, always bore a hasty retreat from the inferno. We no longer simply looked like ham, we were ham. Boiled ham! And if we were pink going in, you should have seen how we glowed coming out. Like flamingo-colored kewpie dolls, bright rays radiated from our molten cores. It was true that I grinned from ear-to-ear over the ecstasy of feeling my entire self warm, but I also grinned over the relief of having survived the melting pot.

Just the same, the yin and yang of such a discordant experience kept me from going to the public bathhouse often, but Bob Fink and Glen frequented it on a regular basis. It was an ideal arrangement for them because neither, you may recall, fit into their Asahi Court mini blue-tiled bathboxes.

On the street just outside of the sento was always an awaiting yaki-imo (yah-kee-ee-moh) cart. "Yaki" means roasted and "imo" means potato, in other words, roasted sweet potato. The taste was beyond scrumptious. Back home in Austin, sweet potatoes were not usually served after we took baths, but rather at Thanksgiving and Christmas, and they were often layered with marshmallows, maple syrup, a drizzle of orange juice and, naturally, a vat of butter. It was a Norwegian thing we Scottish Presbyterians, you butter believe it, quickly latched on to.

Sweet potatoes couldn't have been more different in Japan. Here a wooden cart, standing on two large wheels, was pulled by a vendor. It had long twin poles stretching from the cart to his shoulders. The vendor tooted a melodious horn alerting everyone in the neighborhood he had arrived. The bed of the cart was full of small stones under which a charcoal stove burned. They glowed in the dark night as the vendor constantly stirred them. Embedded in the stones were the sweet potatoes. Their skins were burned black, while their insides were a dark orange—and they were delicious.

> "Cognito ergo spud.
> I think, therefore I yam."
> Graffito

For only a few yen, the vendor wrapped up one large potato in a scrap of newspaper and placed it in our eager hands. They were hotter than Dutch love, but we gobbled them down, unable to stop ourselves. Our outer bodies were already scorched, so why not singe the linings of our stomachs as well? It was just that kind of brain damaged thinking that resulted from a trip to the public bathhouse.

SWEET POTATO VENDORS were part of the music of Japan. They walked all over the place, up and down the streets calling out "yaki-iiiii-mo," raising their pitch in the middle and holding it out for as long as their breath allowed. Whenever we heard one of them, the kids and I would rush out the door falling all over ourselves to catch up with him before he disappeared down the road. Back in the house, we very gingerly unveiled the scorching potatoes from their newspaper wrappings. Then like good displaced Minnesotans—who continued their Minnesota ways no matter where they were on the planet—we slathered on the salt and butter. We couldn't help ourselves. But, of course, we had to pile on the saturated fats and sodium chloride in the privacy of our home—with the lights out—so the neighbors could not see the desecration. Butter safe than sorry.

Forgive me, Lord, for teaching my children unfit—*but, oh, such pleasureable*—ways! They were not to blame. 'Twas their mother!

> "We are born.
> We eat sweet potatoes.
> Then we die."
> Easter Island Proverb

We were surprised one day to see that our yaki-imo peddler had replaced his pull cart with a tiny three-wheeled pickup truck. It looked like he had stolen it straight out of Jeff and Matt's Hot Wheel toy collection. Instead of yelling and pulling, he now had the luxury of a mechanical horn and a gas engine. With such mod amenities, he was able to come right up the driveway to us rather than our going out to the road to him. Frequently he parked right in front of our door, a generous six feet away, and leaned on his horn. If he knew anything in this world, it was that we would never, ever ignore him. The Keeners were a guaranteed sweet potato sale.

There was also the osoba (oh-so-bah) cart. "Osoba" were long honorable buckwheat noodles, and, no, I'm pretty sure they had absolutely nothing to do with The Little Rascals because historically those noodles began way before that naughty gang ever banded together. During the New Year, special auspicious osoba noodles were made as long as three feet, symbolizing a long life for the hopeful eater. To get just one noodle down required a concerted effort. It took a very long and extremely strong slurp—the kind that resulted in our cheeks being sunken inward, meeting themselves somewhere behind our front teeth. A shorter version of these noodles was eaten the rest of the year at which time, I guess, shorter lives were considered adequate.

Out on the street, for the equivalent of twenty-cents, we could get a bowl of this amazing noodle soup. While we slurped standing up, the vendor waited for us to finish and return his china bowl. It was Asia's early version of fast food with no throwaways. Just a dip in his bucket and the bowl was ready for the next diner. For an extra twenty-cents, a tempura fried prawn so large it stretched from one rim of the big bowl to the other, was added. We couldn't help but salivate as we watched the vendor prepare it. Actually, I believe this is where the *Salivation* Army began!

"I eat at this German-Chinese restaurant
and the food is delicious.
The only problem is that an hour later,
I'm hungry for power."
Dick Cavett

I have an old yellowed newspaper photo from the good old days showing an osoba delivery man on a bicycle. With one hand he is steering his bike through the dense pedestrian-and-everything-else traffic, avoiding as best he can the holes in the road, while with the other hand he is balancing a stack of trays. On each tray are four parboil-hot bowls of osoba. Incredibly, the stack is as tall as he is! I heard that shortly after the photo was taken, he moved on to a higher paying job. He became the main scaffolding for Japan's first high-rise building.

Pulling their carts, the osoba men had their own special horn which distinguished them from the other vendors. It was a small brass instrument that sounded exactly like it had been palmed straight from a kindergarten rhythm band. In a highly developed blowing style, the vendors blew in one long exhale from low to high, with melodic chirps in between. To attuned, hungry ears, it was a gastronomic rhapsody.

One evening, Glen and I invited our American friends to come to our home for dinner. Some of them had never eaten Japanese food ... *dumbbells, I know!* For me the party was a heavenly affair for I barely lifted a finger. Instead we hired a chain of four food vendors, each a master of his own epicurean specialty, to come at timed intervals. As each vendor arrived, our guests went outdoors to his cart, stood around it and ate. It was a dreamy way to play hostess. Imagine having four affordable mini restaurants come to your door, cook the food right there for you, serve it hot in their own dishes, and take them back dirty. Of course the chopsticks were always thrown away which also made silverware a non-issue. All that, and some of the most delicious food you'd ever eat in your life.

America has totally missed the boat on this sublime concept, because we probably have some kind of overanxious, nitpicking law that prevents it. Oh, yeah, I remember now. It's the whiny ordinance that says an affordable restaurant cannot conveniently come to your home, cook your dinner, serve it in its own dishes, wash them afterwards, and finally, taste out of this world. Just what I said ... we're dumbbells.

"There ain't no laws
around here! We're trying
to accomplish something!"
Thomas Edison

Glen and I regularly went to the neighborhood restaurants. Each one specialized in one thing only. We went from shop to shop eating till we bulged. After doing this in my Warner girdle once too often ... and later suffering the Doughboy consequences, I got the bright idea of wearing maternity clothes on those outings whether I was pregnant or not. In them, there was no limit to what a girl like me could eat, having no circumference to which a girl like me could not expand.

The music of Japan included many other vendors. For example, there were the otofu (oh-toe-foo, honorable soy bean cake), sellers where the pushcart entrepreneurs blew their horns in one long flat note. You see, each vendor had a distinctive sound with which we could identify him. I can't remember just what the honorable tropical fish vendor blew, but I do remember his cart being the most fun of all, hands down Jeff and Matt's favorite. While he plodded down the dirt road straining to pull his heavy load over the rough surface, the bowl-upon-bowls of seasick gold fish sloshed maddeningly back and forth in their own private, never ending tsunami.

The problem was that Japanese homes were too small for four-legged pets, but one little fish in one little round bowl was, aside from being dreadfully lonely, a perfect fit. And most important on the important list was this: fish did not require the removal of shoes. Very rarely did I see a family who owned a dog, and if they did, the dog stayed outdoors. A tiny lucky smattering of them, albeit, were pampered indoor pets. In such cases, the housewives took the dogs out for a walk. Only two of their collective six feet touched the ground, however, because the dogs, not owning shoes, were always carried in the women's arms so their little feet didn't get dirty. I always wondered which part of "walk" it was that those housewives didn't quite get.

"Cats are smarter than dogs.
You can't get eight cats
to pull a sled through snow."
Jeff Valdez

"If a cat spoke, it would say,
'Hey, *I* don't see the *problem* here.'"
Roy Blount, Jr.

SIXTY-FIVE

GLEN CAME HOME from the office one day—or from wherever he'd been clandestinely lurking—with exciting news! We were going to a sumo match! Besides temples, geisha, kimono, raw fish, World War II, and cheaply made toys, nothing denoted Japan more than sumo wrestling. In every respect, watching sumo matches on TV was like Americans getting to watch the Super Bowl every weekend, even though the Super Bowl hadn't been invented yet, but it was in a petri dish.

In the 1960s, the nation's sumo champion was Taiho. Japan idolized him.

Taiho Koki was secretly, and sometimes not so secretly, more revered than the Emperor. He was born on what is presently the Russian island of Sakhalin, a piece of land off the east coast of Siberia, and one with a very cantankerous history. During much of it, the ownership of the island had been yanked back and forth between Russia and Japan like a gnarly turf game of tug of war. Even today the controversy continues. But when we were in Japan ... primarily because Taiho came from Sakhalin and was a half-and-half blend of Japanese and Russian parentage ... Japan won the yank on that round, latching on to him as one of their own. Had he, on the other hand, grown up to be short and puny, Taiho would have remained Russian, in Russia, and the Japanese would have totally ignored both him and his funky piece of island land.

But, as chance would have it, Taiho did not grow up to be short and puny. Quite the opposite! He was a mountain of a pseudo Japanese

269

man, and due to those hefty Russian genes, also taller than most sumo-san. Additionally, his abdomen was not abominably obese. Although he certainly had a full figure, he was not rippling in undulating flesh as were the other sumo-san. As a matter of fact, Taiho made blubber look good.

Japan worshipped him. Above all, Taiho was regarded as the greatest sumo wrestler of the post-war period, winning a staggering thirty-two tournaments in his career. He was, as well, the youngest wrestler to ever earn sumo's highest rank of Yokozuna, achieving this when he was only twenty-one years old.

As I said, Japan was crazy mad in love with Taiho. I believe there was even an unwritten law that you weren't allowed to be Japanese unless you, too, insanely adored him. With that in mind, Glen and I were, on a daily basis through the power of TV, swept up in the sumo culture right along with the natives which is why we were so thrilled to actually be attending a live tournament.

We arrived at the sumo hall to find an old world, wooden, barn-like building which looked like a living (well, more honestly, like a barely hanging in there) piece of ancient history. It came as no surprise to me to learn that it had been steadily in operation *since* ancient history. Inside was a large round room covered with a packed clay floor that, like a giant funnel, sloped gently down to the one center ring. A very thick rope half buried in the earthen ground outlined the ring, denoting the playing field.

The object of sumo wrestling was to get one's opponent mostly or completely outside the ring. I always cringed when I saw one of those three-hundred-pound monoliths fall directly on top of that brutally hard rope as it must have hurt like sin. But then, that may have just been the idea behind all that corpulent padding. Unlike our American football players who exercised to keep trim and then added artificial padding, the sumo-san built their own padding while not exercising and sitting around sagging dining tables.

> "It's okay to be fat.
> So, you're fat?
> Just be fat and
> shut up about it."
> Roseanne Barr

That night I learned the practicality—the blessing!—of the hard-packed clay floor. Had it been of wood like the rest of the building, the wrestlers would have shaken the structure ruinously each time they crashed down with their theatrical leg lifts, to say nothing of their entrances and exits where they stomped ponderously and pompously up and down the main aisle.

There were no chairs in the large room, but rather zabuton cushions upon which we folded ourselves. Immediately refreshments began arriving along with bountiful amounts of sake. As with everything else in the Japanese society, there was a very strict etiquette for drinking this sacred rice wine. One must *never*, under the threat of social ostracism, *ever* pour one's own. The act must be performed by either the attending server or by one's companion. This solicitous rule spoke volumes for the conviviality and courtesy of the ever imbibing Japanese society.

Generally, sake cups were like large, handle-less porcelain or pottery thimbles. At a sumo match, however, the cups were not cups at all. Rather, they were small wooden boxes of either unfinished or lacquered wood. The edges of the boxes were very bulky to our lips, about a quarter-of-an-inch thick, making the corners the only reasonable way to drink from them without dribbling onto the front of our best sumo duds.

The ultra sophisticated referee was dressed to the nines in multi-layered robes of heavy, richly embellished silk, and his studied, choreographed movements were a kind of aboriginal ballet done in slow motion. Droning up and down the full range of his vocal chords, his voice chanted ancient, rather spooky words, as if they had come straight off an ancient kabuki stage.

Throughout the evening, each new pair of wrestlers entered the ring by alternately tossing handfuls of purifying rock salt into the arena, followed by the sideways raising and stomping of their elephantine legs. Later, when the defeated wrestler fell on top of those crusty crystal devils, it must surely have added to the jim-dandy joy of losing yet another match.

I immediately loved the earthiness and primitiveness of the sumo world. Sitting on the clay floor, drinking sake from wooden boxes, sensing the aesthetics of the heavily twisted rope, observing the agelessness of the salt purification, seeing and hearing the out-of-worldliness of the referee, being viscerally startled by the near nakedness of the wrestlers (each with more skin mass than an exfoliated wooly mammoth), all while being enclosed in the ancient untreated wood of the building, harkened back to the days of simplicity and organicity. In a world that was transforming itself into glass, chrome, asphalt and speed, sumo instantaneously jerked us back to another much older, much slower, and less complicated time.

The food kept coming. It was a tailgater's paradise, sans the tailgate. We were not required to either cook it or to stand outside to eat it, because it was all brought to us fully prepared and indoors. Besides, much the same as the Super Bowl, I'm not even sure tailgating had been discovered yet. How could it have? Like if the Neanderthals still hadn't figured out that those square rock wheels should be replaced with round rock wheels, then they sure as heck hadn't invented the divided rear hatch door!

> "Ask not what you can do
> for your country;
> ask what's for lunch!"
> Orson Wells
> (on reaching 300 lbs.)

Of course, the objective of the get-together (in reality, the audience's sole responsibility), was to get either mildly tipsy or completely soused.

The party animal Japanese, with their biologically very low tolerance for alcohol, were of the latter: completely soused. It looked to me as if most of the audience was from the local branch of Sots-R-Us for as the party revved up, their faces rapidly recast themselves from Mongolian yellow to the butt red of Japan's very own Snow Monkeys. Glen and I, on the other hand, no matter how much we drank, remained as white as two unembellished bowls of Cream of Wheat.

In this eccentric scene, I sat, suspended in time. I could feel the Austin part of me fade to a diminishing speck, as I joined in the revelry of the sacred sumo rituals, as venerable and pristine as all of Japan's hoary history.

Half-way into the evening, I excused myself to go to the restroom. Carefully threading my way out of the big room around the floor-seated, besotted assemblage of inebriated sumo devotees, I eventually found myself in a very long, very narrow, very poorly lit, wooden hallway. The passage was no wider than a space in which two people could comfortably pass. Note I said "two people" and I said "comfortably." What I really meant was two normal-sized people touching shoulders as they brushed past each other. I was surprised by the constriction of the passageway, but being one of the normals, I put it out of my mind. That is, until I left the restroom.

As I stepped back into the hallway, I was surprised by the unexpected darkness at the end of the long corridor. Well, of course I told myself, it was dark because the puny lighting was of nugatory value, as primitive as everything else in this place. I looked again. Hmmm ... it seemed as if a plug of some sort had been squashed into the far end of the corridor, creating a complete blackout of anything behind it. Well, that simply couldn't be, I murmured aloud, for I hadn't opened or closed any doors as I had passed through the hallway only moments before.

Again I looked. That was strange. Now it seemed as if the plug was moving. Moving toward me! Could that be or had I simply drunk too much sake, causing my visual perception to briefly turn wacky? Cautiously I stepped forward, moving down the hall like a person trying to navigate one of those blackened tunnels in a carnival Horror House. Then whoa! Out of the blue, I detected the slightest rumblings under my feet. Holy mother of mothers, this sumo building was no place to be caught in an earthquake! Why, in this ancient tomb, I'd be instantaneously buried alive, never to be heard from again.

The vibrations under my feet grew stronger as the plug drew nearer. Panicked and holding onto the wall, I stopped to get my bearings. Then looking once more ahead, I made out the form of a sumotori. Double cripes! Like a moving wedge, he was absorbing all the light and all the space in the corridor as he plowed straight for me. In the long narrow hallway, there was no place to escape, no niche into which I could duck out of his way. With each approaching step, the ground increasingly trembled

272

under the pounding of his bare feet: those two tiny appendages that had stubbornly refused to gain weight and now alone bore the immense bulk of his immensity. I was as doomed as a piece of well-chewed gum that was about to confront an advancing steam roller. Within seconds, my body would be flatter than a stick of Juicy Fruit.

But, wait! I was young. I wanted to live! With no options other than my own bleeding desire to do just that, it became clear that it would be entirely up to me to save my own life, for obviously this sumo-san was not going to, in any way, alter his stride. Oh, and there was that other issue. Did I mention before anything about the outrageously haughty arrogance of sumo wrestlers? They were kings without crowns—or for that matter, without clothes! Sheesh, everyone, *the whole entire Japanese world*, was their oyster, and everyone and everything in it moved out of their way. But what, I whinnied to myself, was one to do (in particular, a young housewife from Minnesota), when there was no place to escape from them?

His bulk was nearly upon me. Instinctively I flattened myself against the wall like a human espalier, sucked in my belly (good thing I wasn't bloated that day!), and for the first time in my life said a prayer of thankfulness for my small bosom. (Dolly Parton would have been a goner.) Had I been pregnant, my baby would have been sheared right off me for this was going to be heavy-duty squeegeeing, if you know what I mean.

The rotund king pounded up to me, his beady eyes nearly lost in the fleshy folds of his face. He looked in one, and only one, direction—straight ahead. The sweaty pork on both sides of his body slid against the walls. He no more considered my existence than he would have noticed or cared about a blond bug on the wall. I did not exist. It was immediately humbling to realize how non-viable I had instantly become. It was also scary and, you know what, downright rude!

He was upon me. Then on me! As he rumbled past, the bare, greasy, cellulite-filled hide of his right arm, thigh and hindquarters pressed me into the wall like a great big spongy roller applying wall paper. Ish!

It would be true to say that my view of the sumo world shifted that day. I was still drawn into the galvanizing titillation of it all because everyone around me was—and as you know I was trying to blend in with the natives—but, the mystique and my own personal relationship with the sport was tarnished beyond repair. The way I saw it, no matter how all-consuming famous you were, a gargantuan ton of lard wearing only a diaper, still needed to be polite and caring. So there!

LEAVING THE SUMO stable, we wandered along the banks of the Sumida River where Glen and I, in our sake-induced state, were now cleverly singing ... "I Left My Liver on the Sumida River." We were headed for a restaurant whose history was as old as the sumo stable itself. It was called

"The Boar House." Notice I did not say "bore" as in fagged-out listlessly blasé, for this place was anything but. Indeed, this place demanded for you to be on your toes, alert and sharp, for you were entering a realm of which you never dreamed existed in this universe and beyond.

As we approached the primeval, dark, squat restaurant, I was immediately startled by the outside of the building. From a distance it looked suspiciously as if it were wearing a coat. A fur coat! Knowing, of course, that such a thing could not be, I rejected this silly notion. But, by golly, as we got closer, I realized I wasn't being silly at all. It really was wearing a fur coat. But, how could that be? And why would any primeval, dark, squat restaurant want to do that? What did *it* care about being in the fashion parade?

Just then we were upon it, right in front of the place. To our stunned eyes, we saw hanging from the eaves of the roof and encircling the entire circumference of the hairy establishment, animals strung up by their back feet. Dead animals! Dead boar animals! I felt assaulted by the carnage. Like weren't wild boars on some kind of endangered species list—or was it, I couldn't remember—only their endangered feces? You know, the ones Gildna Radner would become so concerned about?

Accompanying us was a Japanese friend, who of course knew everything Japanese, and was now politely explaining to us that the animals were dinner. They were hanging outdoors because there wasn't room to store them indoors. Besides it was winter, and without having a refrigerator, they stayed cold out here. Yeah, I could see that. Uh-huh, it made sense.

But, hold on here. Had Glen and I said anything to him about a burning desire to eat wild beast? I didn't think so. But as usual, like the devil-may-care good chums that we were, we found ourselves roped in, and game, if you will, for this gamey experience. Pushing aside the prickly haired carcasses, we entered the restaurant.

My immediate reaction was that I had just penetrated the tunnel-like home of a ground creature—a mole, a marmot, or a shrew. Hells bells, an aardvark, for all I knew! What was this place? My next guess was that I had mistakenly burrowed inside a fur trapper's hat. It was dark, tight, miasmal and steamy as all get out. But in spite of the heady closeness, the patrons seemed happy, cheerily drinking and chomping up a storm. Okay, so it wasn't White Castle. I could adjust.

We seated ourselves on some rough hewn benches in front of an even rougher hewn table. Glen handed me a menu. It felt as primitive as a tablet of stone, the words seemingly etched by cave dwellers using flint knives. Through the steam I read it. Let's see now... appetizers, nope ... salads, nope ... burgers, nope ... desserts, nope ... stew, yessiree-bob!

Equipped now with the knowledge of the limited selection, ordering became a snap. We would order stew! I turned to our friend who you will remember knew everything, and as composed as I could be so as not to expose my sudden waning love of Japanese cuisine, I offhandedly inquired as to if the stew might possibly contain any parts of the stiff upside-down creatures that were hanging from the eaves outdoors? No, no, he informed me, laughingly. Not to worry.

Normally I am not a food-queasy person, but if I am being brutally honest, I will confess to not having a hankering for liver and all other organ parts that digest and move downward chewed foodstuffs through a creature's system. Rather, I prefer the chunks that are tightly latched onto that same creature's thighs and ribs, which I was now fervently hoping were what I had ordered. But, no matter how spunky I was trying my darnedest to be, nothing prepared me for the appetizer, the entrée and the dessert ... which were all the same thing.

An unshaven Mongol waiter in whiskery burlap garments placed a steaming crockery bowl in front of me. The vapor rising from the contents was so beclouded, I could have carved it. This turned out to be not all that bad, albeit, as it kept me from immediately seeing my dinner. Plowing aside the foggy fumes with my purse, I peered cautiously into my bowl. It was dark in there. Dark as sin.

Now, I know gravy. I was raised by Margaret McLaughlin, don't you forget, who was quite possibly the world's champion gravy maker, so I grew up thoroughly knowledgeable in the ways of the heavenly stuff. But, that evening as I sat there musing over the past gravies of my childhood, I asked myself if it wasn't supposed to be brown? I remembered it being so. This wasn't. This was more on the slushy, unfriendly, licorice side. My gravy looked mean.

While I reflected on this perplexity, our companion eagerly dug in. From out of his bowl he lifted a big chunk of cooked animal that dripped like molten tar. I didn't think I quite recognized what kind of cooked like molten tar animal it was. So I asked. Politely.

"If I may inquire, just what kind of stew *is* this," I queried hesitantly, not really sure I wanted to know the answer.

"Why, this is badger stew!" he informed me. "The best danged badger stew you'll ever eat!"

You gotta be kidding! The *only* danged badger stew *I'll* ever eat, *I* was thinking.

Fearing I'd have to look into its beasty eyes peering back at me from inside the bowl, I was exceedingly grateful to find that the cook had removed its face before serving it to me. The whole thing suddenly felt like it was flying in the face of heavenly law. In his wisdom, I knew God had never intended for a badger to end up on a restaurant menu. Had He meant for it to happen, He would have named it *good*ger instead of *bad*ger. Right?

I sat there. By now Mr. Know-It-All-Including-Badgers was gleefully chowing down, resembling markedly the enthusiasm I had years ago witnessed over and over in my old Zesto customers. I remained immobile, contemplating my next move. I'd have to do something. And do it soon. Willing all the powers within me to rise up, I steadied myself before I jumped into the food fray. After all, our friend still appeared to be alive, which I can tell you, emboldened me greatly.

"Is that a beard,
or are you eating
a muskrat?
Dr. Gonzo

Slowly, slowly the bonhomie, obligingly congenial side of me won over. I took a wee sip. Egads and little fishes! The stuff was awful—an immediate violation of my previously undefiled taste buds. Irrefutably, badger stew was an assault on all things holy, no matter what god you believed in. I suddenly understood the popularity of vegetarianism.

"A vegetarian is a person
who won't eat anything
that can have children."
David Brenner

"The only people with a right to complain
about what I do for a living
are vegetarian nudists."
Ken Bates
(one of California's 700
licensed fur trappers)

Gamey is not a word I had heretofore used in my everyday food vocabulary. Indeed, before that day, I actually had no need of it. All that now suddenly changed. As I sat there with my mouth full and unable to give permission for the thick bolus to slide down my gullet, I recalled that in the dictionary "gamey" was defined as something having a strong, tangy, plucky and high-spirited flavor. Anyway, that's the way Webster had described it. But then what did he know? He was probably a mollycoddled milksop who had been raised on curds and whey.

For sure Noah was a wuss! And it was as clear as cellophane that he had never tried badger stew. Still, in fairness to him, he did at the very end of his definition add the descriptor "tainted," and with that single term, we were now getting somewhere. That was it. Badger stew was tainted; a blot on foodstuffs everywhere.

Not until this bite had I ever applied the word "tainted" to anything in my food world, but now I felt an urgency to add it ... and to know more. A lot more! Immediately I went into reflection mode, again revisiting the candy-assed Webster. There it was, an auxiliary definition: blemish, maculation, scar, pockmark, blotch, splotch, smut, septicity, defilement and poison. Poison! Aha! He'd said it, not me!

I was reduced to shuddering as I brooded over why badgers (whom I had only known as passing acquaintances), were, although friendly, not generally popular in fine dining venues. I now realized that one thing that could have banned them would surely have been the poison issue, for it certainly had a ring of negativity to it. But, it was the septicity issue—wherein lay a pernicious truth—that more than anything hit home. For all I knew, badgers ate septic things. Things like moles and shrews and marmots and aardvarks—and for that matter, even other badgers! In the end, badger, along with any other animal hanging by its dead heels from the eaves of a restaurant, was verboten! Off my bill of what was fair fare.

Recipe for Boiled Owl

Take feathers off. Clean owl.
Put in cooking pot with lots of water.
Add salt to taste.

The Eskimo Cookbook

———

Do not make loon soup.
The Eskimo Cookbook

SIXTY-SIX

IN THE JAPANESE language, everything that does not belong to you, but rather to someone else, is honorable. It is vitally important that you always recognize other people and their possessions as being honorific, while never, ever, *ever* making yourself or your possessions be so. This would be highly uncivil and outrageously vainglorious, besides violating the law of the land. It is pesky, though not difficult, to make any person and their stuff honorable. But, before I tell you how, I must repeat that you have no choice in this. You *must* remember that other people's stuff is worlds' more illustrious, meritorious, sinless and spotless than is your stuff any old day.

To make everything—other than what is yours—more glorious than what is yours, is easy. You simply add an "o" to the beginning of the word. For example, the term for dress is "yofuku" (yo-foo-koo). I would call my own unworthy dress "yofuku," but everyone else's supremely worthy dresses would be "o-yofuku." In English that would come out as o-dress. Got it?

It's the same with the honorific "san." I would never call myself, Peggy-san, but I would *always* address everyone else by adding "san" to their names, no matter if I lived with them, lived next door to them, played and worked with them or even, perish the thought, felt smugly superior to them. It's just the way it is, so get over it!

For me it was a never ending struggle to remember to do this; to remember what was and wasn't honorable. Even things you would never think of as having honor did. For example: soup, or o-soup. The Japanese ate "omiso shiru" (oh-mee-so-she-ru) several times a day. If I made it at home, it was just plain miso shiru because it was mine, but if it came from anywhere else it was omiso shiru.

This tasty concoction was made from a very mild aromatic fish broth mixed with soy bean paste. Tiny squares of otofu (remember honorable soy bean curd?) were added at the last minute. Every restaurant and home served omiso shiru. It was excellent. Trust me when I say that compared to badger stew, it was like eating divinity piled high with frosting, whipped cream, chocolate sauce, caramel sprinkles and a maraschino cherry on top. Plus chopped pecans!

Before I learned Japanese, I had trouble hearing all the unfamiliar words that people were saying because, if you recall, I learned Japanese not by seeing it, but rather by listening to it out on the street. For some knuckleheaded reason, I heard "omiso shiru" as "omiso shiti." It must have been the half trill given to the "r," making it sound like a "t." Therefore, that is what I said while politely ordering soup in restaurants or complimenting friends who served it to me in their homes. I had no idea why whenever I said it, folks reacted in such a startled manner, but I flattered myself into believing my Japanese was so stunningly colloquial, the locals were awed into hang-jawed speechlessness.

After many months, in which I frequently said "omiso-shiti" in social gatherings, Glen one day caught me in my error and corrected me. Like how was I supposed to know everything about everything? Don't forget, I was just a southern Minnesota girl who had a dip of a Minnesota neighbor who thought seaweed was hair dye, and where the pregnant Minnesota natives collected urine in whiskey bottles. Plus, I was now learning the local lingo *all on my own* out there in the snarly confusion of the market place.

To my horror, Glen informed me, I had *not* been asking for honorable bean paste and fish broth soup, but rather for honorable bean paste and *butt* soup.

"Oshiti," as it turned out was "other peoples' honorable rear ends." And no matter how visually connected the words butt and shiti may look to you, you would be wrong. "Shiti," despite its appearance, is pronounced "shee-tee." "Butt," on the other hand is, well, just "butt."

This small matter of mispronunciation was troubling to be sure, but I figured that compared to the shameless blunders my Japanese friends were making in English, it was peanuts. To illustrate this, how about the way they bungled the "s?" Invariably when they pronounced an English word in which an "s" was followed by an "i," they said "shh"—like when you want someone to be quiet. They couldn't help it. "S" just needed a shushing companion. Their honorable tongues were not programmed to handle it any other way, no matter how doggedly they tried.

It was like this. Whenever I visited a Japanese home, the residents would proudly and very politely request, in their finely tuned NHK-TV

English, "Oh, Keenah-san, prease shit here." Or, "No, prease do not shit there, prease shit over here." Or, "This is where you shit." They had me shitting all over the place.

I should, as well, mention that making anything plural in Japanese was not the simple piece o' cake that it was in English. We did it by simply adding an "s" to the end of a noun. For this reason I could not legitimately say that two kimono were kimonos, or that two benjo were benjos, for it was not the way it was done in the Japanese language, and those words were, after all, the Japanese language. I tell you this to explain why throughout this book you have seen Japanese nouns used in a singular fashion, no matter how many I was talking about. Understand?

NATURALLY OUR NAMES were also a challenge, which explained, I suppose, why it was easier to carve the face of Elvis Presley into the head of a pin rather than the words "Glen Leon Keener." The Japanese pronounced our family members' names thusly, including the always necessary honorable "san":

Keener = Kee-nah-san (the "r" ignored)

Glen = Goo-ren-san (an unnecessary "r" included)

Peggy = Peh-gey-san (no challenge there)

Jeff = Jeh-fu-chan ("chan" being the honorific used for children)

Matthew = Mah-phew-chan (the "phew" being a bit disrespectful, though they were unaware)

McLaughlin = Mah-koo-roff-oo-rin-san (my maiden name used at NHK, and off the charts enunciation-wise)

Of course, no one called Glen or me by our first names. Both of us were addressed identically as Kee-nah-san. Folks didn't even call their neighbors of ninety-nine years by their first names. To explain why this was, my theory was that not only were the Japanese over the top courteous, but it also helped maintain a kind of separation ... a polite, but practical barrier, if you will ... from too much familiarity on an overcrowded island where everyone was forced to exist on top of each other. I wondered if the local ants used "san"?

> "Hell is other people."
> Jean-Paul Sartre

Malapropisms—you gotta love 'em!—were as common as pot holes. They were the chocolates in my days. Once I was invited to a very swanky affair where I mingled with the likes of government heads and their wives. Even the Emperor's sister was there, although to my relief, she said nothing about her brother coming over to pick up our/his furnace.

The "heads" were men, naturally, who were allowing their wives a break from their duties at home and PTA. All the women were dressed in elegant nth-degree kimono, except for one woman who stood out strikingly. She did so because of her distinctive and voguish Western style clothing. Could I have come upon someone who feared *not* to be pounded down?

I could only see her from behind, but it was obvious that someone had professionally put her together. (I had my doubts as to this being Sakae-san.) From her spike heels to her beautifully contoured skirt and luscious cashmere sweater, she was harmoniously blended with impeccable taste. As I stood there admiring the backside of her, she turned around. There emblazoned across her rounded cleavage—and sinking deeply into the sumptuous cashmere fibers—was the word "Shithead."

Now, this gal was on the cutting edge of a new trend. She was one of the early Japanese radicals to flaunt English words scrawled across their chests. (Do any of you remember when t-shirts did not have words on them?) Obviously, she was oblivious to the crassness that now traversed her bosom, for she moseyed peripatetically throughout the crowd, her avant-gardism blaring. While she reeked of cosmopolitan savoir-faire, her knowledge of English was as septic as badger stew.

In her fashion choice she was saying to the world, "I am so groovy in my sweater with English on it even though I haven't a clue what it means and could care less because it's in English and that's what makes me so groovy." It was a sure bet the sweater had cost her a tall stack of yen. Being made of cashmere as it was, plus bearing the mark of an expensive designer who also had a thickheaded, tactless knowledge of English, made it a jet-set glad rag of the first order. But, even though I understood her innocence, that tasteless, tawdry shithead business was shocking to my delicate Calvinistic sensibilities. She was lucky I didn't pounce on her and wash her mouth out with soap!

But, as I stood there trying to shake off my astonishment, it dawned on me that no one else in the room was affected *but* me. Heck no! She was clearly in the groove, a true pacesetter amongst her kimono-clad peers, even though to me she was the paradigm for the kind of dumb-dumb who doesn't carry an English dictionary while clothes shopping. Clearly she didn't know a bass from her honorable ... well, er ... behind ... or else she was simply living in the bozone. Surely you've heard of that place. It's the substance that surrounds stupid people and stops any good sense from penetrating through. Unfortunately for her, it was showing little indication of breaking down in her near future.

Many years later during our second tour in Japan, I think I saw—no, I know I saw—that woman's granddaughter. She was equally as dopey and dictionaryless as her shithead gramma had been. Recognizably, Gramma had taught granddaughter everything she *didn't* know. The girl walked towards me on a city street wearing a t-shirt that taunted, "Eat my young puberty!" I've never quite figured out what exactly that meant, but I know for certain that had I ever dared to wear such a thing, Mrs. Wong would have put me in the corner until I turned twenty-five.

"There is a new awareness
of fashion in the Soviet Union.
The premier's wife recently
appeared on the cover of
House and Tractor."
Johnny Carson

SIXTY-SEVEN

SAKAE-SAN, AS you well know, was our babysitter and right hand helper with all things house related. I would never have called her a maid. First of all, the word "maid" just wasn't in my Midwest vocabulary, the idea of being waited upon way too weird, as well as the sound of the word being ridiculously prissy-formal.

> "The town where I grew up
> had a zip-code of
> E-I-E-I-O."
> Martin Mull

To me, "maid" conjured up a woman whose hair was in a bun (whereas Sakae-san's hair was more free-style Brillo pad), who wore a stiffly starched uniform (but then you already know she was into needlework), and fluffed household objects with a feather duster.

Well, I take back that part about the feather duster, for I soon learned it was the Japanese housewife's most preferred housecleaning tool. On her first day on the job, Sakae-san was alarmed to learn I didn't even own one although, I guess, if she could have waited a couple of years, I could have scraped one together from our best dead pet pheasant ... or just turned it around.

Finding us lacking, on the second day Sakae-san (graduate of Dusting 201), brought her own exclusive feather duster from home. To me it was always fascinating in a bad way, and always dumb in a puzzling way, to see the feather-riled dust from one object rise into the air, churn like a mini tornado, hover over a landing place while airborne, and then land mote-by-mote upon the piece of furniture next to it which had just been dusted. Was I the only one who hadn't received the memo on that? Just what gave with it anyway? As for myself, I preferred old underwear and gauzy worn Curities. Besides, who's to say that Sakae-san's feather duster wasn't from some bird we knew personally—like, say, the great-grandmother or third cousin removed of our future pheasant? It just wouldn't have been right.

Sakae-san stood several inches short of five-feet. She was stocky, chunky and reminded me of a soft storm door. On her face were the easily recognizable signs of a pinched and difficult life. As a young woman from a poor family, she had struck gold when a lonely, homesick American G.I. latched on to her affections. They eventually married, had a baby boy (or vice versa), and moved to the States.

In most every respect, this did not work out well for either of them. Sakae-san did not fit into her husband's small-town Nebraska lifestyle, and he quickly became disenchanted with her, his convenient-while-in-Japan-only Asian trinket. They divorced, and she and her son returned to Tokyo, the uncomplicated and-hoping-to-stay-that-way Nebraska undoubtedly relieved to bid them farewell. Back in Japan with no means of support and no profession to which she could turn, Sakae-san resorted to that second to the last recourse of the desperate: housekeeping. As for the last recourse of the desperate, it wasn't in the verbal resume she gave me, and I wasn't asking.

> "The closest one ever comes
> to perfection is on a
> job application."
> Unknown

Because she really needed to hold onto her job, I suspected that Sakae-san was always extra polite when she was at our house, but I also harbored an intuition that once she walked out our door, she quickly reverted to the other objectionably coarse side of her character. Of this I could, from time to time, see hints. But, then, who knew what her real life was like? I could only guess while knowing it could not have been easy.

Once free of being the oddball in Nebraska, Sakae-san's life did not improve when she returned to Japan. In fact, it became heaps more difficult because it was a whole lot worse being shunned by folks like you than by folks unlike you. The problem lay in her son. He was a half-breed, the most repellent genetic persuasion the Japanese could imagine. Who in their right mind would willingly mix their sacrosanct Japanese blood with that of another, lesser race (and trust me, all other races were lesser), plus the fact that the Japanese saw the Japanese as just that: a race unto themselves! No way were they even a part of a unified Asian brotherhood, because Asians were those other people: the Chinese and the Koreans, and heaven help them, those Heinz-57 folks who lived on Taiho's Sakhalin Island. Fervently, they crossed their pure-blooded hearts and hoped to die if it weren't the truth.

The thought of blending blood was a nightmare worse than being born green, with orange hair, a single fuchsia eye in the middle of your forehead and not having a navel. Additionally, on top of that, was the ever-present hammer that commanded: *Be like everyone else! Absolutely never stand out from the crowd!* A half-breed stood out like lipstick in a convent. Verily, Sakae-san's son was a bell clanging loud and clear with the repeated message of his mom's unthinkable past behavior. In his young face was a world of condemnation.

SIXTY-EIGHT

AS BREEZY A picture as I have painted about our life in Japan, it was not all a barrel of laughs. Much of it was deadly sobering. Certainly the Japanese were extraordinary in demonstrating their social graces to us gaijin, but I thought that more than anything, they wanted us to leave them the heck alone. I could detect this every now and then when we were out in their midst. There, I'd ever so briefly catch a glimpse of what was beyond those socially necessary smiles, and into their real thinking.

It happened to me one day as I and a mass of people were waiting to cross a very crowded street near the Ginza. A young man on a bicycle pedaled past us. He was loaded down with tall stacks of business reports that he was delivering to another office. Just as he got right in front of me, his bike hit a hole in the road, causing his front tire to dramatically swerve. In an instant, he was smashed to the street. As he fell, his foot and ankle became badly mangled in the bicycle's pedal and chain.

To my shock, rather than sitting down on the street and attending to his serious wounds, he did the Japanese thing of trying with all his might to not make himself obvious. Within moments his injury was bleeding through his clothing and dripping on to the road. Through his torn pant leg, I could see the gaping flesh and bones of his open lacerations. But, stoically ignoring this small inconvenience for the much more important obligation of saving face, he began hopping around on his good leg while trying to pick up his bike, and then hopping about some more in a frantic attempt to pick up the hundreds of loose papers which were now blowing in every direction. His futile efforts were so pathetically ludicrous, that I stood transfixed, not quite believing what I was seeing. Two minutes into this, I realized the rest of the crowd was as paralyzed as was I.

Looking around at them, then back at the desperate and profusely bleeding man, I waited for his countrymen to rush to his aid. Oddly, no one moved. In disbelief, it struck me that no one was going to help this man. From the pit of my stomach, I felt my blood begin to boil. Then I fulminated, and with a full-throttle rush of adrenaline pushed through the statue-like crowd and into the street of now-stalled traffic. Folks there were leaning out of their car windows watching the blood-soaked fellow hopping about frenetically in his grotesque dance of trying to gather up the loose papers. They, also, were doing nothing.

> "Every normal man
> must be tempted at times
> to spit on his hands,
> hoist the black flag,
> and begin slitting throats."
> H. L. Mencken

As I rushed towards him, I realized my brain was churning out decidedly unfriendly, downright angry, and bordering-on-evil thoughts about the Japanese. Even in the commotion I had to wonder whether or not my loving soul was still loving. And though I was sure *I* understood brotherly love, what was it about brotherhood that *they* were not grasping?

Furthermore, if I was so darned high and mighty virtuous in my rush to judgment, maybe it was I who wasn't such hot stuff in this brotherly business. Maybe my opinionated thinking made me no longer a Christian, one-hundred percent. But as soon as I thought it, I stopped, mollifying my soul that right then there were more important things to do—and to do now!

By this time I was next to the injured fellow. As best I could, I got hold of him by putting his arm across my shoulders. Then with him hopping on his one good leg and leaving a bright red trail behind us, together we slowly moved out of the street. Once across, I carefully, though awkwardly, got him down to the curb. Then without warning, out of nowhere someone began yelling orders to the crowd.

To my surprise, it was me! And, I was as taken aback by my unexpected outburst as was the crowd!

"Call an ambulance! Get the bicycle! Gather the papers! Someone help him!!" I screamed. Even in my agitated state, I could see I was the only foreign face in the quickly enlarging group of spectators. I was also the only one with the ill-conceived, ridiculous assumption that his compatriots would even think of coming to his rescue. How could I have been more wrong?

My appeals for help from those folks were like asking them to jump into a den of flesh-eating troglodytes. Nobody stepped forward. Even so, I could see my pleas were beginning to have some effect for their galvanized stares began to flinch, and then turn away. Still no one offered any help to the man—or to me. In Japan such a move would have required a committee to first be elected, then a plan to be drawn up, and finally the rescuers to be appointed and uniformed. It was beyond exasperation. As Justice Arthur Goldberg once said, "If Columbus had had an advisory committee he would probably still be on the dock." Problem was, I *was* the committee—and I *was* alone out there on the dock.

> "A committee is a group of important individuals
> who singly can do nothing,
> but who can together agree
> that nothing can be done."
> Fred Allen

By then in their embarrassment, or possible lack of any further interest, the crowd began turning away and moving on, their heads bent down so no one (like me, Typhoid Mary!), would call on them. Two people in advanced states of bewilderment remained behind. They were either rattled to the core by my out-gushing or were standing too close to me to escape my wrath. Whichever, they began picking up the papers. Meanwhile, I stayed with the man trying my best to staunch the blood flow.

The poor fellow was obviously scared silly and in terrible pain. But interestingly, even more distressing than his physical anguish was his mortification over having caused a scene. It had come to this. He was now the unspeakable, loathsome protruding nail, and his psyche would never again be the same.

As I sat with him on the curb waiting for the ambulance, something equally as disturbing occurred to me. With a stark wariness, I realized for the first time that if I were ever in need of help, the Japanese—who I had just observed did not take care of their own—would certainly never take care of an uninvited, undesirable, outsider like me. Like a bad, bad omen this did, in fact, come true some years later. It nearly cost me my life.

"The best things and the best people rise out of their separateness," said Robert Frost. "I am against a homogenized society because I want the cream to rise." (In this case, "nail" is what I'm thinking he meant!) With such sentiments, it's a sure bet that Bob Frost avoided the less traveled road leading to Japan. Yes, perhaps someone had already told him about the Japanese recoiling from being anything, in any way, outside the norm.

"There used to be a me
behind the mask, but
I had it surgically removed."
Peter Sellers

CLEARLY ONE OF the most disadvantaged groups that stood out flagrantly from the norm was the orphans. In every sense of the word they were curiosities and different, atypical exceptions to a well ordered society. They had no parents, no extended families, and no one who could wrap up their proof of belonging and stash it in the family's navel trunk. In other words, they were genetically jinxed. The root of their misfortune, of course, lay in having no documented bloodlines registered in a prefectural archive. This was pretty much equal to a really, really crummy future. With no ancestral lineage, job prospects were dim, and marriage only a faint wish.

In the Japanese society there were people who still today work as marriage detectives. We not only do not have such a concept in the West, we also do not have even the hint of a word for it. To understand this, let me explain. The job of the marriage detective was to dig into the backgrounds of prospective brides and grooms. Obviously an orphan had no history in which to dig. He was a brick wall.

Without a family tree (otherwise known as marriage credentials), there was no respectable societal slot in which to place him. No self-respecting family would dare take the risk of not knowing exactly, absolutely, unmistakably the family into which their child might marry. In a culture of arranged marriages, a respectable background, above all, had been a categorical essential down through the ages. It was, I suppose, very similar to what we knew as the rhapsodic joy a Jewish family felt when learning their child was marrying another Jew. It was called Jewbilation! In the case of Japan, this would have translated to something like ... Japonderful! Or Niperior! Mazeltov!

"There are very few Japanese Jews.
As a result, there is no
Japanese word
for Alan King."
Johnny Carson

It is interesting to note that marriages throughout history have been arranged for a myriad of reasons. In Japan, the number one reason more often than not was to improve the standing of both families, or at least not diminish it! If, for example, the bride's family were more elite than the groom's, or if the bride's family name ended with her because she was either an only child or had no brothers, the new husband often took her family name, relinquishing his own for his siblings to carry on without him.

One of my very dear friends was exceptionally tall for a Japanese woman. Among other things, but certainly a primary factor, her husband was chosen because he was short. Somewhere in between the arranged marriage committee hoped to balance out the height genes of the couple's future offspring, making them blessedly taller than him and as equally blessed shorter than her.

For others (the modern free thinking, though unfulfilled singles), there was also the lonely hearts column in the local English newspaper where a desperate, companionless soul could turn for prospects. I cite here one example sent in by a modest, though needy, flower. It was apparent both she, as well as her marriage committee, had not yet successfully snared her Japanese prince, and hence she had resorted to lowering her standards ... drastically! And to make matters more pitiful, neither was she asking for all that much nor did she beat around the bush asking for it: "Charming single lady looks for superior man of America. Send bodyful photo and resume. Want serious intercourse!" I'll bet.

No way in heaven or hell would the Japanese have believed—and certainly not approved of—my decision to marry Glen before I even knew for sure what his last name was. Nor would they have ever entertained the notion that I knew next to nothing about his background, that I didn't meet his mom and sisters until the evening before our wedding, and that I didn't meet his dad until six months *after!* But, even more importantly, they would never in a trillion years have dreamed that I didn't care, because those things were not important to me. Only Glen was. It's sad to think we may not have become a wedded unit if we had had marriage detectives in Austin, and that would have been a serious bummer!

> "One should never know
> to precisely whom
> one has married."
> Friedrich Nietzsche, on Lohengrin

I USED TO visit an orphanage in Tokyo. It was a dismal place. Everything was gray—the children in their drab, washed-out used clothing, as well as the rooms they lived in. There wasn't a spot of color anywhere. For me, this was simply unacceptable; intolerable. These were children; children who needed gaiety and rainbows at least on their walls, because their lives certainly held little of either. After my first visit I went straight home and drew a series of large posters depicting Walt Disney characters. I chose the brightest, happiest colors I could find. Then I returned to the orphanage and tacked them all over their walls. The effect was take-your-breath-away-awesome, like sunbursts exploding in the bleakness of an underground cave.

I also wrote a hasty letter to my dad asking if he would donate enough money for me to buy a rocking chair, clothes and diapers, all of which I could purchase at the Green Park PX. As I trusted, he was as dependable as my love for him. Without hesitation, Gene McLaughin wrote out a check that very day and put it in the mail. With his single donation, I was able to purchase many needed supplies for the children. I doubt the caregivers ever sat in the rocker though, because living in a culture that didn't use chairs ... and certainly not ones that moved ... I'm sure it scared them away. The children, on the other hand, creative and fearless as all children are even though they're orphans, might have played on it like a trimmed-back Jungle Jim. No matter, it eased the hungry voice in me that pleaded for these children to be cuddled and rocked. What kind of childhood was a childhood without being cuddled and rocked?

How well I remember reading in our military paper, the Stars and Stripes, a story out of Los Angeles. It had to do with a Japanese mother and her two young children. While living in California, the mother found herself suddenly widowed by her Japanese husband. For reasons unknown, she had no family in Japan to which they could return. In her mind, and with no means of support and no family connections, there was only one course of action for her to take. Suicide.

But, such a dire move would leave her two children orphaned. Being Japanese she knew how unspeakably dreadful such an outcome would be for them. So, in the end, she went to an L.A. beach where she, conforming to the conscience of her culture, responsibly drowned her children. That freed her up, then, to take her own life. As a loving mother, it was a perfect solution, and she carried it out with consummate love and devotion.

Americans were outraged! It was beyond everything we held dear to imagine a mother killing her own children. To us, she was the foulest of the foul.

In Japan, however, it was quite another story. There folks empathized with her plight, understood her actions, and even agreed, though regrettably, that she had made the right, reasonable and moral decision. What Japan and the young mother did not know was that in the United States her children would have been cared for. There was even a good chance that someone, a perfect stranger, would have taken in those two children and made them his own. We Americans, of the mishmash, goulash, huddled-masses mentality, do not cringe from blending all kinds of ingredients into our family stews. We are so impure, what does one additional maverick pedigree matter to us?

It reminded me of the day we brought Erin home from the hospital. The neighbors in Asahi Court rushed over to get a first glimpse. They stood in our living room clustered around the bassinette ooohing and aaahing over her blue eyes and blond hair. "Gosh," I heard one man say (in Japanese, of course), "Caucasians are just like dogs. You never know how they're going to come out."

"How true, how true," the others around him agreed, "yes, indeed, lamentably wasn't it so?"

And it *was* so! Impartially and guilelessly, we Honkies do not know how we're going to "come out." And that's okay. It's okay to not be okay. As far as we're concerned, how our babies will look *is* the *big* question; the tantalizing spice. Just who and what each child will look like is the surprise, don't they see? For us, we are used to the fact that we are not Xerox copies of each other, but rather a provocative myriad of dissimilarities. We call it individuality.

But, remember, that thinking only belongs to us.

SIXTY-NINE

BEING ORPHANED WAS not the worst thing that could happen to a Japanese. Being Eta was. Eta (Eh-tah) was Japan's dirty little secret.

People outside of Japan, had no idea that on this ancient island there existed a kind of caste system. It was certainly not as extreme as that found in India, but it was nevertheless much regarded and obeyed. It involved the group of people who worked at tanning hides (no, no, not Catholic nuns or Joan Crawford, both champs at spanking children's bottoms!), but rather tanning the hides of animals. Those were the Eta.

Sakae-san was the expert on this subject. She was the person who taught me all I needed and wanted to know. I'll never forget the day of my first lesson.

I stood aghast, with my bottom jaw hanging somewhere around my chest, as she explained that to the Japanese, Eta were very easily recognizable. This seemed unbelievable to me in this ant hill of clones, but wisely I kept that thought to myself. She went on to say that if I couldn't cull out the Eta on my own, that I should pay close attention to the people out on the street for they would signal to each other when one was approaching. This, naturally, was done covertly because, don't forget, the Japanese were supremely, unparalleled, second to none in their politeness towards other people. Oh, brother!!!

Without shilly-shallying about, the oh-brother-second-to-none polite secret signal that one onlooker gave to another began by discreetly holding

293

up both hands. One hand was used as a shield for the other. Behind the curtain of this screen, the thumb on the other hand was turned inward toward the palm leaving the four remaining fingers splayed downward resembling the four legs of an animal ... a four-legged animal whose hide needed tanning!

Dumbstruck, I was about to tan *her* hide for being so egregiously outrageous, when she persisted in continuing. With even more passion Sakae-san then emphasized that if I ever saw such a debased person coming towards me, I should immediately step aside—even cross the street—so that I would not become contaminated by his or her presence. This would be the "polite" thing to do.

Above all, and of paramount importance (the magnitude of the gravity immeasurable), never *under any circumstances* could it be allowed for a non-Eta son or daughter to marry into a family of real-Eta. Great Scot! It spelled ruination for them all, and quite possibly the collapse of the Imperial Dynasty even though that dynasty would be replete with beautiful leather goods.

Of course, in my usual ditzy, over-embellishing way, I had to go and take conditions one step further. How about this, I asked (the horror of it all nearly causing *me* to cut out my *own* tongue), how much more would the Japanese lives be shattered if one of their citizens, perish the thought, committed the double whammy of marrying an Eta who was also an orphan!

Or this, because I couldn't be stopped, how much even *more* ungodly and quite possibly beyond what flesh and blood could bear, would it be if that citizen married a nail-ridden Eta orphan with kinky red hair, six-feet-tall, sporting a pink, fuzzy body, who marched to his own drumbeat and would in a heartbeat help an injured bicycle delivery boy and could pronounce sit "sit" instead of "shit"—and ate butter?

But of course, there was no answer to this speculation since no Japanese, since the beginning of time, had ever allowed his thinking to go to such a horrifying extreme. How astonished and disgusted they would have been to learn this kind of thing happened everyday in Austin. Good ol' Austin.

There's more. Even though it was not as dire as being Eta, it was nevertheless mighty high on the oh-my-god-list. One more disclosure the marriage detective was sworn to reveal was whether or not the groom was the oldest son—or even more goosepimply—an only child. Either condition set up an entire realm of discomfiting scenarios, for such a state of affairs came with multiple blessings for good, as well as heavy curses for bad. It certainly meant a roof over the bride's head because, with no siblings, the groom always took her home to his parents' house. But more than anything, it meant a heck of a lot of hardship for the new Mrs.

She and she alone, from her "I do" onward, bore the responsibility of putting up with and caring for her mother-in-law. In the early stages of the marriage, the father-in-law, like his son, was away at work, so that left the two women home alone. In tight quarters. Every day! Day in, day out! To the end of time and the limits of sanity.

You will recall the Japanese word for "bride" does not particularly conjure up coziness. Sure, one part of its translation tells us she has married, but the other part tells us that she is "the one who comes from outside." See what I mean? Warm and fuzzy not.

Following the nuptials, the bride traditionally moved in with her parents'-in-law where she took on the role of whatever her mother-in-law decided her role would be. Do not forget that to his mother, the son *was* The Sun! Also The Moon and The Stars. He was her reason to live, and to boast about her own umbilical cord trunk where the shriveled up thing stored inside was the proof of her production of him. Do you really think such a mother was going to, all of a sudden one day just because of a very expensive wedding ceremony, change everything and be willing to share Mr. Sun-Moon-and-Stars with his new wife? I don't think so.

I couldn't count the number of Japanese women I knew who lived under the warped thumbs of their mothers-in-law. These prickly, mean-spirited women were champions of their art, having learned first hand the tricks of the trade from their own mothers-in-law. My heart ached for these brides. The best thing they could do was produce grandsons so they would achieve some rank and worth, as well as get some of the focus off themselves.

For the bride, even the promise of a more elevated status after grand-childbirth did not always help, because as the parents-in-law aged, the bride's life became that much more of a grind when she became their sole caretaker. This was a tough bite to chew when you had been mistreated throughout your entire marriage. Yes, the horrible prediction had at last come true and the bride was now actually wiping the nose and bottom of a mother-in-law who had never loved her, but had only put up with "this person from the outside" because her son had married her and she could bear the family's descendants. You've no doubt heard that the Japanese are known for their longevity. In many cases, the care stretched out for years.

"If Vincent Price were to be
co-starred with Bette Davis
in a story by Edgar Allen Poe
directed by Roger Corman,
it would not fully express
the pent-up violence and
depravity of a single day
in the life of the average family."
Quentin Crisp

The good news is this kind of life has changed over the years, as many people have moved from their large country homes to small city apartments where there is no longer room for the extended family. In the really and truly over-squashed existence of Tokyo, (presently a whopping city of thirty-five million people!), who would have ever guessed that the dreaded, horrifically over-priced, dinky apartment would be the saving grace of many a young wife?

"Happiness is having
a large, loving, caring,
close-knit family
in another city."
George Burns

The only light at the end of the dismal only-son-tunnel was that when the groom's parents finally did die, he inherited everything. If there was anything left to inherit. If the bequest included their home, just imagine the joy of the aging bride as she finally had a chance after thirty-five years of marriage, to put up the curtains of her choice.

I must be fair in saying that certainly not all mothers-in-law were beasties. There were a few who were kind and loving. I actually knew two.

None of this is to suggest that the bride alone got all the guff. It was also not an easy road for her husband, the only son. In Japan there was (and probably still is), a society called "The Only Son Club." Here sole sons got together and lamented over how hard their solitary, siblingless lives were; how duty bound they were to their parents, and how stigmatized they were in the marriage arena. But, at least *they* got to leave the house to attend their jobs and meetings!

On the flip side of the coin, there was no such refuge for their partner brides who were left home alone and defenseless, toughing it out while their husbands consoled themselves around the company water cooler or at the clubby get-togethers. I suspected there was many a funeral where throughout the ceremony, middle-aged couples had a difficult time concealing their smiles.

I know I shouldn't be so cynical about Japan. After all, you know that old saying—"before you criticize someone, you should walk a mile in his shoes." But then, think about it. When I criticize the Japanese, I'm a mile away—*well, actually six thousand seven hundred and eighteen*—and I have my own shoes! Nanny-nanny-boo-boo!"

> "Honest criticism is hard to take—
> especially when it comes from
> a relative, a friend, an acquaintance,
> or a stranger."
> Franklin P. Jones

SEVENTY

I KNOW I keep harping on the proud nail metaphor, but you can't imagine how much it dictated the every move of the Japanese. No, you have no idea its power. Take the irony of Sakae-san, for example. As debased as was her social strata, her nail did not stand out as much as the even more debased Eta. Crucified as she was, she still had someone to look down upon.

Praise the Lord, for He in His goodness has made those who are even lowlier than I! (But then, I guess, it wasn't Him. It was those people He made who messed up His plans for equality.)

Nonetheless, Sakae-san's unfortunate life choices certainly were an overt manifesto of her past divertissement. People seeing her son for the first time knew in the twinkling of a winked eye—would you get a look at that boy's face!—that *his* father was *not* Japanese. For a long time I didn't realize how hard it was for Sakae-san to be at our house, knowing she was leaving her boy alone and unprotected after he came home from school everyday.

I learned how stressful it was one morning when she arrived at our house terribly distressed. Upon her return home the afternoon before, her six-year-old son was no where to be found. He had strict instructions to always go straight home and stay there until she returned. On that day, however, as he walked home a bunch of more genetically pure, more elevated neighbor boys grabbed him, tied him up, put him in a dark shed and left him there. After hours of searching, Sakae-san finally found him.

Of course it did no good to report the crime because it would only rain down more attention and contempt upon her little boy. An authority of the hard knocks life, she, above all others, was keenly aware of what a magnet for ostracism she had produced. I had no idea this was her life, and I was shaken to the core when she told me.

I'd like to report that things improved after that incident, but I fear they did not. We did make an immediate plan for Sakae-san to leave our house earlier everyday so she would be certain to be home when school let out, but her boy's lot in life could never have been easy. What am I saying? Both of their lives could never have been easy! You realize, of course, that the boy was beautiful having received the best genes and looks of the two racial groups. Mother Nature, in her all-knowing protectiveness, is sharply aware such children will need both.

> "All God's children
> are not beautiful.
> Most of God's children
> are, in fact,
> barely presentable."
> Fran Lebowitz

Still, despite her pride in her lovely son, Sakae-san was very lonely and any prospects for her situation to improve were highly unlikely. Who was going to marry her? Unlike Wile E. Coyote, she could not scheme and plot away the backwash of her past, because her son's presence did not allow it. She was damned beyond damnation for having a mixed breed child, to say nothing of consorting with the foreigner who fathered him in the first place. How could she have!

I HAPPENED TO look out the window one morning just in time to see our forsaken, spouseless Sakae-san sauntering up the road, stopping every now and then to kick at the dust, while burping out short chuckles of private delight. Obviously, she was just returning from an all-nighter. She looked like an ad for a two-bit hooker—or in the now current, politically correct vernacular, "low cost provider." Her cheap, overly frilly dress (designed by Trollops 'R Us), was, to say the least, disheveled. Her hair was a feral cat's nest of turbulence, and the quarter-inch thick makeup that had once been assigned to individual facial features, was now smeared and sliding outside of its borders.

Clopping awkwardly into the house on plastic sling backs (that had recently slung), the slatternly Sakae-san slumped heavily against the front door jam, grinned at me with saucy chutzpa, and let out one large and looooong voluptuous sigh which set to glowing the self-satisfied grin on her face.

"Ahhhhhh," she exhaled, allowing each breathy "h" its own place in time, "I'm still good!"

Va Va Voom!

Now, I don't see myself as the self-righteous president of the Bay of Prigs, and I'm for sure not here to cast aspersions, *but* I could just picture the tawdry scene of the night before: Sakae-san dancing in the slimelight, cheek-to-cheap with some equally busted soul; a diabolical match like that arranged by the hand of Godzilla.

The truth is I loved it! And I loved her spunk. Even a reformed Mary Magdalene would agree that every now and then a girl needs a sullied, cheap, tacky, rinky-dink of an evening out on the town—just for reassurance.

SEVENTY-ONE

IN ASAHI COURT there was a small band of mixed Hawaiian-Chinese-Japanese boys who Jeff and Matt hung out with. The children almost always played outdoors because no matter how hot it was outside, it was hotter inside. Even though our boys were considerably younger, their Keener bigness fit right in with the diminutive size of their older, but smaller, buddies.

This, notwithstanding, was an especially difficult challenge for Matt who was the youngest gang member. His friends were more than twice his age, a significant difference in the life of a little boy. At age four and as big as they were, Matt more than had his work cut out for him keeping up with the pack, most of the time not having a clue what was going on, but trudging behind them like a persistent wet leaf that was stuck to their shoes, just to belong.

Regardless of his undying gang loyalty, one day the boys-of-the-hood pushed Matt to his limit. After several hours of futilely attempting over and over to be one of them, Matt decided to throw in the towel. He had had enough! He was fed up with the whole lot of them! Into the house he clomped, sobbing his heart out, his wails being in that special category that come from the deepest depths of a child's soul.

Now, you need to know that Matt was not a crier, indeed he was anything but, so I knew I had a serious matter on my hands. I took a good hard look at his suffering, and after a quick perusal was relieved to find neither blood spilling out nor broken bones jutting through. Thereby I

301

concluded this must be a matter of the heart ... as in really, really bruised feelings.

"Wahhhh," Matt implored, the tears covering his cheeks and flowing down like two small rivers converging in the top crease of his round tummy. "Jimmy is the boss of Gilbert, Gilbert is the boss of Alban, Alban is the boss of Ernie, Ernie is the boss of Jeff, Jeff is the boss of me, and I ... I ... I'm not even ... boss of the bugs!"

The wretchedness of his plight ripped the mothering heart right out of me.

> "Moral indignation is
> in most cases, 2% moral,
> 48% indignation, and
> 50% envy."
> Vittorio de Sica

The problem—the very essence of the matter—was that the pecking order he had listed was entirely accurate. There was no getting past it. Matt, being dead last, *was* not even boss of the bugs. And it was just his lot in life that the only resolution to his problem was to grow. But with morale that low, how's a mom to tell her dear crestfallen son a lame palliative like that?

> WARNING TO ALL PERSONNEL!
> Firings will continue
> until morale improves.
> Unknown

Many a time since, each of us Keeners has experienced his own personal bout with being not even boss of the bugs. It was like that platitude the wise Confucius often spouted when he was out for a drive in his Ford Fairlane, "Some days you are the bug; others the windshield." So be it.

The good tidings were that no matter how cruel the outside world felt, Matt always had a best friend right at home. It was true. Even though Jeff *was* his *most* immediate boss, he was also a sincerely caring best buddy and most notable mentor-brother. Why, without Jeff, Matt would never have known stuff. Like, for example, the little known fact of ... well ... what was the tallest mountain in the world? Jeff, the world's most conspicuous expert on mountains, knew—even provided pictures to prove it. I witnessed this very lesson myself as I watched them one evening both squeezed together in the only other chair in our living room (not my Jungle Jim rocker) with a book spread across their chubby laps.

"There it is!" Jeff proclaimed triumphantly, as he pointed to a picture on page thirteen, "Mt. Cletus!"

But then you already knew that.

I MENTION THE word "chair" so casually, as if finding a chair for our boys to sit in was no big, grand, earth-shaking deal. Wrong! It was. Remember where we were? In the land where folks rested their honorable posteriors on honorable floor cushions on honorable straw mats? I was reading The Saturday Evening Post one day when I saw an ad for a La-Z-Boy recliner. Bam! I'd never seen anything so regal, so sumptuous, so cushy, so thoroughly, languorously American. I wondered how it would look all laid out beneath Glen. Off I trotted to the Green Park PX, the picture in hand. Sure, he could order that chair, the manager assured me, but it would take a while. A "while" turned out to be six months.

On a bright summer day, a PX delivery truck rolled up to our door. Packed inside was surely the most beauteous, most fake leather recliner Mr. L. Boy had ever in his supine life fabricated. Flaunting the splendor of the breath-taking PX merchandise, was a cluster of swaggering, short but sturdy, Japanese delivery men. Theatrically, they undid the chair's wrappings outside on the Asahi Court driveway. This was done with the targeted purpose of getting all the neighbors to share in its majesty, as well as pointing out to those same said neighbors, the lofty store in which such majestic merchandise could be obtained ... the very one in which they, themselves, happened to be employed. I couldn't help but notice that busy as they were, they still managed to keep their short but sturdy noses in the air.

As if it were made of eggshells, the delivery crew struggled with the utmost of care, avoiding any damage to the chair's fake hide. The thought crossed my mind of how fortunate we would be—in the event it *did* suffer a rip—if one of the delivery men were Eta and could repair it on the spot. But, it's probably best that I didn't inquire ... if you catch my drift.

Into the house they toiled with the monstrously heavy thing. Then, with one final flourish, the men reverently placed it in the only available spot in our teensy living room—next to Emperor Hirohito's furnace. Can you imagine the glory of coupling those two objects? Why, it transformed the space brilliantly, causing me to look in disbelief at the old rattan lawn chair that it was replacing, which only moments before we had considered fine furniture. Now, in comparison, one could see the truth of the ratty old thing. The mocking demeanor of its unweave-the-weave bamboo strips was suddenly glaringly embarrassing. Gosh, how could I not have noticed it before now? Equating that old chair to the new one and calling them both *chairs* was like saying a St. Bernard and a Chihuahua were both dogs, and expecting anyone to believe you.

But now, the chair! The chair! Oh, what a chair. First it gave unceasing, laid back comfort to Glen, second it provided a roomy squeeze-together place for Jeff and Matt to further their studies of Mt. Cletus, and third it turned out to be a status symbol beyond anyone's illusions of grandeur. Indeed, I felt the flush of the vapors when the neighbors came to salivate over it, even though they—chair weenies that they were—were afraid to try it out.

I could see their point. With all that reclining business it did look menacing—like it had a hankering for a taste of Japanese weenies! But, now, looking at our living room filled with covetous neighbors, I knew our home would never again be regarded as the same old ordinary place. Verily, I could swear I heard a distinct *clink* as we suddenly ratcheted up a notch on the Asahi Court Parade of Duplexes.

Up there in the air, along with it, was my short, but sturdy, nose.

Just like that, we now owned a magnificent pseudo-as-all-get-out leather chair, and I'd wager a bet it was the first of its kind on those distant shores. It was called Naugahyde, and it quickly became a word I could casually throw around at military social events, as if *everyone* knew what it meant. (Oh, the simple folk! They probably still sat around on hollowed-out tree stumps!)

One evening I had my most supreme opportunity EVER to show off my new vocabulary. I was at a party talking with Mr. Noggle when (seriously) Mr. Hyde joined the conversation. Casually I suggested that Noggle's son should marry Hyde's daughter so she could become Mrs. Nogglehyde. It was brilliant and would have for sure gone down in wordsmith history, except that neither of those unschooled, home-décor-bozos knew one iota about upholstery fabrics. Blast it!

But, as things were turning out, I was finding that being on a status-symbol-roll felt so good, I simply could not be stopped. Let's see, so far in my upward climb I had stock piled two symbols: the incredible wringer washer and now the pseudo buffalo hide recliner. I would have included the reincarnated, buzz hair cut, Chinese Ring-Necked Pheasant except that it could no longer be included because the boys had pretty much ruffled its ringed neck past salvaging when they dressed it up for Groundhog Day.

THE THIRD STATUS symbol—and I still tremble at the power of this memory—happened some months later.

> "There must be
> more to life
> than having everything."
> Maurice Sendak

For reasons of which I'll never quite fathom, I, just like that, became disillusioned with hanging the wet laundry in zig-zaggy cobwebs across the living room every darned night of the week. Somehow, unexplained, it had lost its romance for me. Therefore, when I heard the rumor that the Green Park PX had received an order of dryers, I nearly flattened a platoon of soldiers—in tanks—in my haste to be the first one in line!

Never stopping to think where I would put it (my vision now beholding only stacks of instantly dried laundry, soft, fluffy and folded in the blink of an eye), I slammed my money down on the PX counter and signed on the dotted line, requesting, now that I was a regular customer, that my old friends, the short but sturdy delivery crew, bring it right on over.

Before I could say stupid-impulsive-purchase, they were at our door. Once more the men did the status symbol box opening routine right in the middle of the driveway, first looking around to make sure the neighbors were home. To their satisfaction they were, and they were peeking. Fully assured they had an audience and that that audience had exhibited the proper amount of awe, the crew schlepped the grandiose machine into the house, respectfully avoiding any damage to the now famous reposing recliner. I noticed that while schlepping, they did their best to kowtow as they reverently passed by it.

About that time I realized I had a big decision to make. How had I waited so long? Like ... hmmm, where was this ginormous thing going to, for Pete's sake, go? Somehow, in my impetuousness, I had not exactly thought this out at the time of purchase. Now looking at our kitchen, I was reminded all over again that it was little more than a squeeze box of a space, and the only available non-occupied inches were right next to the sink. Exactly in the same spot as the back door to our home!

Back door, did I say? Wasn't that just a plank of wood that swung to and fro on a couple of finger-like hinges? And, of just what importance was that, I wanted to know? Besides who needed a back door? Especially when we had a front door? It was suddenly all so clear. If God, by god, had meant for us to have two exits, would He have invented the dryer?

No space. No problem-o.

I signaled for the team to forge ahead. Ever so carefully they slid the dryer smack dab into the slot right in front of the back door, wedging it in between the sink and the wall like a white enameled foot gliding perfectly into a tight-fitting sock. That was the good news.

The bad news was obvious. It completely, solidly, altogether covered the door. But, la-di-da, let's get real. Our family didn't need an escape from a burning building. We needed dry clothes!

Thus appeased, I began hyperventilating over the splendor of my new acquisition. All I had to do was plug it in and downy, dehydrated, no-iron-needed laundry would be mine. I reached for the plug. My, it was large! And just what was that third pointy thing there? Gosh, the one and only extra socket in our kitchen—the one not used by the refrig, and shared by the wringer washer and every other electrical thing I owned which came to a total of one hand mixer—really looked like it could receive nothing like that peculiar third pointy thing.

You guessed it. The clothes continued to hang across the living room in cobwebby netting for days upon weeks until a Japanese electrician was able to fit us into his hectic electrician's schedule. Once he finally arrived, he had to figure out what the function of this big white box was—like you lame-brained-she-devil, you've got to be kidding ... isn't that what air is all about?—and finally do something about it. As he stood there casting electrical disparagements in my direction, I knew in his small judgmental soul there was no way he believed this thing could actually dry clothes, and how dumb was that, anyway? What I was calling a marvel of a drying machine, he was calling an alien UDO—*unidentified drying object*. Still, it was his duty to politely bend to the wishes of his customers, including this ridiculously boneheaded-obstinate-damfool-of-a-bimbo foreigner.

The electrician sat down on the floor Zen-like, crossing his legs in a loose electrician's yoga pose. This was followed by deep and lengthy electrical contemplation. Finally, when I thought I might have to knock him over to return him to consciousness, he announced the verdict. It came down to one thing: one very simple, uncomplicated, fundamental thing. Rewire the entire electrical circuit for the whole blasted neighborhood!

"Why, is that all?" I feigned, feeling remarkably like Lady Jane when Queen Mary said her head would soon be off. "Well, then, fiddle-de-dee. Just do it, my hearty!"

I would like to report that the rewiring of the entire electrical circuit for the whole blasted neighborhood went well. Alas, it did not. Dryers, don't you know, are intended to not only rotate their drums while blowing like crazy, but to also dry, which is how they got their name. For this they need heat. My dryer was never able to get enough voltage to accomplish the heat part. This is not to say that I did not use it, for I did. Each load simply took two or more hours to dry, and came out as cool as refrigerated pickles. Did I care? Well, sort of, but no one but I knew, so my reputation was safe. And I was no longer a hostage to the belching rains.

Peggy, Peggy Hapless Heatless Lady.

> "If a thing is worth doing,
> it is worth doing badly."
> G. K. Chesterton

SEVENTY-TWO

EIGHT MONTHS AFTER Erin was born, my mom and dad (Honey and Grampa), came to Tokyo. They were hungry to see the new baby, to see us, and of course, to see Japan. For their stay, Glen and I rented an empty duplex in Asahi Court, as with both Erin and the pheasant now in residence, there was no room in our inn. The rental duplex was as close to being the Hyatt as we could get. But, if truth be told, it was a bit closer to being more like the Lowatt.

You will recall that my dad was a retired grocer. Food was his career, his amusement, his hobby, his study, his companion. Although Mom and Daddy had traveled outside of the U.S. before, this would be their first time in the Orient. Just the same, they felt unruffled in facing the unknown for they were confident there was a darned good chance they'd fit right in. I mean, come on now. For years they had regularly consumed canned Chung King chow mein, as well as creamed tuna over Chung King chow mein noodles. And if that didn't supremely qualify them, what did?

They, as well, were the first ones to tell you that besides knowing the word "chow mein," they also knew some other oriental words. Well, actually, only one more. "Suki-yaki!" Except when they said it, it came out more like "suki-yucky." It was with this broad base of knowledge and unflinching hearts that they set out to meet The East, the far one.

Grampa was ecstatic over the idea of discovering new exotic taste treats. He was also a man who recognized that life's very security lay in a larder well-stocked. Ever alert to the magnitude of this philosophy, he brought to Japan with him his own mobile larder. Well stocked.

I mean, gosh! What if famine struck when he least expected it? Daddy was—and this is true—an Eagle Scout, indeed one of America's first Eagle Scouts. He was always, always prepared. In his suitcase, along with a collection of Austin manly fashions, were cans of Hormel Spam, Vienna sausages, sardines, and smoked oysters, plus assorted boxes of crackers to make any sudden famine feel more like a happy hour.

Once settled in the Lowatt, both he and Honey jumped eagerly into the local food scene, relieved as all get out that their stash was not needed, and would remain intact for a true emergency. Everyday Glen and I made certain neither of them missed out on something wonderful to eat, to see or to experience. Shoot, they were like teenagers on spring break without their parents ... but, instead with their children and grandchildren!

Only a few days into their month long stay, a gutsy Grampa began making forays alone to the local market. Arising at the crack of dawn, he left their duplex just as the sun was coming up. His goal: the shops. Each one was enticingly intriguing and perplexingly different from the store he had owned back in Minnesota. In all respects, he was the veritable kid in the candy ... er, make that raw fish ... shop.

When he could carry no more, Grampa would return home just in time for breakfast, loaded down with bags upon bags of Japanese food of which he knew zip, nil (and my old favorite since attempting my first benjo stance), diddly-squat. The food looked alluring, the only invitation Grampa needed.

> "The food in Yugoslavia
> is either very good or very bad.
> One day they
> served us fried chains."
> Mel Brooks

Gene McLaughlin was about as green as a tourist could be and, of course, unable to speak a word of Japanese, yet he carried off all his purchases like they were a piece of rice cake. I was intrigued and asked him how he paid for all those piles of food. "Child's play," he declared, "I'll show you." He reached into his pocket, took out a handful of yen, held it palm up, and showed me how the shopkeepers took out what they needed. There was no question as to its being the right amount. It is a testament to the honesty of the Japanese that I know, as sure as I know you can live a good life without mastering a single PTA dance, that no one ever (well, except for possibly our old crumb-bum-of-a-landlord in Ogikubo), took advantage of him. But, of course if they had, Daddy would never have been the wiser. And that was okay, too, because people on vacation in Japan (when yen was three-hundred-sixty to one U.S. dollar), did not regard yen as real money, anyhow.

With Sakae-san home tending the three cherubs, Mom, Daddy, Glen and I made a number of day trips by commuter trains to downtown Tokyo. This took over an hour on the very fast train. Riding the Japanese trains was not for the faint of heart. Cowards stayed home! Commuter train riding required not only knowing where in heaven's name you were going—not an easy assignment by anybody's stretch of the imagination— but also cultivating an unwavering cheekiness that bordered on incivility. In Minnesota, it had not been necessary to learn these particular survival skills for if we'd gone fast in one direction for one hour, we'd have been over the state line and into Wisconsin where it was okay for us to be rude.

> "In Green Bay, Wisconsin,
> ten bowling shirts
> are considered
> a great wardrobe."
> Greg Koch

But, make no mistake, in the berserk insanity of the Tokyo transportation world, one learned expeditiously, or quickly faded into the mobs of lost commuters to never be heard from again.

If you think I'm making a joke here, think again. I am not. Nobody laughed when this happened to them.

The Japanese train system employed a combative, military-like band of men called "peelers" and "pushers." They did just that—peeled riders back off onto the platform whose bodies were stuck three-fourths outside the closed doors, or pushed riders into the cars whose bodies were smashed three-fourths inside the closed doors. The unfortunates, who were fifty percent in both directions, were left to fend for themselves because it would have been way too problematic to have to appoint and uniform a decision committee in all that hustle and bustle, to say nothing of messing up the precise accurate time tables all trains unyieldingly obeyed. No matter which direction they yanked you, in the end you were sure to be either pushed or pull-verized when they got finished with you.

From childhood, Gene and Margaret had been taught to always ALWAYS step aside and let the other person go first. Wrong! Here the commuters swarmed onto the trains in one stuck glob as if they'd all rolled in Elmer's Glue after breakfast and then hugged. Forged into this single force, they gushed forward like a swarm of furious, untamed, ebony-haired salmon who instead of going against the current, all surged along with it through a single keyhole, the train door. You had two choices: either join in the madness or never leave your house, for as sure as our name was Mah-koo-roff-oo-rin-san, if you didn't barge ferociously forward with them, you would find yourself mangled and alone on an empty platform with the breeze from the last train car blowing in your what-for-the-love-of-Mike-just-happened face.

Knowing the hazards Mom and Daddy were about to confront in their first train skirmish, Glen and I sat them down to instruct them in the fine, but gravely serious, points of train boarding. We stressed over and over the absolute importance of their doing *exactly* as we did. It mattered not, we emphasized, what their refined parents *or* the well-mannered Presbyterian churchgoers (those saintly martinets of strict decorum) had taught them back in Austin ... a place where everybody was Minnesota nice, thereby making these kinds of lessons unnecessary. Also, if I remembered correctly, in Austin we did not have a commuter train system. We did, however, have stop lights ... there was one here and one more over there ... if someone remembered to plug them in.

> "We receive three educations:
> one from our parents,
> one from our school-masters,
> and one from the world;
> the third contradicts all
> that the first two teach us."
> Charles Louis de Secondat

Glen and I knew, oh, how we knew, that they had no idea what they were in for. What a shock they'd experience when the Japanese took off their courteous kidskin gloves and began showing the peevish side of their nature; the one, you may recall, that was so glaringly displayed over Pearl Harbor. On that particular day, they must have been especially peeved!

The reality was that *nothing* prepared my parents for the reality. On our first train trip, we, along with the crush of the herd, shoved and fought our way onto the train, making it through the doors just as they slammed behind us. As always, it took a few moments to jostle about, checking to make sure all four limbs were still attached, people you were traveling with were still in sight, reassuring yourself your carry-ons were still carried on, and lastly, finding a space to either securely plant your feet (if you were so lucky), or to grab hold of a ceiling strap, if foot space did not exist. Both, seldom did.

Usually I dwelled neither in the foot nor the strap camp, and relied on the compactness of the crowd to hold me up. To be sure, there were times when I could go completely limp and it didn't matter a whit. The mash of bodies squeezing into me from all sides held me up commendably until we stopped at the next station where the insane reshuffling dropped me to the floor and we began all over again. One particularly heinous day, the crush was so intense, my rings made deep dents into the flesh of my fingers!

In this rigid, constricted train posture, the last adjustment a commuter struggled with was trying his darnedest to never end up with his face smashed directly into the face of a total stranger. Not good. Like those too-close-talking people that we all know and don't love, I learned that face smashing with a non-acquaintance—in particular an uninvited Philistine

310

like myself—was way too intimate for the Japanese. It took much practice to fine-tune face dodging skills. Unfortunately, such train intimacies only encouraged the seedy side of the local society, providing surreptitious opportunities in which to grope and rub whatever body parts the deviates were either smashed up against or wished to grope and rub. Being the notable pale-faced exception in the crowd made me a target for such fetishes, as curious, covetous fingers often checked out my feel to see if it was any different from the local females' feel.

"Familiarity breeds attempt."
Goodman Ace

The most favored of these palpations was the highly unimaginative pinching of the bottom. What a shock the pervs experienced when they tried it on me. Their lusting, anticipatory fingers reached out (unseen in the tight mass of other lower torsos), to tweak a bit of my ivory rump, only to find their thumbs and index fingers sliiiiiping right off the surface of me like greasy digits gliding off a bowling ball. They must have thought white chicks were made of wood from the Petrified Forest.

If I was the only foreigner they *ever in their life* pinched, they lived and died believing we were honed from really hard timber. Had there been space enough for me to swivel my head, I would have delighted in seeing their shocked faces, for I, as I always did when I went out on the town, was wearing my rib-to-thigh, non-malleable chain mail Warner's girdle. As you know, how else was I going to keep my flesh contained, or my nylons up? For girls like me, armored underwear *was* our petrified forest.

"In the old days, women wore so many
girdles, corsets, pantaloons, bloomers,
stockings, garters, step-ins and God
knows what all, that you had to practically
be a *prospector* to get to first base …
or to even *find* first base."
Danny McGoorty

None of this meant I had to take their lusting standing up. Well, actually I did because what choice did I have? Criminy! Getting to sit on a train was as unlikely as Matt overnight becoming the boss of the bugs or Sakae-san suddenly being proposed to by the Crown Prince. There were, however, two good workable defenses which a probed female commuter could employ. If she had enough room, she could elbow the stomach of the creep behind her, or she could raise one foot and stomp on his, crossing her fingers that both body parts belonged to the letch and not the sweet little old lady crammed off to his side.

As for me, I usually just let it ride, leaving the bottom pinching dirt bag to his astonishment. My wish for him was that he'd live a very long and bewildering nutcase of a life in which he'd try in vain to understand (but never quite do so), the firmness of the Caucasian female buttocks. Additionally, one day while bottom fishing, the mother of all lobsters would bite his own rear, clamping on like a vice from a Snap On Tools set and never, for the remaining duration of his dirt bag life, let go.

Much to my surprise, men were not the only degenerates on the trains. Women were, too. Who knew? Yes, some commuters really went to town when they went to town.

As proof, there was an article from the Japan Times, August 5, 1965. Note that all the individuals were identified by their ages. This was always true in Japanese newspapers. Perchance could it have been their only distinguishing feature?

Indecent Behavior of Some Women

"Is this the result of the liberation of Japanese women after the war? (*See, right off they were blaming us Americans for this, too!)*

"Today many women are bold enough to commit an indecent act on the train. Moreover, there are more women than men who enjoy annoying the opposite sex on rush-hour trains. In other words, Japan is now flourishing with more chijo (chee-joh, women perverts), than chikan (chee-kahn, men perverts), and anyone who is surprised by this is anachronistic.

"According to the statistics of the Tokyo National Railway Superintendence Bureau, fifty-three percent of those committing an indecent act during the last three months have been women! This comes as no surprise, however, since women are now equal with men in exercising their human rights today. (*And what could be more human than being a pervert, I would add?)*

"What is driving women to such an act? And is it intellectual, or not, to release their unfilled desires that way? One professor suggested it is because women's desires are not filled by their husbands, and society as a whole is numb to normal thrills or exciting things. (*Boy, the professor sure got that right!)*

"Railroad security officers are watching for such chikan and chijo. If they catch them in the act, they are taken to the station office and asked to submit a written apology, the only penalty for such public indecency. (*I would also suggest that how about tossing them into a pit of virile, tall and wide, blue-eyed, hairy-bodied immigrants who, after taking advantage of the chambermaid, have moved on to enjoying international goodwill intercourse with train riders?)*

"One exception is the case of a thirty-year old insurance saleswoman. What did she do? She felt a twenty-seven year old company employee who was hanging onto a strap during a rush hour commute. It was reported that the man did not object much to her act because she was an attractive woman. *(No surprise there! And did he grab her hand so she wouldn't stop?)* However, a twenty-three year old office girl *(Secretary of the Bay of Prigs),* who was sitting in front of him, detected it and screamed, "Look, everybody, this woman is doing something funny." *(Or fun, depending on how you looked at it.)* Then this girl jumped at the woman, even though nobody knows why. The result was that the girl got kicked hard by the woman's high heels.

"The offender tried to jump off onto the platform when the train pulled into the station, but she was caught by a railway security officer. The officer had to report her to the police when he later learned that the office girl's injury required ten days of medical treatment. *(Liar, liar pants on fire.)* The woman was prosecuted on a charge of injuring another. *(Note: she went Scot free for groping the guy!)*

(But, here's the kicker…)

"The chijo are not necessarily Japanese! A thirty-eight year old foreign woman is very popular among commuters from Isogo to Tokyo. She was once caught by a Tokyo National Railway Superintendence Bureau man and made to promise not to do that sort of thing again *(or was it not to stop doing that sort of thing again?).* However, she's still doing it and the railway security officers know it.

"It's okay," they agree, "because she does it in such a humorous way, which is characteristic of foreigners. *(We're cute like that.)* Plus, the men cooperate with her *(I'll bet!)* to some extent *(major extent),* although they do so with a sardonic smile *(try lecherous leer!).* Therefore, we can't do anything about her *(awwww),* because her victims are insensible to the fact that they are being victimized." *(Run that by me again!)*

"Said one of her twenty-nine year old *(extremely happy)* victims, 'Her act isn't too vulgar and distasteful. When she is on the train, our trip to Tokyo becomes rather enjoyable.' (*And, I would add, is also the only regularly sold-out trip in all of Japan!*)

"After one particularly obvious grope, the foreign chijo was quoted as saying, 'I married an Oklahoma farmer. Since he died in a tractor accident a year ago, I now have neither hope nor dreams. *(Yeah, tractor accidents can effectively destroy a girl's hopes and dreams).* Yet, I'm still young and lonely, but I'm too proud to become a man's plaything in my home country (*hmmm, would that be plaything spelled 'trollop'?).* While I was thus suffering from this smoldering discontent, *(horny)* my friends who came back from Japan, told me about the thrilling experiences on Japanese rush-hour trains. Now I live in Yokohama and my only enjoyment is to feel Japanese men while riding the Keihin Line every morning.'" (*Spare me. The sign-up sheet was on her back.)*

"Viva Viagra!"

MEANWHILE AS ALL these extra-curricular train riding activities were going on, Glen, Mom, Daddy and I were being propelled onto the train for our first commuter train ride together. After adjusting my position, making sure my clothes had not been shredded to smithereens, I looked around. It was imperative that I locate the other three. Whew, there was Grampa! His face was aflush, not having partaken in this much excitement since Vienna sausages went on sale back in 1959. Thank goodness! He had survived his first train embarkation.

Then I eyeballed Glen off to my right. Let's see ... that makes Daddy and Glen and, uh ... Honey? Where was Honey?

By now the doors were closed and the train was picking up speed as it left Kichijoji Station. Over and around the heads of the other passengers, our three sets of eyes converged alarmingly on each other. Then once again, in one collective reconnaissance, they did a final sweep of the car. Where was Honey? There *was* no Honey. *No Honey?*

Upon realizing this, our rotating eyes simultaneously flew to the windows just in time to see the stricken face of Mrs. Wong standing all alone outside on the platform, executing a perfect meltdown. The stark panic on her now seized-up countenance said it all; she had missed the last lifeboat off the Titanic. Up until I saw it for myself, I had no idea my mom was even capable of demonstrating such terror. She'd always led such a safe, secure, Austin-encapsulated life. Now her gaping, pleading eyes looked like extra-large green olives, and her open mouth—like the voluminous entrance into a toothy cavern—now emitted screams of sheer terror.

Ever ready, ever alert, Glen went into immediate storm trooper mode. Gesturing at the windowpane, he raised his arm and with a repeated downward jab of his index finger pantomimed for her to stay *right there*. Do not move! Do not budge an inch!

In another instant—whoosh!—Mom was out of sight.

Jeepers, just like that I had abandoned the only mother I'd ever known. Daddy had abandoned the only wife he'd ever known. Glen had abandoned the only mother-in-law he'd ever known. And, darn, she had been such a good mother, wife and in-law. It didn't seem fair.

The train sped down the track, already miles away. At the next station, with the three of us holding hands, we fought our way off the train, squeezing out the door through the on-coming commuters like white marshmallows smashing through a mail slot. Clinging in a tight mass, we landed together on the platform. Breathlessly, but firmly—for he was now in command—Glen told Daddy and me to sit on the platform bench and wait. Do not move a muscle! He would run down the stairs and back up to the other side of the train platform, ride back to the last station, and hopefully rescue Mom, *hopefully* being what we were counting on.

One last command before Glen departed: Daddy and I were given the precarious assignment of keeping our eyes glued to the windows of *each* in-coming train, looking for a returning Glen and Honey.

Do you have any idea how difficult it was to peer through hundreds of steamed-over train windows full of jam-packed passengers in search of two albino sardines? Furthermore, there was no clue as to how long it would take for Glen to accomplish his rescue mission, or on which train they would return. Daddy and I had just taken up residence in Improbable Acres.

> "Ya gotta do
> what ya gotta do."
> Rocky Balboa

Meanwhile, Glen was heroically backtracking to the last station. True to his instructions, he found an obedient Mom standing exactly on the same spot where we had abandoned her. She looked to the last hair like Mrs. Lot, of Pillar of Salt fame.

Is there a word in the English language any stronger than elation? Jubilation? Freakin' out-of-your-mind ecstasy? That was the look on Mom's face when she spotted Glen in the crowd, his face being one of only three adult faces she knew in this city of more than twelve million people.

Like Dagrass MacKather, Glen had returned!

By now, being world's more insightful as to the ins and outs of the Japanese train system, plus having little sympathy for the feelings of her fellow riders for they had turned her heart to stone, a psyched-up Mom prepared herself to plow through the crowd like the linebacker she, on short notice, now realized she was about to become. With her fingers twisted like ten screws into the back of Glen's belt (he'd be running interference), they steeple-chased themselves in tandem onto the car. Success! Poetic, though somewhat clumsy, train boarding.

Up ahead on the far distant platform, and walking the tightest tightrope of our lives, my partner Daddy and I were nearly loony from snapping our eyes back and forth from one train window to the next. We looked like giant versions of those cat clocks where the eyes flick from side-to-side in beat with the wagging of the tail pendulum. If we'd had our wits about us, this unfortunate predicament that we now found ourselves in, could have inspired our own version of a human clock. With it we could have made our fortunes, thus providing us with the means to have our own limo and driver whose job it would be to take us anyplace we wanted to go, thereby ditching this train riding business forever! Lucklessly, Donald Trumps we were not. Instead, like devoted family, we concentrated solely on Mom's plight. Flick, flap, flick, flap.

In the years that have followed, I have found myself repeatedly beating myself up for my failure in not glomming onto this gem of an entrepreneurial opportunity. It comes in the form of a sudden night terror. Large hands pick me up from my bed and deposit me in the brackish waters of the East Side Lake Ocean. I am left there until I am fully saturated, whereupon I am removed. Ten strings are tied to my toes; ten to my fingers. I am laid out on a board (a.k.a. the rack), where all twenty strings are pulled tightly in opposing directions. In this taut, unseemly position, I am left to dry. When I am thoroughly exsiccated and it is all over, I am taller, thinner, have only vertical stretch marks, and can no longer find shoes or gloves that fit. Although I can now see over the heads in a crowd, and I wear a pencil-thin size 0 sheath, it does me no good as the opportunity to make my own human cat clock fortune remains irrevocably lost.

About the time Daddy and I thought all hope had dwindled and we would never be a reunited family again, we spotted Glen through a window, his head standing above all the others on a train just coming to a stop. In a flash, hand-in-hand, Daddy and I were off the bench and leaping onto the car. No longer caring about international relations by making polite first-time impressions, we landed like two klutzy Supermen in the midst of the throng. Instantly we began gesturing and crying out victory salutations across the train car to Our Hero, Glen, and to Mrs. Wong, in jersey #911.

To say that our reunion there in the midst of the astonished onlookers was delirious was as ridiculous as saying that a cottage does not make good cheese. The heartfelt bonding of Glen, me and my parental units was one of sheer unadulterated euphoria. I looked across the heads at Mom.

She looked different. During the separation, she had lost seven pounds. Sweat.

I have never been more honest when I say that it makes me shudder to think what might have happened. Had Mom decided on her own to fight her way onto the next train, we would have missed her completely. I cannot imagine how we could have ever found each other again. Not only was there the grim issue of language, even though Mom did know how to say "Chung King" and "chow mein," (but, wait, that was Chinese!), there were the additional concerns of her not knowing our Kichijoji address or, for that matter, our phone number because we didn't have ... well, you know the rest. In the end, the most worrisome outcome would have been that Mom, now reduced to a jabbering fruitcake, would never have been in her happy place again. Her joie de vivre reduced to sludge.

But, the good news, of course, is that none of that happened and we *did* find each other. Once again we were back in our old familiar familial bummer-free zone ... or close to it.

> "There is no such thing
> as fun
> for the whole family."
> Jerry Seinfeld

SEVENTY-THREE

I SUPPOSE IF the outcome of our first traumatic train ride together had been different, the Chuo Railroad could have put Mom in their lost and found department, because they had one. A very good one! All the train companies had very good ones. Passengers constantly left stuff on the trains—although not usually their grandmas. Among the most common forgotten/abandoned items were hats, books, umbrellas and cremains.

Excuse me. What was that last one? *Cremains?*

To be sure, Japan was a tiny, over-crowded island. Not most of … or not just some of … but *all* of its land was owned by some entity, and every square centimeter was designated for a distinct purpose. To demonstrate the strict rigor of this, I cite the incident that happened to one of my Japanese friends. After an intensive two-year search for a new home, the actual purchase was prolonged by six months because of a three-centimeter (that's just a fat hair longer than an inch) dispute over where the property line was between them and the covetous imbedded neighbors!

Having said that, you can easily see there was no extra room for burial plots in the Land of the Lack of Land. Human-being-sized caskets laid into the ground in horizontal fashion and taking up super valuable precious space was just dumb. Such a ridiculous notion was as nonsensical as opening up a business for wet basement prevention in Venice. With this dearth of earth, everyone in Japan was cremated, ending up in powder form in an amazingly compact, one-pound, coffee-can-sized urn. (Sumo wrestlers got three-pound cans.)

Death and cremation were only the beginning of the problem, however. The deposition of the departed was a much more tangled web. Where to find a final resting place for the coffee-can urn was the stickler. Don't you know that such a place cost big bucks, and as it was the world over, there were many families in Japan who did not have big bucks? Actually, little has changed since that time as Japanese funerals were then and still are among the most expensive in the world.

Here's the deal. When Japanese babies were born, they were taken to the Shinto shrine to be blessed. Later when the tots grew to marriageable age, the hottest craze for some couples was to tie the wedding knot in a Christian ceremony, even though the comprehension of this ceremony was lost on everyone but was not considered important because flashy, trendy appearances outranked understanding. Finally when these same people died, last rites in the Buddhist faith won out. Ever cautious, the pragmatically religious Japanese covered all their heavenly bases.

Oddly, now that the freshly departed had entered their Buddhist phase, in some cases they could not be buried with their own names, those monikers by which up until their demise they had been known by everyone in their world. Suddenly upon their death—poof!—not only were their bodies and their souls gone, but also their identities. The purpose of this was to symbolize the attainment of the spiritual awakening in Buddha. I wondered how they knew if this awakening ever actually happened for how could the deceased come back with a report, and Buddha certainly wasn't divulging any information. For the extinguished, it now became necessary for their families to hire Buddhist priests to think up new celestial names in time for the funerals, a rush job. This process cost thousands of dollars, even tens of thousands of dollars for those who were more celestially worthy ... or needed a spiritual awakening really bad!

After not much thought, I told my friends that for me, my money-saving, new-dead-name choice would be Jane Doe-san. I assured them it'd work fine and would be marvelously dirt cheap. Unfortunately, as with my previous suggestion (like releasing belly-button-trapped evil spirits by simply un-layering), they snubbed my plan.

Death also called for outrageous decorations. Enormous displays of artificial flowers wired onto huge hoops, were placed around the homes of the deceased. These gigantic gaudy bouquets stood on long Ichabod Crane like legs and were often taller than the houses themselves. There was no escaping the fact that someone in the neighborhood had left the neighborhood, for these obtrusive, garish emblazonments were as much a contrast to the drab houses, as was a flock of Scarlet Macaws perched on a gravel pit.

But then, that was the point. Death needed to be accompanied by a tricked-out rainbow. In their flamboyant exaltedness, even the least of the faux flowers was conspicuously over-the-top campy. Without a doubt, as each consecutive generation needed to increase its level of funerary showiness, there was now more attention drawn to their family than there had been since they ever became a family, back before Adam and Eve ... uh, make that Shigetada and Tomiko.

I'm not exaggerating when I tell you that other than these glaring in-your-face flowers perking up the neighborhood for a few weeks, there was a void of color in the 1960s. Death certainly sparked things up nicely while they lasted.

But, to top even these displays were the flaming ostentation of the new-store-opening flowers which were equally as huge and boisterous, standing on their towering skinny legs. Each shop would have as many as the width of the shop's front allowed—often even layering. There was enough color in one of those displays (fluorescent pink being a favorite), than had the owner's entire family worn in their entire long history of not wearing any colors entirely. The outlandish bouquets, from the debatable side of decoration, stood there for weeks and months, eventually becoming so dust-cloaked that even their exorbitant fluorescent hues turned to gray; exorbitant pinkish gray.

Colors for people were, it seemed, against the law; a polychromatic world being way too pernicious. Only very young children were allowed to wear something as wild as a red shirt. But then it didn't matter much because their lives from nursery school through senior high were spent in matchy-matchy dark navy blue school uniforms. This also included weekends, because most kids could not afford auxiliary cool clothes. After that, it was on to an adult lifetime of grays, browns and blacks for the rest of their days. Actually, with me and my wardrobe now living in their midst, on many an occasion I became that very obvious outrageous Scarlet Macaw on their gravel pit!

Other than having the Goodyear blimp tethered over either your new shop or your freshly departed loved one, nothing brought more attention than those huge, theatrical, artificial flower arrangements. Talk about a nail! But then, opening a business and expiring did, I suppose, call for something special that *would* stand out. Besides, once you were dead, you were off the hook because making yourself obvious like that could no longer bring you loss of face, although the Japanese would have probably found a way.

The more prominent the deceased was, the more prominent the paper/plastic flower displays were. It was not at all unusual to see the homes of well known defunct persons surrounded on all sides by colossal bouquets, dwarfing to the point of elimination, the view of their houses. This was, indeed, a very good thing. For these very public, very ostentatious, very tacky obituary ads were presented by businesses, colleagues and friends, thereby demonstrating how many prestigious social connections the person had in life ... and still in death ... plus throwing in a plug for the companies who donated the bouquets (and a possible tax write-off?). And, if you can believe this, those expensive flowers were given without the givers having a clue what the new dead names were! Pity the poor FTD man trying to find them. Even those flashy fast wings on his helmet and heels didn't help.

> "The best way
> to get praise
> is to die."
> Italian proverb

Sometimes the body of the deceased was put in an open casket for several days and left in his home where visitors could pay their respects. Because it was believed that Buddha had entered Nirvana by heading north, it was necessary to face the body north. If this was impossible, it could also be pointed west ... in the direction of Austin, although I don't recall anyone in my hometown ever saying anything about seeing Buddha entering Nirvana there. But then, I suppose it could have happened in Bixby, a few miles away. Other times there was only a photo placed in the indoor family shrine. Both necessitated the emptying of the main room of the small dwelling and turning it into a viewing place which now held the shrine and photo, or the full-size coffin, plus the never-ending stream of mourners.

It goes without saying that all guests had to be fed and watered during the on-going, elongated grieving period. Despite the family's heartache and fatigue—in particular the housewife upon whose shoulders most of the work, naturally, fell—they still had to perform those earthly duties in order to properly honor their departed, and hold up the family name.

The guests brought generous gifts of money. In time, the family of the deceased returned this favor with their own gifts given back to the mourners and worth about half of the value, thereby putting the excess towards the funeral expenses. This money, of course, did not begin to cover the costs, nor did it put a dent in the monstrously expensive additional ceremonies required to be performed weeks, months and even years after the person died. Similar to watching acorns become oaks, becoming really and truly dead in Japan was a very long, drawn out procedure.

At the wake, all the lamenters were required to bow three times while burning incense sticks in front of the indoor shrine or the body. Naturally, there were very strict rules for how this was done and they filled me with trepidation as I was never sure of the propriety of my iffy executions. Decidedly, it was no time to be a klutz, as I feared I was, the Christian teachings in my background failing me miserably in the incense and bowing department.

Upon leaving, the mourners were given small packets of purifying salt. Because they had now been contaminated by the close proximity to a corpse, it was necessary to not bring this defilement home with them. Therefore upon returning to their houses, they sprinkled the salt on their doorsteps as well as upon themselves to exorcise any chance of death having accompanied them. With the need to sanitize Japan's sumo rings, as well as to exorcise all her funereal bogeymen, I pondered over whether or not Mortons had ever made any headway into the Japanese salt market. And, if so, was it necessary for it to be iodized? Just wondering ....

> "For three days after death
> hair and fingernails
> continue to grow,
> but phone calls taper off."
> Johnny Carson

Eventually the coffin-encased body was moved to a crematorium. There again the family and friends gathered. Tea and rice crackers were served as they sat around low tables on tatami mats, reminding each other of pleasant memories spent with the departed. As they chatted and sipped, the same-said now soulless, but re-named body, was slid into a fiery oven in the room next door.

I will be the first to admit that I knew nothing about body burning. In my relatively young life, I barely knew any extinguished people. Therefore, I was greatly surprised to learn there was one part of the human body that did not completely turn to ash. Would you believe it was the Adam's apple, that gristly cartilage protuberance that sticks out of our necks? It was a given that men had a bigger problem with this cremation obstacle than did women, but gosh, who knew that lump in our throats was so flame retardant?

Along with this resistant cartilage were other things that did not turn to dust. Some shards of bone survived the heat. These were immediately visible to the mourners who after the cremation were invited to place such fragments in an awaiting urn. Everyone stood in a solemn queue in front of a long metal table upon which rested a large steel tray resembling a gigantic cookie sheet. Instead of sweets, however, this pan was full of the dust and bone particles of their loved one, now crackling and glowing hot. It was very difficult to witness.

A single pair of very long chopsticks (usually iron, because wooden ones caught on fire), was handed down the line to each person as they, one-by-one, respectfully placed a bone scrap into the urn. As this was Japan, there was of course, an order for the retrieval of these cremains. Legs, arms, hipbones, back bones, teeth and skulls—or what was left of them—were collected in that order. The finale was the remainder of the Adam's apple, retrieved by the person closest to the deceased.

After attending several of these events, and in spite of my sadness over the departure of a friend, my curiosity was so strong that I could not hold back from secretly looking hard for the grisly, gristly Adam's apple. I couldn't help feeling my throat go raw. Unfortunately, I could never pick it out from the other ashy chunks and thought it best not to poke around.

In the end, when there were no more solid pieces to be found, the group returned to the tatami room and waited while the cremator scooped up all the remaining remains of the crematee (is that a word?) and put them into the pot. Don't worry, the whole thing only felt macabre the first time you did it.

The pot, or urn, was then escorted to a shrine or temple where, for a hysterical fee, it was placed into a columbarium, a wall of tiny locked door niches that reminded me of the clothes cubbies in the public bath houses which reminded me of the post office cubicles back home.

If everything went smoothly, that was the ideal burial. If, on the other hand, things did not go smoothly because there were no fat cats in the family to fund this kind of shebang, what were folks to do with the ashes? Let's see now ... they could fill potholes, sell them to the Pope for Ash Wednesday, mix them with flour and water and make sculptures ... *or simply leave them on the train!*

No way, in their wildest nightmares, could the train planners on the National Railway Superintendence Bureau have dreamed they'd ever have a lost-and-found problem such as this. Hats, okay. Books, okay. Umbrellas, okay. But, body ash?

Furthermore, at year's end when the train companies held their annual bazaars to sell off all the forgotten items, would it be okay to also sell off used people? They thought not. What choice did the National Railway Superintendence Bureau have but to do the job themselves? So, just as they hired peelers and pushers, they also employed priests whose job it was to pray over the "lost and found" urns. Thereafter, the urns were deposited in a special train vault for safe keeping till, I guess, the end of time. And here you thought Amtrak had problems?

SEVENTY-FOUR

REUNITED AGAIN, GLEN, Daddy, Mom and I got off at Shinjuku Train Station. From there we proceeded on to a tour of their first Tokyo department store. Like the train, the store was equally jam-crammed with people. Only ten minutes into the excursion, as I walked down an aisle chatting away with Mom, I realized she was no longer walking beside me. I looked around. There, twenty-paces back stood Gramma Honey once again frozen in place like Mrs. Lot. Oh, no, was this getting to be a habit with her?

I beckoned for Mom to come, but she responded with an ever so slight back and forth shake of her head, obviously taking extra care not to move her lower body. Having no choice, I threaded my way back through the tight throng of shoppers to see what the problem was. As I approached her, Mom pursed her lips into a long silent "shhhhhh" and cast her eyes down to the floor, a signal for me to follow her muted instructions.

My eyes slowly went down her body to her knees. There wrapped around them were the arms of a tiny child clinging to Mom for dear life. In the mass of humanity, the little boy had become disoriented and reached out to grab on to his mother, not knowing the knees he now clung to were those belonging to the Queen of Darkness.

As I stood there not knowing what to do, the child looked up and saw me. His little face stiffened in astonishment, then disbelief, for never in his short years had he ever seen such an anemic, whey-faced humanoid as the one at whom he was now gaping. This was followed by a look of sheer, coagulated terror; the pure, non-reconstituted kind. Along with it, he let out a piercing wail on par with that of a howler monkey, as he now, like a living tourniquet, wrapped himself even tighter around Mom's knees, making her rigid straitjacket posture that much more precarious. Just about that time his head jerked back as he looked up, seeking protection from the dear mother he thought was up there to save him.

Instead of finding a familiar face at the top of that body, he discovered to his abhorrence Beelzebub's sister—Margaret McLaughlin/Mrs.Wong/Gramma Honey! The poor, innocent lambkin nearly had pediatric apoplexy right there in men's wear.

With all his traumatized might, he began shrieking, "Obakke" (oh-bahk-kay)! Once he'd let it out, it was like the staccato action of a repeating rifle that couldn't stop spitting bullets. "Obakke! Obakke! Obakke!"

Terror, thy name is Mrs. Wong!

"Bakke," wouldn't you know, meant "devil, ghost or apparition," but then, naturally, by adding the necessary polite "o," it became a way-more dignified "*honorable* devil, ghost or apparition." Courteously, even though he was scared out of his young wits, the little kid at least gave Mom that much respect.

By now, every single shopper within a twenty-five-meter radius was staring at Gramma Honey. Poor Mom! She had come to this foreign land with only goodness in her heart towards one and all. Only a short hour before, the train mishap had nearly done her in, and now, here was this awkward and embarrassing scene with General Tojo's grandson. By all accounts, it was even worse than the heartbreak of psoriasis.

There was, however, good news in this story, for in spite of all the humiliation, one thing saved Mom and her quickly dissolving dignity. She had not a clue what Tojo, Jr. was screaming.

Within moments a distraught Japanese mother shoved her way through the crowd. Bowing repeatedly to my mother, she reached out and grabbed the fruit of her loins, clutched him to her, then hustled them both off to the safety of the look-alike throng. As they disappeared into the coagulum of clones, the grimace of anguish on the boy's twisted face let me know his recovery would be slow and expensive.

> "After twelve years of therapy,
> my psychiatrist said something
> that brought tears to my eyes.
> He said, " No hablo ingles."
> Ronnie Shakes

TAKING MOM AND Daddy to the local restaurants turned out to be a blast. They were amazingly compliant, never hesitating to try anything. To be sure, gone were the gigantic hang-over-the-rim Minnesota steaks of their past, but in their place was food prepared in bite-sized portions (hey, man, where's the beef?), perfect for chopstick manipulation. What made ordering worry free for these uninitiated greenies were the front windows where the entire menu of each shop, including the prices, was displayed in wax. Who knew that Madame Taussaud had also invaded the comestibles market? Aside from a little dust, it was pretty much impossible to tell real food from real fake food.

Way back in 1948, one company began making these uncanny replicas, and by the time we arrived, they were selling them as fast as they could be produced—2,500 per day! Imagine edibles made from wax. The look-alikes could be anything from corn-on-the-cob to sushi to noodles to eggs-sunny-side-up to cake to sandwiches; they could do it all. Like the true magicians they were, these clever artists had fortuitously prognosticated the day when post-war illiterate tourists like us would need their help.

The meals in the shop windows were perfect, as if a culinary wizard had used artful trickery to conjure up food that never died, that never needed heating, that never needed replacing. Just the occasional brush with a feather duster restored it to its original glory. There were magical cups of coffee with ghostly mini-pitchers perched high above them from which cream supernaturally poured down in frozen waxy cascades. And, pork strips edged in rich, glistening fat that brought forth swoons of ecstasy from meat lovers like us. The soup in the bowls of noodles never spilled nor did it ever dry up. A glass of beer covered in perpetual foam never evaporated, but lingered for decades awaiting a thirst to quench. They were better than a blow-up Barbie!

Ordering was a breeze. Indeed, the language barrier went right out the window when Mom and Daddy went right out to the window with a waitress in tow, and pointed to whatever they wanted. What could have been simpler, the only down side being that because they couldn't say or read the words, they were once again reduced to being toddlers who could only jab with pointy fingers at what they wanted.

I must confess to having visions of just how these same magnificent paraffin images would play out in a U.S. restaurant. Within my aesthetic core, they conjured up decidedly mixed emotions. Like how would these exquisitely shaped and colorfully coordinated Japanese displays look, say, sitting next to a plate of our beige, unadorned, mucilaginous Thanksgiving dressing that had been slung on a beige plate beside even beigeier piles of turkey, mashed potatoes and gravy, all miraculously frozen in time and space through the magic of solidified petrochemicals? I shuddered at the thought of the phlegmy results.

"When turkeys mate,
they think of swans."
Johnny Carson

Of course, for the gaijin who wished to order food, there was an alternative to wax. Instead of a petrified display of the dinner selections, where there was absolutely no guess work as to what one would be eating, you could also brave the option of reading an adolts (adult's) menu, where there was more guess work than you'd ever again encounter in your life. Such a menu explained everything in clear, concise words: English kinds of words.

For example there was minion steak (*fillet mignon*); lamp steak (*rump steak*); humbug (*no, not Scrooge—hamburger!*); potato cheeps (*chips*); penis butter (*roll that by me again!*) sandwiches; and if you were really lucky and didn't particularly care for penis butter, there was Geek food (*Greek*). In the end, there was virtually nothing to fear in the food department. Well, okay, so maybe the penis butter ....

In some of the more caring, upscale restaurants, certain dishes were fully spelled out descriptively on the menu. This was done, of course, in the remote chance that a foreign diner didn't quite understand. Such explanations were scrupulously thorough, leaving no questions unanswered. Take, for instance, bothered chicken (*battered*): "Our wild chicken is well feeded long enough with only natural food at wild yard which makes their meat more heavier, body flavourful and dericious enjoyable." See what I mean?

There were, on occasion, ala crate (*carte*) selections featuring fresh farts (*fruits*). Let's say, by word of explanation, that you had never eaten a banana. You were not to become fretful and all worked up over nothing, for in Japan bananas came with a thorough clarification:

"The banana are a great remarkable fruit. He are constructed
in the same architectural style as the honorable sausage.
Difference being skin of sausage are habitually consumed
while it is not advisable to eat rapping of banana.
Perhaps are also intrissing the following differences
between the two objects, banana are held aloft while consuming,
sausages are usually left in reclining position. Banana
are first green in cullur, then gradual turn yellowing."

There, you've got it.

At the end of the meal, and if you were able to stuff one more delicacy in your now protruding tummy, there was dessert. One dining establishment cleverly used its resident poet to describe their choices. This worked amazingly well, though it might have been even more successful had that same said poet not been absent on the day his English teacher taught the class that English words work best when their beginning, middle and ending letters are all happily conjoined in single word units:

327

The Original
Hand Made
Confectiona
ry For Your H
appy Tea Tim
e, With Our W
hole Heart ...
Chocolate Ha
s The Sweet
Taste Whic
h Make Your
Life So Happ
y. You Must
Be Interes
ted In the
Dream
Of It.

ENJOY YOUR SWILL DINNER!

OFTEN THE JAPANESE did not wish to go to a restaurant, but chose rather to stay home and still eat lusciously. This was a no-brainer as it could be done with only the bat of an eye. As I have mentioned before, way before it became popular in the West, Japan had already set the pace for the best food delivery system known to man. Any prepared meal your heart desired could be delivered to your doorstep. Sometimes this helpful, handy-dandy service even saved face. In, particular, mine! Here's how it worked.

Let's suppose we were at home one late afternoon when we unexpectedly heard the doorbell ring. There, clustered on our front steps, was a family making a surprise visit (arrrgh!). To further complicate this already unannounced intrusion, they timed it to coincide with—oh, no, not the dinner hour! And, I didn't—shoot, not again—have anything honorable enough to serve honorable them; their fault, not mine!

But, fret not. The solution was as simple as the telephone. Of course, in our deprivation we could not do this, but our over-sexed, Kleenex-using neighbors could. I'd simply interrupt their favorite pastime, borrow their phone, and call the local sushi restaurant. Like witchery, within thirty minutes a man appeared on a motor scooter at our door, balancing a stack of lacquered boxes on either his shoulder (driving one handed), or more conveniently (and safe), on a tray suspended from a high metal framework over the back fender. In the middle of the framework hung a thick metal spring with a hook under it from which the loaded tray hung.

Like the pivoting gimbals on a ship, the tray swayed complacently back and forth as the scooter sped rapidly in and around the potholes. By some inexplicable Asian mysticism, all the contents stayed perfectly in place within their containers.

This marvel of engineering worked especially well for sushi, which although dry, had to maintain its artistic arrangement in its lacquered boxes. But in the wet category, it worked just as splendidly. Take osoba, for example, which came in large bowls of steaming hot broth. Even these honorable noodles arrived without losing a drop to sloshage. I still believe that in the scheme of the genetic evolution chain, we Americans were not bestowed with this delivery DNA.

Voila! A luxury dinner for our noble guests, but even more important, my saved face. Still, I thought it was downright crummy of their honorablenesses to drop in at mealtime without having called first. But, then, that old testy issue of our not having a phone made this impossible, I suppose, and expecting them to write a letter would have been bothersome. In my mind, though, it came down to one thing. They must have been taking unannounced-lessons from the champions of unannounced visits: the Fetid R Us gang!

Still, even though we weren't classy enough to have a telephone, at least we had the dignity, when offering them a chair, to not say, "please, shit here" … although I felt like it.

Trifles aside, at my fingertips was the gorgeous reality that a delivery service would rescue an unprepared hostess like me any old time. Thus, freed up from food prep, I could slip graciously through the evening without having to raise a sweat, other than to make green tea and pour beer. It made for effortless, though expensive—because we had to order *the best* in order to maintain our honor—entertaining.

Moreover, the benefits of this heavenly system did not end there, for the delivery service was the gift that kept on giving. You see, these altruistic restaurants were aware of this unexpected guest problem, and they worked untiringly to save the dignity of their empty-pantry customers. Understanding full well the dread of pantry dearth, the delivery men thought of everything. Not only did they bring consummate food, but they also brought consummate food consummately contained in lovely vessels, and ready to place on the table for the unwanted exalted ones who had so rudely come to call.

But, I am not finished with my praise. Get this! The delivery man *did not expect me to pay him!* That was all part of the plan. As I said, saving my face was as much his responsibility as it was mine. Like what was I supposed to do if I didn't have any cash in the house when those uninvited louts showed up at our door? As if the humiliation of an empty pantry were not enough, now heaped upon it was the mortifying display of our poverty? Hara kiri (ha-rah-kee-ree, self-disembowelment), came to mind.

I feared not, though, for the reality was that I was living in a worry free zone. Conveniently the next day (after a hasty trip to the bank where I re-lined our coffers), I stacked the dirty, *unwashed* dishes (did you get that—*we were not expected to wash them!*) back on the tray, set the whole assemblage outdoors on my front steps along with the money in plain sight (without a care in the world it would be stolen), for the delivery man to pick up. The system worked flawlessly. The venerable-but-brazen guests were treated royally, and I came out smelling like a rose. Of course, a tip for this service was not only unnecessary, it was also not even part of the Japanese mindset. As far from their thinking as were bras with two measurements.

The first time I played the food delivery game, I did the American thing of leaving a tip for the delivery man, hoping to please him and to let him know how much he had pleased me. He was back in his shop before he realized the error in his accounting. Did he squirrel the excess away in his kimono sleeve? No, no, a thousand times no! He immediately—pronto!—made the hazardous, pot-holed motor scooter trip back to Asahi Court to return the over-payment. Thereupon, much to my chagrin, *he* profusely apologized to *me* for the error.

When I tried to explain this monetary tipping gesture to him, he was at a loss as to why I would do such a thing. He just didn't get it. Made no sense whatsoever! In an abrupt reversal of what I had meant to be a sincere, generous offering, I somehow came out of the predicament feeling like a worm in the face of one so principled.

> "Honesty may be the best policy,
> but it's important to remember
> that apparently, by elimination,
> dishonesty is the second-best policy."
> George Carlin

Over and over again this kind of courtesy demanded the question: where, oh, where, was such graciousness when it came to train-boarding time? Perhaps the answer to this baffling deportment reversal lay in the fact that one person (who was outrageously flaming polite when alone), became swallowed up when he was part of a mass; a single identity like that lost in the shuffle. And in this shuffle, there was power: a faceless power. At once you were invisible in the crowd and had, therefore, permission to do whatever the crowd dictated, because you were not really there. Do you see? And, not to be overlooked was the issue of letting go. What a blessed relief to release yourself so completely when with the mob, because all the rest of the time you were expected to be so extraordinarily, ridiculously, unnecessarily, overly polite.

It had, as well, to do with something I'd heard about the Japanese. In their way of thinking, anyone to whom they had not been introduced simply did not exist. Boy! That sure explained some unexplainable behavior! It, a!so, sure sounded lonely. I wondered if individual lemmings held on to their own private, disciplined thoughts even as they rushed along with the pack towards the edge of the cliff? "Darn gonnit, I shoulda turned left back there … aaiiieeee!"

To be sure, the alarming dichotomy of Japanese behavior never ceased to amaze and confluster me.

> "One hundred thousand lemmings
> can't be wrong."
> Graffito

SEVENTY-FIVE

STRANGE AS IT may seem Japanese money was kind. Certainly it bought things and that was considerate, but it went way beyond that. It never left you literally in the dark because it always guided you. To help you understand, let me ask this. What if you couldn't see the money? Like you were blind, *(bless your soul)*. Not to worry. When you paid, there was no disquietude or loss of face, because even a sightless you could discern exactly the value of each paper bill.

Don't you see (or I guess in your case, not see! ... *bless your soul all over again*), right there in the corner was a grouping of Braille dots denoting the value of each bill. How benevolent was that? Now, if only, *(and you really needed your soul blessed for this)*—even though you now knew exactly how many bills to shell out—you were somehow able to *also* discern how to buy the good stuff from the crappy stuff, it would have been heaven. But, it was a problem yet to be solved.

But, there were other money handicaps having nothing whatsoever to do with sight. They weren't a problem for the Japanese, but they were a big problem for us, the military types. You see, we had three different kinds of money to deal with. First there were the American dollars, needed for visits back home. Then there was yen needed for living in Japan, our unhome. But, most importantly, there was MPC needed for everything in between: all on-base transactions.

MPC stood for Military Payment Certificates; that is to say, special Armed Forces money. Unlike any other currency that you've ever heard of, this was the trickiest. How so? Well, like an undecided starlet frequently dying her hair and changing her wardrobe, MPC also periodically altered its appearance. I mean one day it had one look, the next day another—and we never knew when it would restyle itself. Of course, it was all planned and plotted to do this, by who else, but Uncle Sam.

He wasn't just being a pest, mind you; he was containing black marketeering. Armed forces shoppers, looking for a good deal, sometimes sank to the levels of the black market where prices were negotiable and cheap. Of course, the shyster dealers there gladly accepted any form of payment: U.S. dollars, yen and—why not?—MPC. Whatever the buyer was willing to part with was what decided the purchase. That is how the certificates got out of the military's hands.

MPC was just what it said ... *Military* Payment Certificates. It was supposed to stay only within the confines of the military facilities, and not a step outside of those borders. But, as I said, it did. In an effort to thwart these transactions, MPC was reconfigured on a regular basis.

Of course, no one ever knew when this would happen. Sporadic was the name of this game. Also Fend For Yourself. Here's how it worked. Every morning we listened to the 6:00AM news broadcast over the Far East Network to hear if that day was the day we should turn in our MPC. (FEN, our military radio, was transmitted over the entire island and listened to by not only military personnel, but also the Japanese who enjoyed our American music, as well as hopefully learning some colloquial English.) Following this radio announcement, Uncle S., being generous of spirit, gave us till noon to cash in whatever MPC we were now using, and replace it with new, face-lifted bills. There were no coins.

Breakfast was followed by everyone making a mad rush to all the military banks on all the different posts and bases to turn in their money. As you can imagine, the lines at the windows were long because we ALL had to do it ALL at the same time. It was put up with that chaos or lose it, for at 12:01 PM, our MPC was struck valueless, becoming as worthless as wisdom teeth.

As you can imagine, this exchange did not always go smoothly. Make that, it *never* went smoothly. Early one morning we got the announcement. It was turn-in day. Glen went up to our bedroom to the desk where we kept our cash. Only a few days before, he had gone to the bank to load up on MPC for a large purchase he was making the next day. The money was stashed in the locked desk drawer. Reaching in his pocket for the key, his hand came out with nothing.

Also fruitless was every other place he looked for the key. A bundle of money would soon be useless if he didn't get into that drawer. I don't have to point out again, *do I,* how tight our budget was? Every yen, dollar and MPC counted at our house. But, try as he did, he could neither find the danged key nor could he force open the locked drawer. The clock was ticking.

In the end, having used every trick in his lock-picking, drawer-wedging arsenal ... as well as some choice blasphemous words ... he gave up. It didn't matter. The clock said 12:02 PM and all was lost, anyway. That day a small fortune went down the drain.

We were heartsick. Devastated! The world almost came to an end. $40! It was enough to buy a wringer washer! And, way more than the desk was worth. Glen should have toted the desk to the bank, turned it in, and let them fool with it, or simply taken a sledge hammer to it.

> "There are three principal ways to lose money:
> wine, women and engineers—
> *(and, I would add, MPC.)*
> While the first two are more pleasant,
> the third—*(and for sure the fourth!)*—
> is by far the more certain."
> Baron Edmond De Rothschild

> "All I ask is a chance to prove
> that money can't make me happy."
> Spike Milligan

I'VE TOLD YOU how caring Japan was in the Braille-dotted money department, looking out as they did for those whose eyes had failed. They were also heedful of the ears. Especially so the bothersome riddle of how best to execute the irksome task of grooming them. If you wanted clean ears—*and who the heck didn't?*—you did not reach for Q-tips, ballpoint pens or your pinky fingernail. Au contraire, contraire! You reached for your lover!

Yes, ear cleaning was not only hygienic, but also kinky. To understand this you had to first examine the ears. They are delicate instruments requiring conscientious, dedicated, and even adoring care. Now, I ask, who cared more about you and your ears than your sweetheart? And who would you trust more with your precious cochlea than the very one who loved you most? Sure, there was your mom, but then who wanted to do lecherous stuff with their mom?

The mimikaki, (mee-mee-kah-key, ear cleaner) was, and probably still is, the little love tool of Japan. Top-notch mimikaki were made of ivory. Bottom-notch were plastic. They looked like a short, thin chopstick, except that on one end was a mini scoop for digging and retrieving ear wax. (The Japanese have the dry compacted kind which is nettlesome to scour and swab. It's a racially linked thing, honest.) At the other end was either a piece of fluff (the kind that falls off a feather boa) or, on the fancier models, a pluck of rabbit fur.

Do not think this was any old rabbit fur. No, no, this was unique rabbit fur from unique rabbits. And how did one catch these unique rabbits? Well, you niqued up on them, of course. And, so what happened if the rabbits were not all that unique, but were instead just old, run-of-the-mill, ordinary tame rabbits? How did you catch a run-of-the-mill, ordinary tame rabbit? Tame way, you niqued up on it. (Unable to resist, I snitched this off an e-mail.)

The wee rabbit fur ball could be used to either lasciviously tickle the ears or swab out their contents. Or, on a good night, both! Here was the scene. The lights dimmed as the curtain opened on two people languorously lounging about on zabuton cushions laid across a tatami floor. A tympanic tryst was about to unfold. The lovers began their erotic foreplay. Intensity heightened. Then, just when you thought the swain was about to lustfully lurch at his honey bun's buns, he instead laid his head (complete with plugged up ears), on her bared fleshy thighs. That was her signal to, oh, so scrupulously begin working the diminutive scoop in and out of each canal. Before you could say, "the ears have it," he began rhythmically moaning with pleasure.

This surely stressed how entirely appropriate it was to use the fur from rabbits. They must have begged to be plucked. Also their ears, for crying out loud, were ideal. Like who, I'd like to know, raised the ear bar any higher than rabbits? And finally, it must have also explained why they had all those bunny babies. You know how that went—from hare to maternity?

Such ear-reaming lovemaking, gosh darn it, just went to show you how cheap and sensible dating could be. And, just think, it was no longer necessary to pay for an internet cell phone provider with its squads of company platoons standing behind it. "Darling, can you hear me now?"

> "For women, the best aphrodisiacs are words.
> The G-spot is in the ears.
> He who looks for it below them
> is wasting his time."
> Isabel Allende

If, by chance, getting it on with earwax wasn't quite your thing, it was perfectly okay, because you were blessed with another option. The teeth. Particularly appealing to dentists—and others who were dentally inclined/obsessed—was the ever-popular tooth cleaning tool called the "dent pecker." Yowser! For obvious reasons this was not as popular as the mimikaki.

And finally, not to be over looked was something for the last group: the sex-starved, unsound, cuckoo-bird, monastic types who didn't need a partner, but rather enjoyed pleasuring themselves: the self massager.

> "Get it on with private Cecil to touch your
> adventurous dreamy and inquisity.
> For those inability to do themselves well,
> you can make massage or beating on
> your personal self stalk, where you will
> feel your important muscle loosening."

Which begged the question, "But, Cecil, wasn't that loosening muscle business just a bit self-defeating? Why not, instead, stick with that old, but still effective massaging cream, 'Firm Heights?'"

Yes, many things seemed un-understandable. But, I can tell you this. All the above were a thousand times better than what lovers did in old China. There, in the throes of sexual arousal, Romeo suddenly grabbed the tootsie of his tootsie, stuffed it in his mouth and began sucking. These were not ordinary feet, mind you, but rather the bound variety, monstrously deformed, twisted and curled-up beyond recognition. If the binding had been done properly by a loving, devoted grandma and mom, the darling's foot ended up small enough to fit snugly into an average man's mouth! No way! Way!!

Foot binding was done for the man's pleasure. Well, duh! Certainly not for hers! The pain went beyond comprehension, beginning at the age of five when the little girl learned she would never ever run again, to say nothing of walking normally. In exchange for this good fortune, she would live a lifetime of agony.

Any genteel Chinaman would have been out of his mind to consider marrying a girl with "big" (normal, useful, workable, sensible, painless) feet. Such feet were way too ugly to be seen next to him! On the other hand, un-walkable feet were not only intoxicating, but they were also his way of keeping her home. It was obvious. If they had not been a two-palanquin family, how could she have roamed about on her own? Lacking "wheels," she could not have gone anywhere, anyhow, anyway on those teensy throbbing stubs.

Rarely was the question asked, "Just why was it, anyway, that the Chinese males liked to suck on infected, pus-seeping, highly stinky, (look if up if you think I'm exaggerating), grotesquely, gnarled feet? You have to wonder at it all. Moreover, you have to question their savvy while they sucked. Like did the foot-sucking beau use caution as he sighed sweet nothings while slurping? Because, you know, unfortunate slips of the tongue could happen with a foot in his mouth. But then, perhaps that only happened when it was *his* foot and not someone else's? I wasn't sure.

That practice stopped many years ago, but before all these women died out, I actually saw a very old woman in Taiwan attempting to hobble about on bound feet. She was dressed in outmoded traditional clothing, and her legs came down to points like two sharpened pencils. Not only could I feel her pain, but also her captivity. Once was enough. I never cared to see another.

SEVENTY-SIX

WHEN THE PRODUCERS at NHK-TV heard my folks were in town, they requested that they make a guest appearance on one of the programs. By now, of course, I was no longer working there, but before I had said my final sayonara, I had returned for one last time where I finally unveiled my marital status, along with my offspring, to the viewing audience.

Apparently enough fans had inquired as to my whereabouts for it to have become necessary for the director to explain my sudden disappearance from the show. Remember, no one knew I was married. And, if they hadn't figured out something was going on during those last months when they saw me on screen only from the chin up, they also hadn't figured out that I had been heavy with child. At least that kind of ignorance was what the directors were counting on. As you already know, I was not allowed to use my married name because of the sensitivity of Glen's job. Therefore, I had always been known in TV Land as McLaughlin-san, or simply Mac-san, to the linguistically lazy. It had given no clue as to my marital, or lack of, status.

With that in mind, remember that the audience had not seen my swollen body because of the clever cameramen who stayed glued to my shoulders and above, never allowing their lenses to slip low to the nether regions, in particular that one great big nether region! Therefore, when Tazaki-san made a TV announcement in which he revealed the truth about me, it was quite a shock to the viewers to learn that I was not only married, but also the mother of three—*count them three!*— children. To be honest,

337

this did make me feel a bit like a phoney-baloney kind of TV friend, but what was I to do? It was what the life of a spy's wife demanded.

The viewers insisted upon seeing this new revelation with their own eyes. Thus, the children and I were invited to do a guest spot on the show. At the time of the interview, baby Erin was five-months-old. She was about as piliferous as a cue ball. Rather than hair, she had a smattering of white pin feathers. Of course I wanted the world to know I had two sons *and* a daughter (which I feared they might not figure out with that cue-ball head), so I dressed her up in frills and lace, completing the girly-girlyness by affixing, with the help of slabs of Scotch tape, a satin bow to the top of her head.

You see, I was bound and determined to get my due for I had been living without adequate credit for having produced our boys. Glen was getting it all. Everyone said the boys looked exactly like him. Brushed me off completely. So when I had a daughter, I wanted acknowledgement, even if it meant Scotch tape to prove it.

I suppose, for mothers like me, the unfairness in this "oh-he-looks-just-like-his-father" effusiveness has always been, and will always be, an unceasing continuum. You know how it goes—the horse does the work and the coachman gets tipped. But then, I guess, things could have been worse. Jeff and Matt could have ended up like me: five-foot-two with bosoms, and Erin like Glen: six-foot-one with a hairy chest, so I figured I'd better stop my kvetching.

While taping the interview with Tazaki-sensei, I held Erin on my lap, with Jeff and Matt clustered by my side. It was important for me to exude charm all over the place, but it was becoming increasingly difficult with a squirmy baby. Well into the interview and concentrating on my conversation with Sensei, I did not notice that the fidgeting Erin had become infatuated with a microphone sitting directly in front of her on a small table. Magnetically drawn to it, she began leaning towards the table, unsuccessfully grabbing at the air as babies are wont to do. Then as her longing and frustration increased, she began rocking forward and back, forward and back, each lunge getting her closer to the object of her desire. Finally, in one last desperate re-e-e-ach, she grabbed the mike, jammed it inside her mouth and screamed directly into it, also as babies are wont to do.

Awkward! You could say it was the kind of behavior not altogether sanctioned on national TV.

In a flash, an ever-alert cameraman swung his lens around for a tight shot of Sensei's head, blocking everything in the periphery which was Erin and me and the microphone. At the same moment, an equally alert stagehand made a mad leap towards us, snatching Erin from my lap and dashing off to stage right like a Boston marathoner. By then, a thwarted Erin was not only enraged at having the mike—the object of her desire—ripped from her little hands, she was also terrified at having been so abruptly kidnapped from the only mother she had ever, in her mini existence, known. To let the world be aware of her unrest, she let out one of her very long and well-rehearsed Erin caterwauls. The screech was broadcast from the edge-to-the-edge and the top-to-the-bottom of the Land of the Rising Sun, up close, unsettling and window-rattling.

Looking remarkably like a young cheetah in pants, the stagehand, with Erin clutched to his pounding chest, streaked towards the studio door. Like the sound of a diminishing train whistle fading into the great unknown, Erin's wails grew fainter and fainter. Whomp! The padded studio door clumped shut. The set, equipment and walls stopped reverberating. Silence returned. It was deafening. So quiet it nearly blew out the hearing (and not a few mimikaki!) of everyone in TV Land.

Yet, despite this blasphemous behavior, an affable NHK staff did not give up on us—well, correction, not on the taller ones of us. That is why when they heard Mom and Daddy were in town, they insisted I bring them into the studio. Of course, it went without saying that the visiting parents of Mac-san had to be interviewed!

I suspected this might be disquieting for my parents, but I had no clue how much so. They were friggin' freaked out; scared out of their never-having-been-on-TV minds! But, to their enormous credit, and despite Herculean foreboding—tyrannosaurus-sized butterflies dive bombing about in the pits of their formerly contented, Spam-lined stomachs—they squelched their screaming-meemies and agreed to do it.

Mom and Daddy donned their Sunday best and off the three of us went by chauffeured car to downtown Tokyo. Arriving at NHK, we were appropriately gushed over by the producers who laboriously welcomed them to, not only their country, but also their TV domain. Following that, we were ushered into the make up room where the problematic Mexican pancake gook was liberally applied to our Casper-the-friendly-ghost faces, making us look exactly like Scottish-Irish-Mexicans who had overstayed our time in a tanning booth. But only from the collar up.

Daddy and I finished first, Mom last. When it was her turn, the cosmetologist took one overly close, excessively confidential look at her, and let out a long "Saaaaaah, arah maaah!" (loose translation: Oh, my god!), as her eyebrows jumped two inches, landing just under the border of her hairline!

So! There it was! What they said about uncivilized foreigners *was* true. The men *did* beat their wives!

On Mom's grandmotherly face was the proof. The truth was out at last. My cordial, gentle, mild-mannered father was an ogre! A fiend, a remorseless barbarian disguised as a grocer in a Sunday suit! His jig was up.

Earlier that day, an ever helpful Gramma Honey had volunteered to hang Erin's diapers outside on the line. As she carried the laundry basket down the narrow stone path to the clothesline, her foot slipped on the smooth pebbles causing her to fall heavily onto her side. Her cheekbone smacked against the hard stones, precipitously turning it a shocking red. Then slowly, but determinedly, the red mutated to an even more shocking blue. Finally, in a last melding of hues, the new adornment made up its mind and settled into a dismal dark drab of blues and blacks with a purplish undertone. The injury encircled Mom's left eye like a rainbow of wrath.

The job of covering up this distress now fell upon the shoulders of the suspicious, doubting Tom cosmetologist. Doggedly she slathered layer upon layer of greasy camouflaging gunk onto Mom's polychromatic skin, while I tried my best to explain in Japanese the innocence of her black eye. There was no doubt the woman understood me perfectly, but I'll bet you a week's supply of Spam, she still chose to believe her own version, *the juicy version.* Poor Mom, now thrice smacked down by a Bermuda Triangle of glitches. In her march towards global love and enlightenment, she was not fairing well.

HEAVEN ONLY KNOWS how agonizing it must have been for Grampa and Honey to be on live TV. This had, under no conditions, never been a part of their life plan together. But, like intrepid Minnesotans, they muddled through, never laying bare their terror to me, to Tazaki-sensei, to the producers, or to the TV faithful. They came across like champs, holding up their end of the family honor. After all, they were the proud parents of Peggy-san (the lying non-virginal former TV star), as well as the even prouder grandparents of the famous boy-of-many-faces Jeff-chan (of new TV fame), *and* the *in*famous banshee-screeching Erin-chan (of even newer TV fame). Only Matthew-chan, the perfect please-and-thank-you gentleman, who held the lamentable rank of middle child, was unknown. As yet he had not done anything egregiously outrageous enough to distinguish himself on TV. And Glen, of course, remained the invisible man; a Big Screen nobody.

After taping the show, Tazaki-sensei invited us out for a drink. The plan was, he explained, to take a taxi to the Imperial Hotel where we would meet his girlfriend. *Girlfriend?* Why, the old fox! I knew Tazaki-sensei had a wife because he told me so. He also told me she had been institutionalized in a mental hospital for many years. I did often wonder if quite possibly part of her psychosis could have stemmed from her husband having—right there in the epicenter bull's eye of a nail society—named their children Mary and George! But, then, what did I know, and who was I to pass any kind of sanctimonious judgment on either of them, especially on a vim and vigor, but lonely, guy like Sensei. Of course he had to get on with his absent-wife life, and like I told you previously, before you criticize anyone, you need to walk a mile in his shoes. But then, it wouldn't have mattered anyway. Sensei's shoes were too small for me.

The Imperial Hotel, designed decades before by the illustrious Frank Lloyd Wright, was grand in an old, cheerless, tomblike sort of way. (Frank Lloyd *Wrong?*) But, this neither disappointed nor dampened the mood of my parents. Shucks no! They were in high spirits, giddily chanting Presbyterian (and a smattering of Lutheran) prayers of gratitude under their breath now that their TV debut—*Thank You, Lord!*— was over.

As we entered the impressive cocktail lounge, we saw waiting at a small table, the girlfriend. She bowed to us deeply and repeatedly in an elegant robin's-egg-blue silk kimono. There were no gray tones lurking anywhere on this highly polished femme fatale, who obviously being the confident sort, could risk a splash of muted color. Yes, she was the personification of charm heaped upon charm. It overjoyed me to know that my dear friend, Tazaki-san, had such an exceptional private someone, while it tickled me all over the place that he wished to share her with the likes of us.

After several rounds of drinks, Tazaki-san and his glamorous steady announced they were going to take us on a tour of the Ginza. What a marvelous idea! A chance for Mom and Daddy to trip the Tokyo night lights fantastic in the biggest way possible, just as I had done so in the smallest way possible on that first night when Glen and I took advantage of the Gajo-en chambermaid. Holy cow, touring didn't get any better than the Ginza!

We were politely instructed to sit tight and they'd get the car.

"*They,*" my foot! Tazaki-san remained sitting tight, while his girlfriend excused herself and bustled off in her regal kimono, trotting daintily on embroidered satin zori (zoh-ree, elegant thick wedged-soled, thong-like slippers, worn exclusively with a kimono). I, naturally, was in my usual state of affairs; the one in which I didn't have a clue what was going on. I figured she needed to first, before our departure, go to the ladies room to freshen up. After, however, what seemed to me an inordinate amount of ladies room freshen-up-time, I became concerned.

> "When My Love Comes Back
> From the Ladies Room
> Will I Be Too Old to Care?"
> Lewis Grizzard song title

I casually asked if I should go and check on her. Not necessary, Sensei assured me, glancing at his watch. She should be arriving any minute now. With that, he stood up, gestured for us to do the same, and ushered us towards the Imperial's front door.

There *she* was waiting in *his* car! I later found out it had taken her so long because she first had to trip daintily in those elegant, though restrictive zori all the way down to the hotel's underground parking, work her way slowly into a long line of cars plus the exit pay booth, and then finally fight her way through downtown traffic to the Imperial's imperial entrance. Upon learning this, it was a struggle for me to contain myself, that Chinese lover sucking on his tootsie's tootsie coming to mind. Ironically, though, I was saved because of him. He had fortunately, in the nick of time, refreshed my memory, reminding me this was one of those times that a closed mouth (mine) gathers no foot in it, which I'd probably later regret, even though that Chinese guy could have cared less.

With the slamming of four car doors, (I say "four" because, naturally, the honorable girlfriend had to get out, bow to us, then welcome us to *his* car), she propelled us gung-ho into the madness of the Ginza traffic. Every inch was dense with people either in cars or on sidewalks, everyone out cruising one of the world's most tantalizing streets. Zoom!

Jeez Louise, who drove a car like that? And who drove a car like that in an outfit like that? Oh, that's right, it was impossible to drive any other way. In her impractically absurd, even suicidal, skin-tight kimono, she had no choice. Well, actually she did have two: 1. stop altogether—don't drive, or 2. go forth—bat-out-of-hell. Yee-haw!

It was beyond me how well anyone could slice and dice their way through Tokyo traffic while wearing an immovably restrictive kimono, a fourteen-foot-long obi (oh-bee, the heavy silk embroidered sash wound around and around the body), and those two ridiculous zori? Well, *not well*, that's how!

Imagine you were behind the wheel, bound from neck to ankles in a constricted (though exquisite), way too expensive-so-you-don't-dare-damage-it strait jacket. Then just to make sure none of the pure silk yardage budged even one micrometer of a millimeter, you anchored it securely by coiling around your waist a one-foot-wide, fourteen-foot-long embroidered Ace bandage. Encased thusly, you'd be attempting to live, breathe and flex in an unpliable, full-body turban that resembled in every way Tutankhamen when he was unearthed from his pyramid.

Furthermore, there was more, for the meticulously tied obi created a stack of multiple folds roughly the size of a sofa pillow. These folds now rested squarely in the center of the girlfriend's back, forcing her to sit one-sofa-pillow distance away from the seat and jamming her up against the steering wheel. Let's face it, kimono were designed to be worn by a passenger in a palanquin, not a bat-out-of-hell lady driver in a Toyota, even if it didn't have brake problems.

All this and yet I haven't even come to the kimono sleeves. Picture yourself taking a pillowcase, folding it lengthwise, folding that end to end, and then in a flash of genius, safety-pinning it to one of your long shirt sleeves. Repeat for the other sleeve. Having done this, you can see for yourself the good sense for, and the practicality of, the girlfriend's long kimono sleeves. What blasted designer from the under side of the moon came up with that cockamamie idea anyway? One preposterously illogical sleeve now hung nicely around, over, and into the gear shift, guaranteeing that every driving maneuver would be even iffier.

Still not finished. The zori. While burning up the road, it would have been impossible for the girlfriend, in this rigid kimono-obi-confinement, to bend over and put back on the zori which had every chance of slipping off of not only her feet, but also the pedals *because that is exactly what they were designed to do—slide off with effortless ease!* It all spelled the end to simple pleasures.

Fashion! Crack-brained, preposterous fashion!

> "I base my fashions on
> what doesn't itch."
> Gilda Radner

Lip synching a Minnesota version of "Hail Mary, full of grace... *Hail Ole/Lena, full of grace*" ... I tore myself away from our hell-bent chauffeur to catch a glimpse out my window. Catatonic City! The hysteria of the bright Ginza lights screamed at my senses. From all directions was a pompous parade of outrageously blinking neon lights clashing like muted cymbals. It was enough to dazzle a small town bumpkin for a lifetime and beyond.

This was it, the very hub, the highest pinnacle of modern Japan. From the backseat, my hayseed heart skipped a yokel beat as I looked over at my dumbstruck parents, their former optimistic, sanguine faces now gray stony veils of frozen ash.

Unaware of our terror, Tazaki-san and his girlfriend (who I was just figuring out was Japan's current entry in the Daytona 500), morphed into polished tour guides as they began pointing out the sights. This, over here, was a famous something or other, and that, over there, was an even more famous something or other. Incredibly, there were row upon row of famous somethings or other.

Zzzzzing! We passed a railroad station. Not recognizing the train line, I inquired through chattering teeth as to which one it was. "Why, it's my father's," answered the demure, but compressed girlfriend as she swerved to miss it. Talk about liar-liar-pants-on-fire-bull-crap! Nobody's dad owned a train line.

But, hers did.

As I choked on this startling news (egads, didn't only governments own trains ... and do you suppose she could divulge where they secretly buried those lost and found cremains?), we hurtled past a dazzling department store. It stood out from all the rest, clearly designed for only the upper of the very most upper crust of Japanese society. Reduced now to sputtering, I asked which store it was. "Oh, that is *my* store," she replied, careening past it. Holy smokes! That department store was the epitome of elegance, the very pinnacle of shopping even for the richest of the rich. For crying out humble loud, our modest, body-turbaned chauffeur was a tribillionaire!

Glued to the arm rest, my mind groped, then fragmented, unable to take it all in. If I had it figured right, this discordant clash in which Tazaki-san lived was at last becoming clear. Here he was the ultra-mod man leading a gorgeous ultra-mod life, while in contrast back home was that cob-webby old umbilical cord trunk. Jeez! It was the same with this whole country. The yin and yang of it was blowing me away. Just when I thought I had it all figured out and tied up in a neat theoretical bow, this night had come along and pulled the string.

And what was it with this woman, anyhow? Like hadn't I repeatedly seen elderly Japanese couples out strolling, the dominant him ten paces ahead of the subservient her? Here now in the front seat was this other kind of Japanese lady: Miss Money-Bags-Corporate-Exec-Drag-Racing Queen behind the wheel instead of behind her man. And where she should have been wearing a racing uniform, she was in an antiquated outfit as old as all of Japan's history. Furthermore, what was this with *her* driving? In this country where few females did, she contrasted wildly by propelling Tazaki-san's newest model car around at lightning speed like it had been gassed—well, by Baby Matt! She was as big a contradiction as Tazaki-san!

Gee whiz, Japanese folks were sure clever at blending the glittery new with the old-world old. Try as I might to find in my memory bank any comparable historical contradictions that Austin might have, left me with nothing … except, possibly one thing. Yes, that one thing. It always took place in the Presbyterian Church basement and never had a solution. I could hear those heated debates between the young and the senior members of the Women's Guild arguing over how to make coffee; the new or the old way. With or without eggshells. Hmmm, I wondered if that contrast qualified.

As the evening drew to a close (with Mom, Daddy and I in the backseat breathing a sigh of repentance and thanksgiving), I gave up on any further attempts at pigeon-holing Japan, as well as trying to figure out the avant-garde Tazaki-san and his companion. I'd simply brace myself for their next surprise which was … as sure as the Japanese shoot peasants … just around the corner.

> "They were such a progressive
> couple, they tried to
> adopt a gay baby."
> Unknown

SEVENTY-SEVEN

THE FOLLOWING WEEK, Glen, Daddy, Mom and I packed our bags and set off for Kyoto, the lovely ancient capital of Japan. We would be traveling first class on the Shinkansen (shin-kahn-sen), the spanking new bullet train. Once again the blaring contrast of then and now was upon us: Kyoto, the most venerable, ancient city in Japan, and the Shinkansen, the world's most modern train. The Shinkansen was as shiny as Kyoto was patina-ed. Its chromed cars out-stripped the wind, as Kyoto casually wrote haiku while strolling through the serenity of temple gardens.

Only two months before Erin was born, Glen and I had taken this same trip with Bob and Karen. We were privileged to have ridden the bullet train right after it first began operation, and were stunned by how sleek and gleaming it was, the sunlight glinting off its metal curved surfaces like reflections from a thousand mirrors. Settling into seats unflawed in their newness, we had to pinch ourselves to remind us we were, at breakneck speed, moving backwards in time to an archaic city whose history was more ancient than our forefathers could have ever imagined. From Tokyo to Kyoto, the trip took roughly three hours to go the two hundred and thirty-five miles, including station stops. It was a staggering speed in 1965. It still is.

Now eight months later, here we were with my parents seated on the same slightly less unflawed seats and feeling spellbound all over again by the futuristic ride. Just before noon, the passengers got hungry. From out of their furoshiki (foo-roe-shi-ki, wrapping cloths), they pulled obento (oh-ben-toe, small honorable lunch boxes of cold rice, pickled vegetables, and cooked fish), which they had either brought from home or purchased at the last station. In the seats around us, folks began eagerly chowing down. Not wanting to feel or look any odder than the odd balls we were, we joined right in not missing a beat by pulling out our own obento which we had purchased at Shinjuku Station, our departure point. Devouring them along with the group, we watched Japan whiz past our windows. As I chewed—my eyes zapping back and forth at the blurred sights—I wondered if Tazaki-san's girlfriend was at the controls. Heck, her dad probably *owned* the Bullet Train! Probably bought it *from her*!!

> "If you board the wrong train,
> it is no use running
> along the corridor
> in the opposite direction."
> Dietrich Bonhoeffer

Everything seemed so blissful: state-of-the-art train, happy crowd, and us on vacation. We streaked along soaking it all in. As the lunches ended, folks began pouring ocha (oh-cha, honorable green tea). That was nice, I thought, very friendly. I sat there looking at the convivial scene. Suddenly one man raised his cup. I thought he was about to propose a toast. To the new train (*probably*)? To us the foreigners (*get real, Peggy*)? To the occasion (*more like it*)? But, instead of drinking from his cup, he took some sips and then poured the remainder of the tea onto the floor. *What?* I was aghast! Then the others decided they were also through with their tea and poured what was left in their cups onto the floor. Cripes! The pristine, state-of-the-art floor! I was flabbergasted!

I still can't explain it. I know those passengers were not christening their part of the train because I saw no accompanying ceremonies. No, it was just a gesture of convenience, emptying their cups so they could put them away. I was left believing it was what some Japanese did when they were on an outing no matter where they were and no matter what they were in. Years ago Japanese tea houses had dirt floors and when the patrons finished drinking, they poured their remaining tea onto those floors. No problem, the liquid simply soaked into the dirt. But, hells bells, this was 1966, and the Shinkansen floor was not dirt!

As I mentioned before, in some areas, Japan's progress was mystifyingly slow. In the end I decided this tea pouring business was just one more of those issues, like the one which also included the annoying, rude, continuous sniffling of the nose in a hushed concert hall. Or maybe, just maybe, it was simply the lack of ownership thing ... I don't have to take care of it, because it doesn't belong to me. In America, I suppose this would have been as unlikely as expecting a high school guy to dry clean his rental prom tuxedo before he returned it. Never happen!

Oh, for crying out loud, you figure it out because now I'm all worked up into a lather, so I can't. Meanwhile, I'll just stay flummoxed and not a little angry.

"There ain't no answer.
There isn't going to be an answer.
There never has been an answer.
That's the answer."
Gertrude Stein

IT IS, OF course, a must to see Kyoto for it is the ultimate, most sparkling of all the gems in the Japanese crown. Bob, Glen, Karen and I had figured this out on that first visit. Kyoto was how Japan used to be; the very birthplace of its venerable culture. Nothing held a candle to it. It was also—and here I go again spoiling everything with my contrasts—where thousands of years after Kyoto's first shrine was built, the ultra-hip, world-changing Nintendo was created.

To experience the city to its fullest, one had to stay in a ryokan (ree-yo-kan, a small, homey inn run by the family who owned and lived in it). One was never prepared, as we never were, for the impact of a ryokan. The first time it happened, it blew us away. Unaware of the shift we were about to make, we stepped from the bustle and brightness of the day into the unexpected quiet and dimness of the inn. Startlingly, abruptly, in the moment it had taken us to make that single step, we entered Japan's past.

As if it were a rule, the four of us immediately fell into a self-imposed silence as, with an unmistakable hush, the old-world shushed us. The very air inside the inn whispered of its long past, its earliest memories pulsating from the vintage, unfinished wood. This was respected old. This was cherished tradition. From every corner antiquity murmured its simplicity, reminding us of the interminable line of travelers who, before us, had walked on the very floors we were now walking upon, weary and seeking refuge in an unfamiliar place.

There was no paint on any surface. Raw, aged wood was beauty enough. Its unmodified, organic purity blended perfectly with the paper sliding shoji and the luxurious straw tatami.

For you who have never experienced anything but carpet, tile, linoleum and wood under your feet, let me explain. Tatami are made of very fine, exquisitely woven top-mats of rush grass, laid over thick, tightly sewn, rice-straw-filled palettes. The result is not only a soft, slight suppleness under one's bare feet, but also a cushioned blessing for those who sit and sleep upon them. When they are new, tatami are a pale green, but they soon turn to the color of golden dried straw. Of course, the mats don't last

347

forever. They must be replaced every four to eight years depending upon use, but to extend their life they can be lifted out and set outdoors in the sun for airing. In the drippy dampness of Japan, this is a very good thing for it allows them to occasionally be dried thoroughly.

In the West, a room is measured in feet, as in twelve-by-sixteen, for example, and can be built to any size and to any configuration. In Japan, a room is usually built to the exact measurements of the number of tatami it can hold. For instance, a room may be a six-mat room, each mat being approximately one yard wide, two yards long and two inches thick.

The mats are laid side by side in a tight, immovable formation which precisely conforms to the borders of each room. Every mat is edged with a dignified black, brocaded, cotton trim. The smell of new tatami is, in a word, divine. The aroma of its uncontaminated purity stops you dead in your tracks. Once you have smelled it, you will never forget it—and you will wish for more.

To illustrate, during our first year in Japan, Glen, our little boys and I traveled into the mountains of Nikko. We had a reservation at what we heard was a new inn; new inns being an absolute rarity. Entering, we were delighted to find the sparkling new, pristine entry to be as fresh as a daisy. Of course, there was no ambience of the past, because this place had no past. We were immediately greeted by a proprietor who, like his front entry, was also fresh as a daisy. To our surprise, and totally unexpected, the manager began immediately apologizing, pardoning himself to kingdom come. Finally after a very long and ardent appeal, he asked us to wait. Our room, he confessed, was not quite ready.

Well, sure, we replied, absolving him of his distress. (I mean it was either that or watch him self-annihilate from face loss.) No problem. We would wait in his pristine entry.

We did. We did. And, we did. It felt like a perpetual intermission where we couldn't leave because the show still had a second act, although we hadn't yet seen the first. Hours crawled by, and just when weariness and boredom were about to lay us flat on the pristine lobby floor, the owner, no longer looking like a daisy, announced our room was at last ready. Bowing repeatedly, he ushered us down a bright, clean hallway to our awaiting room; a room that announced itself before we ever got to it. Coming from it was the fragrance of new tatami permeating the entire air space of the hall, causing even our very young boys to recognize a change, tilt back their heads, and breathe in deeply and deliciously.

As the innkeeper slid the shoji open, we heard towards the back of the room a scuffling of scurrying feet. Clearly not meant for our eyes were some carpenters with their tool bags hustling out a back entrance as we entered through the front. It seemed that while we had been enduring the long wait, they had been building our room!

That would explain a delay alright.

It took only one blink of our eyes to realize the wait had been worth every protracted minute. If you've ever experienced the commingling sight and smells of new sawn wood, coupled with fresh cut straw, you will understand to what we were treated. We stepped onto tatami that had never before been walked upon by any guest. The slight resilience of its packed sewn layers felt to our feet like they had suddenly grown new cushioning ... as if tiny additional Tempur-Pedic mattresses had been glued to them. The top mat of impeccably woven rush-straw was so silky-smooth, it didn't even snag my nylon stockings. But, then, no tatami ever snagged nylon stockings. It was that perfect.

The wooden supports throughout the room had a bright, unadulterated finish as if the trees had just given birth to them. On one wall was a closet with sliding doors behind which were stored the cotton-filled futon. Like the tatami, they and their quilts had also never known a sleeper. There was nothing in the West to match this combination. For how could we Americans compare the chemically acrimonious smells of our new paint and carpeting to those coming straight from nature? You had to have been in that room to truly comprehend its virginal exquisiteness; to appreciate and absorb its renewing purity. That, in a nutshell, was also what Japan was about.

Stacked beside the futon were the soba gara makura (soh-bah gah-rah mah-koo-rah). These small pillows, designed a thousand years ago, were filled not with the feathers from suddenly naked, shivering geese, but of all things, with the hulls of buckwheat! They were about as far from our fluffy, cushy Western headrests as a pillow could be without being a chunk of wood. After a rough day at work it was at first difficult to be lulled into dreamland by these pillows. Rather, your sleepy senses were convolutedly shocked awake. In particular, your delicate hearing. As the weight of your head pressed into the pillow, a bejillion tiny buckwheat hulls—sounding up close more like their cousins, the harder and tougher peppercorns—began combatively shifting in a noisy, grinding, grating crunch until their jostling finally gave up on the pecking order and settled into place. This place turned out to be the perfect contour of your head.

If you lay your head cheek-down upon this container of grit with one of your finely-tuned ears (whose ability to hear had now, without warning, magnified because of its close proximity to all the racket), it sounded uncannily like the explosions under automobile tires as they drove over a bountiful fall harvest of plump acorns spread across a cement driveway. The ensuing, seemingly endless eruptions continued until all the hulls had at last come to their raspy resting places—the exact imprint of your now wide awake profile. It's a given that Madame Taussaud could have used those molds for her waxy impressions.

I never dreamed I would become utterly hooked on these implements of distress. That I would presently sleep on—not the tiny Japanese version, but (in yet another contest of who can super-size who)—the American king-size, big daddy of all soba-gara-makura. My matching pair was so heavy the mailman had to deliver them with a fork lift (or at least a small back-hoe), their contents alone devouring the buckwheat harvest of a single growing season. Besides the wonderful rest my crunchy pillows afford me … that is to say, wonderful after I have completed the always lengthy procedure of calming them down … yet another unexpected discovery occurred. In an attempt to fluff them up each morning, I have developed good upper arm strength. Indeed, so addicted am I to these bags of boisterous barnacles, that I have a small soba gara makura which I carry in my suitcase while traveling. I cannot sleep without one. God bless the creative buckwheat farmers of the world! Bet the peppercorn farmers are jealous!

> "All creative people
> should be required
> to leave California
> for three months
> each year."
> Gloria Swanson

SEVENTY-EIGHT

BUT NOW RETURNING to Mom, Daddy, Glen and I, we arrived in Kyoto and went immediately to our ryokan. Because our innkeeper's family lived there, the guest rooms were an extension of their home: an ancient version of the bed and breakfast. All Japanese women prided themselves on their cooking because that is what they did. They stayed home and they cooked. Cooking, being such a demonstrative and caring skill, was a major big deal, way beyond even the Betty Crocker mindset of the typical American homemaker. But, as skilled as the average Japanese housewife was, even she paled beside the culinary creativity of the ryokan wife. No question about it, the most wondrous food in all of Japan was prepared by competing inn matrons.

Breakfast and dinner were included in the price, along with a yukata (you-kah-tah, a summer cotton kimono), or a tanzen (tahn-zen, a heavy padded winter kimono), slippers, a toothbrush, toothpaste and a razor. It made packing a cinch. Of course, each ryokan had a common toilet shared by the other guests, replete with toilet slippers. It also had its own small offuro which could be either used by you and yours alone, or shared with the other folks. Your choice. Your degree of modesty.

Sharing the small bath with unknown guests did strike me as a little suspect. It felt way too intimate. You know, later passing fully-clothed strangers in the hallways and knowing exactly what they looked like under their clothes felt like voyeurism gone awry. Oy! I opted for Glen only, as by now I was familiar with what was under his clothes including that smattering of fading Cubism imprints.

The order of the evening was to first bathe and soak (swoon), to eat (swoon, swoon), and afterwards, if you were so inclined, to get into your futon and have a massage (swoon, swoon, swoooon!). In Japan, being a masseur was the occupation of the blind. It was too perfect. Any awkwardness just flew out the shoji door! The recipient felt no embarrassment whatsoever over his lack of gorgeousness, because the non-sighted masseuse (ah-mah-san) could not pass visual judgment on his unsightly body flaws. In a quirky reversal, I suppose this experience was much like Glen had had at that bath house all those years before when that Jezebel of an assistant had covered *his* eyes. Only in that case, *he* couldn't see his own body flaws, but *she* could! Oh, but then I forgot. He didn't have any ... except for those Ban Lon socks.

Having a blind masseuse was ideal in every way; touch, but not see. It did *not* disallow, however, the blind masseuse (while busily kneading your fleshy hills and dales), from having an imagination. I wondered if they found our foreign feel interesting; different from the same-old-same-old Asian feel. I never asked. It felt too good to interrupt with questions.

The system was over-the-top serene. As the freshly bathed, sumptuously fed guest turned out the lights (because no one would need them including the masseuse) he laid beside the futon the appropriate yen payment, then slipped into his futon for the night. Next entered the tip-toeing ama-san who, settling in very quietly, began the magic. When the massage was complete, the payment was collected—and I'll bet checked for those Braille dots in the corner of the bills, just to make sure. Finally the ama-san tiptoed quietly out of the room, oh, so silently sliding the shoji so as not to awaken the now rapturous, comatose guest. In all ways, the ryokan was heavenly. In comparison, Motel 6 felt like sleeping in the trunk of Mr. 6's car!

IN THE INTRODUCTION to this memoir, I promised I would not be a Mr. Fodor. God gave him exclusive rights to travelogues. However, it must be said that one could not go to Kyoto without rhapsodizing over the unique splendor of its temples and shrines. You did not know antiquity until you saw them. Take for example the Buddhist Higashi Honganji Temple which was originally built in the year 1602.

Due to fires, which so regularly plagued these old wooden structures, the temple had been rebuilt several times. Today you will find there a large, dust-coated, glass box containing a kezuna (kay-zoo-nah, a rope made of human hair). This was never meant to be just any old offering to Buddha, but was rather a very personal, very utilitarian gift. When the temple was being reconstructed after the last fire in 1895, the craftsmen ran into

352

difficulties obtaining heavy rope strong enough to hoist up the massive timbers. Rising to the occasion, the female temple devotees generously sheared their long locks and presented them to the monks who braided them into massive hair ropes. The largest is more than one-hundred-sixty yards long, with a circumference of thirty-inches, and weighs more than a ton. Who knew? Hair today, rope tomorrow.

Another fond memory was that of Nijo Castle, the home of a shogun (show-goon ... *ignore, please, the unflattering ring to the second syllable ...* who was a duke or lord). Ever fearing his own assassination by infiltrating ninja, this shogun designed his home/castle with "nightingale" floors. Let me enlighten you. Almost all of the old style Japanese homes were constructed with a porch walkway skirting around the outside of the entire building. As each room had shoji doors that slid open to this covered open-air walkway, it served as a corridor in which one could move from room to room without disturbing others, as well as an air space welcoming the fresh outdoors into the rooms. This gave the warrior shogun some relief from the searing summer heat, as well as a place to view his gardens while penning sensitive haiku about his loved ones—when he wasn't unapologetically plotting blood and guts revenge on his enemies. It was also designed for architectural beauty, much like the way a porch on an old Victorian home binds the building with a finishing wrap.

With his very survival in mind, the shogun contrived his "porch" so that each cupped floorboard was suspended above a support containing special wooden pegs. This allowed the slightly rockered boards to individually move up and down over a drilled frame. Such flexibility then caused the hundreds of pegs to rub against the wood when someone walked upon it, creating melodious cheeping sounds. As Mom, Daddy, Glen and I strolled in our stocking feet along the length of the walkway, the boards did authentically sound like a flock of delightfully chirping nightingales.

But, do not be fooled. The design was not all about foo-foo aesthetics for it, more importantly, caused any approaching assassin to be quickly detected. Luckily, on most nights there were no chirps disturbing the night air, allowing the clever lord to sleep tight without having the ninja bite.

SEVENTY-NINE

MOM AND DADDY had one room in the inn (sounds Biblical), while Glen and I had another. On our first night in Kyoto, we decided to meet in their room before dinner for happy hour (sounds un-Biblical). We would begin with the sake stash Glen and Daddy had purchased for just this occasion. Together, we lowered ourselves onto the four zabuton, all neatly placed around a small, low table on the tatami floor. These five minimal things were the only furnishings in the room, other than a tall folding screen in one corner.

In mid-lowering, Mom took a long hesitant look down at her zabuton and began questioning how the air was at such a low elevation. It had been years since she'd spent any length of time at floor level, and she had a real fear of not getting back up. But with our coaxing, plus the lure of a party, she decided to join us. On her way downward, however, she found it ridiculously difficult. She felt stiff, confined. Perhaps, she pondered, if she could rid herself of her beastly strangulating Warner's full-length girdle *(see, she was the one who made me do it!)*, she could maneuver downward more easily. With that, Mom tiptoed across the tatami to the freshly laundered stack of yukata, plucked off the top one and sashayed to the corner. Within moments, a blouse flipped over the top of the screen. A skirt soon followed.

During the interval, Daddy had settled nicely upon his zabuton and was beginning to feel, with the aid of the sake, his own stiff joints commence to loosen. As it was meant to do, the potent potion was doing its job, unshackling his proper businessman constraints. Just about that time, two stretched-out, seamed nylons came over the screen, landing with a soft swish onto the woven straw matting. Gene's attentions abruptly turned to his Margaret. Ah, tres sexy, he grinned lustfully!

At once, to my astonishment, he began to clap ... then to sing ... then to clap *and* sing. Before long, the strains of *A Pretty Girl Is Like A Melody* came dripping off his lips like maple syrup dribbling over French toast. Was this pas' de deux' my parents' homespun version of a strip tease? I was thinking so. Meanwhile behind the screen, Mom, being highly attuned to her swain's ballad was immediately picking up on its inference. Not one to let a ripe opportunity slip by, she raised one plump arm and with a full rotation above her graying head, let fly a size 38 D bra. To his great delight, its lacey, twin cavernous cups landed squarely on Daddy's head. Tres, tres sexy!

I was seeing a new side of my folks. Gosh, you think everyone is normal and predictable until you go on a vacation with them. This includes, of all people, your parents; the very ones you think you know every last thing about. As I sat there reflecting back, I could have sworn they hadn't acted like that when I was a kid. But, then what did I know? Those rascally senior colts had some chemistry going on. Once again I was reminded that it was no wonder they had birthed us four babies in three years. Whoops, darnnit, it's happened again!

> "Do you smoke after sex?"
> "Gosh, I don't know.
> I never looked! "
> Unknown

I once heard that retirement changes people. For the love of Mike, my children's grandmother was now a bombshell and their grandfather, a lech! About that time, Mom let out a loud whoop followed by a clatter, clatter, thump, clatter, as a real big, rib-to-thigh Warner girdle came thwacking over the top of the screen, its four garters chattering like castanets against the caned panels. I was stunned! Honey, a hoofer! A hooker?

> "I've made so many movies
> playing a hooker
> that they don't pay me
> in the regular way anymore.
> They leave the money on the dresser."
> Shirley Maclaine

Bumping and grinding her way from behind the screen, Mom and her now freed up flesh—presently hanging, swaying *loose and low* under her cotton kimono—gyrated her way across the tatami to the semi-boisterous, borderline-bawdy, just-short-of-bellowing Daddy. Him Tarzan. Her Jane. A tawdry Kodak moment amidst the serenity of old Nippon.

EIGHTY

SINCE CHILDHOOD, I'VE known one thing about myself. I'm a professed window peeper ... and proud of it! Like, come on, folks, isn't that *why* windows are transparent? For criminy sakes, get real! They're an invitation to look! With me, it's like this. Where regular peeping Toms are interested in sneaking a look at the people inside, I only want to see the inside of the inside. I'm into interiors. Is that so bad? It wasn't my fault we moved overseas, dashing my dreams of becoming a Mary Kay Cosmetics lady so that I'd be invited into lots of indoors. And let me add, I was as equally vexed over losing out on the pink Cadillac. Thus full of regrets, and left without a Mary Kay option, I turned to conducting my own furtive surveys in the only way I knew how—at night when interior lights were on.

In this department, I was definitely in the right place. The houses lining the narrow, serpentine roads of Japan, built right up to the edges of those dirt-packed roads, were a dream come true. I nearly brushed against the doors as I walked by. For one of my persuasion, nothing could have been better. (Well, okay, so maybe a Japanese Mary Kay-san I.D. badge.)

Most people I knew planned their vacations with famous sights in mind. I, on the other hand, always preferred to see the houses which, unlike the sights, remained open five days a week, plus weekends and holidays. In Japan, when the weather was hot, the front door opening to the genkan was wide open. But, do not think for one moment this now afforded a clear view of the inside. Not on your life. Japan was on to people like me. To prevent us from peering in, they invented a unique door curtain called the noren (noh-ren).

The noren was a mixed bag of pluses and minuses. To begin on the minus side, it was irritating to have to shove aside a curtain each time you walked through a doorway, to say nothing of the added annoyance of messing up a perfectly contoured doo-wop of a pompadour. It was as well ineffective in providing any kind of security, and it certainly was no hindrance for bugs who effortlessly entered. A screen door would certainly have worked better, but Japan in the sixties did not have a screen door concept. Something tells me that for many, nothing has changed.

Now, the pluses. A noren allowed air to circulate, and it was a sort of barrier to stop people like me from looking in. And with that statement, we have hit on its pulse. What must never be overlooked in this over-crowded island country was the importance of privacy.

Feeble as they were, the noren did create a sense of privacy. They were hung from the top of open doorways in homes, and in shops, the name of the business was printed across the fabric. Wide loops were sewn to the top edge of the noren through which a bamboo pole was threaded, and they were designed to hang flat, fitting the exact width of the door openings. They were easily removed. When a noren was displayed outside a shop, it was a signal to the public the shop was open. This was particularly important in the years before electric lights. Obviously when the shop was closed, the noren was taken down, signaling to disappointed shoppers to come back tomorrow.

The noren was made of individually hemmed rectangles of the same cloth, joined together by a seam across the top only. This allowed the curtain to have two, three or more separate sections, making the whole thing look like it was a ridiculously wide fringe. These slits allowed the noren to be walked through without either disturbing the entire curtain or, heaven forbid, pulling it down. Each noren was a mini work of art. It had to be appealing to the eye because it served as the introduction to, and the advertisement for, one's home or establishment. In shops, the noren were usually dyed a rich deep indigo blue, making a stunning background for the shop's name written in stylized white calligraphy. This was so artistically done, they appeared to have been hand-brushed by a calligrapher. For the home, noren differed as they were considered more often than not to be a kind of artsy decoration for the house. (Another wildly common favorite was calendar art, one in every room, on every wall.)

As I've said, the number one most important reason for the noren was to thwart Peeping Toms and Peeping Peggies. If one of us walked by a house, so close we could touch it, but the weather was so dastardly hot that the door had to be open, privacy was zilch. *Bad!* Hang the noren. *Good!* It was so simple. Just put a curtain over the open door, dummy.

Let me point out here that other things could certainly have been used as a curtain. Take bed sheets, for example, which could have been slung over any door opening. There were two drawbacks to this, however, in the sixties of Japan. The number one drawback was that the sheets were needed to cover not their doors, but their beds, and what kind of crackbrained idea was it (listen up, America!) to make a quick decorating fix by hanging a sheet over an opening, anyway? On a personal note, the number two reason I didn't go that route was that I had used all our available extras to support my overly pregnant, under-slung belly.

Whatever you do, do not get the idea that the noren covered the entire door. No, it hung roughly twenty inches or so from the top of the entryway. This was just long enough to block out the upper half of the door opening. The observant reader will now realize that the bottom half of the doorway remained uncovered. He will also figure out that this allowed a clear view to the lower half of the genkan. This view was called "my chance."

Now let's say you the homeowner were in the habit of going around scantily clothed or even buck naked, because remember it was beastly hot. When an uncouth, wanton, ill-mannered, foreign, Lord-of-the-Flies like me walked by, with my eyes shamelessly peeled on your genkan, I was only able to see the naked bottom of you. Without the top, I had no clue who you were! A rump is a rump is a rump—unless, that is, you were that tight-assed Tom Selleck. See, it was all so clear. With a noren your identity was completely, utterly, totally half safe.

My best thinking tells me that the noren was probably invented as a genteel, delicate, diplomatic barrier to one's home, letting people know they were approaching private property (or people's privates, as the case may have been!), but not being so rude as to keep folks out. The Japanese were always so quirkily polite about things like that.

The subject of noren cannot be finished without mentioning that they could also be found inside the home. They hung from inner doors as soft, subtle divisions between rooms. A foreigner had to be prepared to meet them head-on with dignity, for between getting batted in the face each time you left and entered a room—to say nothing of the destruction of your coif—you also had those previously mentioned burdens of remembering not to wear the toilet slippers in any of the non-toilet rooms, calling everything that belonged to another person honorable, and most importantly, remembering to shit where they told you to shit. Being a guest in a Japanese home boiled down to one travail after another, all making for a trying, but enlightening, experience.

EIGHTY-ONE

WHILE WE WERE in Kyoto, we took Mom and Daddy on a day trip to the city of Nara (Japan's oldest old capital), to see one of the largest Buddhas in the world. There, devout Japanese traveled from great distances to gaze up in awe and reverence at the Buddha. I would be lying if I said the rest of the world did not also gaze up in awe and reverence at the Buddha, because they did—and do. His mere size knocks the wind out of you.

This particular Buddha resides in the equally enormous Todaiji Temple, one of the world's largest wooden structures. The statue sits in the middle of a room built just for it and not a whole lot bigger than it. Without fail, upon entering one's eyes are immediately drawn upward by the gargantuan size of the statue. Circling around the Buddha is a narrow cordoned walkway where the awestruck can see the entirety of it, viewing him from all sides. The sight is so captivating, it is tricky to navigate along the walkway's circular curve while at the same time keeping your eyes permanently riveted upward.

As I previously mentioned, eight months prior to this trip, Bob and Karen made this very same visit to Kyoto, then to Nara, with Glen and me. At that time I was seven months pregnant with Erin and looking remarkably like one of the world's biggest Buddhas myself. As the four of us entered this ancient wooden room where he sat, our eyes—suddenly beyond our control—zoomed upward to take in the immensity of his countenance. Dazed, we slowly began to circle along with the equally dazed crowd, our necks awkwardly craned backwards.

As we rounded the far side of the circle, I suddenly got a cramp in my neck. Ouch! I pulled my head forward to get some relief and as my eyes lowered, I perceived a group of Japanese tourists standing around me. In my captivation with Buddha, I had not noticed them before now. To my bewilderment, not a single one of them was looking up. In fact, all of them were looking down ... *at my midsection!* With their eyes glued to my belly, it had apparently freed up their jaws to unhinge themselves as they now hung open to alarming dimensions. Indeed, even without a ruler, I could see their toothy caverns were plenty wide enough for a small woodland creature to enter, turn around, and exit. Also, I noticed, the people were shaking their heads and murmuring; opining something about disbelief.

"So," I wanted to scream, "you've never seen a preggers lady before? *And*, you're thinking you've never seen one before that looks as preggers as this one? Plus, you're also thinking I'm a whole lot bigger than usual ... and this is supposed to send me to hell in a hand basket? In conclusion, just what am I supposed to do about my bigger than usual preggersness *while* you're thinking? Bonk your unfeeling heads together?"

Anybody got a problem with that?

Golly, it wasn't like I could just pull in my preggersness. Standing there all alone like a bloated capital P, and feeling more memorable than I ever hoped to be (thank goodness I had decided against wearing my maternity Speedo!), I was left with the only spur-of-the-moment recourse I could come up with. I bowed a graceful low bow. Okay, so it was a lame not-such-a-low bow, but it was the best I could do with the circumference of my circumstances. More than anything, I wished I had the nerve to ask their startled faces if they didn't recognize me. Yes, *me*, their Buddha's look alike blond cousin from across the big pond?

But, I didn't, dadgummit. But, I should have.

Ponderously Preggers Peggy, Mortified Lady.

THE LAST MORNING of that trip—before Bob, Karen, Glen and I were to board the Shinkansen to be whizzzed back to Tokyo—we decided to do some last minute buying. Flushed with the fun of being in such a shoppertunisitic paradise, we dashed into a shop in search of glorious things, unaware of the time slipping by.

> "Veni, Vidi, Visa –
> we came, we saw,
> we went shopping."
> Jan Barrett

As the clerk wrapped our treasures, we glanced at a clock and were startled to learn it was nearing lunchtime. My, how the time had flown! Jeepers, creepers, we had a train to catch. But, knowing ourselves as we did—and that number one on our most important to-do list was to never fail to eat ... and to eat a lot ... *and always exactly on schedule*— we experienced the mutual sag of a noontime weakness. Politely, Glen asked the clerk if there might possibly be a nice honorable restaurant nearby where we could have our mid-day meal (a loaded question if ever there was one). "Well, there certainly was!" she assured us, honorably.

With the whirl of a phone dial, she called a cab. In no time at all, it pulled up to her shop where she graciously opened the taxi doors and politely beckoned her kimono clad arm for us to enter. A thousand really deep and choice bows later, she finally allowed us to depart. We were off. As we settled, then resettled our quadruple Caucasian bulk into the narrow seats, we marveled at how "special" the taxi not only looked, but felt, outfitted like it was in dazzling white resplendent linen. In fact, it looked remarkably like the one from NHK! The starched pleats outlining the edges of the seats, as well as the extra-dapper driver, should have been a warning, but we failed to clue into it as we were so wrapped up in the Kyoto-ness of it all. After all, wasn't everything special in Kyoto?

Twelve minutes into the ride, the taxi pulled up to a building. It was as old, sophisticated, and lovely as the ancient temples we had so recently toured. Strangely, there was no sign overhead announcing the name of the place. Again, we should have taken the hint, but in the flush of it all, we did not. Nor did it register anywhere in our touristy faculties that the taxi, which we'd just paid for, was considerably more expensive than any we had ever taken in our four collective lives. Hmmmm ....

Immediately from out of the genkan came a bevy of exquisite kimono-clad beauties. Even we klutzes recognized instantly that we were in the midst of Japanese grandeur. I gulped. Bob, Karen, and Glen gulped, too. From out of the group came an elegantly mannered woman dressed in a quietly amazing silk kimono. Clearly, she in her hushed splendor, was the grand matron; stateliness sublime. Bowing deeply, then gesturing with her out-stretched hand, she ushered us through a refined and fabulous hallway to an even more refined and fabulous private tatami room. Inside were a small table, four silk-covered zabuton, an ikebana arrangement and a lovely cherry blossom scroll hanging in the tokonoma. Believe me, there was not a stuffed dead possum in sight. The place looked beautiful with a capital B. The place looked expensive with a capital X!

In the West, when one encounters a place with polish and propriety it is often overly decorated. In the East, it is the very lack of embellishment that labels it as tasteful. The room's simple minimalism spoke volumes. We were looking at the very embodiment of shibui.

About then it hit us. After repeated failed attempts at recognizing the previous red flags, we were now finally, concomitantly, reading them loud and clear. Oh, m'gosh! We were pitifully out of our league here. Way, way over our heads. But, this far into it, there was no escape.

Bob, you may recall, was in his first year of teaching (really low salary), and Glen was a young army civilian and father-of-two-plus-one-in-the-oven, earning just over a miserly $5000 per year. While on this trip, we four had pretty much blown what meager wads we had, spending almost all the rest of our remaining yen in the shop only minutes before.

What to do? It felt eerily as if we had just won the Wheel of Misfortune. In fact, even worse than that! Instead of being stuck with someone like Vana White, we were stuck with Japan's Grace Kelly, and were now trapped inside her ancient, unembellished-but-first-class establishment. There was nothing to do but muddle through. Perhaps, just perhaps, the best thing was to simply enjoy the experience and not prematurely dwell on the consequence. Yes, absorb it while it lasted for this was more posh than we'd ever again see in our lifetimes. Besides, if we successfully played our pretense, they'd never find out about our plebeian roots! Would they? Well, would they?

By now we had sunken into the voluptuously silken zabuton and were being hostessed over by the gracious courtly matron and her team of flawless maidens. Real honest-to-goodness (not artificial scent from a bottle) apple-imbued oshibori were proffered with which we wiped our hands, the ones now sweating more than usual, while tea was poured into cups that were surely on loan from the national museum. The sumptuousness was intoxicatingly brain numbing.

No menu appeared from which to either order what we liked or to *determine what we could pay for!* To have had such a helpmate would have been beneath the elevated sensibilities of the establishment. Besides, if you had to ask, you were in the wrong place. We were. And we needed to ask. But instead, the four of us sat in studied silence, mentally tabulating just what percentage of our yearly salaries we would soon be swallowing.

The food began arriving. It was over-the-top artistically displayed (as only the over-the-top aesthetic Japanese can do), and was served on dishes which had obviously been intended for the Imperial Family, but now somehow got waylaid to our table. Each delicacy looked like food we thought was familiar. The first bite told us otherwise. Glory be! It was manna from the Heavenly Host, Shangri-la and Beulah Land all rolled up together. Chew by succulent chew, we ascended to epicurean paradise.

There was not a drop of butter in anything!

About mid-meal, as the rest of us were lost in our private ruminations, Karen glanced at her watch. Holy moley, we were running late! Our train was to leave within the hour and we still needed to get to the station ... wherever that was. But, time in this kind of gentility was hallowed; not the time of the universe where ordinary Vienna sausage consuming people dwelled. As composed as he could be, Glen, our linguistically adept spokesman who had suddenly developed an uncontrollable twitch in one eye, courteously explained to Grace K., our stately matron-san, that we needed to wrap things up and get ourselves to the station pronto!

"But wait," proclaimed the alarmed-but-stately matron-san, "you cannot leave now. There is dessert yet to be eaten!"

"But wait," *we* replied, "there is also a train to be caught!"

The woman, comprehending finally ... and eloquently ... our growing boorish hysteria, whirled around in one final display of decorum-perfecto, and bustled gracefully out of the room. Within moments she returned, carrying a splendiferous lacquered tray, the finale of our feast. On it were four black matchless pottery bowls. With ultimate grace, despite her rush, she kneeled like a swan and suavely placed one bowl in front of each of us.

The bowls were sublime. I was stunned, dazed, spellbound by their beauty, a quality I had never before dreamed existed. The sides were straight rather than curved, and molded out of thick, unevenly textured clay, subtly revealing the stroked imprints of the artist's fingers. They were the size of a large cereal bowl, but very deep, and the blackness of their ebony surfaces was as rich and dull as coal dust. Of course, each had been handmade and, of course, each was an original, worth as much as the entire furnishings of both our duplexes, including Glen's new recliner.

I looked at my bowl wondering whether or not I, a mere mortal, was allowed to touch it. There at the bottom rested dessert: two strawberries. Two *perfect* strawberries. Flawless, stellar! They were art; incomparable to any strawberries that had ever before graced the race of man.

We four, of the loaded-banana-split-decadent-brownie-bring-it-on-dessert credo, sat there in silence, hypnotized. We had never before seen anything so simple, so beautiful; so beautifully simple.

But, the time! The train! We were once again pulled out of our aesthetic stupor. We had to leave and we had to do it now! But, alas, being the bumbling lummoxes that we were, how did we exit in the presence, the throes, of such preeminence?

We looked across the table at each other, nodded an unspoken consensus, and each stuffed his two matchless strawberries into his bourgeois mouth like the crass, common-sense plebs that we were.

The bill, the bill, *the danged dreaded bill!* In our astonishment over the strawberries, and then our urgency to down them, we had forgotten about the bill! Bring it now, please, please, and could you call a taxi while you're at it?

In the blink of an eye, a small exquisitely carved tray appeared with the tally brush-stroked by the pen of a master calligrapher onto handmade rice paper.

Never in the history of all our combined math problems had we seen a total with so many digits.

Of course, we didn't have the yen. Of course, we'd have to save up for the next thirty years to *ever* have that much extra yen ... or worst case scenario, our great-grandchildren would be stuck paying it off with a government grant. Left with no recourse, while laboring under the strain of maintaining some semblance of dignity, Glen, with a new quaver in his voice plus his twitching eye, explained to Her Elegance that we did not have the funds to cover the bill. He promised, notwithstanding, that he would send the money by mail as soon as we returned to Tokyo.

Could anything have looked more unseemly, bogus, cheap-white-trash?

The Queen of Grace was unmoved. Standing before us as erect and serene as what we hoped would be our Statue of *Liberties,* she cast down her epicanthic eyes and immediately agreed with the utmost of graciousness to our request ... to our plea. You know the one. It was plastered all over our pale, ignoble kissers.

Being the class act that she was, she would never have dreamed of causing us to lose face any more than she would have wished to lose her own. With a look of implicit trust, she extended a perfectly perfect business card, guided us out of the restaurant, and beauteously assisted us into an awaiting taxi. For all she knew, there was a fat chance in hell she'd ever hear from us clods again.

The taxi roared through the streets of Kyoto and up to the train station. As in all good Japanese train stations, there were stairs. Stairs upon stairs upon stairs, all connecting the various platforms. That day, wouldn't you know, Dame Fortune was smiling on us, for our train was to depart from the most very top, most very distant platform! Bob and Karen ran ahead yelling over their shoulders they would somehow hold the train for us while I, with Glen's assist, dragged and heaved my prodigious paunch upward. As I laboriously climbed, I could hear passengers all around us placing bets. One thousand yen had it that I would have an on-stair delivery.

Anyone who has ever climbed Mt. Cletus with Danny DeVito in their belly can be sympathetic to my plight. I was in agony, and well into an adrenaline overload. By the time we reached Bob and Karen, I was nearly unhinged with the being-on-time crazies. The relief at miraculously making it to our departure point before the train left, plus the solace of being released with our lives still intact from under that too-improbable-to-be-believed restaurant bill—the one which had we loaned it to Bangladesh would have turned that godforsaken place into Trump Tower—were too much. Like a traveling band of psychos, we began to ... what else, but ... giggle.

Giggling felt so good! So palliating! With it we could feel the tension of the last trauma begin to seep away. Our titters quickly turned to laughter, which in no time led to outright howling. So especially convulsed were the jubilant Karen and I, that we could no longer support ourselves. We collapsed to our knees onto the concrete platform and roared like unhinged nincompoops until our anxieties were spent. To the Japanese around us, we surely appeared to be possessed of the devil; especially Karen and her red hair, the exact color of the goosepimply obakke! Without a doubt, Karen was in the throes of publicly hexing me and my belly. In the minds of those onlookers, it made sense all over again. Yes, World War II was just what had been needed to rid the world of the likes of us.

What a shame they had failed. We were still among them.

"Victory goes
to the player
who makes the
next-to-the-last
mistake."
Savielly Grigorievitch Tartakower

EIGHTY-TWO

AFTER THE MULTIPLE faux pas we had made on that first trip with the Finks, we learned to not repeat them on our second trip with Mom and Daddy. Besides, a girl like Mom could only take just so many cultural blunders. Our week in Kyoto ended on a high unscathed note and we returned to Tokyo. There was no question we had gained a truer appreciation for what ancient really meant, something we callow Americans thought we knew all about if we owned a one hundred year old dish.

We had tasted antiquity and were eager for more. Within days we were packing our bags again. This time my parents and I were heading for Hong Kong and Bangkok. Glen, however, would stay home. Not only did he have a job to return to, but true to his word, he had sent the dreaded restaurant payment and was consequently still living a Spartan life, thriftily undoing the financial dent it had created. I, on the other hand, was a lucky duck. My dad was paying for this round.

Up until then I had thought of Japan as a poor country. Nothing prepared me for the poverty we found in Hong Kong. Refugees from northern China were everywhere, flooding the city and bringing nothing with them except more of the displaced, like themselves. With no means of survival, they were reduced to making "homes" on the steep, muddy, barren hillsides surrounding the teeming mass of the city.

Like Tokyo, Hong Kong was a place without space. Even the airport runway didn't get a break from the stinginess of the land. It was little more than a narrow strip. Without enough room to build a conventional runway, the clever—and not a little nutsy—Chinese engineers had fashioned one extending out into the bay like an elongated, stretched-out driveway heading straight out to the sea.

On this first flight to Hong Kong, with no knowledge of how the landing was accomplished, it was creepy beyond terrifying to watch from inside the plane as it suddenly began to descend, heading straight for the ocean. I had the window seat and was the favored one to have a perfect view of this insanity. My folks, thank goodness, were unaware; Mom in her seat applying a fresh layer of lipstick, while Daddy brushed off the crumbs from a snack.

I looked out my window. Mother of God! Nothing down below looked like something we could land upon! Nothing appeared to be solid, as in the kind of nonporous, impenetrable solid we would need for a touchdown! The plane plunged closer and closer to our ocean landing as I stared in disbelief, in utter horror! No joke! This was no nightmare. This was a sunny afternoon daymare! Every prayer I ever learned, all faiths included, flew from my gaping mouth as I prepared to meet my maker. There were only seconds left. With my eyes glued on the rapidly approaching water, I was certain our lives—our perfectly okay Midwestern lives—would soon be over.

Then in the midst of the hysteria, I thought I saw the tiniest glimmer of … what was that? A ribbon? Yes, a ribbon, and it was lying of all places, right on top of the water. For Pete's sake, it looked like a boardwalk for promenading bugs. Could we, it suddenly occurred to me—yes, *we*, be those bugs? Well, if so, like Matt, I can tell you I certainly did not feel like their boss!

With a whump we landed upon that ridiculous insect footpath, bouncing upon it like the repeated dribbles of a very large basketball. Finally, on the last dribble when the rubber tires finally held tight to the concrete ribbon, my heart resumed beating. I looked out the window. Water, water, nothing but water lapping, it seemed, right up to the sides of the plane! I whispered one last hope, my stockpile of ecclesiastical appeals now pretty much depleted, that the pilot knew the meaning of "staying on the straight and narrow."

While the folks in the center aisle were as unperturbed as a lullaby, we unfortunates in the window seats had just taken up residence in Berserkville. Ripped-out tufts of head hair blanketed the seats where we had so recently messed our pants.

> "Flying is hours and hours
> of boredom sprinkled
> with a few seconds
> of sheer terror."
> Gregory "Pappy" Boyington

So much for passenger information on China Air! They had just made a deplorable first impression.

> "Avoid airlines that have
> anyone's first name
> in their titles—
> like Bob's International—
> or Air Fred."
> Miss Piggy

More impressions followed. On the hillsides and rooftops surrounding Hong Kong were hundreds and hundreds of flimsy shacks fabricated from discarded flattened cardboard boxes and oddly shaped pieces of corrugated metal. So tightly crammed together, the refugees had to zig-zag crazily down the steep, muddy hillsides as they wove around each hovel. Open cooking fires were everywhere; a downright invitation to conflagration as the winds blew glowing embers onto the neighboring paper walls. And if fires didn't do them in, the rain did; cardboard walls quickly dissolving under the persistent monsoonal downpours. Both disasters were a regular occurrence.

I was speechless. I was heartbroken. Never had I imagined an existence of such wretchedness, such squalor. Minnesotans, living in their stalwart brick homes surrounded by spacious rolling lawns and fertile fields, could not have imagined this kind of need. All of a sudden the idea of spending money for trinkets and gee-gaws for myself that would only further clutter up my life, vanished. Instead, I needed to find a way to help.

None of us had ever before been mobbed by children; by throngs of dirty, begging, very young children. And, it didn't help one bit that in their smudged little hands were not ice cream cones or candy—but instead chicken feet! Chicken feet complete with toes and talons and all dyed an outrageously glaring tangerine orange. What for crying out loud was there to eat on a chicken's foot, and why did somebody have to go to all the trouble of making them orange? Really now, was a dye job going to enhance them? Weren't chicken feet already beyond ugly; like putting earrings on rats? No, iridescent orange was not the face lift I would have given a chicken foot.

But, even in my skepticism, I could see the children loved them, gnawing to their hearts content, their lips and tongues by association also an outlandish orange. Game as I had always been for most any new taste treat, this one, howbeit, rendered sterile within me any sense of sensory adventure. Even badger stew seemed lovelier. For the Chinese, I guessed it boiled down to not being wasteful, as if chicken feet grew on trees! (Hmmm ... orange trees?)

Despite it being atrociously bizarre, I could nonetheless understand it. You see, I was also economical, and back in Austin we had the Hormel Meat Packing Company. There they bragged about using almost every last bit of the hog, even though they were mystified over the one unused, nettlesome, remaining part. They remedied this profligate squandering by naming their magazine *The Squeal*. Thus, one man's chicken foot, I deduced, was another man's oink.

UPON OUR RETURN to Tokyo, I told Glen of the anguish we had seen. Without hesitation we decided to enroll in Foster Parents' Plan. Through them, we sponsored a young boy and his family who were living in Hong Kong in one of those paper boxes. In the coming years, in a small, but significant way, we changed this family's life, making sure he and his siblings would attend school and be watched over.

In time, the Chinese government took over the sponsorship of the hillside refugees. When this happened, Foster Parents Plan had to leave the country. With their departure, we turned to World Vision so we could continue to help. Now, forty-five years and more children than I can count later, we continue to support them throughout the world. I chuckle as I recall one such youngster from Bangladesh. We began his sponsorship when he was only a toddler. His first photo showed him in a diaper. His most recent photo showed a fully grown man sporting a moustache!

AFTER FOUR HEAVY-HEARTED days in Hong Kong, where the three of us worked at having fun, Mom, Daddy and I flew to Bangkok. Little did I suspect then that one day I would actually be living there. Wow, my family in Siam! (But, then, that's another story; another book.) This time around, I was so hopelessly unenlightened that upon deplaning, I began looking around for Popsicle people ... you know, the kind who are stuck together. Chang and Eng! Oddly, no Siamese twins showed themselves anywhere. One more urban legend down the drain.

Certainly Bangkok was exotic, truly remarkable in its uniqueness, but rather than focusing on it, I was counting the days until I could return home to my little boys and new baby girl. I know, I'm just like that. Take a down-homer like me on a world fling and all she can think about is, well, down home, where her heart is.

There was, nevertheless, one strong memory I have of that city. It involved my dad.

369

On the last day of our Thailand visit, Daddy awoke in the hotel with the realization there was a strong chance he and Mom might not need his suitcase stash of survival food. Things had gone remarkably well thus far. They had both been well fed, never knowing a single moment of hunger induced weakness, thereby leaving his collection of canned goods intact, still untouched. Perhaps it was time to release himself from his security. While Mom and I slept, a plan began formulating in Daddy's mind. Bundling the Spam, Vienna sausages, smoked oysters and crackers under his arm, he tip-toed out of the room and set off for the nearest market.

Gene McLaughlin, professional merchant, had never purchased anything in his life without cash. It was the only way his commercial world functioned. But this, now, was different. He wasn't going to use money; he was going to trade goods. Unsure of just how to do this, and feeling edgy as all get out, he selected the first shop he came to and abashedly went on in. Once inside the door, however, all trepidation flew out the window when he spotted a perfectly resplendent display of wooden elephants. Never having given much thought to elephants—even the resplendent kind—until he saw these beauties, he now realized they were the very thing he needed to perk up his basement recreation room back in Austin. Imagine, up until that minute, he hadn't even known he needed a resplendent elephant. Just shows you how a soiree in Siam could alter a guy's perspective, as well as getting him in the decorating mood.

Gene picked up the biggest elephant in the lot and carried it over to the proprietor. With a grunt he laid the over-sized woodcarving on the counter along with his bag of treasures, making sure to get the man's attention. Then reaching in, he dramatically withdrew a single can of Spam, being extra mindful of prominently displaying the side of the can which showed a picture of its hammy contents. In the palm of his hand it sat in all its tinny, dazzling splendor. Teasing the manager like a seasoned stripper (but then why not, he thought grinning to himself, he was married to one!), he very slowly pulled out another Spam can, the gamble he had in mind now rattling his unsure nerves. *He* knew how delectable these meaty morsels were, *but did this Siamese?*

Little did Daddy know that Spam, that pink palette of potted pork, was known and loved the world over! The clerk took one look at the over-salted, trans-fatted, mystery-meated ham and negotiations began at once. Within minutes, they were finished. Two bartered Spam cans later, Daddy walked out of the shop with a big smile on his face and a teak pachyderm under his arm.

"A supplementary bulletin has been issued
from the Office of Fluctuation Control,
The Bureau of Edible Condiments
(including soluble and indigestible fats,
as well as glutinous derivatives),
and the correction of the Washington, D.C. Directive 943456201,
which concerned the fixed price of groundhog meat.
It should have read ground hog meat."
Bob and Ray

Gene's stash was now markedly lighter. Looking around, his eyes were next drawn to a shop across the street. Brass cutlery! Thirty minutes later he owned a full set of fruit forks and hors d'oeuvre knives, and no smoked oysters. Next the Vienna sausages found a new home in a marble statue shop. What a day! What deals! What stories to tell at the next Rotary meeting! Already Gene was mentally sketching out the kind of two-by-four plywood shelf he'd put up in the basement to display his exotic loot, all of which had cost him not a single baht. For all he knew, His Majesty, the King of Siam Himself, displayed the very same prizes on his own two-by-four plywood recreation room shelf. Rock on, Gene!

Later that night at three dinner tables across Bangkok, platters of Spam, smoked oysters and Vienna sausages were devoured as three foxy merchants regaled their families with three different versions of how cleverly they had, that very day, taken advantage of a lame-brained foreigner. Copiously they patted themselves on their own backs while laughing mockingly at how dimwitted that dough-faced, dullard-blockhead was. Imagine! The guy thought the value of these ambrosial, gourmet delicacies was in the same monetary ball park as their paltry teak elephants, brass cutlery and marble statues! What a schmuck!

At the same time, Mom and I sat around our table and listened adoringly to Daddy's version of *his* wiliness, as he regaled us with the same shrewd story while patting *himself* copiously on *his* back. How totally clueless were those unworldly peasants thinking their exquisite handmade treasures were equal in value to his cheap canned meats! What schmucks!

Gene, Gene, The Bamboozler Machine. Viva free trade!

The good news was that the venerated hunter-gatherer-trader prowess of the four crafty men was significantly renewed in the eyes of their wives and children. That was always a good thing. Yet, it must be said that the story did not end there, for inasmuch as the Thai families enjoyed their meals of unidentifiable by-products—consuming them all in one gulp and ending it there—forty-five years later, I still have the dumb American's treasures. So, who, indeed, was the fox?

"The reverse side also
has a reverse side."
Japanese proverb

EIGHTY-THREE

WHEN JEFF TURNED five, his life changed dramatically. This birthday meant he would no longer attend Musashino Chuo Yochien, his Japanese nursery school, but would instead move up to first grade in the Green Park Department of Defense Dependent's School. With just one flip of a calendar day, he had shifted from the threshold of one school culture to another. In every respect, his days would be starkly different. In fact, so different he would have to rewind himself back to zero, for he was leaving behind his identification as a Japanese school boy. Ahead was a new way of living with a different language, friends, supplies, lunches, clothes, desks, haircuts, toilets, lessons and rules.

He would, also, no longer need his own name stamp, washcloth, towel and toilet paper, and he would not wear a uniform. In other words, without having a clue what to expect, his world was pretty much turned upside down. Unfortunately, this abrupt transfiguration set him on a path of highly unpredictable expectations. As his life unfolded, Jeff followed this pattern through nine different schools in six different countries, all happening before he ever went off to college. Like the honey bucket crew and the kerosene delivery men—only with a new baffling twist—he had one name for every miserable one of those new school starts ... "Bewilderment R Us."

Looking back, Jeff would fondly remember his time in yochien, for not only had he learned to speak Japanese and to be Japanese, but he had also learned how to urinate in a wooden box along with the companionship

372

of his entire class. That skill paled, however, when compared to his really big learning experience. As it turned out, yochien was where Jeff made his first stab at dabbling in American capitalism. There on the dirt-packed playground, he had set up his version of a nursery school Ponzi scheme. It all began with selling tickets to any child who wished to go down the slide.

Get out! Like didn't the slide belong to them? And, besides, its thrills were minimal, for the thing was made of cement and offered nothing in the hair-raising-ride department!

Ignoring these irrelevant facts, (speed, as it turned out, not being a consideration because none of the kids knew, Jeff included, that slides—honest to good real metal slides—slid fast!), my firstborn forged ahead with his lucrative game plan. Adeptly plucking leaves off the playground bushes to use as tickets, he gave one to each daredevil rider.

Oh, what fun! Up the steps they marched like little mountain climbers with the leaves gripped tightly in their hands, then roughly, painfully they scraped downward on the slide that could have grated coconut. Like inordinately short, but principled consumers, the thrill-seekers dutifully paid their leaves back to Jeff as they completed their pumice-coated, snail-paced rides. By the end of each recess, the pockets on Jeff's uniform were bulging with leaves.

Did he take his wampum to the nearest bank, you ask? Well, not exactly. Instead, as playtime wound down, he would—in a grand display of nouveau riche-ness while his devoted bottom-abraded customers looked on—throw all the leaves into the air with a flourish as he made his final excoriating victory lap downward.

Okay, so he was four, not Warren Buffet. Nonetheless, after enough of these blood-letting episodes, Jeff did buy stock in a wax paper company, as well as shares in a local blood bank.

> "He without benefit of scruples,
> his fun and money
> soon quadruples."
> Ogden Nash

FINALLY, ALAS, THE day came when this beautiful—and profitable—nursery school life came to a resounding close. Jeff was on his way to a new beginning! On a memorable September morning, he lined up with his Asahi Court buddies to wait for the U.S. Army school bus. I crossed my fingers that I had prepared him for the extraordinary changes ahead. Along side the children and their moms, I stood with three-month-old Erin in my arms and three-year-old Matt (who now as the only remaining child in the neighborhood found himself severed from the pack), clung to me, his one true abiding friend. The big pea-soup green military school bus pulled up. Jeff boarded the steep steps, grinning so wide I feared his lips would snap.

That's when I remembered something I'd forgotten to tell him! Shucks, I thought I'd covered every important detail: from now on he would perform bathroom business privately (lonely, I know), he would cease and desist from any more Ponzi playground schemes, and finally, Jeff should not expect me to wear Kelly green crocheted accessories to his new PTA. But no, I had overlooked one critical, one, oh, so obvious thing. Setting off after the bus, I staggered down the street with tiny Erin crushed against my chest and Matt clinging like a young orangutan to my left leg. Frantically searching for Jeff's face in a window, I yelled, "Jeff, don't forget to NOT take off your shoes!"

It was a defining moment in his on-going education.

The time had flown by so quickly. Only two weeks before, in lieu of a pint-sized graduation prom, I had invited the entire nursery school to visit our home. Besides being the neighborly thing to do—and certainly in keeping with my international humanitarian mission—I thought it might be interesting for the children to see how Americans lived. Of course, this was utterly bogus from the get-go because, well, we weren't exactly living in America and, therefore, were not by any stretch of the imagination living like Americans really live, if you know what I mean!

Undeterred, I opened our doors to everyone. Led down the long dusty road by the principal and teachers, Jeff, Matt (who was also now enrolled in yochien), and the children in their matching bowl hair cuts, navy blue smocks, and chafed bottoms paraded in a stretched-out line from school to Asahi Court.

My hope was for this to be my moment, my contribution, my opportunity to teach these little people about our American culture. The experience was very important for it would be their first lesson in foreign relations. Well, actually their third, for the first and second were Jeff and Matt, respectively.

Fully dedicated to the cause, I went beyond good sense in polishing up all four rooms of our duplex, fussing over every minute detail. You know, fluffing up the dispassionate-cotton-batting-engorged pheasant, polishing the quail-egg-accident-waiting-to-happen granite stairs, wiping down the majestic wanna-be-real-buffalo-hide recliner, buffing to a blinding luster the brass chrysanthemum on the space heater (with the hope that all would take note of our close relationship with their Emperor), and making sure the cap was screwed securely on the 3-in-1 All-Purpose oil can.

"Housework
can kill you
if done right."
Erma Bombeck

Then to permanently imprint the event on their puerile psyches, I went one step further. I baked cookies. Chocolate chip cookies! This was big; the real American deal. Keep in mind we were in a country where no one owned an oven and where cookies were not cookies at all, but rather rice crackers. If nothing else left a lasting impression, our finger-lickin', mouth-watering American cookies would surely clinch the deal.

I met the children at the door. Leaving their shoes outside, they streamed into the living room. Surely, I thought, they would have a look around and be duly impressed by the splendor: the wringer washer prominently on display, along with the dryer that blew only cold air which of course they didn't know and I wasn't telling—but they were not. Instead they made a communal bee line for Erin.

She was sitting in her stroller with cuteness exuding from her every baby pore like fizz from a shaken pop bottle. Wheee! She was as delighted to see them as they were to see her. As you can guess, she, naturally, stole the show. I could have saved myself one heck of a lot of work. Not one of those children cared a lick about our house, although the cookies *were* a hit. What they really cared about was our little girl. Actually, if truth be told, it was not so much about her as a person, as much as it was about her as a *white haired* person. Up until then, they had not realized there were two people on their planet with white silk growing out of their heads—Jeff *and* his baby sister.

The kids were on Erin's head like cous on cous, as dozens of little fingers stroked, petted, caressed and palpated her luminous locks. How she came out of that encounter with her sparkle still sparkly, to say nothing of not developing early onset male pattern baldness, was a wonder.

"Now someone's invented a wig
to wear to the supermarket.
It has curlers in it."
Unknown

NO TALE OF Japanese children would be complete without a discussion of the Mongolian birth spot. As you've already guessed, this is strictly an Asian thing because it's called "Mongolian." It's like this. When a Japanese baby is born, he has a bluish spot at the base of his spine. Unaware Westerners, seeing this for the first time, are immediately distraught over what appears to be a bruise, and they wonder at what monstrosity of a person could have done such an unspeakable thing to a newborn. The truth is that for the Japanese, this mark is like the kind of assurance a consumer gets from the Underwriters Laboratory tag on a new hair dryer. A mokohan, (moh-koh-hahn, Mongolian birth spot), is a guarantee their baby is pure Asian. Well, as pure as anybody can be in the ceaseless rehashing of evolution, along with the medley of results from lonely, horny, genetically mish-mashed G.I.'s.

We Caucasians, of course, do not have such a mark because we are about as multifariously mix-bred, cross-fertilized and potpourried as a group of people can get. We know we will—indeed we *expect to*— produce variegated children. To be sure, ours is a game of genetic roulette. Take our family for instance who the Japanese could plainly see had obvious differences. There was Glen with his brown hair, me with my strawberry blond, Matt with his light brown, and Jeff and Erin who had been dipped head first into bleach. Why, the Japanese would have been aghast to hear my sister was a chestnut redhead, and my mom had coal black ringlets. Ringlets so corkscrew curly that when I was a teenager, I used to put them in large curlers to straighten them out so people would stop asking if a minstrel singer had given birth to us kids!

Gosh, the last thing I felt was offense at being called a dog, as Erin had on that first day home. We, of the sallow skins, were assuredly an amalgamation, and that was okay. Heck, we should have stressed the fact by simply naming our children Hodge, Podge and Goulash in recognition of their mixed ingredients! That's why being white was so much fun, didn't they see? Didn't they get it? No, they didn't. God forbid, nothing, nothing could have been worse for the Japanese than being that nail thing and turning out to *not* look like the rest of their society. In Japan, sleep was seldom lost over wondering how a child would look. He *would* have black hair. He *would* have brown eyes. He *would* be on the short side. He *would* grow up looking like all the other passengers on the train. Booorrrrring.

> "If I try to be
> like him,
> who will be
> like me?"
> Yiddish proverb.

When we kids wanted to look scary back in Austin, the first thing anybody did (as instinctive as robins building nests), was to pull their eyelids out at the far corners to make their eyes look slitty. We then accompanied the look with a spooky "ooooohing" sound. In Japan, but of course, the kids pulled their eyelids up and down to make their eyes look round, while accompanying the look with the very identical spooky "ooooohing" sound. No translation needed.

> "Prejudices
> save time."
> Robert Byrne

EIGHTY-FOUR

IN 1965, WHEN Erin was only two months old, Glen had the super marvelous idea that we should all go camping. *Camping in our car.* How dazzlingly splendid! You must understand that no one *NO ONE* in Japan in 1965 went camping in a car! Like, why in heaven's name would anyone who had enough money to buy a car (strongly hinting at the fact that they also had enough to buy a house—with beds in it), want to sleep in a car? The answer, of course, was it was just another balmy, goofy, lame-brained American idea.

Our car was, in fact, not a car at all. It was a 1960 Volkswagen Microbus, a quintessential vehicle for safari-like jaunts throughout Germany, Equatorial Africa, and the suburbs of Tokyo. I think we may have had the only Microbus in Kichijoji. Actually, I'd stake my life on it.

I wasn't even aware our bus was a status symbol until one day a blurb in the Japan Times newspaper told me so:

> "The Volkswagen car is a vehicle.
> It is one's friendly resonance box,
> and a medium mirroring one's
> life outlook. With it, we fall
> into love season has begun."

And, there you have it, a perfect description of our resonance box.

With the lure of the great outdoors beckoning Glen to the point where he could no longer resist, the rogue engineer in him drew up a design for a slide-in/

slide-out contraption of bookshelf-like plywood shelving upon which our family of five would sleep, stacked upon ourselves while falling into the love season has begun in the wilds of Japan. There was but one flaw in his otherwise seductive plan. Where were the wilds of Japan? And, did we really want to sleep stacked on top of each other in them?

Scratching his head in dismay, a hired carpenter sawed and nailed together our cubicle deathtrap motel. Glen, in the meantime, scoured maps in search of a secluded camp site. He found it on a beach in Chiba, a peninsula east of Tokyo. Hold on here. *Chiba?* For crying out loud, wasn't that the very same body of water in which we nearly drowned a few years earlier? How jim-dandy was that? This, without question, made the whole idea even more appealing to me. I could hardly contain my pleasure. *Not!*

Golly gee, the tantalizing enticement of nearly drowning all over again—only this time accompanied by our three children—was too swell to bear! But then, I chastised myself, such negative thinking should not get in the way of the debatable joys of our family stockpiling ourselves in stratified layers in our VW. Having figured out this bit of wisdom, I was nearly inconsolable with delight over the up-coming vacation.

Thus, floating in a cloud of tainted rapture, I set about the mission of preparing for our end ... er, adventure. This I did with uncompromising vigor, as I did not want to be labeled the most royal of all party poopers. I organized the food, bedding and clothing for five, and searched throughout the van's uncompromisingly tight quarters for tiny cubbies and niches in which it could all be stashed. Above all, this accomplishment was not made easier by Erin being so squeaky new born, and requiring those mountains of Curities—and everything else. The only cinchy thing was that her food source was me.

Peggy, Peggy, Baby Chuck Wagon Lady. Suck. Slurp.

When the Germans named their van a *micro* bus, they weren't kidding. Neither were they a little deceptive nor were they outright lying. Loud and clear it was right there in the title, "Micro!" As I painstakingly searched for just one more cranny or pigeonhole to stuff stuff into, something prompted me to look up the meaning of this word. Again my old friend Webster had it: "exceptionally little, abnormally small." Well, imagine that! The only thing the Nazis were ever truthful about.

Okay, so they told the gospel truth as far as its size, but nowhere whatsoever was there a mention in the Volkswagen handbook about a Microbus converting itself into a motorized boarding house. But then, Glen, being the innovative thinker he was, paid no heed to the limits of the interior. As for me, I would no more have thought of this than I would have thought of going grouse hunting, but then I had trouble thinking like Glen. He would surmount all obstacles by using this schematic: an almost five-year-old Jeff would have the most luxurious accommodations: the entire front bench driver's seat. Having just turned three, and loved as all get out, Matt was unfortunately still living under the on-going sentence of being the maligned middle child. Thus with his half, but-neither-way status, he would be sentenced to sleep on the floor of the bus, the most claustrophobic emplacement. Only inches above him would be his parents lying on a full-width shelf covering the entire center strata of the bus.

You must realize that for Matt this was an indecent risk. It had every potential of backfiring (even though he had at one time been the prince of this plight), further traumatizing the little lad to such a degree he could possibly spend the rest of his life never again sleeping on beds, but conversely on the floorboards beneath them. Good times!

To finalize Glen's master plan and get the most bang for his buck, Erin would sleep in her pink plastic bathtub on a special mini platform built over the hump of the rear engine compartment. In case you were not aware, it was our family—yes, us—who first introduced the submarine sandwich to Asia.

I'll have to admit that flawed as it was, there was a certain aesthetic flow to Glen's design. It certainly covered our basic sleeping needs, and it did put us in touch with nature. Being humble, I'm not certain that I should go so far as to claim this, but it, and it alone, could well have been the original inspiration for the later wildly popular Feng Shui, or at least I'm thinking it was darned close.

The entire back wall of the Microbus was a door that opened upward allowing full access to the motel, while doubling as a showy awning, a flamboyant plus in anybody's book. At the far back and under the floor was a smaller, narrower door that opened to the snugged-in, bolted-on engine below. Unlike any other vehicle on the road, the Microbus was unequivocally snub nosed. Nothing whatsoever stuck out in front—rather like me without a bra.

Without anything protruding beyond the front window, it certainly taunted the safety crash test ratings (if Hitler even had them), particularly so for the folks in the front seat. But then, the 1960s were the good old days before seatbelts, when the luckiest kid on the block was the one who got to sit in the front seat with his elbows propped up on the dashboard and his forehead pressed against the front window. Uh-huh that one, the very not so shatter-proof windshield. It was a wonder any of us had survived to our teenhoods.

We arrived in Chiba at mid-morning and spent the day playing on the deserted beach. In those days no Japanese went swimming on a beach, much as nobody went camping in their car. There was, as well, a dearth of private or public swimming pools, which I suppose explained the dearth in swimsuit sales. A beach was certainly not a place for recreation. It was simply a sandy rim ringing the edge of their country. This proved to be a good deal for us, however, because our camping site was empty, affirming I suppose, that we had found "the wilds." Along the sandy stretch there was no other living, breathing soul in sight except for the five of us, a few beached fishing boats, and some smatterings of debris here and there.

As the day progressed, I found to my surprise that I was having fun, really getting in the groove of this camping thing. I liked the hushed calm, the openness after the crush of Tokyo, and the smell of the sea air. As the late afternoon approached, I pulled up the big back door (creating that showy awning for no audience to admire), and began preparing dinner on the shelf where Glen and I would later sleep.

We ate a pleasant supper outdoors, sitting on the beach watching the sun go down, and discovered for the first time the taste and texture of sand in our food. (Dieticians would later promote this as "fiber.") Then while I took the boys for one last romp, Glen reconfigured our beach house. Once the boys were in their pajamas, I changed and nursed Erin. The children's day was over. I lovingly plugged them into their individual crevices, and in no time, kiddy sleep-sounds filled the bus.

By now a brilliant moon had risen over us as full, white and grainy as a giant sugar cookie. It was a spectacular evening. By golly, I had to admit the whole thing was amazing. Glen had miraculously pulled it off, finding the one spot in this sardine can of a country where we were utterly alone. In fact, it was near impossible to believe we were still in Japan. There was no traffic blaring, no crowd bedlam, no vendor horns, and no septic tanks being pumped. By george, no sound of anything except the gentle susurrus of the waves tussling with the sand in front of our metal timeshare.

Glen and I spread out two towels and reclined languorously upon them as we gazed up at the moon. We weren't exactly Debra Kerr and Burt Lancaster, but I, in a convoluted sort of way, thought we could have been, only on a lower—much, much lower—scale. As I lay there in my glorious solitude, I could not get my mind off of Debra. I wondered if, all spread out like that, she had stretch marks showing and if Burt cared that she did. Also, did Burt take partial responsibility for those stretch marks, as I was hoping Glen did because, as a matter of fact, they were the result of just this kind of thing ... two randy people lying nearly unclothed in the moonlight on a deserted beach? Furthermore, had cocoa butter helped Deb, and should I write her a fan letter asking?

But it was too exhausting, so I put it on a back burner and instead listened to the heavenly silence of the beach broken only by the sporadic chortlings of our sleeping cherubs, the end result of why I needed cocoa butter ... and Debra's counsel.

I don't know how long we lingered, enjoying the reverie, but eventually the time came for us to turn in and add our own sounds to the slumbering choir. I began to undress. Of course this was done outside the bus because, as you know, there wasn't a millimeter of space in which to perform such a maneuver inside. Plus we were completely alone out there on the beach, so there was no concern someone might ogle me. I was about to pull my pajamas over my nude body when a revelation struck.

"Glen," I exclaimed with an impulsivity that floored even me, "did you know that one of my deepest, darkest, most secret desires has always been to run naked on a beach?"

"Well, gee whiz, Peggy," he declared encouragingly, "*this* is *your* chance!"

With that instantaneous note of support, I dropped my pj's and sprinted off. Within seconds I was in total darkness guided only by the glow of the cookie moon and the feel of the sand under my frolicking feet. Oh, the jollification of it all! The hot, salty, humid air felt heavenly on my bare skin, every last inch of me exposed to the elements for the first time in my twenty-seven years of life.

About fifty yards down the beach, I thought I heard a sound. Silly nilly me, of course it was only my imagination. We were the only ones on this beach, right? But, no, there it was again. Stifling my panting, I cocked an ear as I sped along the water's edge. Yes, there it was again. A girl's giggle. And, it was getting nearer … and clearer.

Just then—as unanticipated as Jack the Stripper throwing open his trench coat and thereby, I would add, getting his pickle into a pickle—two people came into focus. A young man and woman, clearly lovers, strolling hand in hand towards me. Like a lightning bolt out of a still sky, I was nearly upon them, rushing straight at their serenity in what could be a nasty international incident if I didn't do something fast.

If ever there was a time for quick thinking, this was it. Just as I was about to collide with them—flattening them all the way through to Iowa—I veered my unclothed body with an awesome agility off to the right, barely brushing past the shoulder of the astonished, scared-shitless man. Slowing down enough to make an abrupt turn, I then swirled around, circling them in the rear with my rear, and dashed back in the direction in which I had come, once more passing them, and vanishing into the night. Talk about being caught with your pants down ….

Even in my haste, I could see they were paralyzed with terror. Had they just seen what they had just seen—a white, ghostly apparition, untamed, au naturel, Jill-the-Ripper-serpent-of-dread-and-damnation—appearing out of nowhere in the gauzy, phosphorescent light of the moon? Or was it simply the delirium engendered by their blinding love for one another? I didn't see their departure from the beach, because I was busy with my own, but I'll bet to this day that no one— NO ONE—has ever believed their story of the blond, bare-assed, beach banshee. They probably ended up having to marry each other because no one else in town would date such crackpots. Upon later reflection I decided it was really quite a wonderful thing I had done, forging their lives together like that.

BECAUSE OUR VIRGIN camping experience had been such a success, some weeks later we tried it again. This time we drove to Yamanakako, a lake fifty miles east of Tokyo. It was pitch dark when we finally found a vacant area where we could park our friendly resonance box. There was no empty beach this time, but in the inky blackness we found a scruffy patch of land with nothing on it but tall grass and weeds. We figured it was an okay spot because clearly no one was living on it, as far as we could see. Freeing ourselves of this concern, we settled in and in no time at all I had dinner prepared. By all indications this was a pretty close re-run of our previous Microbus dream vacation only this time we experienced the joys of dirt in our food instead of sand.

That night we drifted off to the musical bombinations of landlocked insects rather than the sloshing of ocean waves. Before threading myself into my cubicle shelf—once again empathizing with how a bulky letter felt when it was forced into a narrow mail slot—I made the wise decision not to go streaking. Soon we were all fast asleep.

During the early morning hours, Glen awakened me. With his finger to his lips he motioned for me to not speak, but rather to listen. There, outside the Microbus, was a strange sound—a swishing, rustling, whacking noise we could not identify. With as much stealth as he could marshal in the wedged confinement of our plywood trap, Glen wormed his way downward, quietly opened the back door, and surreptitiously oozed out. If you didn't know better, you'd have thought a Volkswagen had just given birth to a nonterrestrial.

Looking around, Glen found to his astonishment a wizened old man, bent over and with a short handled sickle, cutting the grasses around our bus. He had finished one side and was coming around the front end of the bus.

At the same time, and with equal stupefaction, the man looked up and saw Glen. With untoward composure, he bowed deeply and repeatedly resembling the simple mechanics of a bobble-head doll. Then the man began to speak. It turned out that our visitor was the owner/farmer of the plot of land we were squatting upon. He had arisen that morning expecting it to be like any other morning. Instead he found a big gray box with a snub nose and four wheels parked in his field.

Sneaking down to investigate, the farmer had peered into the darkened windows. There to his shock he discovered a sandwich built of sleeping people. We'll never know if the compacted sight of us brought amusement to his heart or compassion to his soul, but it must have been the latter for it showed in his eyes. How greatly pathetic we must have seemed … so far from home, indeed half a world away … and homeless! Burdened with such misfortune, the kindly farmer had taken it upon himself to make our stay with him as pleasant as possible by creating a lawn of sorts around our metallic homeless home.

Glen, who spoke beautiful Japanese, returned the farmer's bows, stepping forward in a friendly exchange of introductions. He explained the layers within the box were his family and that we were on a camping adventure. Following this Glen offered a sincere apology for coming onto private land, clarifying we were not aware we had done so. To further prove his goodwill, Glen proceeded to thank the farmer by presenting him (like father-in-law, like husband!), with some of our canned food. The delighted farmer assured Glen we were not a problem, his face barely containing the pleasure he now felt upon receiving the foreign cuisine, a dream beyond his rural culinary machinations. Then bowing with a multitude of bobble-headed sayonaras, he marched off to show his wife, a sickle in one hand, Dinty Moore Beef Stew and Hormel Chili in the other.

An hour later we were up and dressed. With the back door flipped up in its awesome awning mode, I began changing baby Erin as she lay on the center shelf. I pulled a tiny knit shirt over her head and folded a fresh Curity around her bottom. Just as I was about to push the diaper pin through the diaper, a strong hand shot out from behind me, reached around to the front and grabbed my wrist. I was stunned, the bejeesus scared right out of me! I had not realized anyone was even there.

Nonplussed, I bolted around in alarm there to discover our friend the farmer, his family and all their neighbors standing behind me like an audience at a sideshow. Apparently every last one of them had decided they wanted to witness first hand the unusual caravan containing the even more unusual tribe the farmer told them was sleeping in his field. As I had been singing and cooing to Erin, they had, unbeknownst to me, silently crept up from behind. There they now stood in a tight congregation, their eyes nervously flitting from one Keener face to the other. Never before had they witnessed anything like this. Up-close and personal they were seeing for the first time the sort of folks who had won the war.

But, could it be? Could this pitiful cluster of vagabond whey-faces—none of whom looked like the other—really be the mighty victors who had forced their country to its knees? Say it wasn't so! Oy veh! How embarrassing.

As I stared at them, I realized all their gazes had switched from us to Erin. Surely if the rest of us had not impressed them positively, she was now in the process of winning them over. There she lay on our plywood bed, looking as close to angelic as any babe they had ever seen on a plywood bed or could have ever imagined seeing on a plywood bed. She was ethereally white from the crown of her silken head to the tips of her lovely toes, verily a gold standard for seraphims ... or was it cherubims?

But then, in a cruel twist of fate, I abruptly realized this very adoration of Erin was the thing now driving the delicate situation. Any infatuation they were now feeling for her, as well as any sympathy they may have felt for the rest of us gypsies, had taken a decided turn when they saw my hand going straight towards the seraphim/cherubim with a huge, sharp, steel pin. In their eyes, I was about to run her through.

The hand continued to hold mine in a firm, unrelenting grip. Then in a flash, it grabbed the pin from my fingers. Looking up, I saw the face of the farmer distorted in grievous alarm. That was the moment I got it. Finally, I understood. It wasn't that we Keeners were savages. It was that Japanese babies wore pinless diapers!

The most popular brand of diapers at that time was descriptively named "My Pee" (get that, *my* pee, not *your* pee)! My Pees were laid flat on top of an open panty with loops into which a My Pee was secured. Snaps or buttons closed it. For My Pee children, no other My Pee hardware was needed. It went without saying that to this stunned crowd, Erin was living in a My Pee-less world, and her mom looked like their version of the Mother from the Black Lagoon.

Without delay I had to expeditiously defend my actions or there would be real trouble. Thus, with a magnanimous smile that rewrote the meaning of neighborly love, I began a series of acute, altruistic bows, stretching my vertebrae further than a circus rubber man. As I did so, the group calmed down because they now had to politely bow back to me, taking their minds momentarily off the pin.

Next, I had to reassure every last onlooker that I meant my child no harm; that I was Peggy who had not come from the bowels of the Black Lagoon, but rather from the superexcellent town of Austin, Minnesota, and was hoping beyond hope no one would confuse them as being the same. I gestured for the crowd to come in closer, right up to the tail end of the Microbus. Then in plain sight I demonstrated how I very carefully placed my fingers *under* the diaper next to my baby's creamy flesh. Holding up the pin I had by now retrieved from the farmer, I pushed it through the Curity where it touched the fleshy barrier of *my* fingers and not the tummy of Erin. With the resounding whoosh of a relieved group exhale, the tension passed like the sibilations from a dyspeptic giant. Their world was once again restored to harmony. It was a shame I didn't know how to say "kumbaya" in Japanese.

Whew! One more cultural clash resolved; one more international crisis averted. But, oh, what amazing fodder for the villagers as they could tell and re-tell in the weeks and years to come, the events of this day to friends and neighbors and anyone who couldn't escape. I'm not sure just how their picture of us Keeners was painted, but I think Saint Jerome, the monk, hit the nail on the head when he surmised …

"Early impressions are hard
to eradicate from the mind.
When once wool has been dyed purple,
who can restore it to its previous whiteness?"

THE FINAL AND possibly most memorable saga of our esteemed resonance box took place when we finally left Japan. Because the bus was our family car, we were entitled at government expense, to ship it back to the States, sans the removable stacked vacation home. Weeks before we departed from Japan, Glen put it on a slow boat to California.

The year was 1966, and our family was facing another one of those grueling marathon flights across the Pacific. As usual, we were loaded down. Still the words "travel light" remained a mystery to me, having never embraced them as part of my globetrotting belief system. Like what was that supposed to mean, anyway? Take less? Poppycock! I'd sure like to know whose nincompoop idea it was to *not* take nearly everything you owned with you, every time you traveled? How dumb was that?

Instead, my approach was the bogged-down-with-lots-of-stuff-including-the-always-needed-kitchen-sink methodology. For example, if we planned to be gone for ten days, we took eleven pairs of socks and underwear in the event that where we were headed did not have either water, soap or rocks upon which I could beat them. Also, our plane could be grounded for de-icing, a regular and highly problematic occurrence for ocean crossing flights during winter. Both, naturally, caused monumental delays, not a few of which turned into really terrific mini-vacations. Due to imperfections in the weather and in the airplanes, there was always the chance our flight could be cancelled and we would have to (*get to!*) stay an extra day or two in some exotic spot on the globe. It happened enough times to know it could happen enough times again.

It must be said that the Maxim of Maximum had always suited me best. Wasn't it Confucius, the first Delta flight attendant, who said, "The weight of every suitcase is greater than the sum of its parts?" For whatever that meant, I recognized some confusion in Confucius, pretty much in line with my own cloudy thinking. Moreover, I was disappointed I never got the chance to tell him this, but if I had had *my* way, instead of using suitcases, I would have preferred to just take my bedroom dresser. It all made perfect sense. Imagine the packing/unpacking time it would have saved.

> "It's really hard
> to be roommates with people
> if your suitcases are
> much better than theirs."
> J. D. Salinger

On this last trip home, we would once more be traveling with a baby. In diapers. Cloth, not disposable. This meant, of course, a separate Curity satchel exclusively for Erin's needs, plus all the novelties it would take to entertain three young children on what could be another "flight eternal." As things developed, though, this paraphernalia was not my most immediate concern. It was, rather, some spots that had popped up overnight and were now covering Erin from her neck to her knees.

As I told you in the beginning of this book, our health records had to be updated regularly. This meant multiple injections for every disease known to man that had an injection. Twelve-month-old Erin was getting all of them in baby-sized portions for the first time. Without a doubt, the most difficult of these was the small pox vaccination. How I dreaded her getting it. All I had to do was look around me at the scarred, perforated upper arms of every grown woman in sight to know I didn't want to blemish my own daughter in this way.

To me it was apparent those scars alone were the primary reason none of those women were either Miss America or Miss Japan. Hadn't their mothers known such disfigurements would someday be looked down upon by scoffing beauty judges? And who's to say that Erin would not grow up to be glamorous and might just wish to enter a pageant someday? Pulleeze. Would besmirching her body, just to guarantee she would escape a horrific disease, be worth risking a pageant title? I didn't think so.

But, I didn't rush to judgment. After a protracted debate with myself, I finally decided it probably was neither motherly of me nor smart for my baby to get a life-threatening, horrific disease, if you get my drift. Thus, I decided on the vaccination.

> "Ever notice that
> 'what the hell'
> is always
> the right decision?"
> Marilyn Monroe

It had to, however, be given on her upper leg. That way she could parade around the pageant stage with a choice of: her hand, a large flower, or a title sash held gracefully over her imperfect thigh. If it came to that.

The Green Park Dispensary, our medical headquarters, would take care of everything. Off we went. A nurse administered the shot. Five days later, with absolutely no visible indication Erin had been vaccinated, I reported this to the dispensary. They said to come back. This time we were attended to by a very young corpsman. He, in his sagacious wisdom, let me know resolutely that the shot had *not* taken. Furthermore, we'd be heading straight for plague and pestilence if we didn't have it redone immediately. Enlightened as he was in the ways of all things medical—like at the age of twenty he was Mr. *Big* on *Small*pox!—he re-vaccinated her again smack dab in the middle of the first site.

Within hours it began to swell, rising up from her baby thigh like a cork pushing itself out of a fermenting wine bottle. The circle, the size of a quarter, rose with a volcanic core so agonizingly red, it was like a lava spill erupting from deep within her. It didn't take any brains (not even one the size of Mr. Big Smallpox's), to know both vaccinations were simultaneously hitting like gang busters. Before you could say "how do we butcher a corpsman with no blood showing," raw red spots broke out from Erin's neck down to her thighs. Her Precious Specialness had turned into a living, breathing pepperoni pizza, size small.

This was a big deal. In fact, a big *big* deal! You see, in only a matter of days we would be passing through international customs. As you can imagine, it was not the best idea in the world to try doing this with a visible, grievously malevolent disease! It was, after all, spots just like these that had turned many an Ellis Island immigrant right back on his heels, returning him to the bleakness of the Europe from which he had fled. None of us particularly wanted to be returned to the bleakness of Asahi Court.

On the day before our departure, Erin's little leg looked as if it were wrapped in a fiercely crimson, scabbed-over band, encircling her entire leg. The diagnosis was cow pox. Yup, that thing the milkmaids of long ago became immune to as they squeezed those dangly things under their cows.

I cringed upon hearing this verdict. I, Darla Disaster, could see our future and with that vision, I murmured an impassioned entreaty that I would never hear this declaration from an airport customs official: "A pox upon your house ... because a pox *is* upon your daughter!"

Of course, there was nothing to do but go forward with our plans, because by then, the entire house had been boxed up and the rental contract torn to shreds, so we couldn't go back. Furthermore, we had done it all in the worst of conditions. On moving day the rain had come down in such torrents the packers had been forced to construct a tent walkway from our duplex door to their moving van in an attempt to keep everything we owned from getting soaked. If you didn't know better, you would have thought a typhoon was on the way.

And, you would have been right! By the time the packers finished their magic and we walked out of a now desolate, soulless, echoing cinderblock house, the winds and the rain were throwing their weight around us as if we were in a wash cycle on high. What in blue blazes was going on? Wasn't this the same sky we were about to take our family into? Had Glen and I, in our zeal to return to the Motherland, become unbalanced dips? Memories of another time, when we really were unbalanced dips, began to creep in. You know the one—the typhoon that had crushed the catamaran (on which we were sailing) into smithereens.

Waving farewell to our empty home, we slogged from our old front door through torrents of rain to an awaiting driver in a military sedan. As our resonance box had been shipped some weeks before, he would drive us to Tachikawa Air Force Base. Like olives in a jar, we five along with all our junk pushed and squeezed inside, filling the interior to the roof. The suddenly overstressed car let out a gasp of alarm and sputtered off on springs and axles now strained with new responsibilities. Strapped to the top of the car was my bedroom dresser.

Just kidding! But Lord have mercy, could the Keeners never do anything with aplomb?

A dripping wet Glen switched on the radio to cheer us with some tunes. Oddly, as he turned the dial, no matter what station he switched to there was always the same report. Something about seeking shelter—and doing it NOW! But, we'd just left our shelter. In fact, we'd been so busy all day long leaving *it* that we hadn't paid any attention to what was going on outside *it*. Now, some person from inside the dashboard was yelling at us to not go outside. Destiny was once again bedeviling us. Outside was just where we were!

Trying to remain calm, the announcer's fear was showing in the tight, high pitch of his strained vocal cords. What was it he was saying? Something about a big daddy of a typhoon ... *heading our way?* Well, I could certainly see he had a point. Things were definitely hairy outside. Visibility was zippo, and sheets of rain were slicing like karate chops into the windshield. We should, I decided, probably pay attention, because it sure did look like the guy knew what he was screaming about; at least all that racket had swayed me to his way of thinking. Son of a gun! If this kept up, we'd be able to fly back to the U.S. *without* a plane.

My body tensed as my bottom began twitching in the way it has habitually always twitched whenever I've wanted to help Glen drive; when I actually wasn't driving, but when *I* knew that he needed my expertise to help *him* drive. Would the driver now sense my twitches? Things were sure looking bad. Like, where was the road? But calming down and reminding myself it was best to always see the bright side of every situation, I noticed we had an unusually unfettered traffic situation. In fact, I couldn't find one other car on the road. Plus we had a remarkably helpful tail wind! Why, it seemed that in no time at all—as if the time had *flown* by—we pulled up to the Tachikawa Air Base Terminal.

Glen dashed out of the car, the torrents of rain soaking through to his bones all over again. Inside and up to the counter he sloshed. There the officers informed him that all the flights—every last one of them ... *helloo, like hadn't we had a look outside?*—had been canceled. Furthermore, all the passengers—and here I know they wanted to add "craniac passengers who possessed workable brain matter"—had, unlike ourselves, taken earlier planes to not only get the aircraft off the island, but to also avoid altogether the disaster we were presently *not* avoiding! They didn't mince words. They also, I would add, could sure have been a little more polite. Why blame us? We couldn't help it if this was moving day. Was it our fault we were subnormal transient clods who just wanted to go home?

"Good judgment
comes from experience,
and experience
comes from bad judgment."
Barry LePatner

The officers, now speaking in air force lingo, told Glen to get his butt and the butts of his wife and children across base to military lodging. And, they wanted to see those butts wiggling *now!* Plowing back through the rain and into the car, Glen conveyed the orders to the driver, making sure he understood this meant only our butts and not his. We drove ... er, wind sailed, over. The boys were, by now, in a high state of excitement/terror while Erin, not having a clue what was going on 'cuz she was a baby, was screaming just to prove she didn't know what was going on 'cuz she was a baby.

At last inside the transient billets, and thoroughly drenched, we were escorted to a room on the third floor. The rains were now bordering on hateful; pelting the buildings like sharp javelins, and growing exponentially more mean spirited with every passing minute. Why was Buddha so mad, anyhow, and why was his message so unclear? Was this anger his way of telling us (in Buddhist air force lingo) that he wanted us and our butts to stay in Japan ... or to get us and our butts off this island and back to where we came from ... the place where all butts looked like our butts? Butter butts!

As the mother of the group, and therefore director of planning, it was my job to quickly formulate a course of action. The first thing that popped into my head was dinner. Why, of course. Food always made any disaster merrier. But, no, it was only the afternoon. The ebony darkness outside had tricked me into thinking night had already arrived. It didn't matter, anyway, because how was I going to prepare a meal? We didn't have any food. Okay, so, plan change. We'd eat the snacks I had intended for the plane ride, and then we'd—night or no night—go to bed. Once tucked under our government billeted covers, we would simply ignore the monstrosity screeching outside our windows and cozily sleep the night away.

Now, just what kind of a dodo lamebrain Pollyanna plan was that? Sure! Sleep away? Why, the Loch Ness monster would have had a problem napping through this storm. As the winds and rain grew increasingly fierce, sleep became a distant wish. And, no matter how scary a threat they were, they were turning out to be only part of our problem. We also had family things to deal with.

Take Erin, for example. The poor child was miserable with eighty-percent of her baby body now covered in wretched, itching cow pox dots. Then there was the traumatized Jeff who was re-experiencing the last time he lived through that other night of terror when he encountered the damned stuffed pheasant beside his bed. And finally Matt, in an ah-ha moment of enlightenment, was figuring out that weather was, in fact, the real and true boss of the bugs, and that we five—the whole pathetic lot of us—were not the boss of anything! Keeners on holiday.

> "If a kid asks where rain comes from,
> I think a cute thing to tell him is,
> "God is crying."
> And if he asks why God is crying,
> another cute thing to tell him is,
> 'Probably because of something *you* did!'"
> Jack Handey

The hours snailed by. As we huddled under our covers, the gales of wind and rain crashed and careened against the building. Electricity had failed hours before and we lay awake in pitch blackness, quivering rhythmically in our beds. Never before had we seen Mother Nature erupt with such fury. If you asked me, she was sure some kind of first class show-off. And, just what was it she was so gosh darn upset about? For crying out loud, Mama N, enough already!

In the middle of the night, Glen and I were shocked out of our trembling by a sudden assault. A fusillade of cold water struck our bed. Like wet buckshot, it slammed into our faces, stinging our cheeks and soaking the covers. Staring in the darkness towards the direction of the barrage, we could just make out the window air conditioner that now seemed to be hanging out of its frame; a wide gap around it open to the outdoors. We couldn't believe it. One side of the heavy unit had been pushed through the window by the force of the winds, and now, with nothing to stop it, the rain was pouring into our room. Hells bells! Within minutes the floor would be a wading pool!

Glen and I leaped out of bed, splashing onto the already soaked carpet, up to our ankles in the sog. Grabbing our now even more terrified children, we carried them out into the long hallway. There we instructed Jeff to remain with Matt and Erin. Then dashing back inside, we began heaving wet suitcases off the floor and carrying them to what we hoped would remain high ground out in the hall. Next we went for the mattresses. They were not as easy. Have you any idea how particularly difficult it is to move bulky, inflexible mattresses in pitch darkness, in water up to your ankles, in a building quivering from battle fatigue, and with a floor plan unfamiliar to you? Oh, and add to that, freaked out. I, to this day, suffer from the mental mars of mattress moving.

Glen and I laid the mattresses in the hall then rushed back into the room for the damp covers. Once again we bedded down our whimpering, convulsive youngsters for the night. As I tucked them in for the second time, I whispered into their ears, "Isn't traveling fun?" Then I turned and began ululating in my wet pillow.

It was the night everlasting. The rivalry between the roar of the wind and the pounding of the rain must have thought they were competing on the Ed Sullivan Talent Show and had to be beat each other out. Would they never stop? Would the world never ever be still again? Jeez Louise! I was only asking for a little peace and quiet here, not a kidney.

Yet, as all things must end, so did the big bully-of-a-storm which at last grew bored with terrorizing us. Streaming through what was left of the broken windows was the morning light; a clean, blinding, new day light. Not a cloud was in sight and the sky was spectacularly blue; a sight we had nearly forgotten while living under the befouled, griseous skies of the polluted Tokyo. The storm had blown all the nasties off our island and, in a gesture of global equality, was now dispersing them to neighboring lands.

If you've never experienced a typhoon, then you don't know about the morning after. It is always, in a shocking way, glorious beyond description. It's very, very quiet (a blissful thing), and it is wet and messy (not a blissful thing). But most importantly, it is over, and your loved ones are standing beside you (in anybody's book, an enormously blissful thing). Actually, I've found this realization comes to you way more easily if your home is also still intact. I guess a person had to be there themselves witnessing the morning after to know what I was talking about. Even if you're not religious, you had to be struck with the idea that this must have been pretty much the way the heavens were on Day One, when God created them fresh and new. That is, if you discounted the bent air conditioner, because I'm not sure if God had air conditioners on Day One.

I stood there thinking about the folks back in Austin. Why, they couldn't even spell "hurricane," let alone "typhoon." Of course, they didn't have a clue how one felt. How could they? The East Side Lake Ocean had never even known a wave. And, if you asked anyone on Main Street, they'd probably think they were called "hurricanes" because the wind hurried, although no one could explain the "cane" part. In Japan, where they really knew stuff about bad weather, the word was "tai-foo"—big wind. Personally, I thought that descriptive "big" was right on, and as for the "foooo" part, it was way better than hurrying winds, because fooo really did sound like something blowing. You know, like some really big pooched-out lips fooooing out birthday candles.

Looking through our broken window, I marveled all over again at the resplendent skies. Ground zero, on the other hand, was anything but. Virtually everything was soused, ripped off and hanging limply over itself like a basket of not yet wrung laundry. We later learned over a million dollars of damage was done to the air base alone. Still, gosh darn, the sunshine was pure and good. From where I stood, I could see across the expanse of lawn (now turned rice paddy) to the base movie theatre. Out in front was the marquee leaning precariously toward the ground. Some ragged letters, all askew and barely hanging on, were advertising the current feature film: *Gone with the Wind*. I kid you not.

OF COURSE THERE was no breakfast. There was also no lunch. It's not like anything could open to serve the public because everyone in the area, like us, had suffered the same wind and flooding damage, to say nothing of the nonexistent electric, water and phone services. By early afternoon, when every last one of our remaining snacks had been consumed, I was becoming seriously concerned over how I would feed my family. Alone and rudderless in those billets, the only iffy options I could come up with fizzled out as quickly as the children's hunger increased. Just when we thought all was lost because no one was coming to our rescue, someone did. It was Glen's very good friend, John Kono.

Good, faithful John Kono, an extraordinary person. I don't say this only because that day he was our hero, but because he was somebody's hero every day. John was just that kind of guy. Born in the U.S. of Japanese immigrant parents and later educated in Japan, John had a unique double upbringing. With it, he belonged to a small class of Americans called "kibei" (key-bay). During World War II, John had somehow avoided imprisonment in an American internment camp. Instead, he ended up in Montana where he worked as, of all things, a sheep herder! This is not to say that John led a peaceful, solitary existence up there in the mountains, camping out in his sheep herder's wagon while strumming a guitar, nor is it to say that up there he ran into a sweet, accommodating Heidi. No, for John loneliness and strife were his only companions.

Above all, his major strife was the local Montana Jim-Bobs who did not take a liking to a Nip living among them, failing to realize that John was an American just like them. But, of course, he was a *waaay* better American than they could ever hope to be.

There were many distinctive things about John. Number one was his body. It was as stalwart a body as there ever was. In fact, I questioned whether his mother had really given birth to him or if he had been, instead, produced in a cement block factory. He stood not so tall, but his legs and arms were as thick as maple tree branches, and his shoebox-like feet were so short and wide (8 XXXXX), that when he later joined the Army, Uncle Sam wanted him so badly, he had custom shoes made just for John.

One day, when Sheep Herder John was down from the Montana mountains doing business in town, he was harassed yet again by the local ne'er-do-well Bubbas. It was the final straw for John. While the bozos guzzled booze in the local saloon, he waited outside. When at last they began exiting, he lambasted them with his mighty fists, one by one, aiming directly for the tops of their empty, pointed heads. From there, John marched down to the nearest Army recruiter's office and signed up as fast as possible to get himself out of sight before the meatheads gained both the consciousness and the strength to tyrannize him again.

With his magnificent Japanese and English language skills, along with his inside knowledge of the two countries, John soon found himself in military intelligence. There, not only did he revel in being appreciated for the outstanding person he was, but he also, for the first time in his adult life, was wearing shoes that fit! All decked out in his new footwear and feeling good about at last fitting in made him a very happy man. What was not to love about John Kono? Glen and John's friendship blossomed instantly, becoming in no time like twin racially mixed brothers .

On the morning after the typhoon, we were favored to have John in our corner. His part of town had weathered the storm better than ours and he still had electricity. Thus, on the radio John heard about the extensive damage to the air base. Knowing we were there, he somehow worked his way to us through the mess of Tokyo. Into the hotel and up to the third floor he splashed, our all-time best friend, hero and now *super* hero, carrying full bags of food in those maple tree arms of his. John's Japanese wife, equal in every way to the goodness of John, had made dozens of seaweed-wrapped rice balls. As John opened the first bag, we pounced on them like coyotes on a downed warthog.

But, as was usual for him, John's generosity did not end there. One look around the hallway and our room showed him the predicament we were in. While we chewed, he gathered up our soaked clothing and headed back out the door. Retracing his drive across Tokyo to his on-post house, where there was a dryer that *did* blow hot air, he and his godsend of a wife proceeded to wash and dry everything. John then hopped back in the car, winding through and around the flooded roads and downed trees, on the long route back to us. He arrived in the nick of time. A flight, we had just been told, would soon be departing. With John's further assistance, we furiously repacked, snatched up the children, jumped in his car, and headed for the airfield. Once there, we hopped out, grabbed our stuff, kissed him goodbye and ran for the terminal.

In life, from time to time, people like John Kono come along. They are sent to us on purpose to restore our faith in mankind. Glen calls this the "Christ consciousness." From that day until now, we have always remembered our dear friend as not just John, but *Saint* John.

ENTERING THE TERMINAL, we found it oddly deserted. There were no G.I.'s or airmen, no harried parents trying to control boisterous children, no nobody. Without crowds to block our way, the five of us breezed right up to the desk where we found it staffed by one lone airman. We asked about the flight. Yes, there certainly was one and it was just outside. It would be ready for boarding in a few minutes.

I was nervous—no, that barely covered it—I was possessed! If you can believe it, on the way out of the transient billets, I had overheard some folks talking about another hurricane heading our way. They were saying it was necessary to get all the remaining planes off the island before it hit. Was this true, and could one of those planes—like the one waiting outside—get us out of here in time? Try as I might, though, I could find nothing advantageous about our three children and us being in an airplane in the sky in the middle of another "Big Wind." Where were our prefrontal lobes?

And do not forget that under all the emotional upheaval remained the reality of our baby and her spots. If anyone saw them, we were doomed; certainly banned from boarding. That would mean a delay … with no home other than those wet transient billets … of weeks, even months. As best I could in the chaos and dampness, I had shrouded the distressed twelve-month-old Erin from her neck down. You may think you know swaddle because you've seen the babe in a Christmas front lawn manger. Trust me, you haven't. Erin looked like a roll of paper towels with only a head and two feet sticking out.

By now the lone airman, with nothing to do, was tilted back in his chair flipping through a magazine. With no passengers to deal with, his duties were pretty much zilch. Lackadaisically, he gave us the once over, cursorily glancing at our vaccination cards, passports and orders, then gestured us through, happy to be returning to his reading. Glad as I was for his indifference, I did think he could have wiped that hint of disdain off his face. So, we were a little on the bedraggled side? For criminy sakes, we'd had a bad night!

Or, was it that John's rice balls had left seaweed stuck in our teeth? Who cared? We were in. Besides, that would only show if we smiled, and we were doing little of that. No, this was no time to either dawdle or floss. Like the wind sucked into an elevator shaft, we likewise whooshed through the doors and into the passenger lounge. There were no lineups this time. The plane was outside waiting; waiting to get off the island to avoid what was coming next. With luggage for five (and only one and a half of us doing the carrying because I was holding the paper toweled Erin), we ran through the departure gates and splashed across the flooded tarmac.

Whoa! We stopped dead in our tracks. Would you get a load of that! This plane was a far cry from the one that had brought us here. Before our disbelieving eyes sat a chartered commercial aircraft! It was not pea-green and it had no propellers. Instead, its sides were silvery gray and it had jet engines which were already revved up. Sweet! This meant I was off the hook; totally absolved of any propeller-monitoring duties.

We climbed eagerly up the steel stairs, arrived at the top and peered inside. Holy smoke! This really was *our* plane! There were no other passengers. Everyone else (those with the good crainiac matter), had either departed before the hurricane or were too freaked out by the one following on its heels. Like holiday shoppers just entering Macy's, we surveyed the cabin with wild, greedy eyes. With no rush and no crush, because we were all alone in there, we threw back our shoulders and moseyed down the aisle, brazenly taking all the time in the world to scrutinize each seat in search of our individual favorites.

Glen says he remembers at least two other passengers. I don't and since this is *my* book and *I'm* doing the telling, it'll be *my* version! (It was a Bickerson moment. Mrs. Bickerson won!) Besides, if there were a couple of other people, I never saw them for they were already out for the count, sunk deep in the caverns of their own claimed spaces.

For some ridiculously farcical reason—as if the world revolved around us Keeners—I had the capricious notion that because there were so few of us, we'd get really good, really star treatment. Negatory! For the very reason that there were so few of us, we were ignored; not worth the bother. Obviously the shiftless airman from the front desk had gotten word to the stewardesses to go lax; any former obligatory duties now being nothing more than nebulous, nonessential trifles.

One strong hint of their apathy was demonstrated later, after we were in the air. A lone stewardess came torpidly sauntering down the aisle carrying a serving tray. On it was a slap-dash display of food choices: a loaf of bread, a jar of peanut butter, a knife (no butter, no grape jelly), and she was wearing her pajamas! Alright, just pulling your chain about the pajamas, but the food choices were right on, which is to say, we were darned grateful it was American peanut butter and not Japanese penis butter! There was a difference, you know. Really? Really.

> "Man cannot live
> on bread alone;
> he must have
> peanut butter."
> James A. Garfield

Not being picky, we got right to it, downing our sandwiches as fast as a bag of spinach disappears in a hot pan. There was no contesting that the strong breezes from the approaching hurricane would hurry us along, and with only a handful of us in this plane, we were as light as a feather. We might even break a speed record. But, then, who was keeping time? Before you knew it, we were zonked out, each in a full center section of seats, armrests removed, with as many blankets and pillows as we could stuff around us. Zzzzzzz ....

After hours of down time, lots of peanut butter, and with not even one stop for refueling, our no-frills flight landed at Travis Air Force Base,

California. We deplaned, collected our cumulus of stuff, and sweated it through one more immigration procedure, poxy Erin somehow again—praise be to Jehovah and swaddling!—slipping by undetected.

Waiting outside the terminal, still on duty, was our familiar friend from five years before, the mottled pea-soup green military bus. Climbing aboard, it transported us directly to Oakland where our Microbus was stowed in a vehicle storage lot. Covered with a thick layer of grime from the long sea voyage, it was barely recognizable. But that snub nose wasn't fooling anybody. To us it looked as welcome as an old faded bathrobe.

We piled in, blowing and swishing off the dust, and immediately set off for our trip across the States. Our plan was to end up back in Austin, the drop-off point for the children and me, while Glen proceeded on to Baltimore for another four-month course in intelligence training. This time it would be counter intelligence. I was not exactly sure what that was—and certainly wasn't going to be Beatrice Buttinsky by asking—but I guessed it was something really tricky. Intelligence done backwards, by chance?

The five of us were like high school kids let out of a long, drawn out detention, wild with glee. Glory hallelujah, we were in America! Again! This time, the boys were old enough to actually get to know and to become one with their country, and Glen and I were the eager ones to show it to them. That very day we set off straightaway, chugging across California, then Nevada, and before long found ourselves in the middle of the Great Salt Lake Desert of Utah, a deserted moonscape of a no place.

As we crossed the desert, creepy in its emptiness, Glen our resident auto expert noticed that the oil pressure light on the resonance box's dashboard was flickering. Being aware of the seriousness of this, he immediately stopped to evaluate the problem. First he checked to see if there was enough oil. There was, so that was a non issue. But, wait. What was that? A leak? Lemme see. Yes, a leak at the oil pressure sending switch.

Oh, is that all, I thought relieved as all get out. Thank goodness! Glen could fix it.

At his side and trying my best to be the helpful co-pilot, I pulled out of the glove compartment a Japanese auto repair manual; something I'd picked up somewhere just in the event we'd ever need it. Like now! I knew our van was a German car, but what the hey, a car is a car is a car, right? I opened the manual and began reading.

Let's see … okay … no, hold on … uh huh … here it is:

"All screws have to be tightened too tough
and checking on this earnestly sometime.
Inside tube where is indented thus circlip
can easily to thru to other side."

"Okay, I've got it! Listen to this, Glen."

"All you have to do is too tough tighten screws inside tube indented where circlip thru to other side earnestly sometime easily." There, I'd done my part.

To my chagrin, he snubbed me completely, grumbling ... if you can believe this ... that he didn't need my help!

> "Talking with a man is like
> trying to saddle a cow.
> You work like hell,
> but what's the point?"
> Gladys Upham

Grabbing the pliers from his tool box, Glen began tightening the loose switch. (*Well, isn't that what I'd just said?*) It was satisfying work, if truth be told, for he recognized all over again he was not only head driver/navigator of his family, but was also our supreme auto repair wizard. What could be better, more prestigious, than that? Glen ruled!

> "A man likes his wife
> to be just clever enough
> to comprehend his cleverness,
> and just stupid enough
> to admire it."
> Israel Zangwell

Silently hoping that we three (except Erin 'cuz she was a baby), would take note of his many credentials, Glen continued with his work. With one final twist—grunt—to make certain it was *really* on tight *this* time, he rotated the pliers. Twwiiiisst ....

Wouldyalookatthat! In Glen's outstretched expert auto mechanic's hand was the detached oil pressure sending switch!

In one small part of my book, the part you are now reading, Glen has given me permission—actually, it was his suggestion—for me to call him not just an auto mechanic, but an auto mechanic lout. So, I will. And, it feels good.

But then, gosh darn, what was there to go and get all worked up about? Like was being stranded in the middle of the desiccated, juiceless, parched, arid, dangerous, treacherous, salty Salt Flats as night was approaching with two young boys in typhoon recovery and a polka-dotted baby really all that bad?

As a mother, I sensed a problem. A voice in my head told me I was right. It also told me exactly what Sakae-san would say about our predicament: "Oh, a terrible what was that!"

But, always the optimist (an optimist, I'd heard, is one who believes a fly is looking for a way to get out) the ever upbeat Pollyanna in me began searching for *our* way to get out. What possible good points could be found in this new grim precariousness? While I was telling myself there

397

must be a way, la-di-da, Glen was telling himself there *was no way,* <*#^/!, on God's green earth he could drive this bus. It didn't matter one iota how much oil he poured into that tank, without a sending switch (the very one he had severed from the crankcase), it would all be pumped directly out onto the briny ground.

And with that, I finally figured out where the word "cranky" comes from.

Hours before, we had survived the wrath of Gone With the Wind, only to now face death once more, this time not by soaking, but by desiccation. Alone out there on the saline flats without a single seaweed covered rice ball between us, we were doomed to shrivel up like old bread crusts behind a sofa; no one, except the ants, knowing or caring that we were there. John, *Saint John*, where were you now that we needed you ... *again*?

Shaking off my trepidation, I knew I must come up with something. Hitchhike. Yes, that was it! We'd catch a ride. But, wait. On further reflection, I had my doubts. Yes, there were huge drawbacks. Like why on earth would anyone pick up a family of five? Was there even a vehicle big enough to pick up an extra family of five? And, what if the driver of that vehicle was the manager of the Bate's Motel ... and he was on his way to work ... where he needed to fix the shower ....

Holy craps!

But, that wasn't the end of it. What if I pulled up my skirt to hail down a motorist—like in one of those stranded-on-the-road Hollywood scenes—only to find that my calves were not really and truly curvaceous enough to get anyone's attention? Additionally, would varicose veins be a turn-off ... and would they even show from a distance?

But, then, maybe those gnarly veins (and just what woman, I ask, needed an umbilical cord trunk to prove her societal worth when she had *those veins*?) might be hidden in the trenches of my cellulite? Success could still be ours ....

I had to remind myself constantly to stay upbeat; erase any self-doubts, any negative negativity. The truth was we had no other recourse. We had to thumb a ride. Raising the awesome awning on the Microbus, I went to work, quickly picking through our suitcases and plucking out the very best attire each of us owned. Brushing off the salty residue that had already collected in our ears and hair, I had the children primped and gussied up in no time, even managing to hide Erin's gauzy wrappings under a wee, flouncy, full-skirted frock. Standing back to assess our group allure, I slapped down a cluster of Matt's wayward hairs with my spit, the only wet thing available.

In a group, we marched to the shoulder of the sodium chloride encrusted road and positioned ourselves like irregular stair steps next to our indisposed bus, its once proud upright oil pressure switch now heartlessly circumcised from its crank. For me especially, I felt that standing close to the van was necessary. There people would immediately understand our plight and not think I was Ma—along with Pa and the Kids—Barker. But, honestly, nothing could have been further from the truth. In reality, what we looked like more than anything was the Partridge family who had become lost while taking an unfortunate circuitous route on their way home from Bible Study.

We waited. A half hour went by. No cars. If we had gone out of our way to have a lousy, lonely vacation, this was it. Our once erect postures began to slump, then lean onto the next person in line as our feet went into a numbed sleep. Stomping to encourage blood flow, we looked around. We were definitely not stranded along the scenic route.

Soon flies began circling our heads, thinking our eyes, mouths and nose holes were oases they could suck dry. Although irritated by the unwelcome varmints, I was also greatly intrigued by them. Instead of buzzing, they were buthing. Dry mouth, I figured.

As we lingered there—our spirits dissolving faster than a bite of cotton candy—we noted, to our alarm, that the sun was quickly sinking in the West. And, it was beginning to take the heat along with it. That's when I remembered that a hot, parched desert gets darned cold at night, and if something didn't happen fast, there'd be nothing left of us but five frozen briny raisins with bloodless feet and exsiccated orifices.

Twilight settled around us. Just when doom was starting to feel like a sure thing, our fortunes suddenly reversed. Off in the distance we spotted a car. Surely it held a Good Samaritan who was now rushing to our aid! The car drew nearer. Hope! It slowed down, not quite stopping. Still hope! As it inched its way up to us, we could see a man at the wheel and his wife beside him peering at us. The looks on their faces told me everything. They were, without a doubt, seeing the toxic waste family from hell. If I didn't know better, I'd even guess their eyes were seeing five frozen briny raisins with bloodless feet and exsiccated orifices.

Picking up speed, they sailed right on past.

Hello and goodbye. Have a good life!

It had all happened in the blink of an eye.

Who knows what jolt of conscience suddenly got the best of them, gnawing at their sense of common decency—i.e. love thy fellow man—for they all at once stopped and began backing up. Slowly approaching us once more, the woman, whose blood was now curdled with fear, rolled down her window the teensiest of a crack. Then twisting our heads to get our mouths up to the one centimeter opening, Glen and I, the Marquis and Marquess de Sade, explained our predicament. When we finished, we asked if we could possibly catch a ride with them to the nearest gas station/motel. Please! Double please ... with salt and a dried raisin on top!

The woman rolled up the window and turned to her husband. They talked, their faces twitching in cantankerous animation. After what seemed an endless wait, she cranked open the crack, again by one exact—no more, no less—centimeter.

Stretching her lips up to the crack, she declared, "No, we will not take you with us, *but* we *will* stop at the first gas station and request for someone to come back for you." The Good Shepherdess had spoken.

I was stunned. What kind of crapola kindness was that? What if there were no gas stations? What is there was nothing until they got to ... to ... Nebraska? And what kind of black-hearted people would leave children out on a desert at night? Come on, folks, have a heart!

Knowing, however, that we must do nothing to mess up our only chance for survival, Glen and I tried our best to appear grateful, gritting our teeth and thanking them copiously for their overly generous compassion. With that they drove off into the cold, quickening darkness. I couldn't help but wish they'd drive over a cliff—after, that is, they sent the gas station attendant back for us.

Left alone, on the Great Salt Flats, our lives now rested upon the shoulders of two people who looked like they'd, in a heartbeat, adopt Charles Manson before they'd let us in their backseat. There was not a thing we could do but trust they were good for their word. Dejectedly, we resumed waiting in our lineup beside the road. Not another car came.

Much later, and about the time we thought all hope was lost, we heard from out of the now ebony darkness the sound of a heavy engine coming from the direction in which the couple had disappeared. Big, strong headlights pulled up to us as we waved for the driver to stop. It was a man from the nearest gas station. The people had come through! They would get a gold star—er, make that a lump of coal—in heaven!

I put in a quick request to God asking Him to cancel that business about them driving over a cliff. I had only half meant it, anyhow.

The man was driving a tow truck and quickly applied his expertise, impressively winching up our bus with his big, over-sized hook. Then all of us Keeners piled along side him into the front and back seat of the truck. If anything good could be said about that salt, it had dehydrated us to the point where we all actually fit.

On the way to the gas station, the man (in whose mercy *he* knew full well *we* were in), discussed with Glen the feasibility of his towing us all the way to Salt Lake City. We knew, of course, that we were in the weakest of bargaining positions. On the other side of those positions was him, the all-mighty driver, and as the possessor of all the power, he was holding out the only chunk of cheese to us the starved, trapped mice.

"Why, sure, we could probably be towed all that way," Glen muttered, "but ... um ... how much would that cost?"

"Let's see," the driver calculated, "it'll only set you back ...."

Holy mackerel! It made those strawberries back in Kyoto look like pinto beans!!!

"You gotta be kidding!" Glen and I wheezed under our breath.

Grinning, the driver knew he had us in his grip. Not grinning, *we* knew he had us in his grip.

Then much to his surprise *and mine*, Glen said that we'd—thanks, but no thanks—get to Salt Lake City on our own. Just take us, if the fellow didn't mind, to the nearest motel.

A testy silence then ensued in which everyone surrendered into a very long, very extra quiet ride. The children, still on Tokyo time, conked out child by child as the truck hummed through the eerie black emptiness, while I remained absolutely still wondering what Glen was thinking. I knew that he, our safeguard, was deep into devising a plan.

An hour later, and by now nearing midnight, the disgruntled driver pulled up to a motel. While I got a room and began settling us inside, he unhitched the van, got paid and drove off. Quickly bathing the children, chipping off the salt build-up as best I could, I got them into bed. Glen, in the meantime stayed outside with the van ... lost in thought.

Formulating a course of action was difficult, but he knew that somehow, someway, he *would* drive the van to Salt Lake City the next day. With morning now only a few hours away, time was of the essence. He, more than anyone, knew the distance away. He also knew the moment he turned on the engine, the oil would start shooting out that gaping hole, the very one in which the switch used to fit so snugly. Darn, if only he could come up with something to plug it.

Searching through his car tools, he came up with nothing. A perusal of the van also proved fruitless. Then he remembered the glove compartment! Yes, the glove compartment, always a treasure trove of unpredictable items, none of which were ever gloves. But then remembering that it had contained the helpful, though questionable, Japanese repair manual I'd read to him, he brightened up. Maybe, just maybe ....

Refueled with conviction, he undid the latch. Lying under a stack of insurance papers, packets of soy sauce, stale rice crackers, a smattering of small toys, a Curity (unbesmirched), and some maps, he struck gold. It was too perfect! Why hadn't he thought of it before? There they were. Chopsticks! Who, for all the rice in China, needed an expensive and highly professional tow for a family of five across the length of a state when he had a pair of chopsticks?

Excitedly he grabbed them and ran into the motel room where he gushed out his plan to me. I sat on the bed listening, wide-eyed. Well, who could argue with using some wooden eating utensils to repair our resonance box, I agreed? If Glen said they would work, then they would work. Well they would, wouldn't they?

And, why ever would I not have anything but complete confidence in my husband?

> "A male gynecologist
> is like an auto mechanic
> who has never
> owned a car."
> Carrie Snow

Yet in all honesty, and certainly not wanting to make a federal case out of it, I'd have to tell you that about that time a wee prickling sensation began to spasm somewhere deep inside my comfort zone. Just who and what, I wanted to know, was I supposed to turn to for bolstering in my time of need?

Gosh, if only I'd been born a Catholic instead of a Presbyterian, I could, right about now, grab hold of one of those emboldening St. Christopher medals. In its absence I guessed my dog tags would do. I clutched them to my breast.

> "In Burbank
> there's a drive-in church
> called Jack-in-the-Pew.
> You shout your sins
> into the face
> of a plastic priest."
> Johnny Carson

Whipping out his pocketknife, I watched as Glen very specifically began to whittle down one of the wooden chopsticks. He was good. He'd begin tonight, he explained, but in the morning he would fine tune it down to the precise diameter of the hole. I had to admit it. Glen's cleverness was bewitching. After all, I reminded myself for the thousandth time, he was the expert at things like this. That bathtub incident back in Asahi Court had certainly taught him everything a guy needed to know about fitting oversized things into undersized spaces. Yup, he knew alright. In fact, there were still a few rogue imprints on his right rump to prove it.

But, Glen further cautioned me, the chopstick alone would not guarantee our success. Careful exacting oversight of the procedure would also be necessary, because who knew when the chopstick might pop out? Once again that vision of Glen in the tub, unplugging himself like a cork from a bung hole—pow!—refreshed my memory. Yes, indeed, he also knew a whole lot of something about how critical the business of popping-out of a bung hole was.

> "Experience teaches you to
> recognize a mistake when
> you've made it again."
> Unknown

Just about that time, Glen began muttering to himself ... something about the critical need for someone to stand chopstick-popping duty. Of course! Why hadn't he thought of it before? That was why we had given birth to children! Oh, how clear everything suddenly seemed. Tomorrow he would post six-year-old Jeff at the back door of the van under which, you will recall, the engine was housed. Sitting there backwards, Jeff's young, but reliable eyes, would never leave the window. If he saw even one drop of oil splash up onto either the glass above or the pavement below, he was to scream bloody murder, and Glen would immediately stop the van.

I fell into a troubled sleep.

The next morning, with Glen's plan now fully in place, we gathered up the children and packed them in the van. Plucky Jeff, like a midget member of a squat ... er, swat team did, in fact, squat, buckling down to his task. My job was to monitor Jeff's monitoring, while Glen drove and monitored me. In the meantime, Erin itched, while dear, sweet, four-year-old Matt, without a special assignment, stewed. Once again that old record of feeling unworthy replayed in his head. Would the dirge never stop spinning? No! He was neither boss of the you-know-what, nor now of the oil spill. Dad gum the dad gummed middle-child luck, anyhow.

Slowly, slowly the Microbus limped across the other half of the Great Salt Lake Desert. The day proved to be very long and very intense. Only a smattering of cars passed us and even fewer towns met us. We were pretty much out there on our own with all our hopes and dreams tied to the steadfastness of one little stick of wood ... and Jeff's vigilant eyes. It wasn't until sundown that we crossed over the Salt Lake City line and pulled into the first motel in sight.

At 6AM the next morning, Glen was up and phoning the nearest Volkswagen garage. They instructed him to come right over. Driving more cautiously than ever without Jeff's help, and doing it early enough to beat the morning rush hour, Glen arrived in no time at all. Whew, he'd made it! He could turn the problem over to a real expert and, at last, take a good, deep breath. He began by explaining to the mechanic the micro bus' long sea voyage from Japan, the drive from California, and finally the odd malfunction. The cocky guy, who thought he could fix everything under the sun auto-related *and* had also *seen* everything under the sun auto-related, opened the rear end hatch to find a chopstick jammed into the yawning orifice on the crankcase.

It seems necessary to pause here and remind you again that this took place in Utah, the Brigham Young Utah of 1966. Asian food was not the usual—or even ever—Mormon fare. What, pray tell, the mechanic thought, was this double-digit-I-Q-numbnuts doing with a chopstick stuck in his engine? But then upon further reflection, he supposed that carrying a mini shovel in your car in case it snowed in Utah would be similar to carrying a pair of chopsticks in your car in case you got hungry in Japan. Yeah, he could see that. Still, it took the cake.

While Glen waited, relaxing for the first time in days, back at the motel the kids and I were ready to break out. Freed of our automobile anxieties, we had the morning off. And, we were hungry. The only decent food we'd had to eat since moving out of our duplex more than three long days before were Saint John's heavenly rice balls and those airline peanut butter sandwiches.

Off we went in search of food. In no time at all we came upon a deli, clean, inviting and beckoning us to enter. Inside we were greeted by a cheerful waitress. As she directed the children and me to a table, we exchanged a few pleasantries, and then without batting an eye, she looked directly at me and queried, "Are you LDS?"

Okay, okay, I'll be the first to admit I probably wasn't looking my Sunday best after being stranded out there on *her* desert, then being deserted out there on *her* desert by *her* people, but just imagine the nerve of *her* asking such a thing in public, and right there in front of *my* three children! And just whose business was it of hers, anyway? Shaken to the core by such impertinence, I ratcheted my backbone to full height and informed her I was *not on drugs!*

Hours later, back at the motel and still steaming, I told Glen about her effrontery. He, in his usual wisdom, inquired as to what exactly she had said. "Well, drugs, of course!" I retorted. "She wanted to know if *I* was on *LDS!* Good grief! Who'd ask a complete stranger a personal thing like that?"

Leave it to say, that was the day I got my first lesson in Mormon acronyms. As you can guess, I wasn't impressed. Just what made them so almighty uppity special that they had to speak in cutesy coded capital letters, I kvetched? It's probably because they couldn't spell. Like who's ever heard of a spelling bee champion from Utah? It's no wonder the Mormons had to walk clear across America in order to find a private place where they could have a cryptic chat! Sheesh!

But then, I second guessed myself. In that situation just what was I supposed to have done? I didn't know everything in the world, you know? However, I sure as heck knew deep down inside where my deepest stuff was stored, that I had risen to the occasion, and done so awesomely. Why, back there at the deli and feeling the sting of that waitress's audacity, I had drawn the line in her salty sand by up and leaving her table. Furthermore, no way Jose was she getting a T-I-P from me! *Ha! Wonder if she could de-cryptify that!*

Still, none of it had solved the problem. My flock remained without food. But, hungry as we were, I resolved that she would have no part in feeding us. Besides, I could see right through her. That brazen excuse for a waitress was just showing off her moral righteousness because she was probably Joseph Smith's great-great-granddaughter twice removed. Incest, I was thinking.

I told the children (except for Erin 'cuz of her being a baby and all), to leave the table at once. The boys, now sensing a strong shift in the local ambience, left with me, our three heads held abnormally high. Together we marched off to the grocery side of the deli, leaving Miss Holier Than Thou in *our* holier than *her* dust. There I bought an over-sized loaf of bread, a jar of mayonnaise and a really tall stack of bologna. I would make sandwiches back at the motel away from her accusatory eyes and her probing public interrogations. Harrumph!

I think—no, I know—just then I caught a gleam of respect in Matt's eye. Like a thump on the head, it had come to him. Could it—yes, it could—be possible that his own mother was, in fact, boss of *this* bug? And, if so (and it sure looked that way), there was hope for us all.

Back at the motel, I laid out the sandwich fixings and we dove in. And, here is where the tale of Glen-the-auto-mechanic-lout took another turn. *The bologna!*

Absolutely celestial! Quite possibly the best bologna in the world!

It is accurate to say that I have not always been a fan of the world's most suspect—even more than Spam—meat, but on that day things changed. Even my religion expanded; Mormon bologna reconfigured my spiritual reckoning. Like an open-minded adiaphorist, I started to use whatever religious customs pleased me. From then on to forever, this now included Mormon bologna.

I could see it all laid out along side a bowl of Presbyterian tuna hot dish. I knew my Deacon dad, Mr. Potted Meat himself, would be initially upset, but after one bite, he of all people, would understand.

In the end, I was left with only this. I'll give you ten to one it was those bad Mormon spellers who put that dumb "g" in bologna!

> "Bad spellers
> of the world,
> *untie!* "
> Graffito

LIKE THE VIBRATING tones of Eartha Kitt, our newly refurbished resonance box purred all the way from Utah to Minnesota. As we crossed the state lines, I sat back listening to its well-oiled thrums. A sense of relief poured over me. Japan was behind us. This was not to say Japan hadn't been good to us, for she had. She had been wonderful and generous and kind and funky. Gosh, without her showing me her quirky side, I would never have had any stories to tell you.

No, it wasn't Japan herself that we were relieved to be leaving, but rather it was her pollution, her rainy seasons, her public toilets and, for gosh sakes, her earthquakes! They were the worst. Not even typhoons were a match for the terror of those deadly jolts. At least a typhoon gave you warnings—if you had the brains to pick up on them while you were out sailing or moving out of your duplex! For instance, noticing the sky had suddenly turned a menacing dark or that the wind had picked up viciously or that the clouds were now vomiting rain. And with those hints, brainiac people would decide there was a high probability of this not being the best day to go to the beach, or for that matter, to get on a plane!

But earthquakes, now, were a whole different can of worms. One minute life was normally normal. The next, you and your world were uncontrollably wobbling, bouncing, jerking. Earthquakes were insidious; sneaked up on folks unawares, jiggling the sense out of their victims like there was no tomorrow ... which for some victims there *was not!* And, pulleeze, don't give me that limp advice about hiding under a desk or a table. Hardly worth the trouble! Just what good would that do me, I ask, when they later found my body as flat as a rolled pie crust *under* a table *under* a four-story building? If Japan had taught me one thing, it was that earthquakes will always hold the record for being nobody's favorite thing.

What we Keeners needed now was to settle down someplace on a solid land mass, avoiding perilously small islands and the equally scary edges of countries and continents. With those words securely cemented in our minds *so that we would never forget them*, we soon did, allowing them, along with all the rest of our good sense, to fly out the window. For where did we move next? Well, of course, where else but San Francisco? Yes, San Francisco and her quivering, quavering San Andreas Friggin' Fault!

And after a few years of vibrating there, we still didn't get it. We moved to the tiny vulnerable island of Okinawa! Okay, so I never said we were geographical Einsteins. And besides, Uncle Sam had a pretty darned convincing way of making these decisions for us. Job yes or job no!

Following Okinawa, Glen went to Vietnam for a year—another really comfortable unsafe haven in anybody's book! Left once more adrift, I decided that the children and I would move to Sydney. Yes, that Sydney! The one perched on the continental edge of Australia!

Hail Ole/Lena full of grace ....

With Glen entrenched in far off Vietnam, and my skull still stubbornly as thick as a stack of official government orders, I took the children and moved once more. Would you believe to that pin-prick of an island, Bali, Indonesia, where we could add intimate tsunamis to our earthquake angst? For crying out loud, military intelligence had screwed with *our* intelligence. Not only had it turned us into dumb bunnies, but dumb bunnies with a death wish! Double sheesh!

You would have thought by now the message had gotten through. But even trembling geography was not enough to enlighten us. After Glen's year-long tour in Vietnam, our family reunited again, this time in Bangkok, on the edge of Thailand. And, five years later we were at it again. That next move would be our last overseas assignment. Where do you suppose we ended up? You got it. Back in Japan! Yes, Japan, *for a dozen more benjo-ridden, monsoonal seasoned, jiggly years!* Fiddle-de-dee.

Do not forget us in your prayers!

"Insanity is doing the same thing
over and over again and
expecting different results."
Albert Einstein

But, of course, all these moves came later, long after our first experience in Japan, and they provided me with enough good stuff to write a continuation of this book. Back then, naturally, I didn't know anything about those future destinations. I was only concentrating on the children and I going to Minnesota, and Glen going to Baltimore. He would report there for another long training where in his spare time he could languorously stretch out in any bathtub he could find, because they would all fit, while the children and I would bask again in the adoring glow of Grampa, Mrs. Wong and the Happy Hour Gang. By anyone's measure, it looked like we were right back where we had started five years before.

In the short, but sweet, interlude before all that happened—before, but by the grace of God, we did *not* turn out like brainiacs, but instead *did* choose the path towards making us the world's most dedicated, hell-bent earthquake magnets—our resonance box purred homeward. I was enjoying the ride across America. She was beautiful, wide, unfilled and full of nails; wonderfully unique nails all over the place, popping up at every turn of my head.

Somewhere in Wyoming we stopped at a restaurant for lunch. A waitress met us at the door. She was just shy of six feet three inches, with bright red, corkscrew curly hair, and her eyes were as viridescent as a putting green. In one hand she carried a dish, while with the other hand she beckoned us to a table.

"Please *sit* here," she said. I smiled to myself as a warm, familiar feeling of home and correct pronunciation flooded over me.

As I did so, I glanced at the dish she had just placed on the table.

Butter!

We were home. Once again potatoes in a potato bowl.

The End

"If the doctor had told me
I would have only
six minutes to live,
I would have typed faster."
Isaac Asimov

ABOUT THE AUTHOR

CONTENTEDLY, PEGGY LIVES with her husband, her dogs, and her nearby grandchildren in Minneapolis, Minnesota. When she isn't writing, gardening or decorating, she works as a professional food taster.

References:

BYRNE, ROBERT. *THE 2,548 Best Things Anybody Ever Said.* New York: Simon and Schuster, 2003.

LLOYD, JOHN, AND John Mitchinson. *If Ignorance is Bliss, Why Aren't There More Happy People?* New York: Harmony Books, 2008.

WINOKUR, JON. *THE Portable Curmudgeon.* New York: Penguin Books, 1979, 1986.

CPSIA information can be obtained
at www.ICGtesting.com
Printed in the USA
FSOW01n1426220217
31128FS